International and Cross-Cultural Management Studies

International and Cross-Cultural Management Studies

A Postcolonial Reading

Gavin Jack
Professor of Management, Graduate School of Management, La Trobe University, Australia

Robert Westwood
Professor of Organisation Studies, School of Management and Centre for Management and Organisation Studies, University of Technology, Sydney, Australia

palgrave
macmillan

First published 2009 by
PALGRAVE MACMILLAN

Palgrave Macmillan in the UK is an imprint of Macmillan Publishers Limited,
registered in England, company number 785998, of Houndmills, Basingstoke,
Hampshire RG21 6XS.

Palgrave Macmillan in the US is a division of St Martin's Press LLC,
175 Fifth Avenue, New York, NY 10010.

Palgrave Macmillan is the global academic imprint of the above companies
and has companies and representatives throughout the world.

Palgrave® and Macmillan® are registered trademarks in the United States,
the United Kingdom, Europe and other countries.

ISBN-13: 978-1-4039-4617-1   hardback

This book is printed on paper suitable for recycling and made from fully
managed and sustained forest sources. Logging, pulping and manufacturing
processes are expected to conform to the environmental regulations of the
country of origin.

A catalogue record for this book is available from the British Library.

A catalogue record for this book is available from the Library of Congress.

10   9   8   7   6   5   4   3   2   1
18   17   16   15   14   13   12   11   10   09

Printed and bound in Great Britain by
CPI Antony Rowe, Chippenham and Eastbourne

This book is dedicated to my mother, Patricia Ritchie, a caring, resilient and talented woman. (GJ)

This book is dedicated to my life partner Chris, quite simply the nicest person I know. (RIW)

Contents

List of Tables

Acknowledgements

This book has been a long time in the making and involved the generous input and support of a large number of people and institutions to whom we are grateful.

We start by acknowledging and thanking seminar audiences at the following institutions for engaging generously with iterative versions of our argument: Essex Business School; Newcastle University Business School; Department of Management, New Mexico State University; Department of Sociology, University of Trento; The York Management School; University of Exeter Business School. Thanks also to stream participants at the APROS Conference in Delhi, India, 2008.

Gavin would like to thank colleagues and PhD students at the University of Leicester School of Management – Joanna Brewis, Martin Parker, Mark Tadajewski, Stefano Harney, Gibson Burrell, Anoop Bhogal, Ishani Chandrasekara, Nceku Nyathi – who read, listened to, gave references or clarified thinking on postcolonial issues. He is also extremely grateful for the financial support and sabbatical leave granted by the University of Leicester to spend time studying at the University of Massachusetts-Amherst and the University of Queensland. Marta Calás and Linda Smircich were extraordinarily gracious hosts and generous with their time and intellect. Gavin would also like to acknowledge the hospitality of Jacqueline Urla, Lisa Henderson, and Lisa's Graduate Seminar Class (COMM 7941) at UMass, especially Christopher Sweetapple who provided help with anthropological sources. Gavin also thanks the financial support of his new employer, the Graduate School of Management at La Trobe University, as well as Ben Fox and Fiona Graetz. Craig Prichard at Massey University and Josephine Maltby at the University of York kindly provided citations and articles.

Bob would like to thank some colleagues who have been supportive – Loong Wong, Johan Beneviste, Carl Rhodes, Carly Edgerton, Steve Linstead, Andrew Chan, Amanda Roan, Dostain Khan Jamaldini, Siggi Gudergan, Donncha Kavanagh, Malakai Tawake, John McManus, Fahad Khan, Ken Taniguchi, Bill de Maria. He would also like to particularly thank David Boje, Grace Ann Rosile and colleagues and students at the New Mexico State University for hosting me and showing interest and support during a sabbatical in late 2008. Also to Gibson Burrell and colleagues at the Management School, University of Leicester for allowing me to be with them on two occasions as Visiting Professor. Bob also acknowledges the School of Business UQ and University of Queensland for supporting two special study programmes that aided the completion of this book.

A considerable amount of patience was required by several people in the production of this text. Dr Guenter Plum took on our copy editing at a late stage. Above all, a very special thanks is extended to Paul Milner, Virginia Thorpe and the multitude of editorial assistants at Palgrave who have keenly awaited the delivery of this manuscript only to be asked for 'more time please'. Finally our partners Karl and Chris deserve a medal not just for the time and help with everyday life they have sacrificed through the writing of this book, but also for their constant love and support, and sometimes cajoling.

The usual acknowledgements are also due to the following for permissions:

Wiley-Blackwell for permissions to use material from Jack, G. (2008) 'Postcolonialism and Marketing', in M. Tadajewski & D. Brownlie (eds) *Critical Marketing: Contemporary Issues in Marketing*, Chichester: John Wiley & Sons, 367–387, parts of which have been used in Chapters 1 and 9.

Gabler for permissions to use material from Jack, G. & Westwood, R. (2006) 'Postcolonialism and the Politics of Qualitative Research in International Business', *Management International Review*, 46(4): 481–501, parts of which have been used in Chapters 2 and 10.

Emerald for permissions to use material from Westwood, B. & Jack, G. (2008) 'Clark Kerr, the CIA and the Cold War, and De/Re-Colonisation: Conditions for the Emergence of International Business and Management Studies', *Critical Perspectives on International Business*, 4(4): 367–388, much of which has been used or adapted for Chapter 5.

Emerald for permissions to use material from Westwood, R.I. & Jack, G. (2007) 'Manifesto for a Postcolonial International Business Studies: A Provocation', *Critical Perspectives on International Business*, 3(3): 246–265, parts of which have been used in Chapters 10 and 11.

List of Abbreviations

AACSB	The Association to Advance Collegiate Schools of Business
AAP	American Association of Publishers
AIB	Academy of International Business
AOM	Academy of Management
AMJ	Academy of Management Journal
AMR	Academy of Management Review
APROS	Asia-Pacific Researchers in Organization Studies
ASQ	Administrative Science Quarterly
BAM	British Academy of Management
CIA	Central Intelligence Agency
CIBERS	Centers for International Business Education and Research
CMS	Critical Management Studies
CSIR	Council for Scientific and Industrial Research Development
DM	Diversity Management
ECA	Economic Cooperation Administration
EDB	Economic Development Board
EFMD	European Foundation for Management Development
EGOS	European Group for Organizational Studies
EIASM	European Institute for Advanced Studies in Management
EIBA	European International Business Academy
EIC	East India Company
EQUIS	European Quality Improvement System
EURAM	European Academy of Management
FBI	Federal Bureau of Investigation
FF	Ford Foundation
FW	First World
GATT	General Agreement on Tariffs and Trade
GDP	Gross Domestic Product
G8	Group of Eight
GI	Global Imperialism
GP	Global Postmodernism
HR	Human Relations
HRD	Human Resource Development
HRM	Human Resources Management
IAI	International Institute of African Languages and Cultures

IB	International Business Studies
ICCM	International and Cross-Cultural Management Studies
ICSU	International Council for Science
IHRM	International Human Resources Management
IJV	International Joint Venture
IM	International Management Studies
IMF	International Monetary Fund
IMR	International Marketing Review
INSEAD	Institut Européen d'Administration des Affaires
IR	Industrial Relations
IRS	Industrial Relations Systems
I-USLPED	Inter-University Study of Labor Problems in Economic Development
JIBS	Journal of International Business Studies
JOB	Journal of Organizational Behavior
JWB	Journal of World Business
JUSE	Japanese Union of Scientists and Engineers
MIR	Management International Review
MNC	Multinational Corporation
MNE	Multinational Enterprise
MOS	Management and Organization Studies
NA	North America
NGO	Non-Governmental Organization
OB	Organizational Behaviour
OECD	Organization for Economic Co-Operation and Development
OS	Organization Studies
OSS	Office of Strategic Services
OT	Organizational Theory
PAR	Participatory Action Research
PCT	Postcolonial Theory
PERI	Programme for the Enhancement of Research Information
PSB	Psychological Strategy Board
SSCI	Social Sciences Citation Index
TNC	Transnational Corporation
TW	Third World
UN	United Nations
UTS	University of Technology Sydney
WASPS	White Anglo-Saxon Protestants
WTO	World Trade Organization

Part I
The Orthodoxies of ICCM

1
Towards a Postcolonial Reading of ICCM

Introduction

This book presents a critique of the related academic fields of inter-national and cross-cultural management (ICCM) based on certain com-mitments, concepts and practices from postcolonial theory (PCT). Our core argument is that these academic management disciplines are Western and Eurocentric discourses (knowledge systems and associated institutional practices) that exhibit historical as well as contemporary resonances with what we might call 'the colonial project' – that is, the formal expansion, conquest and colonial occupation by Western European imperial powers of multiple nations in Africa, the Caribbean, Latin America, South and South-East Asia, and Oceania up to the late-19th and early- to mid-20th centuries. As a contemporary form of cultural imperialism, we will argue that the discursive workings of ICCM render the field limited demographically, skewed theoretically and generative of politically contentious effects on the manner in which researchers, students and practitioners of management across national and/or cultural borders are called to understand the values and behav-iours of their various 'Others' (research subjects, managers, employees, customers, organizations and so on).

Our mode of analysis is historical and cultural. It is historical in the sense that we attempt to trace key moments and the impact of con-texts of production (economic, institutional, political, cultural) on the emergence of our field. It is cultural in the sense that we attempt to delineate the dominant values, interests and knowledge systems that frame how we go about representing, and thus understanding, key concepts of ICCM such as diversity or difference in both our research studies and in student textbooks and training materials. The question of who gets represented and symbolic concerns with the manner in which representational work is conducted are at stake here.

Our driving motivation is not merely one of critical or oppositional engagement with the domain of ICCM. It is not just about dissecting and deconstructing orthodox knowledge for the sake of negative criticism. This project is also transformational in intent. That is to say, our goal is not to 'insert' a postcolonial sensitivity into the field as if postcolonialism were an add-on, an overlooked but now recovered 'perspective' or the latest postmodern theoretical fad. To couch postcolonialism in these ways is to misunderstand its political impulses and to protect the status quo. We attempt instead to mobilize the theoretical and political resources of PCT to contribute to a significant and positive reconfiguration of the philosophical, methodological and institutional arrangements of the field. In the final analysis, ours is a project of provincializing, recontextualizing and politicizing inquiry in international and cross-cultural management.

But why do we feel that such a transformation is needed? Is ICCM not a valuable and dispassionate part of the management academy[1] offering important insights into the complexities of the global economy and its cultural diversity? Are the intentions of scholars not good, just and ethical? Have theoretical criticisms not already been made and accommodated by the field? We have concerns about responding affirmatively to all these questions. In this first chapter of the book, we give a preface to the remainder of the text, offering a clarification of the research problem, the conceptual frame we deploy in addressing it and the organization of the argument. We state why a postcolonial reading of the field is necessary, what this means for us and how the book unfolds in a manner reflective of these concerns.

Parochialism in the management academy

In 1991, Boyacigiller and Adler published their now well-known indictment of organizational science, referring to it as a 'parochial dinosaur'. Key to their argument was the assertion that organizational science had historically been imbued with an 'implicit, and yet inappropriate, universalism' (p. 262). They provided three types of evidence. First, they pointed to a contextual parochialism resultant from the historical emergence and codification of this body of knowledge in the post-World War Two period when the USA expanded economically and became a dominant international economic power. The field developed with an inevitable focus on American firms with a research agenda shaped by their interests, perspectives and questions. Boyacigiller and Adler suggested that in such a context 'it was easy for researchers – including non-US researchers (Servan-Schreiber, 1968) – to assume implicitly that American theories also dominated' (ibid: 265).

Second, a quantitative parochialism was identified, evidenced by the very small number of countries producing management knowledge and concomitantly the very limited contributions from non-US researchers. They pointed to Adler's (1983) paper, which showed that between 1971 and 1980 less than 5 per cent of organizational behaviour (OB) articles in leading American journals focused on cross-cultural issues, and where there was such a focus, it was mainly based on a single-country study. Of the small number of cross-cultural studies, most were designed to 'extend U.S.-developed theories abroad' (ibid: 278) and were driven by 'research methods rather than the problems and needs of managers, policy makers, and students' (ibid: 270).

Finally, Boyacigiller and Adler talked of a qualitative parochialism and the seeming blindness of organizational scientists to the manner in which their own contexts, values, interests and perceptions coloured their production of theory. They illustrated how US values pertaining to free will, individualism and low-context communication preferences, underpinned received understandings of core organizational concepts. Boyacigiller and Adler concluded: 'Organizational science has become trapped, that is, trapped within geographical, cultural, temporal, and conceptual parochialism' (ibid: 278). And further, that 'Americans have developed theories without being sufficiently aware of non-US contexts, models, research, and values' (ibid: 263). But what of international management?

Adler (1983: 226, cited in Wong-MingJi & Mir, 1997: 343) defined international management as 'the study of the behaviour of people in organizations located in cultures and nations around the world' which focused 'perhaps most importantly, on the interaction of peoples from different countries working with the same organization or within the same work environment'. Given the 'international' grasp, and the putative 'eye to the rest of the world' indicated by definitions like Adler's, it would seem appropriate to suggest that ICCM might be less parochial than the broader domain of management and organization studies (MOS). Moreover, it might also seem appropriate to surmise that the time has come for ICCM scholarship to take centrestage in a management academy facing the complexities of a context marked by a globalizing world. The point of departure for this book, however, is a sense of disappointment emanating from a contextual paradox right at the heart of ICCM. That is to say, from a context in which ICCM scholarship should be leading the way with the fruits of its intellectual endeavours, the field exhibits profound limitations and a distinctly narrow vision.

Over the course of this book, we will unpack the deep and troubling contextual, quantitative and qualitative parochialisms we believe afflict ICCM. We ask what is it that ICCM scholars claim to know about the cultural lives of others in globalizing times. How do they claim to know it? Whose knowledge do they represent? For what purposes? With what effects? Guided by these questions, we set ourselves three interconnected goals:

- To provide an historical analysis of the discursive and material conditions for the emergence and development of ICCM;
- To explore the manner in which the strategies of representation and appropriation in the discourses of ICCM can be said to represent forms of cultural imperialism and a continuation of the colonial project;
- To offer alternative theoretical, methodological and institutional frameworks for the study of ICCM.

Our goals and concerns are part of a small but long-established trajectory of criticism and disappointment with international and cross-cultural management studies (for instance, Adler, 1983; Negandhi, 1974; Redding, 1994; Wong-MingJi & Mir, 1997). We are not saying that critical conversations have not taken place in ICCM. But these critiques have been few and far between, and have had little impact on the state of theory and methodology in ICCM. On the contrary, the problems they illuminate have become entrenched. It is likely no coincidence that critical and reflective debate about the nature and logic of the fields' central concept – culture – has a similarly chequered history. In their review of ICCM research, Boyacigiller et al. (1996) pointed out that (with the exception of Roberts, 1970 and Triandis, 1972) very little explicit attention was given to the conceptualization of culture throughout the 1970s, a fact that made all the more welcome to the field Hofstede's landmark text in 1980. Though multiple conceptualizations of culture existed outside the cross-national comparative field of ICCM before Hofstede's, there was no cross-disciplinary engagement. More recently Leung et al.'s (2005) 'state-of-the-art' (p. 357) review of advances in research on culture in international business studies (IB), as well as Tsui, Nifadkar and Ou's (2007) recommendations for 21st century cross-national and cross-cultural organizational research, barely depart from the underlying paradigmatic orthodoxy of three decades of cross-national research.

What makes the contribution of our book distinctive is our use of postcolonial theory to consolidate and extend the small number of critical essays on ICCM and the culture concept. A key demand of PCT is to reveal and disrupt the hegemonic and universalizing posture and mythical status of Western knowledge systems. It seeks to surface the local specificities of knowledge systems, to situate them and thereupon to critique the manner in which local interests and knowledge come to masquerade as universal in nature and universalizing in consequence. In this and other respects, PCT is singularly appropriate for a work interested in the multiple forms and consequences of academic parochialism. But what is postcolonialism?

A selective overview of postcolonialism

Based on the assumption that the reader is unfamiliar with postcolonial scholarship, this section provides selective introductory remarks. There is a plethora of good overview and secondary/introductory texts to the field that interested readers might wish to consult (notably Ashcroft, Griffiths & Tiffin, 1989, 2000; Gandhi, 1998; Loomba, 1998; Mishra & Hodge, 1991; Moore-Gilbert, 1997; Young, 2003). These texts will bring some provisional order to the vast, ever-growing and theoretically and politically contested terrain of scholarly work that constitutes postcolonialism.

The 'colonialism' in 'postcolonialism' refers to the period of violence, conquest and racism associated with the expansion of the spheres of control and influence of a small number of Western European nations (Great Britain, France, Portugal, Germany, the Netherlands, Belgium, Spain, Italy) principally in the 19th and the early 20th centuries. The early European voyages of discovery to the 'New World' in the 15th and 16th centuries and the development of the mercantilist system of trade and commerce in the 17th and 18th centuries provided the cultural imagination and economic grounds whence more formal colonial systems emerged. Loomba (1998) estimates that circa 85 per cent of the earth was physically occupied by a Western European imperial power at the beginning of the 20th century. World history is, of course, marked by the repeated 'successes' and ultimate falls of a number of different empires (Rome, or the Moghul Empire in India for instance). The particular interest shown by scholars in these Western colonial regimes is not just accounted for by their more recent history. It is also, as Prasad (2003) suggests, because they differ in two principal ways from previous forms of empire: one connected to the complex and unequal systems of economic exchange; the other connected to the nature and exercise of cultural imperialism.

First, Western colonialism 'linked the West and its colonies in a complex structure of unequal exchange and industrialization that made the colonies economically dependent upon the Western colonial nations' (Prasad, 2003: 5). The colonies fulfilled two important economic functions: they provided a much needed source of raw materials for the varieties of industrial capitalism developing in Europe at the time, as well as a source of cheap labour power, most notoriously organized through the emergent slave trade. In addition to providing certain factors of production, the colonies also provided a market for the finished goods manufactured in the burgeoning factories of central and northern England, for instance. This commercial structure, based on the creation and exploitation of colonial wage labour, and organized into a world system of core and peripheral dependencies (Wallerstein, 1974), became a key reason for the expansion and success of industrial capitalism in Western Europe. The history of European capitalism is therefore also the history of European colonialism. Second, Western colonialism was as much about cultural and ideological subjugation – about 'cultural imperialism' – as it was physical conquest and economic exploitation. As Bush and Maltby (2004: 9) note: 'colonialism was founded on coercion, the use of armed force to conquer and to maintain dominance, but it was maintained through a "hegemonic project" that involved the imposition of European economic and cultural values'.

There is a subtle, but important, difference in the meaning of the terms imperialism and colonialism. In its most general sense, Ashcroft et al. (2000) describe imperialism as referring to the formation of an empire, a definition that encompasses the many empires noted above. But they go on to cite the distinction made by Edward Said (1993: 8), a leading figure in postcolonial scholarship, between colonialism as 'the implanting of settlements on a distant territory' and imperialism as the 'the practice, theory, and the attitudes of a dominating metropolitan centre ruling a distant territory'. Imperialism is thus a wider term and colonialism is just one example of a strategy for exercising imperialism. Some historical qualifications about the use of the term imperialism as a strategy of national governments are pertinent here.

Ashcroft et al. (2000) argue that the idea of imperialism as the acquisition of overseas colonies is a relatively recent signification of a term connected to the 'Europeanization of the globe', and most especially in the period from the late 19th century until World War Two. They talk of the period of 'classical imperialism' from 1880 onwards, associated with the 'conscious and openly advocated policy of acquiring colonies for economic, strategic and political advantage' (Ashcroft et al., 2000: 122). This policy was pursued aggressively by modern industrial powers, especially in Africa after the Berlin Congo Conference of 1885. Theorists of classical imperialism, notably Hobson (1902), Lenin (1916) and later Hobsbawm (1968), privileged an economic explanation and account of the phenomenon, articulating in different ways how the colonies facilitated the successful expansion of capitalist accumulation. Ashcroft et al. (2000) synthesize the key criticisms of these economic accounts: first, that they overlook the fact that 'the flow of profit from the colony to metropolis was not as great as had often been assumed during the period' (ibid: 126); and second, that it was culture rather than economics that provided longevity for the imperial project. To quote the authors (ibid: 126–127):

> (...) importantly for post-colonial theory, there was a continuous development of imperial rhetoric and of imperial representation of the rest of the globe from at least the fifteenth century. As a continuous practice, this had much more to do with the desire for, and belief in, European cultural dominance – a belief in a superior right to exploit the world's resources – than pure profit. (...) This is, of course, the most significant omission from accounts of economic theorists of imperialism: that the ideological grounding, the language of cultural dominance, the ideology of race and the civilizing mission of European cultural dominance had been accelerating since the eighteenth century. (...) Ultimately (...) it was the control of the means of representation rather than the means of production that confirmed the hegemony of the European powers in their respective empires.

Cultural imperialism was exercised through the creation of a vast assemblage of knowledge about the Other by a variety of means, and by a variety of different people: census-taking, the introduction of taxation, public health initiatives, anthropological study, missionary societies, humanitarian organizations, exploration and travel, museum display and a host of other colonial administrative functions. As Said (1993: 36) notes: 'Knowledge of subject races ... is what makes their management easy and profitable; knowledge gives power, more power requires more knowledge, and so on, an increasingly profitable dialectic of information and control'. To control the Other was to thus create and have knowledge of the Other.

Historians and sociologists of colonialism (such as Prakash, 1999, on India) have studied the so-called 'colonial gaze', to refer to the manner in which this vast collection of different knowledge was also an act of power with surveillance and disciplinary effects on the native subject. Taking from Foucault's (1976) ideas on governmentality, Prakash demonstrates the effects of so-called knowledge-power regimes on disciplining the body and mind of the native through the 'scientific' machinations of the knowledge complex, and in so doing, of turning them into a governable subject (a form of political subjectivation). As noted earlier by Ashcroft et al. (2000), these knowledges were both explicitly and implicitly premised on a belief in the purported superiority of the colonizer and the cultural and racial inferiority of the colonized. Postcolonial work illustrates that colonizers were in the business of 'civilizing the natives', of bringing modernity, 'order' and 'progress' to the putatively primitive nature of the colonized. Colonialism was thus also a moral exercise aimed at 'cleansing' the cultural impurities of the natives (McClintock, 1995).

As McClintock (1995) points out, progress was one of the most tenacious tropes in colonial metanarratives. Colonialism was underscored by a teleology of progress where Europe/Western civilization was always ahead of the Rest, leading the way not only with economic strength and expertise but also with a cultural and moral superiority. As Fabian (1983) argues, this linear teleology worked with a secular, empty and homogeneous conception of time. The West was placing its own historical narrative on the world: the West was the agent of history, fashioning its own modernity and replacing the histories and subjectivities of Others with its own categories. As Chakrabarty (2000) explains, all other histories became a supplement of this European master narrative; colonial natives could no longer write history. The West was at the vanguard of history; the Other was trapped in tradition, in non-modernity. This has been referred to as the problem of Eurocentrism – not just the assumption of the superiority of European history and civilization, but the attempt to posit this 'local' and parochial history as universal in nature. In short, 'worlding the world' (Spivak, 1985).

The 'West' and the 'non-West', or the 'Rest', are terms that we use frequently throughout this book, yet their very meaning is one of considerable ambiguity and tension. It would be fallacious to assume that the term 'the West' refers to a unitary and self-explanatory referent whose content and meaning developed clearly and independently from the 'non-West'. As Said (1978) explains, both ideas of the Occident (the West) and the Orient (the East) are dialectically constructed fictions. Ontologically, both are products of particular knowledge systems (the discourse of Orientalism, to which we return later) that bring into existence, and thus attribute meaning to, these phenomena. In short, they are cultural constructions whose meanings and natures are contingent and mutually dependent: what counts as the West depends on that which it is not (i.e. the non-West).

Following this extremely selective historical and conceptual overview, we can outline some of the tasks of postcolonial studies. First, postcolonialism involves an investigation of the motives, experiences and effects of the interactions of colonizer and colonized across the variety of different colonial regimes. A number of qualifying statements are in order. For one, postcolonial work underscores a concern with particularity and local experience. Since each colonial regime (British, Dutch, French and so on) had a very different history and was played out in distinct and often contradictory ways depending on exactly where it was being exercised, it is fallacious to generalize about the experience of colonization from both the colonizer's and the colonized's viewpoint. One contingency is whether one is referring to a settler-colony or a colony of occupation (Ashcroft et al., 2000). The British Empire controlled Australia through settlement, the murder of many in the small indigenous Aboriginal population and environmental colonialism. In India, which had a larger populace, such settlement was not possible, and a strategy of paying-off local elites and corporate colonialism (notably by the East India Company) became central to the maintenance of power. More than this, we should be wary about homogenizing the categories of colonizer and colonized. Each of these categories contains diversity and group hierarchy: it would be foolish, for instance, to assume that national elites in colonized societies experienced colonialism in the same way as subaltern[2] populations and the poor, or to assume that men and women played the same roles in colonizer and colonized societies. Empire was marked by the differential status of gendered, classed and racialized subjects in metropolitan and colonized locations.

Second, postcolonialism underscores the point that the process of colonization was not simply accepted and passively assimilated by local peoples without considerable struggle and active resistance. The rubric of anticolonialism, as opposed to postcolonialism, is most relevant here and refers to the 'political struggle of colonized peoples against the specific ideology and practice of colonialism' (Ashcroft et al., 2000: 14). The rejection of colonial power and the demand for the reinstatement of local control of the political, economic and cultural domains of colonized societies took divergent forms. The nature of the colonial regime – whether it was a settler colony or colonial occupation – affected the form and intensity of anticolonial struggles. Forms of resistance ranged from silent and passive protest and the subversion of the colonizer's own institutions and cultural expressions, to demands for independence and a postcolonial nation-state (Chatterjee, 1986), often accompanied by armed and violent revolutionary struggle (as associated with Frantz Fanon, 1952/1986). The goal of postindependence colonial states is often expressed as decolonization or the 'process of revealing and dismantling colonialist power in all its forms' (Ashcroft et al., 2000: 63), especially of education systems that had been a core conduit for the reproduction of colonial ideology. To ignore these important aspects of struggle and resistance is to falsely ascribe omnipotence to colonizing forces and to downplay the considerable tension and ambiguity involved in the colonial encounter.

Third, postcolonialism promotes the understanding that whilst 'formal' colonialism may have come to an end, centuries of economic, cultural and political interdependencies do not just wither away overnight. Colonial structures would thus continue to shape the trajectory for postcolonial futures. In this regard, considerable debate has ensued within postcolonial studies about the use of the prefix 'post', and whether one should deploy the term 'postcolonialism' (without hyphen) or 'post-colonialism' (with hyphen) (McClintock, 1995; Young, 2001). The debate has centred on two issues: first the understanding that there is no unitary date for the formal independence of colonies and hence no one point when 'post'-colonization began (with the hyphen debate); second the understanding that, whilst colonialism as the physical occupation of a colony may have been brought to an end, economic, cultural and ideological structures connecting colonizer and colonized have not simply disappeared as a result of independence.

The term 'neo-colonialism', initially associated with Kwame Nkrumah,[3] captures some of these ideas in its reference to 'the new force of global control operating through a local elite or comprador class' (Ashcroft et al., 2000: 64). Considerable debate exists, for instance, about the postcolonial status of nations such as Australia and Canada, former parts of the British Empire. Since gaining independence, it can be argued that these nations now pursue their own form of internal colonialism towards their ethnic/linguistic minorities, that is the Aborigines in Australia and the French-speaking minority of Canada. The question of Ireland can also be interpreted as an anticolonial or anti-imperialist struggle. Moreover, Young (2001: 67) refers to the contemporary global system of late capitalism

(Young, 2001: 67) as containing forms of both neo-colonialism and new instances of imperialism associated with the domination, for most of the post-World War Two period, of the United States and its associated commercial-military complex. The various machinations of American power form a key part of any contemporary postcolonial critique, especially in this book on management knowledge.

Fourth, since colonialism involved the attempt to suppress and replace indigenous knowledge systems with those of the colonizer, a central concern of postcolonial scholarship has been to forge a space to give back voice (Bhabha, 1994; Spivak, 1988) to the experiences, cultures and languages of the Other. This is seen as a key part of the process of decolonization and takes form in calls for a revival of indigenous languages (Ngugi, 1981) as a mode for changing attitudes to indigenous cultures. Postcolonial scholarship emerged from the discipline of literary criticism, and most often by scholars from the Third World who have emigrated to the USA, with a concern for 'writing back' to the centre through fiction, biography and autobiography. Over a series of iterations of the same essay, Spivak famously debates the possibilities for the subaltern to 'speak'. A further concern lies with the rewriting of colonial history from the perspective of the colonized. The work of the Subaltern Studies Group (Guha, 1982) has played a central role in this aspect of postcolonialism, by focusing on the role of the subaltern (that is, non-elite groups) in India and South Asia as agents of protest, change and history. They have fostered considerable, interesting and complex debate and rewriting of the histories of colonialism 'from below', and thus reinstating the subaltern voice to colonial historiography.

In sum, and for the sake of terminological convenience[4] at this point in the book, we can say that postcolonialism can be used as an umbrella term for many, though not all, scholars who wish to pursue a critique of colonialism, neo-colonialism and imperialism, as well as resistances and responses to them in the form of anticolonialism and decolonization. Postcolonial scholarship seeks to deploy theoretical scholarship and analytic practices that aim to reveal and disrupt the hegemonic and universalizing posture, and mythical status of Western knowledge by provincializing them (Chakrabarty, 2000). It is about overturning the use of a European teleology and disrupting it, of legitimating the knowledge-systems of Others and of working towards progressive and radical solutions to the economic and cultural inequalities between the 'West and the Rest'. Postcolonialism is, therefore, a critique of modernity as imagined by the West, and an attempt to reclaim history, and a particular path to, or rejection of, modernity amongst formerly colonized nations. It provides 'a uniquely radical and ethically informed critique of Western modernity' (Prasad, 2003: 33).

Postcolonialism is not, however, a homogeneous body of work. It contains a number of significant internal fissures and tensions, and has also been subjected to external critique. Recent debates in postcolonial scholarship have involved a critique of the High Theory represented in the works of Said, Bhabha and Spivak, the 'Holy Trinity' of postcolonial thinkers. Moore-Gilbert (1997) describes postcolonialism as a combination of postcolonial theory on the one hand, and postcolonial criticism on the other hand. In this text, we use the terms postcolonial theory, postcolonial analysis and postcolonialism in the manner articulated by Moore-Gilbert (1997). This is not semantic hair-splitting on the part of Moore-Gilbert. Trenchant, and sometimes quite personal, criticisms have been levelled at postcolonial theory by Ahmad (1992), Dirlik (1997) and JanMohamed (1983) for its lack of what they consider a political agenda. Driven by historical materialist and neo-Marxist theoretical frames, they consider postcolonial theory to lack an emancipatory politics, a clear path for social change and to be elitist, cosmopolitan intellectualizing. Huggan (2001) illuminates the aestheticizing tendencies of certain forms of postcolonial writing and critique (for instance in relation to the literature on Salman Rushdie), and refers to the manner in which the 'margins' are now marketed as part of an 'alterity industry' in the West. Moreover, some historians also feel that the work pursued under the 'new' label of postcolonialism is just old wine in new bottles, and that (especially Arab) scholars had been doing the kind of 'postcolonial' work associated with Edward Said long before it became popular in comparative literature and cultural studies departments in the US.

Postcolonialism is not, however, merely an interesting concern of relevance to the disciplines of the humanities whence it emerged, disconnected from the disciplines of the social sciences, management and organization studies. As Prasad notes, it is the case that: '... the continuing imprint of colonialism and anticolonialism is discernible in a range of contemporary practices and institutions, whether economic, political, or cultural' (2003: 5). Management and organization are examples of such practices and institutions. Postcolonialism asks questions of profound importance to those of us working in the management academy. It raises questions of how the history of management was also the history of colonialism; the role of business and management in the reproduction of economic and social inequalities between the West and the Rest; the espoused superiority of Western management theory; alternative modes of organizing available in non-Western contexts; and, importantly, what counts as progress in our discipline (Calás & Smircich,

2003a). In the next section, we outline the ways in which postcolonialism has hitherto been received in the management academy.

Postcolonialism in the management academy

Postcolonialism has had a profound effect on academic work across a number of disciplines in the humanities and social sciences, most notably in literary criticism, history and cultural studies. Its inception in the academy is conventionally associated with the publication in 1978 of Edward Said's monumental work *Orientalism: Western Conceptions of the Orient.*[5] Despite the popularity of postcolonialism in the humanities, its impact and reception in the various disciplines of the social sciences has been uneven. Within 'the business school', a postcolonial interrogative space has finally emerged in the study of organizations and organizing, and is principally associated with organizational and accounting scholars whose institutional bases are the USA, Canada, the UK, Australia and New Zealand.

The contributions of Anshuman Prasad and Pushkala Prasad have been paramount in establishing a postcolonial organizational analysis, especially through their inception of the postcolonial stream at biennial critical management studies (CMS) in 2001, which led to the publication in 2003 of Anshuman's edited collection entitled *Postcolonial Theory and Organizational Analysis: A Critical Engagement.* Postcolonial work has been primarily conducted through CMS conferences in the UK, pre-conference workshops and streams in the AOM's CMS and gender and diversity divisions, and at EGOS and the APROS conference. Its influence even at CMS, once marginal, would seem to be changing. The postcolonial track at the 2007 CMS in Manchester was very healthily attended (typically 50 in the sessions) and resulted in a further edited book (Banerjee, Chio & Mir, 2009).

Postcolonial work in the management academy has drawn selectively from theoretical frames and issues of concern in the broader domain of postcolonialism. A review of the literature suggests three key trajectories of work: history; knowledge, discourse and representation; and materialist and transnational analyses. It is vital to note that these three trajectories are not discrete or mutually exclusive areas of inquiry. There are examples of work where analytic concern transgresses the distinctions we have made above: in some historical analyses, for instance, there is a dual concern to understand how categories for representing the Other became important aspects for developing a political economy of colonialism, that is, a concern with both representational and materialist phenomena.

To begin, then, there is a strong historicizing tenet to postcolonial organizational analysis that underlines the imperative of understanding Western organization and Western management principles and practices as emerging from the colonial encounter. As Prasad (2003: 31–32) notes:

> (…) postcolonialism can help management scholars examine and understand the influences of colonialism in constituting/producing current practices and discourses of management. One result of such analysis would be that, rather than being viewed as autonomous Western productions, management practices and discourses would come to be understood as having emerged from (and/or bearing the imprint of) the colonial encounter between the West and the non-West.

Postcolonial theory allows us to tell a different story (or stories) about the genesis of our disciplines, one that better acknowledges the often disturbing contexts in which ideas and practices that we now take for granted were induced. As Frenkel & Shenhav (2006) note, the constitutive role of the Other in Western management discourse has typically been edited out of canonical representations of our discipline to create the illusion of cultural unity and purity. Cooke has produced a number of important historicizing works (1998, 2003a, 2003b, 2004), which often, though not always, adopt a postcolonial tenor,[6] to interrogate critically the colonial evolution of a number of management practices. For instance, he illuminated how what was later labelled classical management theory was developed *inter alia* on cotton plantations in the American South where four million slaves were subject to the bureaucratic principles and practices of 38,000 managers by the 1860s (2003a). Furthermore, Frenkel and Shenhav (2006) reveal the explicit and implicit Orientalism and racism of early treatises on management, including Lord Cromer's explicitly Orientalist writings on bureaucracy, which are typically expunged from conventional management historiography. So too are the implicit Orientalism and early African anthropological influences on Mayo's work. There is also a well-developed stream of historical research in accounting[7] (and some in taxation studies) that deploys postcolonial theory. (We will review some of this work in Chapter 4.)

There are multiple interests within the trajectory of work on knowledge. The first aspect relates to the identification and critique of the continued practice of Othering (*pace* Said, 1978) and Eurocentrism across a variety of Western representational forms associated with management, organization and marketing. A number of studies have focused on the presence of Eurocentrism and colonial ideology in academic fields such as cross-cultural or comparative management (Kwek, 2003; Westwood, 2001, 2004) or organization studies (Ibarra-Colado, 2006); particular areas of theoretical or conceptual discourse such as management control (Mir, Mir & Upadhyaya, 2003), organizational culture (Cooke, 2003c), globalization (Banerjee & Linstead, 2001; Banerjee et al., 2009), sustainable development (Banerjee, 2003), concepts of political risk (de Maria, 2008) and qualitative research in IB (Jack & Westwood, 2006); or through critiques of particular texts, for instance Hofstede's *Culture's Consequences* (Ailon, 2008). Others have focused on questions of pedagogy and the presence of Eurocentric assumptions and Othering practices in the teaching of cultural diversity in universities and business schools (Jaya, 2001), and in private sector cross-cultural training materials (Jack & Lorbiecki, 2003). A final area of interest in this area is the reproduction of Othering strategies such as Orientalism, tropicalization and exoticization in various aspects of business practice or commercial life, including product marketing (Jack, 2008), tourism (Echtner & Prasad, 2003), business journalism (Priyadharshini, 2003) and the production of oil (Prasad, 1997a).

A second element of the postcolonial organizational interest in knowledge relates to the description, legitimization and discussion of non-Western forms of organization, management and accounting. Justification for this approach relates to the concern expressed above about the domination of Western knowledge in management theory and practice, and its positing as a universal phenomenon. The well-developed Maori approach to research across a number of different disciplines in New Zealand represents the best developed example of a non-Eurocentric alternative to mainstream management, which develops out of Maori cosmology (Henry & Pene, 2001). Other recent promising empirical studies of non-Western forms of knowledge include Nyathi's (2008) study of Ubuntu organization in South Africa and Chandrasekara's (2009) ethnographic work on the accounting and financial practices of subaltern women in Sri Lanka.

A third element concerns what happens to knowledge (such as a business model) when it 'travels' between the West and the Rest, and is enacted in local, non-Western contexts. Key to this area of analysis is a critique of simplistic, homogenizing views of the transfer process, which assume the omnipotence of Western models in replacing local knowledge systems. Studies of encounter reveal a considerably more complex, ambiguous and subtle process of cultural accommodation, resistance and hybridization where elements of both the transmitted model and local practice come to change as a result of their inter-action. In this vein, Frenkel and Shenhav (2003) examined the transfer of British and American productivity models into Israel. Mir, Banerjee and Mir (2008) and Mir and Mir (2009) present a fieldwork-based analysis of knowledge transfer between a MNC and a contracting firm based in the 'Third World'. Chio (2008) explores the formation of modern market citizens in Malaysia through the transfer and subject-ivation of local Malaysians by 'foreign' discourses. Bhabha's psycho-analytic concept of the colonial encounter offers particular analytic promise in this field, as illustrated in Frenkel's (2008) application of the idea to the study of knowledge transfer in MNCs.

Finally, there is a small but strong strand of postcolonial organizational analysis informed by political economy and transnational perspectives. Authors here focus on systemic questions of capital accumulation, the expropriation of land and natural resources (Banerjee, 2000) by private interests and wider postcolonial dilemmas associated with economic development, especially in postcolonial nations such as Malaysia (Chio, 2005). Questions of death, destruction and the military in the post-colonial world (Banerjee, 2008), and the treatment of Aboriginals by the Australian state (Sullivan, 2008; Tedmanson, 2008) also form part of the postcolonial terrain in organization studies.

At a broader level, and taking these three interconnected areas of academic work as a whole, perhaps the key implication of an emergent postcolonial interrogative space in the business school is that it offers possibilities: 'for *thinking about thinking* and for *radically rethinking* the modern idea of "progress" in organization and management studies. The stories we have written in much organization theory, our concepts and representations, no matter how "global" (or precisely because of this), represent the ways of thinking of certain peoples and not others' (Calás & Smircich, 2003: 45, italics in the original). Usually noted in relation to history, progress in organization studies has traditionally been written by its 'victors', that is those whose interests are perhaps most clearly aligned to those of capital. We are therefore offered an invitation of thinking differently about what constitutes (theoretical) progress in ICCM, and to offer other voices for progress.

We now offer an account of the particular postcolonial theoretical framework that underpins the analysis presented in this book.

Neo-colonial discourse analysis and organization field

Expressed in the terms of neo-discourse analysis, our framework prin-cipally draws upon selected writings by Edward Said, Dipesh Chakrabarty and Aamir Mufti, and to a lesser extent work on organization fields and dependency theory. Later in the book, and as appropriate to the material analysed, we will introduce the ideas of other postcolonial writers including Homi Bhabha and Gayatri Spivak. We deploy this combination of writers and associated concepts in order to conduct an analysis of the 'theory culture' of ICCM in a postcolonial context. That is to say, whilst we wish to make a primary contribution of a textual and cultural analytic nature to postcolonial studies in the business school, we wish to contextualize our commentary by demonstrating sensitivity to the historical and institutional contexts for knowledge production in these fields. Three key concepts articulate these concerns: provincialization; recontextualization and politicization.

First, we address our concerns with the universalizing posture of most international and cross-cultural management studies by setting out to provincialize it (Chakrabarty, 2000). Provincialization is a key task of postcolonial scholarship and it involves the goal of unveiling and critiquing the Eurocentrism of the knowledge-systems that constitute received wisdom in the Western academy, the management academy included. In this book, we set about the task of provincialization in three ways: first, through historicizing work; second, by locating presumptions of universality and tying them to particular cultural contexts and interests; and third, by outlining ways in which the pretence of universality has been accomplished through the workings of institutional hegemony. This is a task of defamiliarization, as noted above: that is, of re-reading and rethinking our discipline and of opening up a space for debate about what counts as academic progress.

Second, the point of any piece of postcolonial scholarship is not just to inspect something critically, but to disrupt, change and transform it. We use the phrase recontexualization to index this goal, as noted earlier in this chapter. Recontextualization is a political project in so far as its goal is to challenge the dominant values, interests and institutional practices and structures of ICCM by opening up a space for alternative ways of thinking and doing in our discipline. Notably we will ask how we rethink our relations to Others by rethinking and 'practising' differently the culture concept in ICCM in philosophical, methodological and institutional terms. It is also to admit, however, that whilst changes to these 'representational' aspects of ICCM might represent some kind of progress, they are problematic in a wider material context weighted in the favour of a history of the capitalist present. Our third concern is thus to politicize ICCM and to draw attention to its ethical practices and responsibilities.

In the next two sub-sections, we add theoretical flesh to this skeletal outline, combining insights from postcolonial theory with work on organization fields and dependency theory.

Whilst charges of Eurocentrism are familiar to scholars working in comparative literature and other humanities disciplines, perhaps even provoking 'yawns of familiarity' (as noted by Mufti, 2005), the problem of Eurocentrism in the management academy is all too rarely acknowledged, far less understood. Eurocentrism is an epistemological problem that lies at the centre of the hierarchical organization of global culture. According to Mufti (2005), Eurocentrism refers to a set of knowledge structures that 'normalize the idea of Europe as the birth-place of the modern', and render it 'the theoretical subject of all historical knowledge'. As noted earlier, the historical emergence of this cultural logic is associated with the colonial history of Europe and it rests on the military and economic power of colonial regimes to expand their horizons of interests. According to Mufti, the outcome of Europe as the theoretical subject of all historical knowledge is that historical and cultural accounts of non-European societies can only be rendered through the knowledge structures of the West. The history of Europe is thus the grand narrative through which the histories of other nations become intelligible, a position that reflects the cultural domination of European knowledge structures within the academy. It is also a logic that embodies what Mufti calls an 'informal developmentalism' – history happened first in the West and then elsewhere.

How does this relate to those of us outside Europe? If Eurocentrism is about the history and knowledge of Europe, surely the charge does not apply to knowledge generated in North America, which includes, of course, most management and organization theory? This is not the case. As Chakrabarty explains in his work *Provincializing Europe* (2000), the Europe in Eurocentrism does not so much refer to the geographical entity as much as it refers to 'figures of the imaginary', to modes of 'identification and organization of cultures' (Chakrabarty, 2000: 28, in Mufti, 2005: 27). Eurocentric knowledge structures travel and continue to do so. As Mufti argues:

> The modes of cultural authority that the idea of Europe regulates are *Western* in an encompassing sense, underwriting narratives of American universalism as well as those of a uniquely European polity and culture in the geographically specific sense. It is the social and cultural *force* of this idea of Europe in intellectual life, as in the

phenomenal world of global power relations, that I am referring to here as Eurocentrism (2005: 474, italics in the original).

Mufti echoes the criticisms of previous writers, including Said and Spivak, that his discipline of comparative literature (in the US and Europe) exhibits a Eurocentric theory culture. In short, Eurocentrism is built into the shared knowledges and practices in literature depart-ments in North America, according to Mufti. In relation to our critique of ICCM, these concepts of provincialization and Eurocentrism provide materials for an investigation of the multiple parochialisms of our field in a manner reflective of a postcolonial lens.

In other words, they can be used to recontextualize and inflect in a postcolonial manner the discourse of parochialism in MOS of the sort illustrated by Boyacigiller and Adler. Thus, to what extent do we consider ICCM to embody a Eurocentric theory culture? How is it a problem as, like comparative literature, ICCM strives to 'respond more adequately to the hierarchical situation of global culture' (ibid: 473).

Neo-colonial discourse analysis is an interpretive procedure that enables scholars to illuminate the textual strategies and practices of Orientalism that belie the wider problematic of Eurocentrism described above. It is therefore an appropriate methodology for addressing the question of the extent to which ICCM can be considered Eurocentric and the precise forms that this takes. To explain it, we need to under-stand that colonial discourse analysis is the name given to the kind of analysis pursued by Edward Said in his landmark text *Orientalism: Western Conceptions of the Orient* (1978), the first in a trilogy of reflec-tions dealing with Western representations and experiences of the Other. The success of Said's work resides in its systematic and complex un-ravelling of the way in which Western scholars (historians, geographers, anthropologists, linguists, philologists) and others (travel writers, artists, curators, administrators) constructed knowledge of the 'Orient' (refer-ring to the Middle East and North Africa, rather than Japan as many might think) (Gandhi, 1998; Moore-Gilbert, 1997). Said explored the sets of representations (categories, classifications, images) utilized by these scholars and commentators in producing accounts of the Oriental 'other'. In doing so, he emphasized the notion of the Orient as a cul-tural production rather than a reflection of an already existing reality. For him:

(...) as much as the West itself, the Orient is an idea that has a history and a tradition of thought, imagery, and vocabulary that have given it reality and presence in and for the West (Said, 1978: 5).

Orientalism is, therefore, a Western set of ontological assumptions, epistemological practices and cultural constructions which serve to create[8] its object of study, rather than a descriptive set of methods for articulating the contours of an *a priori* reality called the Orient. In short, Orientalism is a practice of Othering where the construction of the Self is dialectically achieved through the simultaneous construction of the Other and becomes naturalized. This process of naturalization means that the ideological practices required to produce these knowledges are erased or repressed, such that the effect, the Orientalised Other, is made to appear as a form of truth, 'free' of ideological domination or political distortion. What Said shows is that the 'naturalization' of the knowledge of the Other is neither neutral nor value-free, as noted earlier in this chapter. We describe what we do in this book as neo-colonial discourse analysis to exhibit our theoretical debt to Said and, through the prefix *neo-*, to highlight the continued presence in contemporary (ICCM) texts of the very strategies and practices of Othering that Said illuminated in literatures from at least the last three centuries.

In Said's analysis, the identification and critical discussion of the ways in which the Other comes into existence as an effect of Orientalist discourse is in large part based on analysing how binary oppositions work to create asymmetrical relations between the Occident and the Orient. Prasad (1997a) illuminates a whole series of binary oppositions (see Table 1.1) mobilized in the construction of a superior West to an inferior non-West. These binaries work through the devaluation of the one by the other and the resultant idea is that 'difference' means 'less than' rather than simply 'different from'.

It is on the basis of these binary oppositions that the discourse of progress was organized in a manner that suggested that: some 'races' were inferior to others; colonizing powers had a moral obligation to assume control and help develop lesser peoples; the knowledge-systems of such people were inferior; only the 'developed' and 'educated' people of the colonizing world were capable of producing valid knowledge; the subaltern should not be allowed to speak for themselves, until judged as 'progressed'. As Ashcroft et al. (1995) explain, 'knowing' other people through this type of discourse underpinned imperial dominance and, more insidiously, became the mode through which the colonized were persuaded to know themselves.[9]

Table 1.1 The Hierarchical System of Colonialist Binaries

West	Non-West
Active	Passive
Center	Margin/periphery
Civilised	Primitive/savage
Developed	Backward/underdeveloped/
	Underdeveloped/developing
Fullness/plenitude/completeness	Lack/inadequacy/incompleteness
Historical (people with history)	Ahistorical (people without history)
The liberated	The savable
Masculine	Feminine/effeminate
Modern	Archaic
Nation	Tribe
Occidental	Oriental
Scientific	Superstitious
Secular	Non secular
Subject	Object
Superior	Inferior
The vanguard	The led
White	Black/brown/yellow

Source: Prasad 1997a: 291

The work of these binary oppositions in Orientalist practice often coalesced in the circulation of particular colonial myths. The 'myth of the lazy native' is carefully documented in Alatas' (1977) account of the colonial history of the Malays, Filipinos and Javanese. In these contexts, this myth circulated to 'justify compulsion and unjust practices in the mobilization of labour in the colonies' (p. 2). With regard to Africa, the 'myth of the dark continent' has a complex history traced by Brantlinger (1985) from the years prior to 1833, when slavery was abolished in British lands, up to the partitioning of Africa in the latter part of the 19th century. The myth functioned ideologically to demand that Africa, and its 'savage customs' (notably cannibalism), be colonized and thus 'civilized' and 'enlightened' on 'moral, religious and scientific grounds' (pp. 167–168). As Brantlinger points out, at the core of this mythical ideology was a projection of European fears and desires on to the Other. It was underpinned by a psychology of 'blaming the victim' (p. 198) for their own colonization.

A further example is the 'myth of the tropics'. Here images of the tropics lay claim to a 'lush earthly paradise, full of exotic flora and fauna', an 'Edenesque abundance ... held responsible for the lethargy and idleness of the tropical natives' (Prasad, 2003: 157). Crang (1998)

notes how images of Africa (and elsewhere) in imperialist and Orientalist discourses were typically highly sexualized and feminized, a likely outcome of the fact that the fears and desires projected onto the continent were those of white, male colonialists. According to Crang, fascination with male dominance, female sexual availability and the 'menace' of black sexuality lay at the heart of white colonial male fears and desire for the Other.

The use of a Saidian-inspired discourse analytic approach is, to be sure, not without its limitations.[10] One of these is the fact that he offers little commentary on the material context of production for the various forms of representation in which he is interested (Moore-Gilbert, 1997). According to Hardy (2001), whilst discourses (such as Orientalism) are embodied in texts, they also stretch beyond any one text. A key challenge for our analysis is to consider how we might account for these 'stretches', and the history and wider structures of domination that find expression in institutional life (in our case, in the institutional life of the management academy). That is to say, our interest also lies in the role of various actors such as journal rankings, editors, academic conferences, leading business schools, leading names, editorial policies and so on, in shaping and reproducing a normative framework for the conduct of 'good' research and teaching in ICCM. Furthermore, our wider interest lies in the fact that ICCM is itself a global discourse – its core ideas, practices and agenda can be found in a number of different national and cultural contexts. An interesting question, then, is how does ICCM travel? And what kinds of claim might we make about its influence and import outside the leading centres of ICCM knowledge production? (See Chapter 3 on this issue.) Certain comments are therefore appropriate about how we think that texts and 'knowledge' more broadly are circulated through certain discursive, material and institutional practices.

Organization field and structural dependencies

We use the concepts of organization field and imitation as a way of conceptualizing modes of circulation. According to Hedmo et al. (2005), field is an analytic concept that enables us to talk about the links between individual actors, their identities and meaning-making processes, and the wider patterns of actions and norms that facilitate collective life between a number of actors. In following Bourdieu, Hedmo et al., take a structurational approach to argue that 'the field is a system of relationships in which dominant actors occupy central positions; more peripheral actors continuously seek greater influence and more central positions, challenging central actors and dominant understandings in the field' (2005: 192–193). Fields therefore have two important qualities. For one, they display a series of regularities that exist beyond the context of any one individual action. Second, fields have a 'dynamic stability' in which the tensions between different social actors and the accommodation of certain challenges to the status quo are reconciled.

According to Hedmo et al., practices and intertwined processes of imitation are central in the development of fields as areas for institutional life. In fact they see them as so significant that they demonstrate and discuss so-called 'fields of imitation' (ibid: 191) in their fascinating account of the development of management education in Europe. For these authors, imitation is a performative process where the results of imitation may mean that the model/idea/practice being imitated is significantly altered through the copying process. Imitation opens up the possibility of new relationships and identifications, and is perhaps better seen as a moment of translation rather than the faithful copying of an imagined original. This process is also captured in terms like hybridization, recombination, translation and editing. In relation to European management education, they distinguish between three processes of imitation: broadcasting, chain and mediated imitation.

Imitation, they argue, is typically conceived in terms of single actors imitating other single actors. The broadcasting mode of imitation is perhaps closest to this, with a specific model or core of ideas being incorporated into local practice by a set of actors. Hedmo et al. suggest that this kind of imitation can lead to the homogenization of practices and the adoption of a single model that can be imitated by further actors in a local setting. In their study of management education, the broadcasting mode involved the initial promotion and imitation of a US management model in Europe (and in particular the MBA). As this model was embedded by particular actors in particular places, a chain of imitation then occurred, not of the US original (and with little explicit reference to it), but of the European imitation. Through this chain mode of imitation, similarity and variation emerged, rather than a process of homogenization. So, the MBA was deployed as a cultural form, a recognized category, whose contents were filled out in ways that reflected different local contexts and specificities of European educational systems.

Finally, 'the third mode of imitation is one in which the relationships between those being imitated and those imitating are *mediated by other organizations and actors*' (Hedmo et al., 2005: 196, italics in the original). Hedmo et al. pay particular attention to the carriers of ideas: those organizations and actors that play a key role in the circulation and translation of ideas in a local context through processes of discussion, codification, interpretation, certification and stigmatization. In a European context, these include accreditation bodies like the EFMD and EQUIS, and rankings tables in the media, for instance *The Financial Times*. These 'editors', as the authors call them, 'form templates and prototypes outside the local context of schools and beyond interactions between these schools' (ibid: 196). Social relations within these chains of imitation involve 'a combined logic of individual actors searching for reputation, status, recognition, and respect as well as following individual actors' rule-following logic' (p. 211).

In order to render the concept of organization field more relevant to a postcolonial frame, we layer it with ideas from dependency and world systems theory (Frank, 1975, 1978; Wallerstein, 1974). World systems theory, simply stated, is premised on the idea that from the 16th century on, the world's economies and societies were bound into an unequal system of relationships by the development of the capitalist system of production during the colonial period. Three principal structural positions existed in this world system – the core, the periphery and the semi-periphery – and unequal relations were the result of the differences between these structural positions. Unidirectional flows of power were assumed to flow from the core, to the periphery and semi-periphery, an assumption that has given rise to the criticism that world systems and dependency theory are overly deterministic and too certain about where the centre resides, and where a periphery. Appadurai (1990), for example, believes that ideas of core and periphery are redundant in a contemporary world marked by increasing transnational flows of people, capital, ideas and cultural symbols. Dispensing with the vocabulary of core and periphery does not, however, get rid of the 'real' material inequalities that continue to exist in the postcolonial era between economies and societies.

Whilst we share the broad idea of a world system, our view would be that the globe constitutes multiple cores, peripheries and semi-peripheries, and that where and how we choose to demarcate and understand the nodes and networks that connect them, and the manner of these relations, very much depends on what one's object of inquiry is. As we shall see to a greater extent in the next chapter, and more broadly through the remainder of the book, the fact that our object of inquiry is skewed by particular interests with particular implications for other parts of the world gives a very particular starting point for investigating the world system of ICCM.

Organization of the book

The book is structured into four key parts that enact in different ways, and with different foci, our key concerns to address the potential parochialisms of ICCM through the conceptual imperatives of pro-vincialization, recontextualization and politicization. This introductory chapter is one of three that constitute Part I. In the next chapter we clarify exactly where we place boundaries around the study of international and cross-cultural management in order to give us an object of inquiry, and then go on to show why a postcolonial critique is necessary for the theoretical and political development of these fields.

In Part II, we carry out important historicizing work, excavating and critically analysing the historical conditions of possibility for the emer-gence of the study of ICCM. Chapter 4 examines the 'birth' of modern scientific and anthropological knowledge systems, and their alignment with the commercial and military interests of colonial power mainly through the example of the British Empire. Chapter 5 focuses on the emergence of the USA as an imperial power in the immediate post-World War Two period and explores the importance of discourses of modernization, industrialization and development to the early field of IB/ICCM. Chapter 6 explores the continuing but reconfigured forms of imperialism and neo-colonialism propagated, but often masked, by economic and cultural processes of globalization.

Part III continues the work of provincializing international and cross-cultural management. In this section we conduct a neo-colonial discourse analysis of the representational practices and tactics of a sample of different kinds of work from ICCM, notably, but not only, student textbooks, through which the central figure of the Other has been invoked, constituted and positioned. Here we trace the legacy of ICCM's colonial roots through the manner in which these strategies and tactics appropriate and subjugate the Other within the Western gaze of academe, whilst at the same time providing the conditions for multiple forms of engagement and resistance to such forms of domina-tion. Parts II and III illuminate what we consider to be a latent struc-ture of domination in ICCM.

In Part IV, we address how the field might move forward by decolon-izing its constitutive theory, methodology and institutional practice. The answers are multifaceted and cover issues of ontology, epistemology, method, politics, ethics and the institutions of the academy. Whilst Chapter 10 places a particular focus on decolonizing methodologies for ICCM, Chapter 11 offers alternative institutional arrangements for knowledge production. Chapter 12 provides a reflexive evaluation of the arguments pursued in the book, and their potential implications for future scholarship in ICCM.

2
The Commitments and Omissions of ICCM

Introduction

This chapter, and the one that follows, set out to demonstrate why a postcolonial interrogation of international and cross-cultural management is essential for its theoretical and political development. We will identify in ICCM the multiple parochialisms (contextual, quantitative, qualitative) that Boyacigiller and Adler found in organizational science. Consequently, we will argue that the field is marked by a lack of demographic and epistemic diversity, ineluctably embedded in the values and interests of the West (and more especially North America) and reproductive of a highly limited and limiting functionalist and positivist theory culture that eschews the possible development of a critical trajectory for theory development. The multiple resources of postcolonial theory can thereupon be used appropriately to guide us to different locations from which different questions might be asked by a greater diversity of voices from a greater number of positions about our domain of inquiry.

This chapter is divided into three sections. First we place some definitional boundaries around our object of inquiry – the theoretical and empirical study of ICCM – and clarify what we mean when we deploy this conceptual label. The following two sections carry out some of the provincializing work necessitated by our PCT frame. Specifically we present a brief analysis of the contextual and qualitative parochialism in the field (developing this to a much greater extent in Chapter 3), followed by an outline and discussion of the forms of paradigmatic entrenchment and hegemonic practice that have resulted in a disavowal of epistemic reflexivity and a trajectory for heterodox theory development.

Some ground-clearing

One of the difficulties of any project intent on critiquing and contributing to the transformation of a substantive domain of intellectual inquiry is coming to a shared agreement on how one represents that domain before one subsequently interrogates it. To represent is necessarily to construct partial (in both senses of 'selective' and 'skewed'), and therefore highly subjective, frames through which an object emerges. Our portrayal of ICCM is therefore unlikely to be shared by all readers, but we offer some specification of our view of the field not least because it is such an uneven, nebulous and discrepant terrain. The topography of this terrain is inscribed by the variety of theoretical and empirical work conducted by business and management scholars and others. Work predominantly relates to the nature and effects of the practice of management as conducted in an international and comparative context with, frequently, a common focus on culture as the 'variable' of focal interest through its presumed capacity to account for differences in observed practice. However, the terrain is complicated, firstly by the scrutiny of these broad issues from a range of sub-discipline areas such as organization theory (OT), human resources management (HRM) and organizational behaviour (OB), as well as by the adjacency, if not overlap, with another field of inquiry that identifies itself as international business (IB). This last field incorporates investigations of international trade, MNE/TNC operations, internationalization processes, investment decisions and contexts, international strategy and so on, but may still include issues such as managing international operations, expatriation, and the effects of culture on international business.

The abutment with IB is problematic since it makes any boundary between IB and ICCM imprecise and so interferes with an uncluttered specification of our domain of interest. It is an issue complicated by the fact that IB has an extensive heritage, historically embedded as it is within 300 years of classical political economy. Of course, we more commonly think of the contemporary study of IB as an offshoot of the economics discipline in the US and UK in the immediate post-World War Two period. Indeed, the study of international trade theory, with its historical focus on the reasons for, and benefits to be gained from, trade between nations, as well as more recent developments in technology-based trade and capital investment theory at the level of the firm have become conventional learning materials in IB curricula. Conceptual work often dovetails here with the strategy literature (notably via the influence of Michael Porter and his national diamond) and links to work on the internationalization of the firm and industrial and national competitiveness.

A cursory glance at the key IB journals in recent years (notably the *Journal of International Business Studies* – JIBS), however, suggests that all is not well with the discipline. Questions have been raised by eminent IB scholars in relation to two inter-related issues: first a consistent concern with a perceived lack of clarity about what is actually distinctive about IB inquiry (Shenkar, 2004); second a perception that the IB research agenda may be 'running out of steam' (Buckley, 2002; Peng, 2004). Such concern with the putative absence of a substantive domain of inquiry signals a degree of disquiet, perhaps even paranoia, amongst IB scholars about the legitimacy and respectability of their endeavours. It is a concern that, in our view, is further signified by what appears to be a repeated preoccupation with addressing and assessing the state of the art prevailing in the field. This is particularly manifest with an apparently obsessive desire to demonstrate the currency, growth and impact of the field through its publications and citations performance – and not just in dedicated IB journals, but more broadly (DuBois & Reeb, 2000; Inkpen, 2001; Phene & Guisinger, 1998). This self-absorption has an incidental benefit for us in that it has led to a detailed documentation of the profile of publication in the field, showing who has published what, about whom and where (more detail to follow in Chapter 3).

The perception of a lack of clarity in relation to the substantive nature of international inquiry in business schools spawned by the paranoia of IB is repeated among and compounded by those who self-define as international management (IM) scholars. The meaning of IM also exhibits significant variability. Firstly, there are those who see it as a mere sub-set of IB and hold it to be emergent from a strategic concern with the management of MNEs and/or the internationalization of the firm. Secondly, there are others for whom IM is different from classic IB through its focus on a range of specifically management issues. However, this view still sees it anchored around the management of a MNE or international enterprise of some form. For example, taking just one well-known IM scholar, Peterson (2004: 25) suggests that IM is a complex of a number of sub-areas including 'international strategy, human resource management (HRM), organizational behaviour, ethics, industrial relations, and international joint ventures (IJVs)'. Thirdly, IM is taken as substantively different from IB by expressing a wider concern for the impact of social, cultural, historical, political and institutional issues on the activities of economic actors in the contemporary global economy. Fourthly, there are those who define IM in terms of its comparative and cross-cultural concerns, that is, it is focused upon a comparison of management issues across national or cultural boundaries. Boyacigiller et al. (1996) label this as the cross-national comparative research approach, the longest established tradition in ICCM,[1] which along with more recent intercultural interactive and multiple cultures approaches, form a broader terrain for the culture concept. It might also be noted that there are those who see the whole notion of IM as a chimera in that, for them, management is management – whether it occurs in a domestic or an international business and hence there is no need for any special focus of study. Despite this uncertainty and diffusion, IM is for us, at least as an academic discourse, real and needs to be conceived of in ways other than a narrow focus on the management of MNEs or internationalizing firms. It is real too in that it constructs a discourse and the appearance of knowledge that impacts upon practice and participates in the reproduction of power inequalities and certain hegemonic structures.

These divisions within the 'field' were apparent very early on. As we shall see, IB and ICCM emerged fully within the Western academy (primarily in the USA) in the post-World War Two era with economics initially the lead discipline informing its emergence. Indeed, Nath (1975/1988), in classifying the strands of historical development of ICCM, locates the work of Kerr and colleagues (such as Harbison & Myers, 1959; Kerr et al., 1960) as paramount in a particular strand he labels the 'economic development approach'. As the name suggests, it was informed primarily by economics and was interested in the comparative analysis of the role of industrialization and management in economic development. (A more detailed account will follow in Chapter 5.) Nath refers to a broader approach that presumes to examine the relationship between management practice variability and a range of external factors such as the legal-political, the economic and the sociocultural, as the 'environmental approach' and sees the early work of Farmer and Richman (1965) as an exemplar.

Work that focused more narrowly on culture as the key factor in examining cross-national differences Nath tags as the 'behavioural approach'. He notes the work of Barrett and Bass (1976), Davis (1971) and Haire, Ghiselli and Porter (1966) as examples. A fourth approach, identified as an 'open systems approach', adopts the type of systems thinking already present in theorizing in organizational and management studies. Here management practice is viewed as impacted by a series of inter-related sub-systems structured in terms of a broader, general or indirect-input environment as well as a more specific, task or direct-impact environment. Nath aligns the work of Negandhi (Negandhi, 1983) with this approach. Regardless of the perspective, the focus for investigation was still the internationalization of US firms into Europe and beyond, and the encounter with difference engendered in that process.

A central bifurcation, and one that continues to problematize the field and make it difficult to offer a clearly and unambiguously defined object of inquiry for us, is that between culturist and institutionalist approaches to understanding management and organization across nations. The former emphasizes culture as the primary unit of analysis for explaining and understanding similarities, differences, convergences and divergences in IB/IM issues. It is often considered too narrow a conceptual framework by the latter for which economic, historical, social-structural and political factors are considered more vital for analysis. In Nath's terms it is a division between the behavioural and the environmental/economic development perspectives.

The institutionalist perspective has sometimes been promulgated under the rubric of a 'societal effects' approach in which the institutional frameworks within different national contexts are held to account for differences in management and business practice (see for instance, Inzerilli, 1981; Maurice, 1979; Maurice, Sorge & Warner, 1980; Sorge, 1991; Sorge & Maurice, 1990). There are also aspects of an institutional perspective more latterly in the work of scholars such as Whitley (for instance, Whitley, 1991, 1992, 1999, 2002, 2006, and Morgan, Whitley & Moen, 2006) and Redding (2002, 2005). It ought to be acknowledged that despite the differences of focus, it is not the case that culturists reject out of hand institutional issues in explaining research findings, nor that institutionalists are uninterested in culture. Rather, we note that there are degrees of difference in emphasis and priority, with some foregrounding culture and others institutional factors. Recognition of both institutional and cultural factors was apparent in some of the earliest works in IB/ICCM, such as the work of Farmer and Richman (1965).

The culturalist perspective was informed by anthropology, particularly as mediated through the work of Parsons (1951, 1967, 1973), Kluckhohn and colleagues (Kluckhohn, 1951; Kluckhohn & Kroeber, 1952; Kluckhohn & Strodtbeck, 1961). It was identified as a key issue in IM as the field emerged to such a degree that by 1970, Ajiferuke and Boddewyn (1970) were able to review 22 studies in IM that had culture as the prime independent variable explaining differences in management practice. As Boyacigiller et al. (1996) note, however, such work proceeded with no clear definition of culture, simply assuming the role of independent variable. Moreover, these authors note how such work assumed nation-states and national cultures could be conflated and that national culture and identity was 'a given, single, and permanent characteristic of an individual' (1996: 162) (with the exception of Triandis, 1972). This emergent culturalist perspective continued into the 1970s with a flurry of interest in the impact of culture on management behaviour (see for instance, Barrett & Bass, 1976; Davis, 1971; Goodman & Moore, 1972; Graham & Roberts, 1972; Graves, 1973; Harris & Moran, 1979; Kraut, 1975; Miller & Simonetti, 1974; Pazam & Reichel, 1977; Roberts, 1970; Schollhammer, 1969, 1975; Smith & Thomas, 1972; Terpstra, 1978; Weinshall, 1977). The work on managerial values by England and colleagues was particularly influential (England, 1978; England & Lee, 1971, 1974; England et al., 1974; Whitely & England, 1977, 1980). There was also an interesting attempt to tie social and economic development to culture and to national differences in motivation mechanisms through the work associated with McClelland, exemplified best perhaps in his books *The Achieving Society* and *Motivating Economic Achievement* (McClelland, 1961 and 1969 respectively).

Latterly the culturist approach is perhaps most closely associated with the landmark publication of Hofstede's (1980) *Culture's Consequences: International Differences in Work-Related Values,* a research study that has since proved paradigmatic in terms of its epistemological orientation and research design for those investigating national cultures from within management and organizational studies. The debt to Parsons and to Kluckhohn is very apparent in Hofstede's conceptualization, and indeed in his empirics. The 1980s saw the emergence of the concern with organizational cultures partly through the popularization of the notion in the work of Peters and Waterman (1982) and Deal and Kennedy (1982), but also associated with perceived differences in organizational culture derived from differences in national culture (Ouchi, 1981). Indeed, the last is significant, since the rise of Japan as an economic force, and particularly its penetration into markets in which it competed heavily against the US (including the US domestic market), had very much exercised the minds of politicians, practitioners and academics alike within the US. Abegglen (1958) provided one of the earliest accounts of Japanese management and business systems, but through the late 1960s to the early 1980s this had become something of an obsession among sections of the US academy (Ballon, 1967; Pascale & Athos, 1981; Trevor, 1983; Tung, 1984; Vogel, 1979), not to say a point of nationalistic alarmism (Wolf, 1985).

The impact of Hofstede on the field cannot be doubted and for some he is the contemporary founding figure for ICCM. His work, however, has not been without its critics and detractors (such as Ailon, 2008; Westwood & Everett, 1987; McSweeney, 2002; Søndergaard, 1994). His perspective, and particularly his methodology, came under attack right from the outset, and that continues. For example, the exchanges between Hofstede and British academic Brendan McSweeney (see McSweeney, 2002) make for a highly interesting read for those interested in issues associated with a Hofstedian analysis. Criticisms aside, Hofstede's five dimensions,[2] and the positivist methods used to develop them, have certainly fostered an expansion in the amount of comparative work conducted by IB and IM scholars and must therefore be given credit for engendering the space in which IB and IM projects, including this one, become possible.

Whilst Hofstede filled a vacuum in organizational research for an explicit and putatively rigorous definition of culture (Boyacigiller et al., 1996), his work continued the tradition of viewing culture as an independent variable purportedly explaining the dependent variables described/measured. More recent debates on the culture concept within the pages of *JIBS*, especially the exchange between Hofstede and members of the GLOBE projects and commentaries thereon (Earley, 2006; Hofstede, 2006; Javidan et al., 2006; Smith, 2006) do provide an interesting trajectory for understanding what is perceived by leading and, in the main, orthodox researchers as significant conceptual and methodological issues in future cross-cultural organizational research. Whilst we consider issues of level of analysis (Earley, 2006), or the question of when and how cultural effects happen (Leung et al., 2005) potentially interesting, two glaring problems stand out. First, the unexamined continuation of a functionalist and positivist trajectory for theory development, a moment in which these authors in the field have chosen to continue with metatheoretical 'business as usual' rather than pursue a more heterodox agenda. Second, the unexamined continuation of sufficient connection between the cross-national approach with the interactive intercultural and multiple cultures frameworks.

An inter-related problematic in the history of ICCM from the 1950s through to, say, the late 1980s, is that there are few scholars outside of the USA or North America making a contribution. It is important, however, to recognize significant exceptions and to acknowledge the work of people like Anant Negandhi, Raghu Nath, Simcha Ronen, Moses Kiggundu and Musbau Ajiferuk. It must also be noted that such people were often working within the Western academy and deploying its knowledge frames and resources. Over the same period, there was a severe limit on the number of cultures/countries examined in IB/ICCM. This was largely determined by the interests of the US/Northern Europe and those cultures with whom they had strategic and commercial interest (a point we shall return to in Chapters 3 and 5). There was also little work and limited space for studies on the indigenous management and organizational practices out of the Western-centre. Again there were exceptions that need to be acknowledged such as Wright's (1981) analysis of Islamic business/management, Dore's (1973) comparison of British and Japanese factories, Sinha's (various in the 1970s) work on Indian management, Badawy's (1980) account of Middle Eastern management style, Redding's (various) considerations of overseas Chinese management and Orpen's work in South Africa – among others.

This slanted and parochial approach to much ICCM research is compounded by some taking the view that even single country studies, when conducted by a researcher in a country that is not her own, can count as 'international management' (Peterson, 2004). In other words, a scholar from the USA conducting research in, say, China, might commonly be held to have produced work within the ICCM ambit. On the other hand, single country studies conducted by people indigenous to that country/culture are often excluded as legitimate ICCM studies. The very notion of 'international' is thereby constructed with respect to some very specific locations and is ineluctably made a relational construct.

Taking this very brief and certainly highly glossed overview as a whole, we can see that the conceptual terrain of ICCM is diffuse and marked by competing boundary-constructions and forms of vocabulary. Simply in order to move forward, for the purposes of this particular book we heuristically delimit our focus to: (a) international management rather than international business; (b) approaches that are culturist and pursue the concept of culture rather than institutionalist approaches or those deploying notions such as national business systems; (c) comparative/cross-national and (where they exist) interactional frameworks of analysis that focus on areas of organizational and managerial behaviour and where the unit of analysis is either individual, dyad, group, or sometimes organizational.

We acknowledge that there are areas that might be counted as ICCM that share the political and theoretical aspirations of this book, such as in parts of international labour relations or in heterodox international economics. However, our sketching of 'the problem', inevitably involves some ghostly losses such as these, as we provisionally tighten up a focus. The kind of visibility we bring to our object of inquiry comes with the problems of all forms of visibility: it simultaneously occludes other perspectives and aspects. In other words, it entails strategy and its effects that both enable and constrain our understandings. Having put these partial boundaries in place, the next section begins our critical analysis of the apparent commitments and omissions of ICCM, which at times incorporates parts of IB as an adjacent domain.

Contextual and qualitative parochialism in ICCM

The accusation of parochialism and ethnocentrism against IB/ICCM has been levelled for many years now. We prefaced such accusations in the last section, and will argue here, and in Chapter 3 more fully, that they are still part of the current landscape of the field. Simultaneously, though, there have also been those that have resisted and detracted from these accusations, and examination of one of those gives us an entrance into the tenor of these debates. Adler's (1983) labelling of cross-cultural management as an 'ostrich', in tandem with similar observations by others, provoked consternation a decade later from Steers et al. (1992). They took umbrage with Adler and others' argument that 'the academic establishment impedes or constrains the conduct and dissemination of international or cross-cultural research efforts', through 'the use of parochial and culture-bound American theories of management, (...) the insistence on traditional research methods as the criteria for journal acceptance, and through the downplaying of cross-cultural studies in our doctoral programs' (Steers et al., 1992: 322).

They particularly wanted to counter the assertion that key journals 'systematically – if unintentionally – constrain[s] progress' in international research; and that they present a 'not-so-subtle and structural bias against international work' (ibid: 323), for example, in terms of the composition of editorial boards and the lack of recognition of foreign sources in articles. Whilst we may agree that the field has not necessarily intentionally or consciously set out to exclude non-North American or non-Western European voices from the academy, lest we are read this way, we will show that the evidence from surveys within the field itself does suggest structural bias and exclusionary effects. Part of the explanation by Steer et al. is that 'journal editors can only publish what they receive. When we talk to journal editors about the relative paucity of international research in the journals, the typical reply is that they would certainly entertain more such research' (ibid: 326). They argue that editors complained of the few international submissions of an acceptable quality from outside North America and also that non-standard methods such as ethnography do not suit the format of a journal article. They conclude that: 'many of the purported impediments to such research either have diminished or never existed in the first place' (ibid: 328). Our analysis suggests otherwise.

The surveys from the field, which we will report to a much greater extent in Chapter 3, reveal a systematic and persistent bias in the institutional frame surrounding ICCM, as do other elements of the frame, such as parts of the publishing industry, professional associations and universities themselves. The field is dominated by North America with a second level of representation from parts of Western Europe, Australasia, Israel, and selected parts of Asia. Editors and editorial boards, as significant gatekeepers, continue to show a clearly skewed geographic dispersion. We believe that the assessment by Steers et al. is based on a misunderstanding of the nature of hegemony and the way that institutional structures and dynamics, shared practices and norms, rather than individual intention, function in exclusionary and inclusionary ways. Parochial impediments have dogged the field, and the idea that they are diminishing involves a very particular reading of the situation and of the survey data. It is not enough, in our view, simply to claim, as Kirkman and Law (2005) have, that five years' worth of AMJ articles with a greater presence of non-US authors and datasets represents a significant disjuncture in the institutional structures for the production of knowledge in ICCM. If anything, it is to obfuscate the field's most fundamental yet unacknowledged problem (Jack et al., 2008): the continuing dominance of structural-functionalism and neo-positivism as a paradigmatic location (see also Lowe, 2001; Redding, 1994). One brief illustration of this comes from Steers et al. themselves.

Steers et al. argue that whilst it might be acknowledged that most extant management and organization theories are developed by American researchers, based on past American literature, and using American samples, this does not in itself imply a biased intent. We might agree. They also suggest that it does not mean *a priori* that the resulting theories are culture-bound. Here we depart. Making reference to a cross-cultural study using equity theory (Kim et al., 1990), and suggesting that the equity norm is cross-culturally generalizable, Steers et al. seem to validate approaches in ICCM in which research propositions based on theory and methods developed in the US are tested for their potential generalizability via observations from countries other than the USA. This reflects the dominant approach through the 1980s characterized by attempts to *'compare* and *validate* Western nation-based management theories and principles across cultures' (Kirkman & Law, 2005: 379). It does not even meet Richman's (1965) expectations for ICCM way back in the 1960s that it move on to detailed 'developmental research'. To assume that the ethnocentrism of a theory can be 'resolved' by research design is to gloss naively over profound ontological and epistemological issues.

What this critical assessment makes apparent is that the parochialism of ICCM is not just a matter of a limited and limiting intellectual horizon within the field, nor of the clear locational specificities – in terms of history, culture, politics and economics – that in fact constitute the field and define its agenda and modes of representation. Nor is it even one of just counting who is doing research, where they come from, and for whom they produce. More fundamentally, it is also about the philosophical assumptions researchers make, be they implicit or explicit, through which 'truth' about ICCM issues can be constructed. Our interest lies, then, in the philosophical discourse of ICCM that enables, constrains and thus regulates what is taken to be true and valid knowledge about its objects of inquiry. ICCM diverges with some conspicuousness from other areas of management and organizational inquiry in that it has managed to avoid an active engagement in a reflexive theoretical conversation of a cross-disciplinary nature about its underlying logic, aims and practices (Jack et al., 2008). Functionalism and positivism achieved early hegemonic status in ICCM (Kerr et al., 1960; Redding, 1994), and this philosophical orthodoxy has been doggedly pursued and defended over the years with only too infrequent scrutiny of the assumptions embedded therein.

Paradigmatic entrenchment and hegemonic practice

Hegemony is an active social form (Gramsci, 1971), in the sense that it needs to be maintained and regularly accomplished, and challenges to it accommodated or staved off. Dominant structures of interest need to engage with challenges to its legitimacy and authority through the policing of its boundaries. In the case of ICCM, this would refer to the management of processes of knowledge production and dissemination, as well as the institutional frame in which the field functions (its points of access, development, progression, and assessment; the nature of universities, journals, publishing houses and academic bodies). We will deal more fully with the institutional frame in the next chapter. In this section we illustrate and discuss the principal ways in which the hegemony of the field has been exercised, and in doing so we draw from our previous work, some of which we have written with other colleagues. We do this in part with reference to the culture concept in ICCM, showing how particular intellectual practices (in the sense of both philosophical assumptions and the assumptions of a 'scientific method', as well as the values and behaviours of academics) have acted to sustain continuously a particular orthodoxy and at the same time disavow the possibility of the kinds of epistemic reflexivity necessary for the establishment of an alternative and critical trajectory for theory development.

In the editorial introduction to the recent special topic forum on international management, the editors (Jack et al., 2008) outlined what they considered the four key 'moments' of epistemological disavowal that have sustained an entrenched paradigmatic orthodoxy in ICCM: faulty generalizations; essentializing the culture concept; ignoring connections of metatheory and methodology; resorting to old literature (in sociology and anthropology). They viewed these practices as part of a collective institutional inability to move out of the field's knowledge-making limitations, and thus promote radical critique and change in the field. The preference for empirical work rather than theory development in IM-specific journals was also cited as a compounding factor in this regard. We go on to outline and extend these four moments of epistemological disavowal.

The 'as-if' syndrome

The construction of a discourse in which the relationship between culture-free and culture-bound knowledge, between that which is deemed universally applicable and that which is locally specific, rests upon the assumption that it is possible to make such a distinction in the first place. That is to say, that it is possible to delineate something that could be called universal knowledge. We consider this to be a chimera; but it is one that is profoundly embedded and continuously reproduced in orthodox research practice in ICCM. There is a degree of irony, then, in the fact that scholars in the field simultaneously point to the parochialism of their pursuits whilst pursuing positivist research whose conditions of possibility efface this very fact. This is the 'as-if' quality of ICCM research (Jack et al., 2008), a fundamental philosophical contradiction through which hegemony is practised. Let us explain.

The theoretical hegemony of ICCM has been informed by and recursively resulted in a number of forms of universalism. These universalisms are grounded in the early establishment of a structural-functionalist paradigm in the discipline (via Harbison & Myers, *inter alia*), drawing as it did on orthodox economic theory of the time, the functionalism of early management theory (*à la* Taylor, Drucker and others), the sociological structural functionalism of Parsons, the structural functionalism of Kluckhohn and colleagues, and some aspects of positivist psychology (for instance McClelland). The culture-free assertions of the Aston School under the auspices of 1970s contingency theory are also a significant signifier of this orientation. This intellectual frame conditioned various modes of universalism including: ontological universalism, where elements of organization and organizational behaviour are taken to be objectively real and universal in nature with only contingent variations; a universal model of development, based upon the economic rationalities of the West and its development theory; a form of scientific method seen as universally applicable and which engendered the dominance of quantitative methods (Peterson, 2004). Together these universalisms are part of a paradigmatic location that also sustains the epistemological separation of object from subject, and the myth of a detached, rational, objective observer accessing an *a priori* fixed reality (Westwood & Jack, 2007) and results in a radical decontextualization, atomization and simplification of phenomena.

In relation to discussions of context and culture, the above paradigmatic location manifests itself in paradoxical beliefs, and misunderstandings, of an ontological and epistemological nature. In a survey of international research published in the AMJ, Kirkman and Law (2005) suggest that international management studies through the 1980s were preoccupied with the attempt to 'compare and validate Western nation-based management theories and principles across cultures' (p. 379). They do go on to assert that the 1990s witnessed more of an attempt to develop management theories cross-culturally. The work of Steers et al. (1992), suggesting the cross-cultural applicability of equity theory based on a multi-country sampling strategy, is a case in point. But the problem here is that the methodological embedding of multiple contexts in a research study does little to bring attention to the researchers' specific location and the interests and values prevailing therein, which, in the first place, define and regulate the ontology of the object of inquiry and the epistemological basis from which knowledge about it is pursued.

The problem of the 'as-if' syndrome is not just one of logical inconsistency however: the stakes are higher than this and relate to matters of power and politics.

Ontological essentialism is the 'hidden' facet of the as-if quality. It comes with a number of effects. First, from the paradigmatic location orthodox ICCM finds itself in, culture has a tendency to be considered as a fixed entity, a view that, as noted by scholars too numerous to mention in the organizational culture and organizational theory literatures, fails to understand the full complexity of cultural life.[3] Processual approaches to culture, which bring into being its nature from a different ontological standpoint, are suggestive of the contingent, socially constructed and non-unitary nature of culture, and the manner in which it is infused with dimensions of power and inequality. When culture is framed in essentialist terms, we will only ever fail to understand the manner in which power relations and inequalities are produced through everyday social and organizational interactions. For us, this would be to adopt a position that is profoundly misaligned with, and misrepresents the realities of, everyday life and to render ICCM researchers complicit in the reproduction of power inequalities. Such a misalignment between this mode of essentialist theorizing in ICCM and the experienced realities of the world, and particularly its economic and political processes and structures, seems a defining feature of ICCM. Boyacigiller and Adler (1991) similarly noted that the parochialism of organizational science means that it is poorly placed to understand the global complexities of organizational life. Theory is thus left trailing behind reality, as our frameworks provide blinkers rather than lenses.

From a different perspective, Sullivan (1998) provides a cognitive framing explanation for the 'narrow vision' of IB research, which leads researchers to construe their research agendas in particular ways. It is a narrow focus, according to Sullivan (*pace* van den Ven, 1989), that leads to the conclusion that IB's increasingly 'impeccable micro logic is creating macro nonsense', by 'encouraging cognitive processes that precisely pinpoint the trees to the neglect of the forest' (Sullivan, 1998: 838). He presents a cognitive scientific analysis of research presented in JIBS from 1970 to 1997, and more specifically the ways in which IB scholars have represented their logics of interpretation. Whilst we do not share his cognitive approach, we find his two key findings highly interesting nevertheless. First, scholars' representations were dominated by analogue reasoning about which he comments:

(...) analog reasoning is prone to devolve into rigid, linear analysis that encourages consensus-building quantification as an end unto itself. Unchecked, the search for ultimate causes and effects can inspire an 'over-rationalized' representation whose disregard for nonlinear processes may lead to technically significant connections, but intellectually sterile findings (Morgan, 1986, p. 229). The use of analog representation, if unchecked, encourages logics of interpretations marked by narrowing comprehensiveness, connectedness and complexity.

Second, and relatedly, he found a narrowing range of less-complex schematic representations within the logics of interpretation deployed from 1970 to 1993, the very period during which increasingly, IB researchers complained of a lack of decent theory and expressed uncertainty about the distinctiveness of their body of work. In our view the predominance of structural functionalism within ICCM and IB research with its realist ontology, objectivist epistemology, atomizing and decontextualizing tendencies, provides the intellectual conditions for such narrow research trajectories, limited forms of interpretation, and analogue modes of representation. The result is a stunted exploration of critical phenomena that might be legitimately of interest to the field.

Context, selective reporting and non-inclusive generalization

The manner in which the field of ICCM manages the selective reporting of context and generalizability in its research studies is one of the key practices through which hegemony is exercised (Clegg et al., 2000; Westwood, 2001). Almost invariably, for example, research findings that emanate from American contexts are presented without accounting for their historical, political, economic, cultural and ideological context. They are typically then expounded as universal in nature as if the specifics of location, the contingencies of context, are of no consequence. In contrast, non-American research, say from India, is required to attenuate what it reports and discusses, giving specificities of location and context. Such research has to account for and specify the localized nature of its context, for example, in terms of culture, economy or other aspects of social organization. Typically this translates into an expression of the limits of generalizability of what the research reports, limits not deemed to attach to US-centred research whose universality is simply taken for granted.

A perusal of any journal in the field will reveal this disparity in these representational requirements. This is very much also the point made by Wong-MingJi and Mir (1997) when they talk about the high percentage of studies found in their review of the literature claiming universal applicability for their arguments and/or failing to specify any contextual information. It is resonant too with the earlier explanation of Boyacigiller and Adler (1991) for the unexamined assumptions about the applicability of US theory in non-US contexts. As noted by Jack et al. (2008), reflexive statements as open as the following about the contextual relativity of theory are highly unusual in ICCM. The statement comes from the concluding section of an investigation of cross-cultural negotiations in which, in contrast to the majority of participants, the American sample exhibited a consistent interactional pattern:

> Finally, the most profound limitations of this and similar studies may be the theories and methods themselves developed by American behavioural scientists. Perhaps the American behavioural consistency across intra- and intercultural negotiation situations reflects a similar obstinacy in American theory building (Adler & Graham, 1989: 532, quoted in: Jack et al., 2008: 874).

If from the outset, the theories and methods to be deployed had been considered as such 'profound limitations', perhaps the study would have never been enacted as planned. It is ironic perhaps that an empirical study that might be considered a failure in terms of its capacity to deliver results as expected is seemingly required before this type of reflexivity is delved into. Ironic too that such a study with such equivocal findings might typically have not made it past review processes and into publication – the fact that it did at all is perhaps more a tribute to the status of the authors than to the openness of the field typically to such reflexive and reflective practice.

   This neglect of context continues, as exposed by the fact that as recently as 2001 the editors of a lead journal in mainstream organizational behaviour – the *Journal of Organizational Behavior* (JOB) – felt obligated to challenge deficiencies in considering context in OB research (Rousseau & Fried, 2001). They note that whilst the organizational context has increasingly been acknowledged in theory building, it remains neglected in empirical work, something the editors argued needed rectification. Interestingly, they believe that the internationalization of organizational research has partly impelled this plea through surfacing 'challenges in transporting social science models from one society to another' (ibid: 1), but acknowledge that the neglect of context is very apparent in domestic research. However, still under the sway of the neo-positivist, functionalist purview, for them the reason for including context is to ensure that models are more 'accurate' and interpretations more 'robust'. There is no reflection on the fundamental nature of the epistemological, ontological, ethical and political commitments made in the modes of research they advocate, nor any call for increased reflexivity in research practice (see also Lim & Firkola, 2000).

Indeed, reflection on inclusion of context leads to rather banal statements of the obvious such as saying that when a set of factors is considered this can lead to 'a more interpretable and theoretically interesting pattern than any of the factors would show in isolation' (ibid: xx). The editors offer some guidelines to researchers on how to include context, and this includes incorporating it in the write-up and presentation of results where it can, they tell us, be included in their journal in a 'Sidebar'. Thus, whilst calling for the inclusion of context, it is, in the same moment, assigned to the margin – only as supplement to the main text.

More radically, Brett et al. (1997), among others, suggest that cultural differences may be so great as to necessitate wholly different concepts to address the same research question in different cultures. Doing so requires the examination of 'emic' concepts (that is, those with meaning unique to the particular setting and to those within the local culture) as opposed to 'etic' concepts (those that represent an 'outsider' perspective and which are concerned with cross-setting generalizability). As Brett et al. suggest, emic research is still relatively infrequent in organizational research. More common is 'imposed etic' research (Berry, 1980), wherein the theories, models and meanings of the [Western] researcher are imposed on local contexts and over-ride local meanings. In the orthodoxy of the field there has been a tendency to argue that for comparative research, etics are necessary in order to enable comparisons to be drawn. But progressively, it has been argued that both emic and etic approaches are required (for instance Berry, 1999; Helfrich, 1999; Morris et al., 1999). The issue has long been debated and continues to be so. The originator of the terms, Pike (for instance 1967) argued that it is emic knowledge that is of concern and that etics are primarily a way of approaching and developing emic understanding. He maintains that etic knowledge does not have a privileged position over emic.

This is in contrast to Harris, the other person with whom the expressions are foundationally related. For Harris, etics represent objective knowledge and should be the goal of scientific work. Emic knowledge is subjective and non-generalizable, it may provide insights or the groundwork for etic knowledge, but etic knowledge is necessary for developing universal theory (Harris, 1964, 1976, 1979). The aspiration for universal knowledge is, of course, part of what is at issue. Pike would argue that all knowledge is subjective and local (see Headland et al., 1990). For contemporary and reflexive anthropologists this is a false binary that needs dissolving (Clifford & Marcus, 1986).

In the context of discussing race in organizational studies, Nkomo also notes this type of practice and refers to it as part of the 'faulty generalization or noninclusive universalization' of mainstream theory (Nkomo, 1992: 489, quoted in Jack et al., 2008: 874). It is an error, according to Nkomo, that:

> (...) occurs when we take a dominant few (white males) as the inclusive group, the norm, and the ideal humankind. (...) The defining group for specifying the science of organizations has been white males.... We have amassed a great deal of knowledge about the experience of only one group, yet we generalize our theories and concepts to all groups' (ibid: 489).

Such practices are part of a wider, and longer standing, imbalance in the thinking about science and its practice. In that sense, as Nkomo, *pace* Harding (1986) argues, the faulty generalization thesis is reproduced via the bias inherent in Western science. Science, as noted by Harding and many other philosophers and sociologists, reflects 'the values and concerns of dominant social groups' (p. 490) and masks the localized and particular nature of those values and concerns.

The qualitative panacea?

The manifold criticisms we have just outlined can also be said to pertain to certain qualitative modes of research in IB and ICCM. Marschan-Piekkari and Welch's (2004) edited *Handbook of Qualitative Research Methods for International Business* is a state of the art statement about this domain. Qualitative and specifically ethnographic approaches in international management are hardly new (for instance Brannen, 1996; Dore, 1973; Wright, 1996), but as these authors point out 'qualitative research still remains a minority and even marginalised pursuit within IB'. Further evidence for this position is found in Andersen and Skaates's (2004) work on the nature and explanation of validity in qualitative research in IB. They presented a survey of 1783 articles from 297 issues of JIBS, Management International Review (MIR), Journal of World Business (JWB), IMR, Journal of International Management and

International Business Review (between 1991 and 2001). Categoriz-
ing research into qualitative, quantitative and reviews/modelling/
commentary, they found that:

> (...) a consistent distribution in the sense that quantitative research
> strategies have a dominant position in English-language IB research.
> In contrast, qualitative research strategies are the road least fol-
> lowed. Taken together, approximately 10 per cent of all published IB
> research is of the qualitative variety. Approximately 50 per cent is
> based on quantitative inquiry, whilst the remaining 40 per cent of
> studies reviewed concern conceptual contributions dealing with
> model development and/or theoretical reviews (Andersen & Skaates,
> 2004: 467).

Of further note in their findings was the discrepancy between the journals in terms of the amount of qualitative research published: only
three per cent in JIBS during this period, compared to 20 per cent for
JWB. Similar results were found by Peterson (2004) in his survey of
JIBS, AMJ and ASQ. He found 78 empirical studies of international
management published in the period between 1990 and 1999; only
seven of these used qualitative methods.

Marschan-Piekkari and Welch (2004: 5) note something of a paradox
in IB relations to qualitative research: 'while its status remains stub-
bornly low, its benefits are nevertheless widely acknowledged' (ibid: 6).
They point to the following benefits: IB lacks the sophisticated theory
development to be a mature discipline, and so more exploratory and
theory-generating research is needed rather than empirical testing;
qualitative research allows for deeper cross-cultural understanding and
for emic perspectives to emerge; qualitative research tries to understand cultures in their own terms through a more holistic approach
and with contextual sensitivity, going beyond the measurement of
observable behaviour towards the meanings attached to particular
social actions. Despite these advantages, 'as a methodological alternative, it [qualitative research] is considered second best – even unsci-
entific and too "feminine"' (ibid: 7). It might even be taken to suggest
that the researcher is not sufficiently skilled in statistics, or that a
survey was not a feasible research method.

Qualitative research is thus not perceived as a 'legitimate science',
with Marschan-Piekkari and Welch citing as evidence Cavusgil and Das
(1997) and Schaffer and Riordan (2003), who declare that they look
forward to a time when IB will have sufficiently matured as a discipline

to no longer need qualitative and conceptually-based studies. What this all suggests is that the invocation of a lack of scientific maturity, situated within a gendered discourse of research methodology (where positivism is masculine, interpretivism is feminine), frames qualitative approaches in ways that diminish their intellectual and political potency and frighten new researchers into thinking that it 'carries the stigma of being a poor career move' (Marschan-Piekkari & Welch, 2004: 5).

Though progressive, qualitative research approaches are no panacea for the broader philosophical issues we have touched on so far. Taking our cue from Marschan-Piekkari and Welch, we would develop this assertion in two ways. First, there is the problem of mistaking method for methodology. As noted earlier, the deployment of qualitative approaches is typically shored up by the use of case studies and more importantly in-depth interviews. The use of in-depth interviews is taken as a guarantee that one is a qualitative researcher. Marschan-Piekkari and Welch suggest, and we would agree with them, that the limitations and complex nature of carrying out interviews have received little critical examination amongst qualitative IB researchers (exceptions include all chapters in the third part of the Marschan-Piekkari & Welch handbook), despite heated debate about them else-where in the social sciences. But the point is not just a technical one. We will elaborate further on these methodological issues and suggest alternatives to them in Part IV.

Second, and too often, the pursuit of in-depth interviews, and of putatively qualitative methods more generally, is typically done without discussion of the wider paradigmatic frame in which it is taking place. This is a profound problem, which we have articulated at length in a previous paper (Jack & Westwood, 2006). To focus on method as the guarantor of a philosophical position is to misunderstand the connections between methodology and metatheory, and to pursue a problematic separation between theory and method indicative of a slavish adherence to a neo-positivist position. Indeed, it results in the pursuit of a kind of qualitative positivism, which is hardly commensurate with a constructionist epistemology.

In turn, and in common with positivist approaches, we argued that the unwitting separation of theory and method by some qualitative IB researchers has the effect of depoliticizing qualitative research. As researchers focus on method, rather than metatheory, they disavow their own implication in the knowledge they produce as well as the political and ethical facets of writing theory and research more generally. Research in such a mode can do nothing but reproduce the status quo: '... IB researchers tend to limit themselves to describing the existing social order (Osland and Osland, 2001), and have largely steered clear of theories that are critical of capitalism and globalisation' (ibid: 15).

Problems and impediments to indigenous research

The arguments in pursuance of emic perspectives give recognition to the localized specificities of knowledge, knowledge systems and knowledge production, and caution against universalizing and totalizing tendencies. Indeed, recent, and on the surface seemingly more progressive, debates on the relationship between the global pretensions of management knowledge and the local specificities of their formation, have emerged in the management and organization studies literature under the aegis of 'indigenous' perspectives on management (for instance, Gopinath, 1998; Meyer, 2006; Tsui, 2004; Warner & Ying, 1998; Wright, 1994). At first blush, this literature appears as a celebration of local knowledge as it might pertain to management and organizational issues and is mobilized to counter the universalistic pretensions of North American theory. However, there are reasons to be cautious and a need to recognize that barriers persist. A significant portion of the literature on indigenous management takes the form of resurrecting indigenous knowledge related to resources and land management (for instance, DeWalt, 1994; Rist & Dahdouh-Guebas, 2006; Ross & Pickering, 2002). This resurrected indigenous knowledge is often then considered in conjunction with Western/ modern knowledge systems in 'knowledge alliances' (Puri, 2007) for a presumed beneficial synthesis. However, some see this as yet another appropriative move that still captures indigenous knowledge for purposes other than those truly determined by indigenous people, and too often as simply serving the needs of Western capitalism, often with the complicity of NGOs (Fernando, 2003; Smith, 1999).

In spite of this belated interest in indigenous approaches to management and organizational issues, it remains a minority interest and the simple truth is that much of the Third World (TW) or periphery remains effectively silenced in terms of having a space within ICCM in which to articulate any indigenous perspective. It would be relatively straightforward to point to the apparent absence of theory and research from a whole range of Third World contexts, but it might be more revealing to examine the problem of finding theoretical space for a location that whilst not within the North Atlantic axis, is at least close to the centre and with strong Western roots and leanings.

Clegg et al. (2000) illuminate some of the wider dynamics pertaining to the paucity of 'Australian' organization theory. They start by recounting the tale of one Australian colleague self-congratulating over the acceptance of an article in a top-rated American journal. Using Connell's (1991) reflections on similar processes in Australian sociology, they argue that Australians are keen on developing 'international reputations', though what is actually meant by 'international' is North American or European. They quote Connell (1991: 70; Clegg et al., 2000: 104):

> To publish in prestigious journals in North America or Europe you have to write like a North American or European, cite North American and European sources, situate yourself in North American or European debates. That is what the editors and referees demand. And why shouldn't they? That is to say, to gain maximum prestige in Australia you need to see the world from the North Atlantic.

The academic's celebration of his international credentials is, then, to be read against Australia's colonial past, its Anglocentric imaginary and what Clegg et al. refer to as the 'North Atlantic intellectual hegemony'. This narrow relationship means that there is nothing distinctively Australian about Australian organization theory; it is a mimic, a copy of a putative original. The disavowal of Australian context and Australian knowledge in relation to the bigger US management academy has a history, according to the authors, particularly associated with the funding strategies of leading charitable foundations from the USA, notably Ford, Rockefeller and Carnegie, and the wider geopolitical, economic and ideological context of rendering the world ideologically safe for American capitalism (Clegg et al., 2000: 106) (more to follow in Chapter 5).

Clegg et al. are not entirely defeatist in their prognosis. They point out, firstly that, as with any hegemonic structure, there is some backflow between the periphery[4] and core, such backflow enables some of these marginalized voices to be heard and the idea of legitimating alternative, and sometimes contradictory voices, within already existing arrangements is, for these authors, an important part in changing the balance between centre and (semi)-periphery. They are not suggesting that Australian social science should ignore, give up, or reject the US-dominated mainstream – they see this as 'neither possible nor desirable' (ibid: 109) – but do argue for a more constructive mode of engagement. To this end, they call for Australian researchers to bring to bear that which is distinctive about Australia, its location, its context, in creating an Australian organization theory. They view Australia as a unique place geographically, ontologically and epistemologically, a set of distinctions that can be used toward some kind of independence from the NATO mainstream. Similar concerns have also been articulated in the context of Aotearoa New Zealand by Prichard, Sayers and Bathurst (2007)[5] and others.

We also need to note, however, that the call for greater sensitivity to context and local perspectives contains problematic elements; or to be more specific, reactionary elements clothed in progressive guise. To give one example, Tsui has been a key figure in the Academy of Management and in the encouragement of indigenous perspectives on management, in her case in relation to Chinese management and advocacy of Asian-Pacific perspectives on management and organization.[6] She recently suggested the need for more context-embedded and context-specific research strategies and called for theory development built upon high quality indigenous research (Tsui, 2004). For her, context-embedded research seems to echo concerns about the cultural relativity of theory and research expressed earlier by Hofstede, Laurent, and Boyacigiller and Adler, whilst a context-specific orientation calls for the inclusion of the particularities of a local context for understanding management and organization. Whilst we certainly endorse Tsui's calls for more sophisticated relations to context in ICCM, there is a fundamental problem for us in her position (also articulated in Jack et al., 2008).

According to Tsui, high quality indigenous research should:

> (...) test or build theories that can explain and predict the specific phenomenon and related phenomena in the local social cultural context. By scientific studies, I mean methods of inquiries that follow the logic of science adopted widely in both physical and social science (Kaplan, 1964; Wallace, 1971) (Tsui, 2004: 501).

From Tsui's perspective, any indigenously constructed research accounts still have to be refracted through Western theoretical, ontological and epistemological lenses and made available to positions of intelligibility within Western discourses. To us, this repeats the same error committed by Steers et al. and many of the contributions to recent JIBS discourse on culture. There is no questioning of the localized Western specificities inherent to the particular view of science that is promulgated and of the particular ontologies and epistemologies it ratifies. The effect is to cast ontological and epistemological issues in mere methodological terms – Tsui's context-embedded and context-specific strategies are still subject to the hegemonic status quo of the field and thus serve to reinforce it. Whilst it appears to advocate an emic position it is, in fact, still an imposed etic one. In commenting on Tsui, Meyer (2006: 121) notes that work produced in and for the Anglo-American academic centre rarely articulates its local, contextual specificity. Citing Whetten (2002), this means that often Anglo-American authors make implicit claims for context-free, or universalistic validity, when they are actually only providing context-specific knowledge (Meyer, 2006: 122).

Partial interdisciplinary engagements: The case of anthropology

A different kind of turn to indigenous knowledge in management inquiry also illustrates the problem of apparent progress obscuring persistent problems: the turn to anthropology by those interested in the management practices of people in indigenous contexts. This might seem an appropriate thing to do and indeed some within MOS/ICCM have suggested as much (Bate, 1997; Czarniawska, 1992, 2008; Wright, 1994). However, too often such a move is suggested without an apparent awareness of the methodological contortions that anthropology has gone through in recent years and its critically reflexive turn (such as Clifford & Marcus, 1986; Hymes, 1974). In other words there is a call to invoke an orthodox, prereflexive anthropology of the kind implicit in the colonialist project and which remains appropriative.[7]

Banerjee and Linstead (2004) illuminate the neo-colonial impulses detectable in one recent anthropological study. This was a study of the indigenous environmental management practices in the Cree Nation published in the AMJ (Whiteman & Cooper, 2000). The paper was based on an ethnographic case study of one indigenous beaver trapper, describing the ways in which he related to and managed his environment. Whiteman and Cooper use descriptions of his practice to formulate their concept of 'ecological embeddedness', an idea promulgated in the pages of AMJ to evaluate contemporary environmental management practice amongst corporate stakeholders.[8] Whilst Banerjee and Linstead are keen not to downplay many positive aspects of the fieldwork, they argue that in disembedding the Cree trapper's environmental practices and indigenous consciousness from the economic, social and political historical context that informs and indeed instantiates them, Whiteman and Cooper, in effect, create a 'loose analogy or even caricature of indigenous behaviour to its own practices' (ibid: 222).

They argue that such cultural disembedding is typical in much anthropological work, despite numerous and long-standing warnings about the dangers of translating categories and practices from one knowledge system into another (Marcus & Fischer, 1986), and produces reductionist and romanticized versions of the Other. Whiteman and Cooper's practice is seen as neo-colonial in its appropriation of the Other's knowledge practices and its failure to account for the socio-cultural, political, economic and historical conditions that frame and constitute those practices. Thereby no prospect is offered for the transformation of those conditions. The failure of reflexivity in this case is such that the locational specificities of the research practice and the privileges and power asymmetries on which it rests are not acknowledged or attended to.

There have been consistent, if intermittent, calls for IB and IM research to become more multidisciplinary in conceptual and methodological outlook. It is curious then that some very selective reading has thwarted such apparent openness to the insights of other disciplines. In the few cases when ICCM has gone to other disciplines for inspiration, it comes back with very selective theoretical treasures. Take for example the interest in ethnography and anthropology, an obvious interest for researchers pursuing work on culture, as Marschan-Piekkari and Welch note: 'In response to the inherent limitations of interviews, some IB researchers turn to anthropology, with its long tradition of cross-cultural research, as a way of enriching research practice in IB' (2004: 14).

Based on even the most cursory look at an anthropology textbook, one would have expected ICCM scholars to notice that for at least three decades cultural anthropology has undergone an extraordinary reconsideration of its primary ontological, epistemological and methodological commitments. Anthropological reflections on the rhetorical specificities of 'writing culture', the colonial history of ethnographic practice and the concomitant power relations inherent in modes of knowing the Other (significantly more detail is offered on this in Chapter 4) have all been glossed over in ICCM, even at its 'qualitative' margins. The result is a failure to engage with the complex rhetorical, ethical and epistemological aspects of an ethnographic tradition.

Perhaps because of this selective use of interdisciplinary resources, ICCM has been ignorant of paradigmatic controversies and philosophical debates that have recently marked humanities and social science discourse. This has meant a refusal to consider differently the ontological and epistemological underpinnings that constitute received wisdom on its core concepts – such as culture.[9] ICCM has thus failed to respond in any meaningful way to the challenges of post-positivistic, critical theoretical, poststructuralist and postmodern theorizing, and the concomitant liberalization of methods elsewhere in the academy.

In the next chapter, we continue the work of provincializing the fields of ICCM. Its focus, however, lies explicitly in the institutional practices that sustain the kind of parochial, positivist hegemony illuminated in this chapter.

3
The Institutional Present

Introduction

> White men from middle and upper class backgrounds and with
> other arbitrary entitlements, attributes, and symbols of status dom-
> inate elite institutions of research. By virtue of their position, they
> are the dominant groups in prestigious journals as editors, board
> members, authors, and reviewers. (Özbilgin, 2009: 114)

In Chapter 2 we attempted to delineate the target for our critical interrogation and map the current intellectual terrain of ICCM. We identified
a dominant discourse in ICCM in which particular modes of knowledge
and the epistemologies and ontologies upon which they depend are
valorized: a functionalist paradigm, positivist methods and Western
interests. As with all discourses, there is an inclusionary/exclusionary
power effect mirrored in the commitments and omissions we have
explicated. The maintenance and sustenance of such a dominant
discourse and intellectual orthodoxy is dependent, naturally, on a particular institutional frame. ICCM, as a discourse and as a domain of
disciplinary and professional practice, has an elaborate institutional
frame associated with it. This frame serves to manage and control the
processes of knowledge production, dissemination and consumption
for the field. It also constitutes mechanisms and practices that regulate
the points and modes of entry, the nature and extent of participation,
and the processes of evaluation, assessment, development and progression of persons, groups, other institutions and knowledges in
the field. It is the nature and dynamics of that institutional frame,
as it is presently constituted and enacted, that we examine in this
chapter.

We seek to emphasize how, in many respects, the current status quo can be seen as an extension of the West's wider domination of the discourses of science, development and education (Carnoy, 1974; Kelly & Altbach, 1984). The Western model of education, including its institutions of higher education, was to some extent replicated around the colonized world and beyond, made possible, as Alvares argues, through the conditions of colonial dominance since 'as power defined knowledge, the process was easily facilitated' (Alvares, 2002; see also Selvaratnam, 1988). Western style education has been exported globally – in terms of, *inter alia,* curriculum, pedagogy, content and institutional form. From kindergarten to university, through colonial imposition and then through imperialistic exportation, the world has been 'educating' in an increasingly homogenous fashion. The institutions of higher education in particular are among those that sustain Western hegemony: they are 'key sites of cultural and epistemological invasion, where inappropriate and irrelevant forms of Western culture and knowledge are thrust upon an unwitting student population' (Pennycook, 1996: 64). This sustains a distorted structure wherein, to quote Alvares (2002) again: 'The intellectual centres are located in the West, and they supply the categories and terms for all intellectual debates. We play along. They remain the center, while we keep ourselves at the periphery. They create; we copy and apply'.

Loubser (1988) refers to the 'vertical' relationships between academics in the Western Academy and those in the non-West, a view echoed by Alatas (1996, cited in Lee, 2000) who referred to a core-periphery relationship in world social science. Loubser expressed concerns about the dependency of the non-West on the West and 'the implied, if not explicit, intellectual imperialism and colonial exploitation involved' (ibid: 179). The international social science community, he argues, has encouraged limited and elitist 'patterns of participation' with 'exclusive networks of communication, and domination by the European and North American centres, perpetuating the glaring asymmetries and dependencies in the international social science system' (ibid: 187).

We see the situation Loubser describes in the social sciences as being mirrored in MOS in general and ICCM in particular. To explain the chapter begins at the broadest level in terms of societal relations and infrastructure and then moves through the management, structures and practices of universities, the operations of professional associations and down to the detail of the academic publishing machine and the present structures and policies relating to journals and journal publishing.

Structures of dependence/independence and societal support

Loubser (1988:183) states that the capacity to pursue an indigenous perspective in an academic discipline is dependent on a range of factors that relate to the 'historical, cultural, economic, political and geographical' relations of the local society to others. An indigenous approach is more likely to be viable, he argues (ibid: 184) if the local society:

- is economically independent and not determined by the economy of another nation-state;
- is politically independent and militarily strong *vis-à-vis* other nation-states;
- is different in language and culture from larger, more powerful nation-states;
- is comparable in development to dominant nation-states;
- is committed to independence and autonomy *vis-à-vis* other nation-states;
- is relatively closed in protection of its culture and activities of its own members;
- strongly supports its own scientific community and protects its independence and autonomy;
- has a strong tradition of literate culture and intellectual life;
- has a well developed system of education, including higher education.

Whilst some of this is contestable and perhaps the criteria are somewhat idealized, it is quite apparent that many 'Third World' and previously colonized societies currently struggle to meet a number of these criteria given the present order of things. However, it is important to acknowledge, as Loubser does, that whilst the problem might be more acute in developing nations, problems of indigenization are also apparent in developed contexts. He cites Canada, but we might also cite Australia and New Zealand and reiterate our comment from Chapter 1 about the charges of ongoing internal colonialism within these nations.

Whilst Loubser's argument is simply put and glosses enormous complexities, it exposes the struggle for any fully indigenous academic practice in much of the non-Western world. He remains somewhat pessimistic and suggests that the contextual matters limiting indigenization are beyond the scope of the academic community. For him, real change is dependent on the establishment of a 'new international socio-economic order'. The situation is compounded if local elites are seduced by Western economic, cultural and intellectual hegemonic practices and lack confidence in, and fail to support, local academic aspirations to autochthony and independence. In consequence, there is often more support for local scholars to participate in the international (that is Western) academic community and less support for localized efforts and less recognition of the value and uniqueness of indigenous knowledge systems.

Loubser notes the role of national research councils in this regard. Given their control of key funding, national research councils are in a position to shape research agendas and orientations. With appropriate political will, they could be involved in encouraging and supporting research that is indigenously driven and derived, or at least reflects local concerns and interests. They also not only influence research agendas, but play a part in the whole ethos of research within society, international collaborations, and the conditions under which researchers work and function. Too often such councils appear more interested in supporting work that aligns with 'international' research and institutions and publication in the international journals of the centre.

A postcolonial perspective adds a particular hue to these questions of local elites and national funding councils. Blaut (1993) maintains that Western education systems created local elites imbued with the ideology and tenets of Western political and economic thinking and who held the view that Third World development depended on retaining colonial systems and institutions. Within a decolonized, nationalist, neo-colonial context, the perpetuation of such systems leads to a continued dependence on the West and a belief that development and modernization rests on continued Western importations of education, knowledge, systems and technologies. These structural relationships extend to higher education and serve to perpetuate inequalities between the universities of the centre and of the periphery. Altbach (1987, as summarized in Subramani & Kempner, 2002: 240) has identified five aspects that perpetuate such inequalities:

(1) 'The educational institutions that were established by the colonizers were Western' (ibid) – in terms of models adopted, pedagogy, curricula, materials and so on.
(2) The colonizers' insistence on using their language as the language to be used in higher education with mastery of the colonizers' language functioning as a local status marker.

(3) Developing nations become positioned as consumers of knowledge – rather than producers and disseminators.

(4) Western 'hegemony over the means of communication' (of knowledge). In consequence: 'As scholarly journals, publishers, bibliographies, libraries, and the internet are predominantly in the West, the concerns of the developing world are hardly considered or their needs met.' (ibid) Furthermore, the authors and audiences for the journals are also Western, further leading to a neglect of local issues and concerns. 'Thus the international intellectual community continues to be structured under the old colonial international order' (ibid).

(5) 'The substantial number of students from the developing countries studying in the industrial nations.' (ibid)

This brings us to universities and, subsequently, to other bodies associated with research and teaching in the field. We maintain that the dominance of Western science and the promulgation of Western education through the colonial period and beyond have resulted in a clear dominance of not only Western knowledge systems, but also educational systems. This dominance extends to business and management education, indeed is amplified there given the particular genesis and development of those fields.

Whilst we can certainly point to important precursors in Europe (such as the Ecole Supérieure de Commerce of Paris, now ESCP-EAP established in 1819; and the Aula do Comercio established in Lisbon in 1759), it can reasonably be argued that in its contemporary form, management and business education was founded in US graduate schools and universities. The first US business schools, as dedicated graduate schools of business education, were Wharton (1881), Tuck (1900), Harvard (1910) and Chicago (1920). The MBA was first offered by Harvard in 1910 but did not arrive in Europe until the 1940s, and even then was slow to spread, whereas it spread quickly in the US. By 1997–8, the number of MBAs awarded was over 100,000 (Zimmerman, 2001: 3, cited in Steinbock, 2005). There has been a slight decline latterly. Regardless, the US model for business and management education and research has been exceedingly influential and has in large measure been exported around the world, a process of imitation and diffusion that continues. The increasingly homogeneous workings of Western and non-Western universities offer an insight here.

Universities, management regimes and academic careers

Universities and business schools are a key element in the institutional frame for a number of reasons. First, they are the location for prime research activity, dominant recipients of research funding, and set the research agenda. Second, they are central not only to knowledge production, but also to knowledge transmission and dissemination, often having a key stake in the dominant mechanisms of publishing. Third, they train and socialize newcomers to the field, inducting them into dominant paradigms, research traditions and the politics and etiquette of professional academic work. In many respects they are the repository of the field's orthodoxies, keepers of the traditions, managers of the field, and policers of the boundary. The current context for these roles is one of increasing managerialism.

The internationalization of managerialism

People working in the fields of MOS or ICCM are academic professionals who are subject to the exigencies of career and professional practice. Part of the complexity of the situation is that these contexts and regimes are no longer purely local, but have become internationalized and globalized. Standards of performance and hence career security and progression are in many instances shaped by, or at least influenced by, those pertaining to the Western academy. At issue here, then, is the whole question of the management of the employment, career and performance of non-Western MOS/ICCM academics.

Academia has, in general, become increasingly subject to processes of corporatism and managerialism (Deem, 1998; Meyer, 2002; Prichard & Willmott, 1997; Trow, 1994; Webster, 1994). This echoes the types of moves that have characterized more broadly the public sector reform movement that swept through the OECD countries and beyond through the 1990s (Clarke & Newman, 1997; Consadine & Painter, 1997; Pollitt, 1993). Academic work has been increasingly subject to control through the application of managerial ideologies and practices typically located hitherto in private sector corporations. In particular, the new managerial ethos has sought to manage and control academics and their work, principally through the instigation of performance management regimes and metrics.

Further, entry into the profession, and progress within it, are now highly dependent on these performance metrics and systems. These regimes have been collectivized and nationalized under schemes such as the Research Assessment Exercise in the UK, the Performance Based Research programme in New Zealand, and the emergent 'Excellence in Research for Australia' exercise in Australia. The internationalization of the performance management systems and regimes of the centre means they have infiltrated the academic employing institutions of the non-West (Nkomo, 2009). Together with the desire non-Western elites often hold for the Western academy, this has meant that these institutions have often pursued human resources management (HRM) and performance management systems from the West with profound implications.

Performance management

Undoubtedly the prime performance criterion for most academics has become published output and increasingly, this is more narrowly construed in terms of journal publications. Those charged with making evaluations of performance in these terms commonly engage in reductionist strategies wherein they reduce the complexities of research and writing, of the production and dissemination of knowledge, to a set of simplified metrics (Adler & Harzing, 2009; Giacalone, 2009). These metrics consist of counts of numbers of publications, their location on some ranking system and a proxy measure of impact through citation counts. The issue from a postcolonial point of view is that the dominance of the Western knowledge/education system means that increasingly the performance assessment of academics from the non-centre is incorporated into the assessment regimes promulgated by the centre (Nkomo, 2009). Thus MOS/ICCM scholars located in non-Western universities are having their performance assessed by the same criteria and in pursuit of similar standards as those prevailing in the centre. In other words they are expected to publish in what are taken to be the lead journals with the accompanying metrics of rankings and citations. These leading journals are by-and-large produced in and managed by the West, and all are in English. Moreover, the citation databases only use those journals published in English. Meyer (2006: 131) notes that it is thus 'highly problematic if Asian (or European) institutions adopt lists of top journals from US institutions'.

These mechanisms may reveal impact within the Anglo-American academy, but as Meyer points out, a leading scholar from Russia or China, who impacts thousands of students, publishes influential papers in the local language and publishes in local journals, affects social policy, and has the highest reputation might well receive an impact score of zero following SSCI protocols (see also Giacalone, 2009). Increasingly, however, professorial and other academic appointments in non-Western universities are dependent on publishing in 'international' (i.e. Anglo-American) journals and upon citation counts. This leads Meyer to observe wryly that 'an expert of the Californian electricity industry would have a better chance of obtaining a professorship in Hong Kong or Singapore than an expert of the Chinese electricity industry' (ibid: 133).

This situation has a number of effects. Firstly, as the lead journals are produced by and managed in the West they reflect the interests and orientations of the West. Research agendas, the assessments of what is current and valuable, the modes of theorizing, the epistemological commitments, the methods deemed acceptable, indeed the whole structure and tone of academic and disciplinary discourse, are constructed by and for those engaged with scholarly activity at the centre (see Adler & Harzing, 2009; Nkomo, 2009; Özbilgin, 2009). Of course, this shaping and narrowing of the research orientation and agenda is argued to impact even those of the centre so that scholars tend to 'tailor their choice of topics, methods, and theories to the perceived tastes of these journals' gatekeepers'.

Local scholars, pragmatically reflecting on the signals they get and what they see as determining rewards in their career, often choose research agendas, problems and topics because of their receptivity and fashionableness within the Western academy. We have witnessed colleagues in non-Western universities choose lines of research purely on that basis.[1] The extreme version of this is a form of empty technicism wherein research is conducted only because the researcher has developed some facility with the latest statistical technique known to have currency with the key journals of the centre. Research is only done on issues and in ways that meet the expectations of the journals of the centre (Meyer, 2006; Nkomo, 2009; Özbilgin, 2009; White, 2002). In consequence, even champions of indigenous research (in the Chinese context in this case) like Tsui are compelled to admit '(…) original theorising on Chinese business organizations and management is still in a primitive stage, especially in the behavioral areas' (Tsui et al., 2004: 37). Furthermore, as Meriläinen et al. (2008) have argued, simply copying and mimicking the practices of the academic centre actually results in bolstering its dominance and hegemonic position.

Recruitment

In addition to the increasing adoption of Western-style performance systems and criteria, non-Western academic institutions have also moved towards Western recruitment standards. Thus, in addition to the requisite certification, potential recruits are often asked to show a capacity or potential to publish in 'international journals' – in other words the journals of the West, and its dominant metropolitan centres (Prichard et al., 2007). Thus, entrance to the discipline is based on a perceived ability to participate in it in the manner prescribed by the centre and, concomitantly, to avoid localized or indigenized interests. The issue of requisite credentials cannot pass without comment either. One assurance that a candidate is properly schooled in the discipline is to employ a 'ready made', that is to recruit people who have been educated in the centre. Meyer (2006) created a database of over 1400 academics from business schools and departments located in 16 leading universities in Asia and Australia. Analysis revealed that almost 66 per cent of the faculty members had received their PhDs from the US, reaching as high as 90 per cent and 84 per cent at top universities in Hong Kong and Taiwan respectively. Meyer also notes the weak links within Asia and the substantial influence of the UK. He is led to assert that: 'Anglo-American educated scholars dominate leading Asian business schools' (ibid: 129).

There was a time when universities in the non-centre were heavily populated by expatriates from the centre. For example, through the 1970s and 80s and even into the 1990s, the major higher education institutions in Hong Kong – Hong Kong University and, what were then, the two polytechnics (City Polytechnic of Hong Kong and Hong Kong Polytechnic[2]) – had significant numbers of expatriate academics, primarily from the UK. There has been a progressive localization of staff since, however, these 'local' staff are invariably educated overseas, with PhDs from the US being the preferred credential. There are also an increasing number of mainland Chinese nationals being employed who also typically have research degrees from the US. Such researchers are often deeply imbued with the theories, conceptualizations and methods of their training grounds.

Meyer also notes that the Anglo-American influence is sustained through the presence of incentives for Asian scholars to write for Western audiences and publish in Western journals. As has become the norm in universities of the centre, so those in the non-centre are applying performance metrics that count journal papers, their position on Western-derived ranking systems, and citation figures to assess performance as part of local performance management systems (Nkomo, 2009). In consequence, career progression depends on meeting these performance standards.

Local academics from the non-centre have to make rational calculations about their financial situation, their careers and job security like anyone else. In other words they will make calculations of effort-reward relationships within the context of performance-reward systems operable in their immediate work environment. In the current scheme of things, they are more often receiving signals that the rewards lie in participating in the research activities of the centre and playing in their publishing games and not in focusing on local issues and developing indigenous theory and method. There is a compounding dynamic wherein these mechanisms elevate those who conform to this regime and when elevated to positions of power there is a tendency to value, support and perpetuate the orientation and regimes that got them there, a power dynamic Özbilgin (2009) also explores.

Training and development

Local universities need a supply of talent that is trained and qualified. It is apparent that in many parts of the non-centre, local education systems seem to lack confidence in themselves and their own products, seemingly preferring to send staff overseas for graduate training or, as noted, recruiting staff already trained in the West. However, even if local universities pursue policies of developing home-grown talent, this still does not overcome the problem. It can be observed that local universities often deploy programme and curriculum design, pedagogy and content adopted from or in imitation of the centre and that they are in danger of simply reproducing the Western knowledge system and its theories, methods and orientations.

If we focus simply on materials and content, then non-centre universities face a considerable difficulty. The Western dominance has been in place for so long and has been so hegemonic that it has tended to almost completely dominate the discursive space surrounding MOS/ICCM. The vast bulk of pedagogic materials are produced and disseminated by the centre and consist of content that reflects Western theories, concepts and orientations. An obvious instance of this dominance is the textbook market (on which more shortly). Lee (2000) attests to this in the context of East Asia, and argues further that there is little innovation and indigeneity in the development of curricula and pedagogic materials. Local academics, even when trained domestically, are typically still imbued with Western materials and theories, despite local 'adaptations' of famous American textbooks e.g. Kotler's *Marketing Management* with European or Asian editions.

Professional academies and associations

The practice of management research and scholarship has, like many other professional activities, established for itself associations providing a concrete institutional frame for its work. For general management and business studies the American Academy of Management (AOM) is widely seen as the pre-eminent association. It was founded in 1932 and today has 17271 (active)[3] members (AOM Online, 2008) drawn from 102 nations. However, a breakdown of membership reveals that the vast majority are from the First World (FW) and even then from a very limited number of countries: from North America (over 68 per cent) and Europe (18.1 per cent – the majority from the UK). There are approximately 8.7 per cent from Asia – but again further breakdown reveals this as limited to certain countries/areas such as Korea, Hong Kong and Taiwan with others, Sri Lanka and Indonesia for instance, being very poorly represented. There is less than 1 per cent from South America and less than 0.5 per cent from Africa. If one puts North America, Europe and Australasia together, then almost 90 per cent of the current membership is accounted for. There are many countries in Africa and the Middle East that have no registered members. This is despite the fact that the Academy has made claims about its internationalization for some time and includes among its formally stated Strategic Themes that it is 'a member of the global and pluralistic profession of management scholarship. Attention to global issues and concerns is encouraged among all members of the Academy...We value the contributions and multiple perspectives of members from all countries and regions' (AOM Online, 2008).

One might expect the Academy of International Business (AIB) to have a greater array of international members. It reports (AIB, 2008) that it has a little short of 3000 members from 71 countries[4] and claims to be a 'global community of scholars'. However, once again representation is disproportionately from North America, accounting for virtually 50 per cent of members, and Europe, where the UK alone accounts for 7.3 per cent. After Germany, with around 2.5 per cent, there is a smattering of members across Western Europe, but with no country having more than 50 members. There is representation from Asia, but again concentrated in a limited number of countries, with the largest numbers coming from Japan (133) and Taiwan (101), with China, Hong Kong, South Korea and Singapore also featuring. Barely one per cent of members are from South America and less than 1 per cent from the Middle East and Africa combined. There is only one member each from Central Asia and Russia, and very few from Eastern Europe. It is also important to note that the AIB is housed and managed from within the US, with all of its current (2008) administrative staff and all its current Executive Board being drawn from US universities and related institutions.

The AIB does have 'chapters' with a regional focus, but over 40 per cent of those are in North America. Including Western Europe brings that up to almost 60 per cent. The remaining single chapters are in China, Japan, South Korea, Southeast Asia, India and Australia/New Zealand. The AIB also houses one of the key journals in the field, the *Journal of International Business Studies* (JIBS). The current[5] editor is from Canada and all past editors have been North American. Further, in the current editorial team of 12, only two are from outside North America – and that includes 'area editors'. It has 30 'consulting editors', of whom 20 per cent have institutional affiliations outside of North America, but only two outside of Western Europe or North America.

It is very clear that in terms of the influential institutions that help govern and police the discourse of management and ICCM, there is a significant distortion in favour of the Western centre with firm institutional control residing in the US. There have been moves to establish management/business academies in other parts of the world, but many of these are satellites of the US academies or in other cases are replications of the model with their own limited horizons and representations. The AIB chapters are one example of this. The AOM has five domestic affiliates and two international ones: the Asia AOM and the Iberoamerica AOM. The former was established in 1998. Its current president is based in the US (AOM, 2008). The latter was established at a similar time (1997) with a similar mission.

The above notwithstanding, there are, unsurprisingly, professional academic associations in many places around the world – for example the Brazilian AOM (est. 1976), the Irish AOM (est. 1997), the Nordic AOM, the Academia Italiana di Economia Aziendale, and the Japan Society of Business Administration. Whilst obviously fulfilling a domestic function, few of these have international impact and cannot be taken as having a shaping influence on the broader fields of MOS and ICCM in the way that the US AOM or AIB do. There are, however, other academies that are influential in shaping the discourse, and these tend to be built on the US model. These include The British Academy of Management (BAM), which was founded in 1986. It freely acknowledges that: 'The initial inspiration was the (American) Academy of Management, although BAM has evolved in peculiarly British ways over the last 20 years' (BAM, 2008).

Another example of a European association that is modelled on the US is the European International Business Academy (EIBA), which was founded in 1974 under the auspices of the European Foundation for Management Development (EFMD), but in close collaboration with the European Institute for Advanced Studies in Management (EIASM). As stated on the official website (EIBA, 2008) 'EIBA act[s] as the Western

European chapter of the Academy of International Business'. EIASM is a broader-based international network for management research and teaching that includes more than 40,000 management scholars from Europe and internationally. It was founded in 1971, and in a reflection of issues to be discussed in Chapter 5, received significant funding from the Ford Foundation for its first five years. As well as its involvement with EIBA, EIASM also manages the European Academy of Management (EURAM), which, reflecting Europe's late (relative to the US) turn to the contemporary academic investigation of management and business, only held its inaugural conference in 2001. Despite its initial funding and modelling, EIASM and its subsidiary associations, like EURAM, have attempted to pursue more uniquely European perspectives on business and management.[6] EIASM, in pursuit of its mission over the years, has come to recognize that 'rather than having to depend solely on American models of management development, higher educational institutions in Europe can now refer to their own bodies of knowledge' (EIASM, 2008). This means, it claims, that it can contribute to distinctly European management education and the development of European faculty.

This latter reference to the development of academic professionals is noteworthy, since it signifies some of the institutional influence and control these associations have over people in the field and their career trajectories, as well as over the construction and dissemination of its knowledge. As professional academic associations, such bodies are involved in a range of activities, among the most salient of which are the construction of networks for scholars. This includes the organization of conferences, workshops and other fora as vehicles for these networks. Indeed, membership of such associations can itself play a part in tenure and other career-related decisions. Additionally, these associations are also involved in training and development relevant to the field, including the introduction of neophytes through various graduate student engagement activities, and doctoral colloquia. It is typical for them to also be involved directly in the job market through recruitment related activities. They are invariably involved in developing codes of professional practice, including ethical practice, intended to guide member behaviour.

We have shown that the international academic institutions related to ICCM are typically, and despite protestations to the contrary, still mostly Western dominated both numerically and in terms of their governance. Thus, although there are some very vibrant local academic associations, there is both a pull to the centre and a promulgation of the Western academies internationally.

The publications apparatus

The publishing apparatus connected directly or indirectly to the Western academy is a critical element of the institutional frame through which the hegemony of Western knowledge and knowledge systems are produced, reproduced and sustained. The publishing machine is multifaceted incorporating as it does publishers of monographs, textbooks and other books, magazines, on-line content, videos, CDs and other audio-visual media. The component dealing with the academic arena encompasses commercial, quasi-commercial and public-sector operations in a multi-billion dollar business. Of most relevance are those publishers of journals, books and other materials related to ICCM.

Textbooks

The role of textbooks is critical since they capture the core canon of material for the field that is deemed essential to those learning about it and seeking to enter its domain and claim competence in it. Textbooks are central to curriculum design and pedagogy within universities and other bodies charged with educating and training those with a professional interest or aspiration in the field. One effect of textbook construction is a tendency towards conservatism and orthodoxy. They tend to summarize and reproduce what is widely accepted and agreed upon, which means that less orthodox, more peripheral, contentious or controversial ideas and research tend not to be included. It also tends to mean that research and ideas from within the Western centre are more likely to be incorporated than material from the periphery or semi-periphery.

The higher education textbook market is massive. A recent report by the American Association of Publishers (AAP) states that within the US there are more than 8000 publishers, who currently make available some 262,000 titles to college bookstores and on which the average student spends US$650.00 per year (AAP, 2006).[7] The value of the US market is put at US$6.5 billion a year based on data for the academic year 2005–06 (NACS, 2008).[8] The market is oligopolistic, being dominated by a small number of large multinational companies such as Thomson, McGraw-Hill and Wiley. There has been significant industry consolidation over recent years with many smaller publishing houses being acquired by these large corporations: another trend that tends to engender conservative publishing of the orthodox. Of significance for us is the penetration of Western-based, mainly American, textbooks into institutions of higher education around the world.

Gopinath (1998: 270) for instance argues that most management text-books in Indian education are either Indian editions of standard US or British texts, or are by Indian authors schooled in and replicating the Western tradition. Local content is confined to case illustrations and there is 'little effort at incorporating [local] theory' (ibid). Gopinath notes that in such work you will find coverage of the motivational theories of Maslow and Herzberg, but not of Gandhi (a point also made by Jaya, 2001). Students around the world are being educated primarily through a core canon of work condensed into standard textbooks produced and dis-tributed out of the Western centre or in mimicry of them. As Alvares (2001: 2) notes, 'Too many texts from the "centre" are automatically taught in the "periphery" simply because they originate in the "centre" and not because of any inherent quality of the texts or originality of the authors, or their relevance to our part of the world.'

Surveying the field: the institutional bias in journal publishing

Our task of assessing the state of journal publishing in ICCM is aided greatly by its own obsession with accounting for its own practices: ICCM has something of a self-survey fetish. To quote Wong-MingJi and Mir (1997: 343) (with specific regard to international management [IM]): 'IM has engaged in a curiously substantial amount of navel gazing with over 50 review articles of the field published between 1965 and 1994'. This self-absorption has continued and is present in IB research too, where surveys of the state of knowledge in the field appearing in the field's journals, such as JIBS, are very apparent. Such surveys map out IB/ICCM's contours, tabulate its most studied topics and concepts, articulate its preferred methodologies, locate its key authors and their institutional affiliations, and identify the key contexts and countries of study. This enables us to document and comment on the skewed and particular nature of this core component of the field's publishing apparatus with cautious confidence.[9]

It is useful to outline firstly some parameters in relation to the various surveys, since they do not all attempt to measure or track the same things. First, some are surveys of IB (rather than IM or CCM) research; others pertain to IM or CCM and not IB; others are mixed. Second, many are surveys of research published in particular journals. Thus, some examine the amount of 'international' work published in leading and general management journals (for instance Kirkman & Law's 2005 survey of the AMJ), others survey the changing content of well-known IB and IM journals (for example Thomas, Shenkar & Clarke, 1994 on JIBS). Third, some look at more than one journal at a time, comparing results: for example, Peterson (2004) uses three journals (JIBS, AMJ, ASQ) for analysis. Wong-MingJi and Mir's (1997) survey of the IM literature examines 16 journals and comprises a sample of 3649 articles. Finally, the surveys we refer to all appeared in journals whose language of publication is English[10] (itself already reflective, of course, of the institutional location of ICCM).

A point of consensus across the surveys we examined is that international management research as a discipline is deemed to have grown over the last 30 years. In relation to the content of dedicated IB journals such as JIBS, Thomas et al. point to a 'maturing' phenomenon (Thomas et al., 1994). And more recently in the general management area, Kirkman and Law (2005) presented a historical analysis of the amount of international research published in the AMJ, which gave them grounds for 'cautious optimism' (to which we return later). There is, then, some consensus around the growth of IM/IB study and, according to Kirkman and Law, this has accelerated markedly during the early 2000s; confirming Wong-MingJi and Mir's (1997) earlier prediction of growth.

The growth of published work in Western journals with supposed IM/IB content is, however, not the same as the internationalization or increased inclusivity of the field. Given the continued expansion of IB and the furtherance of globalization processes, that more study of IB/IM matters is undertaken is hardly surprising. Indeed, for Wong-MingJi and Mir the reason for growth is largely in terms of an institutionalized response in business schools, academic and regulatory bodies and elsewhere to the pressures and articulations of the globalization discourse, a view with which we largely concur. Surveys of international journal content, however, paint a different picture.

Some of the most extensive evidence for parochialism comes from Wong-MingJi and Mir's (1997) analysis over the period 1954 to 1994. Key results of their study were:

1. IM research is predominantly conducted by scholars from the US and a small number of Western European countries;
2. IM research focuses largely either on generalized and deterritorialized conceptual issues or on matters related to the US, Western Europe and Japan;
3. IM research draws overwhelmingly from sources published in the US, and to a lesser degree on those coming out of Western Europe (Wong-MingJi & Mir, 1997: 360).

This assessment echoes a number of earlier surveys. For example, Thomas, Shenkar and Clarke's (1994) review of articles published in

JIBS between 1983 and 1993 found that IB consists of research 'conducted by scholars from the United States, Canada and Western Europe about the United States, Canada and Western Europe' (p. 492). Peng et al. (1991) reached similar conclusions. A survey of 15 leading management/ organizational behaviour journals for the period 1981 to 1992 demonstrated that over 85 per cent of authors were from the US; including the UK increased that to 91.1 per cent (Engwall, 1996). Following up a little later, Danell (1998, quoted in Clark et al., 1999–2000) reported that whilst European journals had become more international, US journals had not.[11] In another survey, the international content of 79 'leading' journals also revealed a strong North Atlantic bias (Pierce & Garven, 1995). They report that almost 23 per cent of this set of top management journals had 'no international content and 62 per cent had less than 10 per cent' (ibid: 76). In summarizing the 'international orientation of the journals' they say that:

> The majority of authors were from North America, primarily the United States. There was a tendency, however, for non-US-based journals, particularly those located in Europe, to publish more work from non-US-based authors. The readership of most journals was geographically highly concentrated, with three-quarters of the journals having more than half of their circulation in the US. Only fourteen journals had 10 per cent or more of their subscribers in each of three or more regions of the world' (ibid, 1995: 75).

A similar picture emerges from the Clark et al. (1999–2000) survey of 29 lead journals that published work on 'the management of human resources' broadly construed. This meant that not only HRM journals were surveyed, but also general management journals such as the AMR and AMJ, ASQ, and OS, as well as specialized journals in fields adjacent to HRM, such as psychology and industrial/labour relations. The survey covered the period 1977–97 and included over 20,000 articles. A mere 338 (1.7 per cent) met the criterion for inclusion: being concerned with the management of human resources *and* having a comparative or international approach.

The first thing to note, then, is the small proportion of 'international' papers, lower, as the authors clarify, than reported elsewhere, a reflection of their criteria perhaps. Clark et al. report that the US, the UK, Japan, France and Germany accounted for 48 per cent of the countries studied. Other countries featured were Canada, Australia, or Western European (Sweden, Spain and the Netherlands), and parts of Asia (China and Singapore). When comparisons were conducted they were also in relation to a limited number of countries: US and the UK; the UK and France or Germany; the US and Japan.

They also classified 59 per cent of the studies as 'ethnocentric', meaning that they utilized theory, conceptualization, research design and methods developed in one location and used by researchers from that location in relation to a different location with the aim of standardization in pursuit of universal or etic findings (ibid: 10).[12] Clark et al. (1999–2000: 11) conclude that research in IHRM is characterized by marginality, ethnocentrism and parochialism: a disciplinary parochialism in which IHRM does not articulate or learn from work in adjacent disciplines such as anthropology and psychology; and a cultural/ geographical parochialism in which the work is inextricably imbued with an 'Anglo-Saxon' orientation and bias (ibid: 14).

Taken together, the dominance of the West in terms of the authorship and contexts for IM research is indicative of an apparent unwillingness to investigate and take seriously the problems and concerns of vast proportions of the world's population. Wong-MingJi and Mir present some very telling data (see Table 3.1) showing the exclusion of large parts of the world in IM published work.

Wong-MingJi and Mir (1997) identified a further parochial aspect of IM research, which relates to the reading habits of scholars. Analysis of the articles' bibliographies shows that IM scholars draw very selectively from the work of the same small set of Western scholars. There is a narrow and narrowing citation practice, which serves to privilege Western knowledge, and through years and years of citation of the same authors, to sediment references and create authority for a select number of authors. Özbilgin (2009) commented critically on the use of citation networks as a strategy for bolstering journal rankings and fostering careers. A self-replicating trajectory ensues, where previous citation demands further citation, and legitimates the exclusion of other, non-Western knowledge since it does not 'fit' the canon.

Baruch (2001) wondered if the geographic location of authors impacted on whether their papers got published in lead journals or not. He examined 1091 articles from close to 2000 authors published in seven top management journals, four located in the US (AMR, AMJ, ASQ, Group & Organization Management) and three in Europe (OS, HR, Journal of Organizational Behavior) for the years 1980, 1985, 1990, 1995. The observation driving the analysis was that non-North Americans (non-NA) seemed to be under-represented in North American (NA) journals. He also hypothesized that NA authors would be under-represented in European-based journals and that such biases would exist despite differences in base

Table 3.1   Countries Excluded from IM Research

Countries not participating in IMR	Countries ignored in IMR
Afghanistan	Afghanistan
Albania	Albania
Angola	Algeria
Antigua & Barbuda	Angola
Bahamas	Antigua & Barbuda
Bahrain	Bahamas
Barbados	Bahrain
Belize	Barbados
Benin	Belize
Bhutan	Benin
Bolivia	Bhutan
Botswana	Bolivia
Brunei	Botswana
Bulgaria	Brunei
Burkina Faso	Bulgaria
Burundi	Burkina Faso
Cambodia	Burundi
Cameroon	Cambodia
Cape Verde	Cameroon
Central African Republic	Cape Verde
Chad	Central African Republic
Comoros	Chad
Côte d'Ivoire	Comoros
Cuba	Côte d'Ivoire
Cyprus	Cuba
Djibouti	Cyprus
Dominica	Djibouti
Dominican Republic	Dominica
Ecuador	Dominican Republic
El Salvador	Ecuador
Equatorial Guinea	El Salvador
Ethiopia	Equatorial Guinea
Fiji	Ethiopia
Gabon	Fiji
Gambia	Gabon
Ghana	Gambia
Grenada	Grenada
Guatemala	Guatemala
Guinea	Guinea
Guinea-Bissau	Guinea-Bissau
Guyana	Haiti
Haiti	Honduras
Honduras	Iceland
Iceland	Iraq
Iraq	Jamaica

Table 3.1 Countries Excluded from IM Research – *continued*

Countries not participating in IMR	Countries ignored in IMR
Jamaica	Jordan
Jordan	Kenya
Kenya	Korea (North)
Korea (North)	Laos
Laos	Lesotho
Lesotho	Liberia
Liberia	Luxembourg
Madagascar	Madagascar
Malawi	Maldives
Maldives	Mali
Mali	Malta
Malta	Mauritania
Mauritania	Mauritius
Mauritius	Mongolia
Mongolia	Mozambique
Morocco	Namibia
Mozambique	Nicaragua
Myanmar	Niger
Namibia	Oman
Nepal	Panama
Nicaragua	Papua New Guinea
Niger	Rwanda
Oman	St Lucia
Panama	St Vincent & Grenadines
Papua New Guinea	Sao Tome & Principe
Paraguay	Seychelles
Peru	Sierra Leone
Philippines	Solomon Islands
Qatar	Somalia
Rwanda	Sri Lanka
St Lucia	Sudan
St Vincent & Grenadines	Surinam
Sao Tome & Principe	Swaziland
Senegal	Syria
Seychelles	Togo
Sierra Leone	Trinidad & Tobago
Solomon Islands	Tunisia
Somalia	Uruguay
Sri Lanka	Vanuatu
Surinam	Vietnam
Swaziland	Western Sahara
Syria	Western Samoa
Togo	Yemen
Trinidad & Tobago	Zimbabwe
Tunisia	

Table 3.1 Countries Excluded from IM Research – *continued*

Countries not participating in IMR	Countries ignored in IMR
Uganda	
United Arab Emirates	
Uruguay	
Vanuatu	
Vietnam	
Western Sahara	
Western Samoa	
Zimbabwe	

Source: Adapted from Wong-MingJi and Mir, 1997: 350, 355.

rate.[13] He also reasoned that the level of publishing would be related to language, acknowledging that all journals selected are published in English. Finally, he speculated that the locational distribution of published authors would be related to the locational distribution of editorial board members.[14]

The analysis confirmed that non-NA authors are significantly under-represented in NA-based journals. Indeed, the percentage of non-NA papers published in NA journals did not exceed 10 per cent for any year under investigation and was below 7 per cent through the 1980s. Only in one journal, Group and Organization Management, did the non-NA contribution go above 10 per cent, with an average across the whole period of just 11.7 per cent, and even this showed a declining trend. Noticeably, NA authors were not, overall, under-represented in non-NA journals (ibid: 116–117). In fact, almost 60 per cent of authors in non-NA journals were from NA.[15] It is important to note that although Baruch talks about non-NA, he is really referring to a very restricted part of the world, acknowledging the dominance of UK authors in the non-NA category and the 'almost non-existent represen-tation of the Third World'[16] (ibid: 118). In fact, the UK, Israel and Australia account for 67 per cent and 52 per cent of non-NA papers in non-NA and NA journals respectively. Thus publication is not only skewed in favour of NA, but there is significant skewedness within the non-NA category too.

It is incumbent upon us to point out that there have recently been some more positive assessments of IB/ICCM research and suggestions of 'improvement' in the situation. Peterson's (2004) review of IM research detected a growing number of articles in AMJ and ASQ focus-ing on countries other than the US. However, the authorship of papers still appeared biased, with 66 per cent of the articles having only one or two authors, typically from one country and typically from the US. Even when authors are from outside the US often they have taken their PhD in the US.[17] Clark et al. (1999–2000) also promoted a more optimistic tone in suggesting that 'HRM can no longer be considered a marginal area of interest, that it is increasingly less constrained by geographical or cultural parochialism, and that there is a growing recognition among researchers of an ethnocentric bias within the field that has led many to adopt alternative approaches'. This is despite their own survey findings and it is an optimism we are not convinced is warranted.

Perhaps the most positive assessment of recent times comes from Kirkman and Law's (2005) analysis of the 'internationalization' of the AMJ over the period 1970–2004 noted earlier. The impetus for their article was Eden and Rynes' (2003) (then Associate Editors of AMJ) explicit encouragement of the submission and publication of more international work in the journal, appealing particularly to non-North American researchers. Kirkman and Law acknowledge that the international content and orientation of the journal was weak in the earlier years of the journal, but were led to describe the first five years of the 21st century as something of a golden age for IM research in AMJ. They claimed a substantial increase in the amount of IM work published and took this as an indication of a 'real "internationalization of AMJ"' (Kirkman & Law, 2005: 380). Their conclusion is that the AMJ is a 'truly international journal', 'one with, (1) many authors who are international scholars, (2) many samples collected outside North America, and/or (3) many topics related to international or cross-cultural management' (ibid: 383). We do not concur with this celebration and suggest that their own analysis does not justify such conclusions.

First, across the whole period they found that only 14 per cent of AMJ publications were on IM topics. Interestingly, they note that it was in the 1970s and not the 1980s or 1990s that AMJ published most international research, and this despite the increasing competitiveness of Japan and other Asian economies in the 1980s, and the concomitant spread of Japanese management techniques to North America and Western Europe. It was also in spite of the emergence in the 1980s of key approaches such as that of Hofstede. It was not until the 2000s that Kirkman and Law found a substantial increase in the amount of international research published in AMJ. In 2004, for instance, they identified 46 per cent of AMJ publications as 'international'. It is this figure that leads to their optimism about the internationalization of

AMJ and their conclusion that IM research in AMJ is 'alive and well' (ibid).

However, it must be noted immediately that they define as 'international' 'any article that satisfies any *one* of the following three criteria: (1) at least one author is a non-North American scholar,[18] (2) the sample is collected outside North America, or (3) the topic is related to international or cross-cultural management issues (regardless of authorship or data collection location' (ibid: 377, emphasis in original). Given that any one of these satisfies the definition of international, the inclusion of the first criterion is extremely problematic. Simply because a paper has a co-author from outside of North America only makes the paper 'international' in the very narrowest of senses. Indeed, it could be the case that the author recorded as 'international' was actually a US citizen working overseas. Furthermore, such an article may have nothing to say about international management and be entirely focused on internal US matters. The paper reports that 30 per cent of these so-called international papers had no North American authors. However, this was a proportion that had declined in the 2000s.[19]

Examining the international affiliation of authors reveals that just under 50 per cent were from Europe, and within Europe 83.6 per cent came from the UK, France, Italy or the Netherlands. Another third of the authors came from 'Asia', but over 29 per cent of them were from Australia or New Zealand, and 66 per cent from Hong Kong, Singapore, Taiwan or Japan – thus 95 per cent of 'Asia' is represented by authors from these six countries. Other than Europe and Asia there is no other clustering offered; the authors simply lump remaining locations under 'other countries'. Among those 'other countries' the whole of South America is represented by just two authors, and Africa by one. The largest representation in this 'other' category is Israel with 33 of the 39 authors counted; indeed of all countries contributing international papers, Israel is the second highest after the UK. These figures are mirrored in data reporting the countries on which studies have been conducted. In terms of location, close to a third had data only from within North America, 43 per cent had data from Europe (and 42 per cent of those were from the UK or Netherlands), 40 per cent from Asia (with a third from Japan, and another third from China, Korea or Hong Kong) and of the 'other countries', Israel was again easily the most studied.

Kirkman and Law's celebratory claims need to be tempered by such detail and by the limitations in their definitional frame and methodology. In fairness, they do acknowledge the continuing over-representation of authors from North America, Western Europe, Israel, Australia and limited parts of Asia, along with the obvious under-representation of Africa, Eastern Europe and Latin/South America.[20] However, this does not prevent them from offering a glowing endorsement of AMJ and its international qualities. In truth the claimed internationalization, if accepted, is under a very narrow construal and only includes a limited number of countries and regions.

Keepers of the journals: editors and the editorial process

What gets published and why is a complicated issue, but clearly has much to do with hegemonic forces, prevailing orthodoxies, and the politics of publishing. Editors and editorial boards play a crucial role here. It is these people who determine editorial policy and manage publishing practices: it is they, more than anyone, who police the boundaries of academic discourse. Usefully, there have been some surveys of the editorial structures associated with IB/IM/ICCM journals.

Most significant in this respect is a survey of the editorial structures and editorial policies and guidelines of 22 'top' IHRM journals (Özbilgin, 2004). Although Özbilgin provides an analysis of the editorial membership of top IHRM journals,[21] he also includes key general management journals that publish HRM-related papers, such as the journals of the American Academy, ASQ, the European Management Journal, and the Journal of Management, as well as specialist journals from applied psychology and labour/industrial relations. To explore editorial geographic distribution, he uses the United Nations list of countries and then clusters these into countries from Africa, Asia Pacific, Europe (excluding the UK), Latin America, the Middle East, the UK, US and Canada. The editors and editorial board members from the journals are then cross-tabulated with country cluster based on the address given for the board member in the journals.[22] Crucially, Özbilgin's (ibid: 205) analysis serves to surface the 'skewed geographic distribution of editorial membership' of these journals.

We note firstly that more than half the countries on the UN list had no representative on any editorial membership. Further analysis leads to an idealized classification into 'blind spots', 'shadows' and 'spot lights'. The last are those locations that are well represented editorially and unsurprisingly include North America, Western Europe (particularly the UK), and parts of the Asia Pacific (principally Australia, Japan and China). Indeed, 55 per cent of all editorial members are from the US, with a further 12 per cent from the UK. Adding Canada and the rest of Europe takes that up to 87 per cent indicating typical North Atlantic dominance. At the other extreme are the 'blind spots', the countries/regions with only a very 'rudimentary level of editorial parti-cipation' (ibid: 214). The Latin American, African and Middle East clusters are in this category, each having only 1 per cent of the total, and within those clusters Brazil, South Africa and Israel respectively dominate.

The 'shadow' regions are in between, with moderate representation, and include other parts of Asia and Europe, and, as with other features of institutional IB/ICCM, representation here is again likely to be slanted towards just a few countries[23] – in Asia, Hong Kong and Singapore for example.[24] It needs to be noted that editorial board members are invited for all kinds of reasons, including giving a journal the appearance of being international, and their actual role can often be quite passive. In this regard, Özbilgin's declared motives for undertaking this research are telling, since it involved his meeting with two Turkish professors[25] who had been invited onto the editorial boards of IM journals but then were never contacted again over a two-year period (ibid: 206). Importantly, beyond editorial board membership, *all* the chief editors of the journals were from North America, Europe or Australia.

Özbilgin's insightful work receives confirmation from a survey of the geographical location of the editorial board members of 30 leading IB journals published a year later (Chan, Fung & Lai, 2005). It was found that 63 per cent of editors were from North America, 25 per cent from Europe and 9 per cent from Asia and the Pacific. Only 3 per cent came from the 'other' category, which included South America, Africa and the Middle East. Confirmation too, from Pierce & Garven's (1995) review of leading English-language journals that publish IB research. Of the 79 journals examined, 60 (76 per cent) of the editors were from North America. Of the remainder, editors from the UK were the most prominent with 14 (18 per cent), and only four from the rest of Europe. In another study of the editorial influence of the top 25 MOS journals (determined by citation impact), it was reported that the editors-in-chief of 20 of them were based in the US, with the remaining five being from the UK (Meyer, 2006). Indeed, 20 of the journals are US based and the US editorial influence[26] was 100 per cent in nine cases, over 90 per cent in all but three, and never lower than 75 per cent.

Özbilgin also conducted a discourse analysis of the editorial policy statements and other materials related to these journals. He reports three major constraints on a proper realization of internationalization. First, that journals make claims regarding their international status and orien-tation, but none acknowledge the existing skewed nature of their content or editorial membership. Second, none recognize nor have policy guide-lines related to the problems associated with their monolingualism.

Related to this is the juxtaposition of claims to be international and to have international readership, whilst making no proactive moves to pursue geographic or positional diversity in content terms. Third, and as noted earlier, there is an over-reliance on large-scale empirical studies that become canonical. Furthermore, authors are required to cite the canon and anchor work to existing theory and literature, which serves to reproduce the orthodoxy that is already exclusionary with respect to large parts of the world. Additionally, some journals charge processing fees that disadvantage authors from peripheral contexts, precisely those contexts already marginalized editorially.

Academic dependency and captive minds

Our account of the present institutional frame for ICCM may be read as signalling asymmetrical relations, bias and inequality, but also as revealing of relationships of dependence and/or exclusion between centre and periphery. Numerous commentators have identified and discussed the academic imperialism and dependency that has developed in a core-periphery relationship enabled by and constructed under colonialism, but which persists as a condition of postcoloniality (for instance Alatas, 1974, 1996, 2000, 2003; Prakash, 1992; Raman, 1983). It is a critique that has a long pedigree going back to the anticolonial analysis of Fanon (1961/1963; 1952/1967), Memmi (1965, 1968), Césaire (1955/1972) and the critical pedagogy of Freire (1970). As Alatas (2003) points out, academic imperialism began with the colonial control of schools, universities and publishing, and structured the thinking of colonized people as a complement to political and economic imperialism (Alatas, 2000). It was a way of colonizing the mind; an interpretation introduced by Fanon (1963, 1967) and elaborated on by Alatas (1974), Ngugi (1981) and others. It is suggested that in the 'postcolonial period what we have is academic neo-imperialism or academic neo-colonialism as the West's monopolistic control of and influence over the nature and flows of social scientific knowledge remain intact even though political independence has been achieved' (Alatas, 2003: 602). Alatas (2003: 604) has enumerated the various 'dimensions of academic dependency':

1   Dependence on ideas;
2   Dependence on the media of ideas;
3   Dependence on the technology of education;
4   Dependence on aid for research as well as teaching;
5   Dependence on investment in education;

6 Dependence of Third World social scientists on demand in the West for their skills.

We might suggest a step further back and refer to the dependence on Western-based ontologies and epistemologies, but Alatas' first dimension clearly refers to Western knowledge systems, theory and metatheory. The second dimension refers to the elements of the Western publishing machine that has been much of the focus of the early parts of this chapter. By the dependence on the technology of education, Alatas means the sophisticated computer and information retrieval, storage and analysis technologies owned and managed by Western governments and agencies that are able to generate data and analysis in relation to Third World contexts, but according to Western choices and interests. The fourth dimension refers to the TW dependence on foreign aid to support educational institutions, for example through provision of scholarships or expertise. The next dimension signifies the direct investment in higher education by Western educational institutions into the TW and includes the, by now, extensive exportation and mounting of degree programmes in the TW by First World (FW) universities, a phenomenon very apparent around Asia for example.

As Alatas points out, the final dimension could be referred to in terms of a 'brain drain'. Many aspiring TW scholars are attracted to study in the FW, and indeed, will often go further and seek employment in FW universities or research institutes. However, Alatas refers to a perhaps more pernicious form of brain drain, one that does not involve physical relocation. By this he means that the inducements of the Western academy and the incentives to participate in it are such that all the energies of TW scholars are oriented in that direction and away from local and indigenized concerns.

The structures of academic imperialism and dependency also naturally result in inequalities in the nature of participation in knowledge work between centre and periphery. Specifically a division of labour, initiated and instantiated under colonialism, has persisted that continues to disadvantage the TW scholar and works to sustain the structures of dependency. This division of labour has the following profile:

1. The division between theoretical and empirical intellectual labour;
2. The division between other country studies and own country studies;
3. The division between comparative and single case studies. (Alatas, 2003: 607)

In relation to point one it is argued that FW scholars are enabled to undertake both theoretical and empirical work, whereas the work of

TW scholars is mostly confined to empirical work. In the social sciences, as a scrutiny of journals reveals,[17] FW scholars feel enabled to undertake not just studies involving their home context, but also to study other countries, whereas TW scholars typically are confined to studying and writing about their own location with limited comparative work. When comparisons are undertaken, they are most often in relation to a FW country and often in collaboration with FW scholars. It is rare indeed to see comparative studies focused on just TW countries. We are of the view that this is true in MOS/ICCM also. Indeed, the last element of Alatas' profile suggests quite simply that comparative work is much less common in the TW context, where single case studies prevail and usually on the domestic context. Alatas concludes that: 'The division of labour, therefore, functions to perpetuate academic dependency and academic neocolonialism' (ibid: 608).

The assessment by Alatas suggests structural inequalities in the relative participation of TW and FW scholars in the social sciences. It also points to incentives and processes by which TW scholars become incorporated into FW knowledge systems and modes of academic practice. Indeed, it can be argued that part of the hegemony of the Western knowledge system and discourse, including that of ICCM, is that it provides processes of incorporation whereby those outside of the Western academy are provided with opportunities for inclusion *only if* they construct accounts of the phenomena, in our case management and organization practices, within their locations in a manner compatible with Western theory and delivered *via* Western methods and textual strategies.

In this sense, non-Western scholars participating in Western institutions and publishing within Western paradigms and in Western journals might be considered to have become 'captive minds' (Alatas, 1974), held by the Western knowledge system. Within the geopolitics of contemporary academia, the West has managed to achieve a globalized hegemony for its knowledge systems such that many from non-Western contexts have been imbued with its values, assumptions and practices. Many feel professional, careerist or institutional pressures to refract their research and thinking through a Western academic lens. Indeed, Hofstede (1984) maintains that it would take an act of 'considerable personal courage and independence of thought' (1984: 397) for a TW scholar to disavow Western theory and question the relevance and applicability to non-Western contexts. The consequence is a tendency for non-Western scholars to participate in precisely those research and representational practices that essentialize and exoticize the Other and to reproduce the West and its knowledge systems.

In formulating the notion of the 'captive mind',[18] Alatas (1974) was exploring his deep concern about the intrusions of Western knowledge and educational systems into colonial contexts and the continued ramifications of that for indigenous ways of thinking and acting, particularly among a nation's intellectual elites. Such intrusions created conditions for the minds of local people to be captured within the knowledge systems and ways of knowing of the West, which then stunted their capacity to think independently and creatively about the pressing issues and problems confronting their own society.

In sum, we would conclude that ICCM remains ineluctably an intellectual practice embedded in and driven by the economic, strategic, political and sociocultural interests of the West and a constitutive and supportive institutional frame. A disciplinary power is constituted by this complex system of institutions. Its institutional elements, practices and policies establish relations of dominance and facilitate a subjugation of subjects, particularly those academics seeking to function in the periphery and semi-periphery (Foucault, 1981). That institutional frame is multifaceted but journal production and its relation to regimes of performance management are a central and critical component and key in the reproduction of Western hegemony. And as noted in the previous chapter, it is also framed by the limitations of a functionalist paradigm and positivistic methods.

In the next part of the book we go on to give an account of the historical conditions of possibility for this state of affairs in ICCM.

Part II
Historicizing ICCM

4
Colonial Legacies

Introduction

To pose the question whether ICCM represents a continuing form of the colonial project is to ask questions about the nature of colonialism, with particular regard in the first instance to its knowledge systems. As Said (1978), and others, have demonstrated, the non-West has been subjected systematically to the West's intellectual and scientific technology which has scrutinized, labelled, categorized, taxonomized, codified and ultimately invented the Other. This discursive invention provided a ground upon which all manner of material practices have been launched (and vice versa): from the scientific, administrative, anthropological and commercial practices of the colonial past, to the globalizing and multiculturalist management and trade practices of the neo-colonial present.

This chapter is organized into three key sections. In the first two, we examine the colonial histories of Western or, what Harding (1996) calls, 'Northern' science, and the discipline of anthropology. It can be argued that both emerged in the colonial encounter and had their own justificatory rationales and systematic modes for representing, and claiming to 'know' the Other. Such representational strategies rendered the Other comprehensible, palatable and amenable to the West's systems of knowledge and colonial administration. Furthermore, the interests of science and anthropology were aligned, fractiously at times, with the 'business' of Empire, the subject of the final section in this chapter. Colonialism and capitalism were mutually constitutive structures, as perhaps best illustrated by the history of merchant enterprise, and especially the East India Company (EIC), which drew extensively upon varied forms of scientific and anthropological knowledge.

Colonialism and modern science

As noted in Part I of the book, ICCM scholarship has sought contin-uously to gain academic legitimacy and institutional credibility. Like most management disciplines, scholars have addressed this goal by making appeals to the scientific status of their work. Such appeals have taken root in positivist methodology, hypothetico-deductive approaches, a faith in the possibility of value neutrality and a split between the observer and the observed. Above all, such appeals are also embedded in a belief in science's ability to create superior truths *vis-à-vis* non-scientific methods and alternative forms of rationality. However, the scientific method in which ICCM is currently invested is, despite appear-ances, far from a universal or in any way neutral body of knowledge, as this sub-section sets out to show.

Recent historical work from postcolonial science and technology studies, feminist philosophy and sociology, and the history of science, demonstrates the isomorphism between colonialist expansion and the development of modern Western science. That is to say, just as the colonial project was dependent on the development of a particular mode of scientific endeavour (one in tune with prevailing Eurocentric empiricist, rationalist and objectivist predilections), science was also dependent on the colonial project (Harding, 1996; Jasanoff, 1995). We illustrate this co-dependency by examining science both as an acad-emic or applied set of formal knowledges, and also by looking at the broader role of science and technology in colonized societies.

Historicizing and politicizing science

To understand the history of science is to be able to critique the kinds of internalist accounts of science that frequent the pages of many text-books and popular cultural texts. According to Harding (1996), inter-nalist accounts start from the premise that science is an intellectual achievement only possible and extant in the West. Science is often viewed as the greatest achievement of the Enlightenment, part of man's (sic) route out of the dark towards the light. With faith in reason and in progress predicated on scientific and technological advance-ment, a worldview emerged in which a new human subject (rather than a set of divine forces) became the agent of change and of history. Harding describes how science, when caricatured in textbooks, 'springs up out of a few brilliant ideas and some hardworking genius' stubborn insistence on fiddling with pieces of wire and glass' (1991: 218). This image neatly sums up the idea that Western science is most often associated with the 'intellectual genius' of the Western male mind. This internalist view not only restricts intellectual and scientific achievement to the West, but also disavows the material contexts that made it possible.

To hold on to such a story, as Harding (ibid) ascerbically remarks, requires 'an altered state of consciousness'. Recent scholarship from history, philosophy, sociology, and women's studies *inter alia* renders this view intellectually suspect and ultimately untenable. With their point of departure in the 'science wars', and intellectual roots perhaps before then, a number of different 'counter cultures of science' (from ecologists and feminists, to workers' movements and anti-imperialists) (Harding, 1991) offer an alternative view. Accordingly, the internalist and universalizing account of science is an ideological expression of the need for the West to mask its reliance on the knowledge systems and methods of non-Western cultures as it proceeds to assert its superiority. Harding encapsulates the point using anthropological discourse:

> What is at issue for all these critics, including feminists, is not only the easily identifiable theories, methods, institutions, and technological consequences of the sciences but also something harder to describe: the Western scientific view or mind-set. The 'indigenous peoples' of the modern West – those most at home in Western societies – have culturally distinctive belief patterns in which scientific rationality plays a central role. These 'natives', like all Others, have trouble even recognizing that they exhibit culturally distinctive patterns of belief; it is like discovering that one speaks a distinctive genre-prose. From an anthropological perspective, faith in scientific rationality is at least partly responsible for many of the Western beliefs and behaviours that appear most irrational to people whose life patterns and projects do not so easily fit with those of the modern West (ibid: 3).

In addition to identifying the 'distinctive genre-prose' of North Atlantic sciences, the remainder of this sub-section is premised on a view that the spread and 'success' of Western science is a facet of its external contingencies, its historically-evolving material relations to other societies and cultures. This externalist account should serve to decentre the history of science from the geography and time of the North Atlantic, point to competing and older achievements of non-Western scientific rationalities, and relink the West's cognitive structures with its material contexts of production.

The first point of departure for decentring this internalist narrative is simple: to understand that Western science is only one form of scientific rationality. The history of science literature is replete with studies of the scientific rationalities of civilizations outside Europe, notably work on Chinese (see for instance, Needham, 1969), Indian and Islamic civilizations. Scholars have paid particular attention to the mathematical systems, astronomy and medicine of these civilizations, and demonstrated their ancient, complex and sophisticated cosmo-logies, beliefs and understandings of the natural world and the human body (for instance, Lindberg 1992 on ancient Egyptian and Meso-potamian science). Not only does this give an awareness of alter-natives, it should also draw our attention to the fact that there were many achievements in these scientific cultures that predated Europe's proclaimed advances.

In this latter respect, the idea of Greek science as an originary point whence all scientific thought developed can be considered a myth. Greek thought was not immune from external cultural influence and, moreover, was not the sole or constant influence on the development of Western science. This insight is developed most comprehensively in Lindberg's (1992) study. Whilst previous historians of science had tended to separate the history of science into discrete periods, and to analyze these periods independently of each other, Lindberg traces connections between the ancient and the medieval periods in Western science. For one, Greek thought was importantly influenced by Egyptian and Mesopotamian science during the ancient period. During the medieval period, the interaction and mutual influence of Greek and Islamic scientific thought was notable. Later, Islamic scientific thinking would go on to play a paramount role in the revival of European seats of learning in the medieval period. For instance, Islamic translators and thinkers exerted a profound influence on how Aristotle was received in Europe's ancient universities. The early history of Western science is therefore a history of intercultural encounter, and of cultural hybrid-ization. This tradition of mutual influence would continue, and Wes-tern science would take on a character with which we are now most familiar during the colonial period of European history. This history of mutual scientific encounter and cultural influence would, however, be expunged from orthodox accounts.

According to Gilmartin (1994: 1127):

In the eyes of many colonial administrators in the nineteenth century, the advance of science and the advance of colonial rule went hand in hand. Science helped to secure colonial rule, to justify European domination over other peoples, and to transform production for an expanding world economy.

Science and colonialism were mutually constitutive practices that contributed to the development of a capitalist system of production (and consumption) between colonizers and their colonies. On the one hand, science provided colonizers with technologies of shipbuilding and engineering necessary for exploration and settlement as well as military hardware for physical aggression and violence. It also cultivated cultures of rationalism and empiricism wherein human reason evolved to eclipse religious belief as an arbiter of progress. Science thus provided the tools as well as the vision and ambition for colonial expansion. Its task was therefore ideological as much as it was material. On the other hand, as much as colonialism needed science, science also needed and co-evolved with European expansion and colonialism (Harding, 1991, 1996; Jasanoff, 1995).

At the heart of this scientific relationship was a profound asymmetry. Just as colonialism allowed the development of the science of the colonizer, and more importantly the development of an industrial and commercial system that would generate wealth, it simultaneously created the 'de-development of the societies of Africa, Asia, and other Third World countries' (Harding, 1991: 220). Harding advises that '(...) we should refer not to the development of Europe and the underdevelopment of the Third World but to the *over*development of Europe and the *de*-development of the Third World' (ibid: 234, italics in the original). Whilst the West and the Rest shared a common history, they were not identical histories and the scientific dependencies between centre and periphery established a zone of power between the two. But how exactly did these dependencies happen? What was the nature of the interaction?

Basalla's (1967) three-stage model of the spread of Western science is a useful, if not unproblematic, heuristic for framing and addressing parts of these questions. He portrays these phases as interlocking but temporally consecutive phases. The first phase of the three in his heuristic uses the metaphor of the 'laboratory' to describe the non-European or 'non-scientific'[1] society. Basalla (1967: 611) characterizes this period as follows: '(...) the European [who] visits the new land, surveys and collects its flora and fauna, studies its physical features, and then takes the results back to Europe. Botany, zoology, and geology predominate during this phase, but astronomy, geophysics, and a cluster of geographical science (...) sometimes rival them in importance'. He suggests that science is an extended part of the well-documented voyages of discovery.[2] For example, the primary outcome of Cook's voyages between 1768 and 1780, with Sir Joseph Banks' botanical and zoological explorations of Australia, was the description and analysis of the natural resources of the non-European society.

Processes of transformation and change are central in stage two and three of Basalla's heuristic. Whilst the second phase of his model describes a period of 'colonial science' encompassing an asymmetrical relation between the colonizing and the colonized nation, the third involves 'a struggle to achieve an independent scientific tradition (or culture)' within the colonized nation (ibid: 611). Colonial ideology assumed that European science and, of course, European culture, politics and so on were intellectually superior, whilst those of other nations trailed behind. It is not much of a leap from there to define progress, development and modernization in European terms and to see the colonial project as the legitimate export of such 'benefits' to the rest of the world.

The transfer of these purported benefits of European civilization typically involved violence in a number of forms. The history of colonialism is also a history of killing, death, displacement, dispossession, rape, torture, physical servitude and slavery. Modernity was not just a symbolic construction – it was also created down the barrel of guns, and through the use of technologies that killed. As Crosby (1993) describes, the extermination of local populations took place as a result of, sometimes intentional, sometimes not, environmental colonialism. There are several examples of colonial powers introducing new animal species or even diseases into local populations in order to kill the native population.

The spread of Western science can also be viewed as a form of cultural imperialism that committed epistemic violence *vis-à-vis* local knowledge systems. There are at least two ways in which this can be understood. First, recent scholars of science point to the violence that is endemic in the very cosmology of Western science (Alvares, 1988). Bajaj (1988) explores the power relations in Bacon's work (for some the 'father' of modern science) and its dominance and violence as 'encoded in the cosmology that gets telescoped into the culture of modern science' (p. 13). Bajaj argues that the violence is written into Bacon's concept of true and useful knowledge, in his homocentric vision of the natural world, and in his masculine perception of nature, including human nature. Nature was an enemy to be defeated and tortured for the benefit of the human race. Bacon was the first to provide philosophical legitimacy to the human quest for omnipotence through science, the first to 'reconceptualize the non-human cosmos as an experimental subject fit only for manipulative intervention' (ibid: 14).

Moving beyond the cosmology of Western science, epistemic violence can also be considered a facet of the interaction between colonizer and colonized. Scientific colonialism systematically produced not only knowledge, but also ignorance (Harding, 1996). 'Modern science' positions other knowledge systems as non-scientific, pre-scientific, pseudo-scientific, prelogical, superstitious, magical, alchemical, or folk. These terms functioned to demote non-European knowledge systems and traditions. In terms of interaction, it would be wrong to assume, however, that scientific colonialism simply involved the 'diffusion-by-receipt' of European civilization (Blaut, 1993). Historical evidence suggests that the cultural and institutional life of science was much more complex than such diffusionist explanations suggest, and that epistemic violence took a number of twists and turns.

Colonial science and the university: The example of Australia

Studies of scientific knowledge in the academic arena during the period of 'colonial science' illustrate well the asymmetrical dependencies plus the tensions and ambiguities of scientific relations between centre and periphery. Postcolonial analyses of science in particular teach us that any simplistic notion of diffusion-by-receipt significantly misrecognizes the local specificities and 'external factors' that shaped the encounter between Western sciences and non-Western cultures (Reingold & Rothenberg, 1987).

Schedvin's (1987) study of the development of Australian biology in the period between the so-called classical (1770–1836) and modern ages of science (1930s onwards) shows how Australian biology developed through a series of 'stops and starts' connected to a set of local and interacting economic and environmental factors (such as drought, the detrimental impact of introduced pests on the local sheep population, excessive land clearing, economic collapse) which forced Britain to rethink its development policies for Australia. To address these problems, the colonial administration put considerable funds into applied (rather than pure) science since it was seen to contribute more directly to the economic goals of industrialization. A new funding regime organized through the CSIR (Council for Scientific and Industrial Research) created an imperialist structure for scientific knowledge transfer – the

CSIR was formed so that Australia could 'receive' British science in the role of metropolitan client.

An uncomplicated receipt of British knowledge, however, was pure wishful thinking. British scientists were sent to Australia as 'experts' to play key roles in the development of applied scientific research programmes in the late 1920s and early 1930s. Their work was ineffective however, since they did not have enough knowledge of Australia, and its particular geographical and environmental conditions, to create useful scientific programmes. Furthermore, Australian scientists, unhappy with the economic aspirations of Empire, and exhibiting what Schedvin calls an 'independent spirit' in the interwar years, managed to create a certain distance from the pressures of metropolitan science. It would be unwise to overstate this 'distance', however, since, as Schedvin notes of biology and other scientific fields, the development of proprietary normative structures in Australian science was often thwarted by imperial control.

The fractious relationship between metropolitan and peripheral scientists often proved detrimental, rather than facilitative, to the development of new knowledge. Dugan's (1987) study of the history of zoological knowledge in and about Australia is illustrative here. The development of zoological knowledge was stunted in both Britain and Australia by a kind of mutual intransigence. Given the prohibitive geographical distance, European scientists needed to rely on local data collectors to conduct scientific investigation on their behalf. Whilst local Australians collected and structured scientific data and sent it to Europe, theoretical work on the data only took place in Europe. The reason for this, according to Dugan, was that European scientists at the time had little trust or respect for their data collectors. Australians' diminution to 'data collector' was compounded geographically by their distance from scientific networks in Europe, and institutionally by their own lack of adequate scientific training, good scientific collections in Australian university libraries, and the slow trickle of scientific knowledge in the form of journals and books from Europe to Australia. Consequently, Dugan suggests that data collected in Australia were subject to a greater degree of theoretical manipulation than data generated in Europe. When Australian data appeared to transgress extant theoretical beliefs and scientific classifications, the evidence was typically ignored, explained away or deemed unacceptable or flawed.

The 'discovery' and subsequent scientific categorization of monotremes (egg-laying mammals) and marsupials was a case in point. Previously European taxonomy assumed that all milk-giving animals gave birth to live young; that all warm-blooded, egg-laying animals were birds; and that all egg-laying quadrupeds were placed among reptiles. Monotremes (impossibly) had all these characteristics – the assumption was that the local collectors must have been wrong. As Dugan notes, it was a full 85 years after the discovery of this species that European scientists would accept that monotremes laid eggs, despite the consistent evidence presented by local Australian collectors. A principal reason for this scientific intransigence on the part of British scientists was the denigration of local Aboriginal knowledge in these colonial scientific interactions. Dugan cites the case of the Australian scientist Bennett, who, when collecting data and told by Aboriginals that monotremes laid eggs, chose to ignore what he had been told, assuming that either his questions had been misunderstood or he had misunderstood the meaning of the answer he received. In any case, and whilst language might have been a barrier, he reported that no dependence could be placed on native accounts of zoological knowledge, since they were 'outside' the scientific community.

Dugan documents a clear strain of racism that underpinned the denial of Aboriginal knowledge. To illustrate, Dugan presents selected excerpts from the memoirs of William Caldwell, a University of Cambridge scholar who conducted research in rural Queensland. Caldwell chose Queensland as the location for his research because it supplied him with a large and cheap labour pool for the collection of data. His memoirs suggest that he considered his Aboriginal labour pool racially inferior and their knowledge as lacking validity and value. Dugan quotes the following excerpt:

> A skilful black, when he was hungry, generally brought in one female Echidna, together with several males, every day … The blacks were paid half-a-crown for every female, but the price of flour, tea, and sugar, which I sold to them, rose with the supply of Echidna. The half-crowns were, therefore, always just sufficient enough to keep the lazy blacks hungry (1987: 93–94).

Staging science in India

The tugs, tensions and epistemic violation of colonial science were certainly not reserved for the academic arena. They also characterized the diffusion of Western scientific knowledge in the civic and public cultures of colonial societies. Prakash's (1999) landmark study of science in pre- and post-independence India is illustrative here. He explains the limitations of assuming that Western science was 'pre-formed' and ready to wield authority in India. Instead he shows how Western science was itself made in negotiation with local Indian cultures and was subject to a power struggle between colonizer and colonized.

As noted by Said, the goal of cultural imperialism was to transform local cultures into something more recognizably European such that local populations could be controlled and governed. The diffusion of science into local knowledge systems was an important tool for achieving this goal, but it required that Western science would be understood and valorized before it could replace local knowledge systems. In Prakash's words, Western science was a 'sign' that needed to achieve cultural authority 'functioning as the name for freedom and enlightenment, power and progress' (1999: 3). Science functioned as the prime arbiter and guarantee of modernity for the Indian state by putting into wide cultural circulation a set of norms, values and understandings that would transform the myth and superstition of the Indian population into an 'Enlightenment mindset' and thus, in theory at least, render them governable.

Prakash examines two interconnected facets of science in India: first, the staging of science; and second, the role of science in governmentality.[3] With regard to the former, museums and exhibitions were key sites for colonial pedagogy in which Indians were 'invited' to: 'identify and learn universal principles of classification and function in objects encased in colonial power and exhibited as spectacle' (ibid: 34). Science was 'performed' in order to gain Indian acknowledgement of a foreign logic with the goal of replacing local superstition. Museum curators sought to transform local knowledges of natural history by refracting them through Western systems of classification. Knowledge of nature was thus reordered, dislocated from the diversity of local Indian epistemes into the supposedly universal schemes of Western classification. Local artefacts were 're-cultured' or 're-invented' as objects of colonial discourse. As for exhibitions, these contained displays of Western technologies (such as agricultural machinery or engineering feats) which instructed Indians in the new cultural category of function and aimed to encourage locals to engage in and enhance agricultural and economic production in India (for British benefit). The discourse of colonial science, expressed in terms of classification and function, was a distorted one according to Prakash. He describes how just at the moment when science is staged, the key binaries upon which it rests ('universal' scientific knowledge v. 'local' superstition and belief) were necessarily dislocated. Colonial discourses based on the staging of science led a 'discordant life of dominance' marked by ambivalence, paradox and subterfuge.

Science was also a vital basis for structures of governmentality in India since it was seen as enabling the colonizer to improve the security of the colony. The British did so through the creation of an elaborate system of governance based on 'modern institutions, infrastructures, knowledges, and practices' (ibid: 4). Science filtered through a plethora of different forms of social and economic life in India, not just health, agriculture or economics, but also religion, literature and philosophy. It was the body of the native that was the key site for colonial control and regulation. Furthermore, state bureaucratization created a common political structure for local elites, subaltern populations and the British. Prakash describes it as a 'reconfigured space of power' in which the local Indian population came to have particular and differential forms of agency depending on their social position.

Indeed, the authorization of Western science provided a key arena in which Indian class relations became reordered or reinscribed. On the one hand, Western-educated Indian elites (men) played a central role in 'reforming' local culture. This class of men came to represent, and to translate modernity in India by promoting a scientific culture based on a belief in natural laws to reform religion and society. Primarily emanating from Bengal, these locals fostered a new scientific culture that only later would spread to other provinces in India. Without necessarily dismissing Western modernity out of hand, they were able to develop a version that would later go on to form an important basis for Indian nationalism.

As with the elites, the subaltern population (defined and discussed later) also demonstrated the limits of colonial science. The idea of the transformation of the local by the scientific was a necessarily untenable goal: how would the British justify colonialism if they succeeded in converting the superstitious masses? What would be left? As such, Prakash notes they became an 'intractable presence in the discourse of science' (ibid: 46), simultaneously (and necessarily for the continuation of colonial discourse) knowable yet unknowable. Prakash uses the example of rumours (for example that agricultural machinery was a plot to increase land taxes) to demonstrate that the subaltern was a tricky presence for colonial rulers, never passive in the process of domination. The 'native supplement' (ibid) would always remind the British of the limitations of trying to translate and objectify local knowledges. These kinds of epistemic structures and elite interests have not vanished since India gained independence (Nandy, 1988; Shiva, 1988).

Colonialism and anthropology

Just as science is a core knowledge system upon which the construction of orthodox international and cross-cultural management research rests, so too is a certain anthropological understanding of human culture. It is typically a functionalist understanding of human culture, wedded to a certain 'scientific attitude' (Redding, 1994), that dominates ICCM and has a very particular genesis and historical development. To suggest how anthropology emerged from the colonial encounter is to understand the problematic colonial genesis of the kind of anthropological knowledge we have received in ICCM. To this end, the section is structured into three key sub-sections. The first clarifies exactly what we are referring to when we talk about anthropology. The second critically discusses the relationship between anthropology and scientism, and the resultant objectification of the Other by early anthropologists. The final sub-section addresses the relationship between anthropological theory and methods, and funding structures.

Situating anthropology

There are many kinds of anthropology (social, cultural, linguistic, forensic, medical and so on) and there are many national variations of the anthropological discipline (British, American, French, German and so on). This section is primarily based on readings of the historical development of British social anthropology and its relationship to colonial administration in Africa, in particular in the period between the two World Wars. The British Empire was the largest compared to the other European powers. By 1919 it had reached its peak of geographical influence following the distribution of German colonies after World War One. These facts presented the British Empire with considerable administrative challenges. As the interwar years unfolded, they turned to an increasing degree to anthropology for assistance. The discipline of British social anthropology, and its functionalist orthodoxy, emerged just after World War One and is predominantly associated at this early stage with the writings of Malinowski and Radcliffe-Brown. The discipline went on to achieve academic credibility only later after World War Two (Asad, 1973) during the period of late colonialism. ICCM's cultural orthodoxy is related to the legacy of this particular period.

Just as certain counter cultures of science came to prominence in academic debate from the 1960s onwards, so too did certain counter cultures of anthropology. By the early 1960s, there were a number of highly critical essays on the colonial history of the discipline. Critics (such as Leach, Worsley, Needham, Gough and notably Hymes) lamented the manner in which functional anthropologists neglected the impact of politics and economics in their accounts of cultural development. From this context emerged some of the best known critical writings on anthropology in the 1970s and 1980s (including Asad, 1973; Fabian, 1983; Marcus & Fischer, 1986). Together these counter cultures of anthropology revealed the bourgeois, Eurocentric and androcentric basis of the historical development of the discipline. Our historicization of functional anthropological thought is organized in ways that attempt to showcase elements of these key critiques. Our point of departure is encapsulated in the following long quotation from Asad (1973: 14–15):

> (...) anthropology is ... rooted in an unequal power encounter between the West and Third World which goes back to the emergence of bourgeois Europe, an encounter in which colonialism is merely one historical moment. It is this encounter that gives the West access to cultural and historical information about the societies it has progressively dominated, and thus not only generates a certain kind of universal understanding, but also re-enforces the inequalities in capacity between the European and non-European worlds (and derivatively, between the Europeanized elites and the 'traditional' masses in the Third World). We are today becoming increasingly aware of the fact that information and understanding produced by bourgeois disciplines like anthropology are acquired and used most readily by those with the greatest capacity for exploitation. This follows partly from the structure of research, but more especially from the way in which these disciplines objectify their knowledge. It is because the powerful who support research expect the kind of understanding which will ultimately confirm them in their world that anthropology has not very easily turned to the production of radically subversive forms of understanding. It is because anthropological understanding is overwhelmingly objectified in European languages that it most easily accommodated to the mode of life, and hence to the rationality, of the world power which the West represents.

The exploitative capacities of early anthropology find foundations, as Asad notes above, in the structure of anthropological research, and the particular ways in which anthropologists objectified their knowledge. Both these issues can be said to have mitigated against the establishment of a radical critique of anthropology during the interwar period in particular. How did anthropologists go about objectifying their knowledge? How was anthropological research structured, and in what way was subversive thought concomitantly marginalized? And to what extent, therefore, was anthropology the handmaiden of colonialism?

Anthropological knowledge and objectification

Fabian (2001) argues that 'domination for the sake of civilization' became an outcome of the new field of anthropology as a result of the manner in which anthropology engaged in objectifying processes of knowledge creation using discourses of scientism and visualism. According to Fabian, the seeds of an objectifying, scientistic and domineering anthropological gaze have a heritage in the writings of a varied group of early travellers to the colonies. These included: government officials or administrators, traders, missionaries, aristocrats and those of independent wealth and interested in exploration, and travel writers. Several authors (including Said, 1978) describe the panoply of texts produced by these varied travellers, including travelogues, administrative texts, political pamphlets, manuals for travel and maps. Fabian (2001) argues that together these texts constituted a 'proto-anthropological perspective' that prefigured the later scientific object-ification and political subjectification of native populations.

Fabian illustrates through an analysis of the travel writing of the noted 19th century social scientist, and 'armchair anthropologist', Francis Galton (1822–1911). Galton's book published in 1853, entitled *The Narrative of an Explorer in Tropical South Africa*, recounts an expedition up the Swakop River. According to Fabian, Galton's scientific pretensions were manifest in his continuous observations and documentation of the native population's notions of time, local economic systems, measurement and language *inter alia*. Galton's book presented the many differences between local tribes, a proto-anthropological approach in so far as it indexed an 'anthropological theorization of variation' based on 'natural terms' and utilizing 'scales of nearness and remoteness' (Fabian, 2001). Galton was no mere benevolent note-taker on local cultures; he was tasked by the British government with bringing order to this area of South Africa. These observations of cultural variation were a necessary part of the political subjectification of the native population, bringing them through juridical means (as well as physically violent ones too) into colonial systems of order. Galton's 'science' was certainly not, however, the same kind that would later become institutionalized in anthropology's first major paradigm – evolutionism. This is because *Origin of Species* had not yet been written. It was only later that Darwin's influence, combined with extant social evolutionary theories, would form the bedrock for anthropology's evolutionary paradigm.

It was in the emergence of the evolutionary paradigm across the social sciences of the late 19th century as a whole that anthropology would become aligned with science, and thereby subject to the prevailing 'scientism' of the time. The alignment can be illustrated through the manner in which evolutionary thinking engendered the 'spatialization of time', a development that would ultimately facilitate the exercise of cultural imperialism and colonial governance. Fabian (1983: 143–144, italics in the original) famously notes:

> Anthropology emerged and established itself as an allochronic discourse; it is a science of other men in another Time. (...) they [Western imperial nations] required Time to accommodate the schemes of a one-way history: progress, development, modernity (and their negative mirror images: stagnation, underdevelopment, tradition). In short, *geopolitics* has its ideological foundations in *chronopolitics*.

Chronopolitics is exemplified through the manner in which the objectification of knowledge about Others is performed through the category of time. Fabian (1983) traces the conditions of possibility for such a chronopolitics back to the historical and philosophical transformations in the nature and meaning of time in the Enlightenment period. Specifically the Enlightenment served to secularize the meaning of time, and to render it amenable for particular social and political purposes. In the case of the social sciences, it enabled relationships between different parts of the world to be understood as temporal relations. Notions of geological time, in which time was seen to 'accomplish things', underpinned the evolutionary interest in identifying the different things that different times brought with them. The category of time was deployed topologically and, aligned with a scientific disposition, manifest in a number of representational practices: the categorization of the human race by stages in historical development; the classification of societies as peasant, modern, traditional, premodern; the emergent notion of a global history and a concomitant idea of universal progress. The category of the 'primitive' became a staple of anthropological discourse, with 'savages' viewed as survivors of ancient forms of cultural development. Evolutionary anthropology worked then to spatialize time, engendering a taxonomic approach to cultural analysis drawing upon discourses of natural history (physics and geology).

Fabian (ibid: 325) characterizes the effect of these developments as follows:

> It is not the dispersal of human cultures in space that leads anthropology to 'temporalize' (….); it is naturalized-spatialized Time which gives meaning (in fact a variety of specific meanings) to the distribution of humanity in space. The history of our discipline reveals that such use of Time almost invariably is made for the purpose of distancing those who are observed from the Time of the observer.

Visualism is also important here. Fabian argues that the taxonomic practices of anthropology were one instance of the rhetoric of vision which dominated modern social scientific disciplines. The spatialization of time was a visual practice, most obviously perhaps in so far as classifications and typologies could be represented diagrammatically and through different forms of visual representation. The visual domain was a principal site for the exercise of colonial control which Prakash (1999) illustrates well with regard to exhibitions in 19th century India that had 'ethnological stands' documenting local races in terms of various dimensions.

The problem of time in Fabian's (1983) text is, however, more centrally focused on ethnographic writing and anthropology's schizogenic relationship with time therein. That is to say, whilst anthropological knowledge in the field is created through intersubjective communication – dialogically in the co-presence of the Other – when it comes to be reported and represented in ethnographic monographs, these dialogical features of simultaneous knowledge production are suppressed. Fabian refers to this as the denial of coevalness and identifies two principal representational strategies through which it is achieved. The first is the use of the ethnographic present in the writing up of monographs, which serves to reify and dehistoricize the Other. Second, and as a consequence of the first strategy, there is a lack of autobiographical voice in traditional, realist ethnography. These representational moves, based on a scientific attitude in which the anthropologist strives for an objective voice, mean that the anthropologist and their reader come to occupy a different timeframe from the cultural Other being described. This is the anachronism, or to use Fabian's twist on the word, the allochronism and foundational problem of anthropology: it serves to dehistoricize the relationship between the anthropologist and the native. This continued to be a problem in varying strands of anthropology, notably in functionalist anthropology, the discipline's next major paradigm.

The structure and colonial patronage of anthropological research

British social anthropology became aligned most closely with functional anthropology during the interwar period and as a consequence moved closer to colonial administration and cultural domination. To understand this realignment, it is imperative to pay attention to contemporaneous historical and material factors that can help explain the purported lack of radical or subversive critique in anthropology of oppressive colonial systems. A key material factor here was the emergent structure and colonial patronage of anthropological research.

Feuchtzwang (1973) provides an extensive analysis of the historical development of the colonial patronage of British social anthropology from the mid-19th century up to World War Two. The Royal Anthropological Institute emerged as the key professional body of anthropologists during the second half of the 19th century. Until the 1890s, it had been able to provide funds for anthropological research through the levy of membership subscriptions. This stopped in the 1890s, however, and so anthropologists turned to government for funding and patronage of anthropological research. Feuchtzwang notes how anthropologists initially exercised a duality of approach to funding bodies, emphasizing their capacity to provide not just scientifically valid, but also instrumentally useful knowledge such as the training of colonial administrators in the languages and racial characteristics of tribal societies. The creation of the IAI in 1926 – the International Institute of African Languages and Cultures principally funded by the Rockefeller foundation – was a key turning point in the attractiveness of anthropology to colonial administrators. Its aims went beyond training and information provision, setting itself the goal of 'educating the natives in modern ways'. The IAI cemented the duality of approach, and in particular the scientific aspirations of the discipline when, in 1931, it constructed a five-year research plan based on Malinowski's famous essay *Practical Anthropology* 'to study the processes of change in a purely objective scientific manner' (Feuchtzwang, 1973: 84).

The second key historical factor that brought anthropology and colonial administration more closely together was the policy of indirect rule which the British government sought to implement in a number of its colonies, notably in Africa, after World War One. The erosion of Britain's economic and political power, as well as the expansion of the British Empire following the end of World War One, meant that it could no longer afford to continue with its extant colonial arrangements. With the redistribution of German colonies, Britain controlled an expanding slice of the world's territory which created practical, administrative challenges. Its answer of indirect rule involved a paternalistic system of tutelage where the British perceived the need to 'teach' the locals how to govern themselves and engage in economic production independently from, but without disrupting the political status quo of, colonial relations. The government had a new interest in understanding how social order worked, and how it might be able to manipulate such systems to ensure that a policy of indirect rule could work. Anthropologists, in need of funds, and government officials in need of applicable knowledge, now had shared interests. As Feuchtzwang notes:

> There are grounds for considering the turning point of the late 1920s as a move either toward an anthropology more suited to colonial administrative need or else as a change which met with new colonial administrative needs more than the previous anthropology could (ibid).

But how did anthropologists engage with these contextual factors in ways that resulted in the disavowal of critique of the colonial system? Feuchtzwang impels us to look more carefully at the theoretical knowledge and methods of functionalist anthropology that came to prominence in the interwar period.

The British government's new interest in understanding social order, mechanisms for cohesion, and plotting a trajectory for controlled social change (toward indirect rule) was highly complementary with the theoretical underpinnings and methodological practice of functionalism. Functionalist anthropologists offered government an account of how social order, cohesion and stability worked and could be manipulated to imperial ends. The focus of anthropological study was small-scale units of tribal societies, and it started from the presumption that, prior to European colonization, tribal cultures had achieved a state of equilibrium through centuries of development. European contact was thought to have brought disequilibrium to these societies, and new institutions were now required to adjust this imbalance and to bring back social order. Anthropologists were tasked with describing systems of order and cohesion in these societies – their essential characteristics, the nature of variation within them, and key factors of social cohesion. For anthropologists like Malinowski, the goal was to apply anthropological knowledge for the benefit of the native. Anthropological knowledge could be deployed as part of the scientific planning for indirect rule, a view articulated in his 1930 book *Dynamics of Culture Change*.

It is in this institutionalization of the scientific attitude through functional anthropology that one explanation can be found for the lack of subversive critique. The argument put forward by Feuchtzwang is that this lack can be taken as a sign of the complicity of anthropologists in colonial domination, an outcome of a form of self-censorship that precluded anthropologists from studying their sponsors and the wider colonial system. This self-censorship is however more than just a self-interested decision not to critique the funding body from which one is seeking support. It can be traced to the institutionalization of distance encoded in the core theoretical framework and methodological procedures of the discipline.

First, Feuchtzwang describes a belief in the possibility of pursuing knowledge in the abstract, of carving out a space for knowledge, which was codified in methodological aspects of functionalist fieldwork. This abstraction created a distance between knowledge and its use, echoing the duality of approach noted earlier, and thus distancing anthropologists from administrators' use of their knowledge. Second, and relatedly, functionalists pursued the neutral observation and description of small-scale units of analysis – not the whole – 'the seeking of knowledge of total systems or structures from small-scale social units by direct personal observation with as little participation as possible' (ibid: 72). Indeed, taking Forster's (1973) summary of French anthropologist Leclerc's (1972) well-known book, it can be said that: '(...) functionalist anthropology had no conception of colonialism as a system ... In contrast to the Victorian evolutionists, who *did* have a conception of colonialism [justifying it], classic functional anthropologists saw colonialism in a neutral manner, as a specific form of social change'. This espoused neutrality and methodological distancing from the wider systemic context of colonialism proved politically attractive to colonial authorities.

Crucially, however, it would be unwise to extrapolate from the material above that the relationship between colonial administration and anthropologists was a completely comfortable one based on the claims that their interests were aligned materially and historically. For one, as noted above, anthropology was organized at a certain distance from the practical application of its knowledge. Anthropologists trained the administrators, but it was the administrators who carried out the work of colonial authority. Second, the historical record also suggests that anthropologists struggled for years to gain funding from government sources. There are documented instances of antagonism, suspicion and downright dislike between administrators and anthropologists (Lackner, 1973) – the former suspicious of the utility of highbrow academic knowledge for practical, everyday purposes of governance. Third, there are different, less reactionary readings of the research of leading anthropologists of the time. James (1973) for instance would seem to be more comfortable painting certain anthropologists as 'tempered radicals' rather than complicitous colonialists. She outlines evidence of more radical views (by radical she talks of a 'moral' rather than a political or activist form of radicalism) of certain individual anthropologists including Evans-Pritchard, Frith and even Malinowski, so closely associated with the ahistorical nature of functional anthropology. In the realpolitik of research funding, however, an appearance of co-operation had to be maintained, according to James. Anthropologists needed to defend their work when confronted with sceptical administrators, and 'science' provided them with a necessary respectability.

The business of Empire

Thus far our aim has been to historicize two of the principal knowledge systems (science and anthropology) that have formed the basis of received wisdom and dominant approaches for cultural analysis in ICCM. In setting many of the key assumptions we make about science and anthropology into their historical context, we begin to understand them not as neutral or universal, but as local knowledge systems that were deployed towards the scientific objectification and political subjectification of native populations. The relationships of dependency and asymmetry between the metropolitan centre and the colonial peripheries in which this took form were not smooth or unilinear exercises of power. Instead, and as suggested in both previous sections, they were zones of power in which indeterminacy and resistance were paramount.

It is important to keep in mind that these knowledge systems are intimately connected to economic factors. The colonial system developed webs of economic dependencies populated by a complex and historically evolving set of interconnected economic actors including individual merchants, trading companies, national governments and emergent multinational firms, and military actors, notably local armies and state agencies. Scientific and anthropological knowledges can be considered to be aligned with these commercial and military interests of colonial powers. We refer to this alignment as a colonial com-mercial-military-industrial complex. In this section, we examine the business of Empire,[4] that is to say the economic organization of a particular colonial system, from two perspectives. First, we outline and discuss the organization of slavery. Second, we explore the organ-ization of colonial trade by trading companies, with a particular focus on the East India Company.

Managing and accounting for slavery and racism

In this sub-section, we illustrate the alignment of forms of cultural imperialism and cultural domination with the pursuit of economic interest through the example of slavery. The organization of slavery was vital to the capitalist industrialization of Great Britain. Importantly from a management and accounting perspective, slavery plantations were key sites for the birth of modern management techniques and accounting discourse and practice. That is to say, management and accounting can be read in important and challenging ways as products of slavery and of a related white supremacism and racism.

Over a series of publications, Cooke (1998, 2003a, 2003b, 2004) has produced studies of management history that tell alternative stories to those sanctioned by received wisdom. One particular study illuminated the role of slavery in early management history (2003a). According to Cooke (ibid: 1896), the 'birth' of modern management is typically located by management historians in the development of the US railroads from the 1840s onwards, part of a 'heroic, frontier extending episode in the history of the US'. Cooke however argues that ante-bellum slavery in the US can be considered as an alternative site, one that provides a different and far less heroic account of management history. Standard histories have been written in ways that deny the important place of slavery in management studies, with authors either failing to make any mention of it in their pages or, when they have, arguing it out, or using reason to exclude it from an account of modern management. Cooke argues that slavery has been excluded from modern management because it has been argued to belong to a premodern or a precapitalist period on three counts. First, slavery was viewed as devoid of wage labour, a defining characteristic of the capitalist epoch. Second, slavery does not display sophisticated enough levels of organization. Finally, it lacks a group of people who can be said to have a distinctive identity as managers.

Cooke refutes all these charges, presenting counter-evidence that slavery was very much a 'modern' management practice. First, he presents historical evidence that ante-bellum plantations were managerialist, and that slavery played a key role in the pace and nature of capitalist industrialization in Britain (also noted by Bowen, 2006). Second, he points to the complexities involved in the operations of plantations, notably through the use of what we might now recognize as Taylorist scientific principles as well as classical, modern management practices (division of labour, chain of command, span of control and so on). He suggests that these modern principles were already in place and evolving on plantations even before their use on the US railroads. Notably, he describes various and evolving managerial strategies for discipline on the plantations (for instance the use of the gang system), a necessary response to the ever-present forms of resistance in plantation labour processes, embodied in the figure of the 'overseer'. Third, Cooke regards these overseers as managers, since they occupied a distinct occupational category and had a distinctive managerial identity. To quote Cooke:

> By 1860, when the historical orthodoxy has modern management emerging on the railroads, 38,000 managers were managing the 4 million slaves working in the US economy (ibid: 1895).

Cooke also called attention to the 'managerialist consciousness and reflexivity associated with slavery' (2003a: 1910), which directly expressed racism most visibly through a number of essays and publications on management from the time. Cooke cites titles such as *Moral Management of Negroes* and *On the Management of Slaves*, to argue that the modern category of management that emerged at this time was founded on white supremacist racism. The managerial imperative was based on an assumption that blacks were morally and intellectually inferior to whites, a view that could serve to legitimize slavery and to organize problematic racial differences.

Scholarship from the history of accounting and taxation also tells of the genesis and practice of modern management and accounting discourse and practices, notably connected to industrial discipline, in the context of slavery (Fleischman & Tyson, 2004; Fleischman & Oldroyd, 2004). Accounting work on slavery, especially in the plantations of the American South and the British West Indies, is an important parallel read to Cooke's work in organization studies. Tyson et al. (2004) for instance explore the history of tasking methods (with its emphasis on individual work rates and practices of surveillance and measurement) for the organization of labour as the forerunner to modern-day standard cost accounting. Tyson et al. (2004) look at the period of apprenticeship in the British West Indies after slave labour was abolished in 1833 and wage labour introduced. Using archival research, they document how: 'accounting measures (slave-keeping costs, output levels, and task rates, for instance) and valuations (slave prices, leasing prices, notably) were used to rationalize a particular labor structure and, more broadly, to normalize the practices and sustain the institutions of slavery' (p. 760).

Whilst six million Africans provided a source of labour that contributed to the industrialization of Britain, those who remained in Britain's African colonies typically became subject to new taxation regimes. Bush and Maltby (2004) for example studied the introduction of taxation in British West Africa from the late 19th to the mid-20th centuries. Taxation forced locals out of their traditional, non-money subsistence economies and into a new monetary economy. Levied on local Africans only, many were forced to sell their new labour power for wages (mainly in the context of cash-crop production) in order to pay their taxes. Although Africans had taxation and alternative systems of accounting long before colonialism, the introduction of this colonial taxation regime (which differed across African nations) caused resentment and resistance since it was seen as a cultural imposition that assumed African societies were incapable of any logical management of resources. Wage labour also exposed Africans to racism and to Western conceptions of time, as well as Eurocentric and ethnocentric assumptions of superiority connected with self-discipline, honesty and duty.

As much as they were used to raise revenue and to create a pool of wage labour that would contribute to economic goals, accounting and taxation practices can also be considered as exercises in governmentality and cultural imperialism. Neu's (2000) study of the role of accounting in the exercise of British colonialism in Canada 1830–1860 is illustrative. Through archival research, Neu describes how: '(...) government strategies towards indigenous peoples changed. We see the emergence of technologies of government (especially accounting technologies) with these technologies being used in the attempt to change the habits, customs and behaviours of indigenous peoples' (Neu: 181). In other words, accounting emerged in the service of disciplining the bodies of indigenous population. Neu gives the example of the changing character of 'presents' (annuity payments on land purchased by the British to the indigenous communities). Over this period the British aimed to change the indigenous people's relation to land, to root them to a fixed location rather than continue their nomadic lifestyle and to engender a British morality in their behaviour. To this end, the British replaced goods (especially liquor) with stock and agricultural equipment as annuity payments, held back hunting supplies, encouraged schooling, and ceased the distribution of ready-made clothes. Instead they provided locals with the materials to make their own clothes, an attempt by the British to combat the perceived indolence of the locals.

Merchant enterprise and the East India Company

As the first nation to industrialize, thanks in large part to the colonial system and to slavery, Britain was an economic powerhouse especially during the 19th century when international trade doubled in the first half of the century (Jones, 2000). This was the time of the so-called pax Britannica in which British naval power and control of the seas enabled Britain to build an effective system for import-export trading and for spreading its imperial political and civic cultures. Merchant enterprise played a crucial role in this historical context, both benefiting from, whilst also extending, these facets of British territorial and economic expansion. In focusing on the history of merchant enterprise, and in particular the history of trading companies, we gain an insight into the intertwining of imperial interests with those of commerce, politics and industry.

Jones (2000) argues that the origins of British multinational enterprise lie in the long and evolving history of merchant enterprise. Merchant enterprise flourished in the 18th and early 19th centuries, with merchants based in London playing a key role in the organization and intermediation of the booming Atlantic trade of the 18th century. Though most merchant houses started off by specializing in trade of a particular commodity (such as sugar or grain) or in a particular region, their histories reveal a marked diversification in their business activities over the 19th century. Particularly so after the dissolution of government monopolies for the chartered trading companies opened up new opportunities for private enterprise. By 1850, the British mercantile enterprise was pervasive around the globe, and companies were showing signs of moving beyond the intermediation of trade and into the making of capital investments. Some historians have claimed that this period saw the emergence of the first modern multinational enterprise – the East India Company. Whilst other historians (such as Bowen, 2006) disagree with this characterization, the history and transformation of the EIC from a trading company to an imperial agency of considerable power and influence certainly illustrates the complex knitting-together of commercial, political, military and cultural interests.

Following its formal inception as the United Company of Merchants of England trading to the East Indies in 1709, the EIC based in London was the British version of a number of European colonial trading companies organizing commerce to the east of the Cape of Good Hope. According to Bowen (2006), it enjoyed a period of even-paced expansion and internal stability until the mid-1750s, during which political and military events in India would trigger seven decades of territorial expansion. The conquest and colonial rule of India was not a state-sponsored achievement; rather, it emanated from the developing relations of a privately-owned commercial organization.

Bowen (2006) presents a historical analysis of this period of major transformation for the company (1756–1833). He notes how, in order to defend, govern and exploit these vast new territories, the Company transformed its internal organization, and in turn its standing and reputation, in Britain. In the 1770s and 1780s in particular, the EIC was under constant criticism from many in British politics and in the public for its reputed corruption, greed and misrule in India. Discussion abounded as to whether the EIC was sufficiently well organized to govern India, part of a broader debate between the Crown and the Company concerning who owned these new territories and their revenue streams. By the 1790s, however, such political and public concerns were allayed to a great extent through the many and publicly-acknowledged administrative reforms to the Company, especially in India through Governor-General Cornwallis. The transformation of the Company into what many refer to as a 'Company state' in India by the turn of the 18th century and into the first decade of the 19th, was based upon the development of an extensive revenue-gathering system plus an increasingly sophisticated administrative system protected by a large Indian army.

The new and sophisticated administrative system brought a sense of order and purpose to the domestic affairs of the EIC, and was held up as a model for other institutions to emulate. Bowen (ibid) even quotes Whig writer John Kaye, who describes it as a 'paragon of virtue, a force for civilization and progress'. On the one hand, its new claim to virtue rested on the inception of a set of guidelines meant to regulate and control the behaviour of the EIC's so-called 'overseas servants'. In addition to this code of practice, the desire to improve the administration of the Company was also manifest in the creation of a new cadre of overseas servants through new mechanisms for formal training. In India, for instance, Wellesley established the College of Fort William for the teaching of Indian languages. And in Britain, in 1806, the East India College was opened at Hertford Castle for training its administrators and functionaries. The opening of the college was viewed as a commitment to reform, improvement and good governance, and endowed its administrators with particular metropolitan attitudes related to order and efficiency for transfer over to India. The training of administrators was also, in part, a reflection of changing attitudes in the EIC towards the local Indian population. The shift was one from 'securing' the natives through military and political force, to bringing benefits to them and 'improving' society through government and control by the 1820s.

This change in attitude was not only a reflection of the fact that military security meant that attention could be paid to other things, but also to do with the increasing influence of evangelicals and reformers within the Company in London, especially in its court. They exerted political pressure on both the Company and on Parliament to make full use of the EIC's position to promote change and improvement. The 1813 Charter Act allowed Christian missionaries into India and obliged the Company to spend one lakh of rupees a year on education. The striving for educational and religious reform became very explicit in despatches from the 1820s onwards, as in this one from 1825 quoted by Bowen (ibid: 204):

> There is nothing, we have informed you, which we regard as of greater importance than the diffusion of the English language, and of European Arts and Sciences among the natives.

The new code for corporate behaviour, training for administrators and the shift in attitude regarding the native population were certainly not the only manifestations of the Company's attempts to exert control over its expanding territories in Asia through administrative means. The more mundane, but nevertheless crucial, practices of recording, writing and reading information were paramount to the Company's emerging control of its Empire. The EIC created an 'Empire in writing' (Bowen, 2006) – a mass of written documentation was collected, and collating information became a mark of EIC's corporate culture. A principal goal of these extensive searches was to create better knowledge of the territories it had under its control, a desire that eventually gave rise to the Company's patronage of research. For instance in 1770, they sponsored John Ferguson's *Dictionary of the Hindostan Language*, one example of many works connected to linguistics and translations that they felt would improve the language skills of overseas servants. According to Bowen, scientific fieldwork (on geography and topography) was also a core component of enlightened governance. The EIC sponsored the trigonometrical surveys of the subcontinent by

Lambton, Everest and others in the early 19th century. This research and knowledge enabled the Company to conceptualize India – to have knowledge of it in writing and through visual representations.

In the next chapter, we bring our historical account of the historical conditions of possibility for the emergence of ICCM forward in time, to the period immediately following the end of World War Two, and in place, to the United States of America.

5
Modernization, Industrialization and Development

Introduction

In the previous chapter we outlined and discussed the historical conditions of possibility, and thus the material and discursive precursors, of the fields of international and cross-cultural management: Western science, anthropology and imperial commercial and organizational practices. This chapter looks at how these knowledge systems became entwined and inter-related through the discourses of modernization, industrialization and development that emerged in the US post-World War Two period. We shall argue that these discourses reflected the manifold economic, military, political and cultural concerns of the United States, the new dominant power at this juncture in history. These contextual factors and associated discourses would find direct expression in the early classics of ICCM: Harbison and Myers' (1959) *Management in the Industrial World: An International Analysis,* and Kerr et al.'s (1960) *Industrialism and Industrial Man: The Problems of Labor and Management in Economic Growth*. We offer a critical analysis of central aspects of these texts.

The emergence of a discourse of ICCM

Weber and truncated historicism

In seeking to trace the emergence of the full-blown academic pursuit of ICCM it is difficult to offer a precise point of embarkation. One candidate is Weber's account of the effect of different religions on the development of cultures, societies and economies, most notably his essay *The Protestant Ethic and the Spirit of Capitalism* (Weber, 1905/2002). The work is partly comparative in its examination of the effects of the

Calvinist puritan spirit, and the Protestant ethos, on society and the development of capitalism in Europe. It also initiated subsequent analysis of other religions and their effects on societal and economic development, as pursued in the *The Religion of China; Confucianism and Taoism* (1951) and *The Religion of India; the Sociology of Hinduism and Buddhism* (1958). In the latter, Weber claims that within Indian religious and philosophical traditions, the mundane material world is deprecated and made secondary to the spiritual and the infinite. Such a philosophy, together with the Hindu caste system, was inimitable, according to Weber, to an indigenous development of modern capitalism. In the former, he compared aspects of Chinese society and culture, particularly Confucianism and Taoism, with Europe and the Protestant ethic and asked why China had not developed a capitalist system despite exhibiting several factors favouring such development.

His arguments are complex and offer a number of reasons for this. First, that the Confucian ethic, with its focus on maintaining good relations in extended families and on cultivating a cultured person, together with the 'otherworldliness' of Taoism, conspired to promote harmonization with, rather than control over the environment, to dampen technical innovation, and to limit an action orientation. Second, the Confucian ethic constituted a form of rationalism through its provision of a system for ordering social relations and society, and promoted values of self-control, moderation and thriftiness – all compatible with wealth accumulation. Moreover, it also promoted social inclusionism and coherence that mitigated risk and provided a personalistic social ethic that inhibited the development of an impersonal, rational legal system. Third, a familistic societal structure together with an entrenched and elitist status hierarchy prevented the emergence of an urban middle class of the kind that drove capitalist development in Europe. Finally, the emphasis on Confucian scholasticism and the presence of a privileged mandarinate[1] provided a more prestigious and efficacious career path than one based on mercantile or business activity.

There is clearly some logic in taking Weber as a context for the emergence, if not a starting point, for ICCM, particularly in view of his concern with the problems of economic development and his belief that rationalism was the prime mechanism through which modern capitalism would develop. That is, rationalism as facilitated by Protestantism, but also as embodied in a (specific) scientific endeavour, the development of a system of jurisprudence centred on an impersonal legal framework, the systematization of government administration and, of course, in the transformation of economic enterprises into bureaucratic forms.

Discussion of Weber is also appropriate, given the field's subsequent early development, in view of his opposition to Marx's account of economic development. Put simply, Weber inverts Marx's thesis that all human systems and institutions are based upon the materialist foundations of economics by suggesting that religious values, and in effect culture, provide the conditions for the emergence of particular economic systems. There is a bifurcation here, initiated with Weber, which percolates into much subsequent theoretical and perspectival development. On the one hand, there is a strand that sees ICCM with a provenance in the economic discipline and which finds an interest in comparative systems in terms of explanations of disparate economic development across countries based upon economic rationalism. On the other hand, there is a culturalist position, in part initiated by Weber but also reinforced by Parson's functionalist concerns with cultural values and their shaping of social systems. Moving forward, it was not until after World War Two, however, that theorizing about management from within the Western academy turned to international and comparative matters.

International management in the US academy

The emergence of ICCM discourse was facilitated by some very specific conditions of possibility connected to this post-War period, as we have argued elsewhere (Westwood & Jack, 2008). First, the US economy was booming and it engaged in a rapid expansion of its international business and trade activities, including an increasing amount of foreign direct investment and the establishment of business units in overseas locations. Such activity naturally entailed encountering new and difficult business situations, cultures, and social systems. This spurred an interest in examining and comparing management systems as a way of enhancing the efficacy of US international business (Boyacigiller et al., 1996). Second, there was the start of the Cold War. The US was very concerned about the threat of Soviet expansion and of communism more broadly, a threat it sought to counter in a variety of ways. Third, the world was entering a period of radical decolonization as newly independent states emerged. The US was concerned with this situation from both a commercial and a strategic perspective. It wanted to ensure that such states were not seduced into aligning with the Soviet Union or becoming socialist, but also that they became incorporated into the Western economic order providing both new markets and provision of materials. ICCM began to develop in relation to, and some might argue in support of, this commercial-political-military complex.

The academy, international business and the Soviet threat

For some in the US, the expansion of US business interests internationally was considered in relation to the perceived need to contest the Soviet Union and the 'Eastern Bloc' in international markets. This contestation was to unfold not only in strategic, military and political terms, but also in terms of economic and commercial interest. The Cold War was clearly not conceived of as a military campaign (although there were militaristic elements), but one involving economic, cultural, social and even intellectual theatres. This strategic and geopolitical aspect of US international business was made quite explicit in certain quarters, illustrated as follows. The example resides in the papers of the 26th National Business Conference sponsored by the Harvard Business School Association in June 1956 (subsequently published in a version edited by Fenn, 1957). Unlike previous ones, this National Conference turned from the domestic scene '(...) to the growing interest and activity in overseas business operations' (Fenn, 1957: v). Fenn[2] sets the tone and outlines the central problematic in the preface (ibid: vi):

> The balance sheets of our businesses, the daily life in our country is affected in a myriad ways by the vigorous competition we face from an opposing philosophy. The democratic and the communist ideals are vying for the support of vast millions of uncommitted peoples, and that competition is felt throughout our society.

Fenn puts the contestation between US values and interests and those of the Eastern Bloc in stark contrastive terms, but crucially locates business and commercial interests on the frontline. It is for Fenn, and others at the conference, an ideological battle of opposing philosophies and value systems. Included in the stakes is the alignment of other countries, particularly those newly independent, decolonizing countries that might be tempted to turn towards communism and away from US interests. As Fenn puts it: 'They will choose the best from the competing systems which are seeking to attract their support; it is up to us to see that they choose more from us than from the communists' (ibid: vi). The need to be proactive is reinforced by the Indian Ambassador to the US, A.L. Mehta, who reminds the others of his country's wariness about foreign investment given India's colonial experiences. The ideological nature of the battle is signalled by having business and management aligned with and constitutive of the values of democracy, productivity, individualism and freedom. International business has a part to play in the 'strengthening of the democratic cause in its conflict with authoritarianism wherever the latter may be' (ibid: vii).

Fenn's view of the world and this interpretation of the ideological role of international business are reiterated by almost all the other conference delegates consisting of US academics, managers and officials. Unsurprisingly, the clearest statement regarding the Soviet threat and the need to meet it came from former Under Secretary of State Herbert Hoover Jr. who referred to the 'Soviet economic offensive' and 'a new type of Soviet aggression' and the need to counter that and promote the values of the 'Free World' (ibid: 20–21). In a similar vein, Blough, Professor of International Business from Columbia University, argued the US' goals 'might be achieved by strengthening our friends economically through overseas investment, as part of the effort to promote the broad objectives of our foreign policy' (Blough et al., 1957: 210). Academic research on economic development would come to fill an important role in addressing that goal.

The Inter-University Study of Labor Problems in Economic Development

Of prime significance for the emergence and growth of ICCM within the Western academy was the formation of the Inter-University Study of Labor Problems in Economic Development (I-USLPED) and the industrialization thesis that emerged from that (Jamieson, 1980). This was a 'cooperative research enterprise' (Harbison & Myers, 1959: vii) that included faculty members from the Universities of Harvard, Princeton, California and Chicago as well as MIT. Funds came from the Universities but also, significantly, from the Ford Foundation (FF). The leading lights of I-USLPED were Frederick Harbison (Chicago and Princeton), John Dunlop (Harvard), Charles Myers (MIT) and Clark Kerr (University of California), but Kerr is seen as the initiating and leading figure (Kaufman, 2005).

Kerr was an influential person who pursued a complex career. He had a PhD in economics from UC Berkeley (UCB), worked there as an associate professor of industrial relations (from 1945) and became the founding director of its Institute of Industrial Relations. In the late 1940s, at the height of the McCarthy era, the regents of the University of California introduced an anticommunist oath and required all university staff to sign it. Kerr complied, but did speak out in support of those threatened with termination for not signing. He became the first Chancellor of UCB in 1952 and President in 1958. However, in the 1960s he was embroiled in free speech debates again when he denied students the right to engage in political protest on campus (Lustig, 2004). Ironically, the FBI, who had already done a clearance check on Kerr because of the University's nuclear arms research, decided he was a 'liberal' and began to investigate him. They gradually constructed a negative picture of him, even going so far as suggesting he might be an undercover communist. Hoover compiled a dossier on UCB and its Faculty and liaised with the Regents of the University (Rosenfeld, 2002). Kerr was sacked by the Regents in 1967, not long after Reagan became State Governor.

John Dunlop is seen by many as a founding figure in industrial relations studies. He received his PhD in economics from UCB in 1939 and then taught at Harvard University until his retirement in 1984. His reputation rests not just on his academic work but on his engagement with practice. He began his work as Director of Research and Statistics for the War Labor Board in 1943, and held a whole stream of positions thereafter including Secretary of Labor (1975–1976), Director of the US Cost of Living Council (1973–1974) and Chairman of the US Commission on the Future of Worker/Management Relations (1993–1995). In addition to his involvement in I-USPLED and as co-author of *Industrialism and Industrial Man* (1960), he is also very well known for his *Industrial Relations Systems* (IRS) (1958), which has been extremely influential. It resonates with the I-USPLED project in its belief that actors in an IRS (labour, management and the state) working with their own ideology and power produce outcomes that govern the relationship between them. In this regard he participated in the great debates about the role of organized labour and the problems of industrial conflict in the US system. This was something that Frederick Harbison was also embroiled in immediately prior to his work with the I-USPLED (Harbison, Burns & Dubin, 1948; Harbison & Dubin, 1947). These concerns with domestic IR, conflict and its resolution/avoidance, and notions of unitarist systems in which there is a presumed commonality of interest, are all taken into the I-USPLED situation and are part of the context for the emergence of ICCM.

To return to the establishment and activities of I-USPLED, in 1951 they applied to the FF for a grant and in 1952 were awarded an unprecedented $475,000 over three years to 'finance a multi-year and multi-country comparative study of the genesis, evolution, and management of labor problems that accompany the industrialization process' (Kaufman, 2005: 413). The I-USLPED project extended beyond the life of the grant (in fact they secured over $1 million in other grants, including additional grants from the FF in 1954 and 1955), being active for over two decades. The project ultimately involved about 90 academics and generated some 40 books and over 50 articles (Kaufman, 2005: 413; see also Cochrane, 1979 and Dunlop et al., 1975).

Despite its large scale, two texts were central and extremely influential in the emerging discourse of ICCM. The first of these was Harbison and Myers' (1959) *Management in the Industrial World: An International Analysis*, the other *Industrialism and Industrial Man: The Problems of Labor and Management in Economic Growth* co-authored by all four key figures (Kerr et al., 1960). These two texts have arguments and frames of analysis that are in many ways overlapping, although the focus of the former is upon the significance of professional management for economic development and the conditions that facilitate, or otherwise, the development of professional management within the context of different national systems. The latter is more concerned with the industrialization process and how that develops and is in dynamic interplay with the societal context, particularly with respect to labour-management relations. The commonality resides in a frame of analysis, which posits a kind of technological imperative, the effects of which are partially mediated by societal elites. The technological imperative is embedded in an industrialization thesis that asserts that all societies aspire, or will aspire, to industrialization and the benefits it is presumed to bring, and that once they have embarked upon an industrialization process certain changes will be precipitated, not just within management and organizations, and employment relations, but more widely in other structures within society. There will be some variance in this trajectory, especially in terms of pace, depending upon which elites have dominance in society. Whilst we expand our analysis of these themes later, for now we note the development of contemporaneous discourses that impacted upon those of I-USLPED.

Managerialism and functionalism

Kerr and colleagues participated in the elevation of managerialism and in the construction of a particular conceptualization of management. Crucially, they argue that management is a necessary element for industrialization and economic development. Theirs is not an entirely original view of management and they draw upon, and in some cases reference explicitly, other management thinkers who at about the same time were responsible for articulating these new conceptions of management. Among those explicitly acknowledged are Frederick Taylor, Herbert Simon, Peter Drucker, Elton Mayo, Douglas McGregor, Rensis Likert and Robert Gordon. Let us comment briefly on some of these and the type of managerialism they were contributing to and which influenced Kerr and colleagues.

Drucker was already an influential figure by the time the I-USLPED came into being. He was undoubtedly part of the intellectual climate in which it developed and was instrumental in the emerging discourse about management, organization and industrialization in which it engaged. As an immigrant from Vienna in the late 1930s, and as someone who warned against the threat of totalitarianism, Drucker was a passionate advocate of individualism and individual freedom as prerequisites for sound and stable economic development (Drucker, 1942). He prefigures Kerr and colleagues to some extent in outlining the inevitabilities (and the hazards) of industrialization, but also in positing an ideology that needs to accompany it. He elaborates this ideology in his account of General Motors, which he pursues as a kind of paradigm of a modern successful organization, effectively structured, organized and professionally managed (Drucker, 1946). The *Concept of the Corporation* is one of the first works to take the organization as the appropriate level of analysis and it plays a significant role in the imposition of the functionalist paradigm in MOS by constituting organization as an ontological object amenable to empirical investigation. It was an influential book, not just at the time and in the US, but subsequently and internationally.

Also influential was Herbert Simon. Simon's early work was in public sector measurement, reporting and matters of efficiency. It was not until the 1940s (Simon, 1944) that he began to pursue more obviously the interest in decision making and broaden out into a wider ranging consideration of administration and management (such as Simon, 1945). But he was perhaps most influential at the time as a microeconomic theorist, albeit one that forged bridges between economic theories of the firm and organizational theories from administrative science and sociology (Simon, 1952). Significantly Simon, like others, was positivistic and functionalist in his approach. In addition to the influence of economists and early exponents of a new managerialism, Kerr and colleagues were also cognizant of the recent work on human relations in managing the workplace and the humanistic, democratic, individualistic ideology of the Human Relations Movement. There is expressed admiration for Management by Objectives as promoted by Drucker (1954) and the idea that people freely come to exert self-motivated effort on behalf of organizational outcomes. There is, thus, reference to the work of Mayo and Roethlisberger as well as to the motivation theories of the Michigan group as exemplified by Likert (1953).

This work is used to construct an account of worker motivation and productivity that is based not on 'the fear of discipline, incentive wage payments, or close supervision' (ibid; Harbison & Myers, 1959: 31), but upon managerial techniques that convince the worker that his/her interests align with those of the organization. It is a view bolstered by reference to the work of another supporter of the Management by Objectives ideology, Douglas McGregor (1957) and others promoting an organizational humanistic, democratic, liberalism such as Argyris (1957). The discourse, then, is part of that rhetoric that continued to hold sway right through to the present and that seeks to incorporate the worker into the capitalist order of things by suggesting an isomorphism of interest.

Systems thinking was also burgeoning at the time, with a collective organized under the auspices of the Center for Advanced Studies in the Behavioral Sciences at the University of Michigan tasked with developing general systems theory and its applications. This group included Kenneth Boulding, Harold Laswell, Paul Lazersfeld and Clyde Kluckhohn. Dunlop's development of his 'IRS' model owed much to general systems theory, as does the orientation of the whole I-USLPED group. Dunlop had also been much influenced by Talcott Parsons. Parsons' functionalism was pervasive and central in shaping the paradigmatic location of MOS. Kerr and colleagues reference and make use of Parsons repeatedly in their texts, especially his work on social values and so-called *pattern variables*, which, it is argued, shift radically as processes of industrialization and modernization take place. It is also important to note the presence of Kluckhohn in the systems group above. Both Parsons and Kluckhohn have been extremely influential in conceptualizations of culture and in the emergence of a culturalist perspective within ICCM. Their work was foundational for the culturalist models of Hofstede, Trompenaars and others. It can also be noted that structural-functionalism was the predominant perspective within anthropology at the time.

The complex knowledge networks across academia, government and commerce at this time are further signified by the fact that Kluckhohn was appointed Director of the Russia Research Center within Harvard University. Funded by the Carnegie Corporation, but reportedly supported by the CIA (Diamond, 1992), the centre conducted 'overt' research on contemporary Russia and its affairs and influence as well as 'covert' research of strategic benefit to the US government in its pursuit of the Cold War. Indeed, Nader (1997) is extremely critical of not only Kluckhohn, but also Parsons, other anthropologists and indeed the whole practice of academic anthropology for their involvement in agencies of the Cold War and complicity in covert research and activities that were part of what she terms 'hidden anthropology'. Through the sponsorship of the Ford Foundation, management education was also to become deployed directly in the Cold War struggle.

The Ford Foundation and management education

The FF was established by Edsel Ford in 1936 to support educational and charity institutions, and its stated mission remains: 'to reduce poverty and injustice, strengthen democratic values, promote international cooperation and advance human achievement' (Ford Foundation, 2008). However, it has been argued that the FF has always maintained close links with the US government, its foreign relations and security branches in particular (Saunders, 1999). This was held to be especially true in the post-World War Two period, moving Saunders to suggest that:

> At times it seemed as if the Ford Foundation was simply an extension of government in the area of international cultural propaganda. The Foundation had a record of close involvement in covert actions in Europe, working closely with Marshall Plan and CIA officials on specific projects (ibid: 139).

There is certainly a noticeable pattern of FF senior officials having ties with the CIA. For example, Paul Hoffman was President of the FF from 1950–1953 and prior to that was head of the Economic Cooperation Administration (ECA), which was the administrative vehicle for the implementation of the Marshall Plan. The Marshall Plan was ostensibly introduced to rebuild Germany in the post-War period, but has also been interpreted as the US chief strategic device for preventing Soviet or communist encroachments into a weakened Europe (Chester, 1995). Hoffman was considered to be a 'firm advocate of covert operations as an important component of Cold War strategy' (ibid: 43) including psychological warfare and propaganda. Some of this psychological warfare was guided by the Psychological Strategy Board (PSB). The ECA had worked closely with the PSB and the CIA. Indeed, Hoffman brought a number of ex-ECA staff with him to the FF, some of whom had a record in covert and strategic activities. For example, Milton Katz was involved with the Secret Intelligence Division of the Office of Strategic Services (OSS) and its European missions. Richard Bissell, who also worked for the OSS, became head of the ECA and also worked for the FF before joining the CIA as special assistant to its then head, Allen

Dulles. Chairman of the FF from 1958 to 1965, John McCloy, established a special administrative unit within the FF to liaise with the CIA (Saunders, 1999).[3]

Moreover, it is also claimed that various CIA 'front' organizations, particularly cultural, anticommunist, and anti-Marxist organizations such as the Congress for Cultural Freedom, received grants and support from the FF (Coleman, 1989; Saunders, 1999). The FF established the East European Fund (originally the Free Russia Fund) in 1951, a body that was a support organization for Soviet exiles and active in anti-Soviet campaigns. It was administered by George Kennan, another person with strong CIA connections (Chester, 1995: 45). A further organization funded by the FF was the Chekov Publishing House, which published and disseminated materials in Russian outside of the Soviet Union, supporting Russian émigrés.

Very importantly and significantly, the FF contributed to US efforts to promulgate US management and business education and its accompanying ideology throughout Europe and beyond (Adams & Garraty, 1960; Gourvish & Tiratsoo, 1998; Kipping et al., 2004). It is suggested that: 'The flow of aid for developing management education was part of strengthening security ties' (Kipping et al., 2004:101). Through this support and these programmes the US sought to introduce their models, practices, pedagogies and management education systems into Europe. A number of European business education institutions were established at this time with support and at least partial funding from the FF, US corporations and/or other US-based bodies. These included the Institut Europeén d'Administration des Affaires (INSEAD) in 1958; the Instituto Superior de Estudios de la Empresa in Spain; the Isletme Iktisadi Enstitüsü in Turkey; and the Instituto Postuniversitario per lo Studio dell'Organizzazione Aziendale in Italy. It needs to be noted that this influence of US-style management education and its programmes and institutions was not homogenous across Europe, but rather was developed and responded to in complex and dynamic ways (Alvarez, 1997; Engwall & Zamagni, 1998; Hedmo et al., 2005). Nonetheless, the impact was real and intentional.

It is clear then that the emergent discourse on ICCM was deeply embedded in convoluted networks within the US commercial-political-military complex in the post-World War Two period. There was another key condition impacting on the emergence of the ICCM discourse: the decolonization processes occurring around the globe and the possibility that newly decolonizing and other Third World nations would align with the Second World.

Decolonization and the discourse of development

By 1945 most of Africa, the whole Indian sub-continent, and parts of the Middle East, South East Asia and South America were still colonized by European nations. The post-World War Two period saw an intense wave of decolonization, which stretched over 50 years and encompassed the independence of India and Pakistan in 1947 and thus far has concluded with the return of Hong Kong to China in 1997. Springhall (2001) argues that the decolonization process has been far from uniform. For many of the former French colonies, independence only came after protracted and bloody conflict, as in the case of Algeria. In other places, decolonization was more benign and peaceful. In Betts' (2004) chronology, there were three 'clusters' within the post-World War Two period: the first in the late 1940s saw independence in much of South East Asia; the second was in the 1950s with North African independence events; and the latter was a rapid and intense period of decolonization for sub-Saharan Africa, in which 24 new republics emerged.

There is a confluence of movements and discourses, then, in the post-World War Two period. Modernization becomes signified through industrialization and both are entangled in the notion of development, particularly in the period of decolonization. It is this discursive triumvirate that Kerr and colleagues engage in their research: '(...) 'industrialization' is a central dynamic at work around the world. It is, of course, only a part of the modernization process which includes political and cultural developments as well...but industrialization is usually a basic aspect of modernization' (Kerr et al., 1960: 279). Into this discursive terrain came associated notions of development.

Development Studies was a direct product of the decolonization process and the reorganizations of foreign policy, both political and economic, it generated in the metropolitan centre. Its institutional origins were thus closely linked to the formation and trajectories of agencies, policies and practices of development aid. Indeed, it has been suggested that the agencies involved in 'development' simply occupied the same spaces as those just vacated by colonial administration (Escobar, 1995). 'Development' was a somewhat multifaceted discourse. As we have implied, in some quarters it became an imperative driven by Western economic and security concerns. On the one hand, economic and social development of the Third World was seen as necessary to further fuel Western economic growth. On the other, incorporating the newly decolonizing and underdeveloped nations within the fold of the emergent capitalist world order was a necessary bulwark against creeping socialism/communism and Soviet expansionism. For still others with more academic interest (not that these realms can be separated, as we have already shown), the central issue was to address the question of why there was such apparent development variability at the time. Why had some countries been able to develop and follow a modernizing path, whilst others, from a Western purview, continued to languish in states of non- or underdevelopment? The answers were varied, with many, unsurprisingly, emerging from economics or the domain of political economy. Western models of development demanded modernization strategies, which in turn often implied embarking on some form of industrialization process.

There were others though who promulgated a culturalist analysis, which argued that there were culturally-derived impediments to 'modern' development within some societies. It needs to be noted that within sociology, Parsons constructed a view of societal development in which development was intimately related to cultural values (Parsons, 1951, 1977; Parsons & Shils, 1951). Parsons aligns certain cultural elements, including value orientations, with the possibilities of development. These value dimensions, or pattern variables, are mapped onto a capacity to move forward with modernizing development. The positive values seem anchored to Western culture and there seems no reflexivity about their cultural and locational specificity. They enable analysis and arguments wherein the absence of the requisite values profile is held to mean that a culture is not conducive to development and will remain 'underdeveloped' unless the values alter and with that social structures and the very social formation. Cultures not exhibiting the right values set are castigated as being at various stages of the premodern and as suffering from a deficit. The rhetoric of 'lack' resurfaces and governs relations between First and Third Worlds as it had under colonialism.

Part of the problem here of course, is that 'development' is really a Western notion, and was defined, and its parameters and contours inscribed by, Western academics, policy makers, politicians and others. Thus the very idea, the models for and the criteria related to development were Western developed and then applied to the Third World, often without any collaboration or inclusion of local perspective. It also became the case that development interventions, be they direct through aid, NGO action or other mechanisms, or indirect through advice or insistence from bodies such as the United Nations, the IMF or other bodies, were uninvited intrusions that presumed to reconfigure an underdeveloped system and society in ways chosen by the West. It is little wonder that for some the resonances and continuities with colonialism were very apparent.

Indeed, for some the whole notion of 'development' was ineluctably embedded in the colonial project. As Ludden (1992: 250) says: 'Development was linked in instrumental ways to the growth of the modern state, the preoccupations of colonial rule, and a general commitment to economic progress'. Colonized locations had already been subject to various and multiple intrusions as the colonizer sought to manage and make use of their colonies. Modes of administration, organization and education had been put in place along with, in many cases, modes of production, trade and commerce. These were in part impositions, but they also articulated with the local context, and were subject to modification and hybridization, with local elites often playing a key role at the points of intersection. Hence systems of political economy, organization, and government were already in place as decolonization processes ensued.

In continuing to interact with the decolonized and other parts of the Third World, the West was able to make assessments about level and state of perceived 'development' largely defined in their terms and to decide upon modes of action or intervention accordingly. As Westwood (2001: 253) says: 'Disparities between the colonizers' conception and expectations of these issues of governmentability, and the perceived situation in the colonized locations, marks out the 'development' space. Put another way, the gap provides a rhetoric of motive for the discourse and practices of development'. It has been argued that 'development' was never really about improving the Third World; it is about furthering the economic development of the West and sustaining its hegemony, and in this way exhibits clear continuities with the colonial project (Dossa, 2007; Escobar, 1995; Hobson, 2004). It is argued that development is actually a reconstituted mechanism of domination through which the '"developed" countries manage, control and even create the third world' (Tucker, 1999: 22), and one associated with, as Doosa (2007) argues, the 'metaphysics of white mythology' (Derrida, 1982: 213). For ICCM 'development' provides a parallel discourse and a point of intersection. The language of development provides a specific model that links to modernization and suggests trajectories that TW or underdeveloped nations need to embark upon. In this sense it articulates with the I-USPLED project, in that they participated in the discussions about development and used ideas from that discourse in their assessments of modernization and industrial development.

The parameters of the discourse

In the first part of this chapter we have sought to outline some of the critical conditions for the emergence of the academic discourse of ICCM in the post-World War Two period: the expansion of the US economy and the growth of its international trade and business; the strategic situation confronting the US, specifically the perceived threat of Soviet expansionism, and the Cold War; and decolonization processes. We now consider the nature and content of the emerging discourse, seeking to map out its main parameters through a close reading of the two texts we have argued are foundational for ICCM (Harbison & Myers, 1959; Kerr et al. 1960). We focus on three key elements of these texts. The first is the industrialization thesis itself, which comes to assume the quality of an imperative with significant teleological overtones. Second, the convergence thesis embedded in the texts. Finally, and running through all the sub-sections, we outline and critique the inherent universalism and ethnocentrism of the thesis they construct.

The industrialization thesis and its imperatives

In both Harbison and Myers (1959) and Kerr et al. (1960) there is a more or less explicit industrialization thesis, which asserts that the industrialization process contains an ineluctable logic that projects societies that embark upon the process along a common trajectory. That societies will elect to do so is taken as virtually axiomatic, as the advantages of industrialization are deemed to be so apparent and seductive that it becomes the desire and goal of all societies (Harbison & Myers, 1959: 3). The core thesis is expressed in very clear terms:

> Industrialization is an almost universal goal of modern nations. And the industrialization process has its own set of imperatives: things which all societies must do if they hope to conduct a successful march to industrialism. This is what we call the logic of industrialism (Harbison & Myers, 1959: 117).

The convergence aspects of the thesis are also expressed early in the text: 'The logic of industrialization...leads to uniformity rather than diversity among industrial organizations and organization builders' (ibid: 5). It is important to note the inclusion of 'organization builders' here, since it signals that the industrialization process transforms people as well as organizations. In its full articulation, the convergence thesis includes an economic, sociocultural, technological, organizational and a managerialist imperative, as we shall show.

The economic imperative argument links directly to notions of development and modernization. Simply put, if societies are to develop economically and pursue the path to modernization as displayed by the 'developed' nations of the North Atlantic, they need to embrace industrialization. Industrialization, for Kerr and colleagues, constitutes not just an imperative, it is also a universal goal, and there are teleological overtones in the way they discuss this. They assert that: 'By 1918, industrialization was so obviously the road to power, to better health, to higher standards of living, and to education that it became the goal of mankind and the essence of national aspiration' (Kerr et al., 1960: 80). They are in full recognition of the likely impact of industrialization: changes to societal power systems and hierarchies, to the role and institutions of religion, to class formations, to the political and legal frameworks of society as well as to family structure, and other social and cultural aspects of society. As Kerr et al. (ibid: 104) state: 'Industrialization imposes its own cultural patterns on the pre-existing culture'.

Industrialization is positioned by Kerr and colleagues as the primary (if not only) pathway to modernization and economic development. These are processes that are held to run up against that which precedes them – which become conditions of preindustrialization, underdevelopment, the premodern and the traditional. It is these things, or at least aspects of them, that are deemed to have held societies back and that stand in the way of the supposed progressive processes of industrialization and modernization. Indeed, Kerr et al. identify five core factors present in preindustrializing societies that affect the nature and rate of the industrialization process:

(a) an extended family system which weakens industrial incentives to work, save, and invest, and which reserves key managerial positions for family members regardless of competence; (b) a class or social structure based on traditional social status rather than on economic performance; (c) traditional religious and ethical values which emphasize 'place' and 'duty' unrelated to economic gain or advancement, and oppose change and innovation, particularly in science and technology; (d) 'traditional customs and social norms which deny individual and property rights and fail to guarantee observance of contracts'; (e) divisive groups in the society which hinder or prevent the emergence of a strong nation-state (ibid: 105–106).

Hence, in relation to (c), traditional religions are depicted as not conducive to the incentives and motives required by modern industrial development. Following Weber, the Protestant Ethic is seen as an exception. Presaging notions that have resurfaced latterly, Kerr et al. also maintain that traditional Islamic legal precepts are not resonant with modern industrialization. It is further argued that a permanent and stable nation-state is necessary for industrialization. This puts significant pressure on any cultural context and is resonant with the effects of colonialism in establishing nation-states at its various points of engagement and with the promotion of the nation-state during the decolonization processes in the post-World War Two period. In terms of class structures, industrialization introduces a different order, supplanting older and traditional hierarchical arrangements with new hierarchies based on capital and on professional and occupational formations.

With respect to the first factor identified by Kerr et al., they expressly state that the extended family and its associated patriarchy and systems of obligation and reciprocation are inimical to healthy economic growth. If industrialization occurs, extended family structures are destroyed. In pursuing this argument they invoke Orientalist tropes. For example, Harbison and Myers (1959: 40) argue that management based on the sovereign rule of a patriarch or single family is the 'most primitive' form. It is compatible with primitive patriarchal systems and tribal, village life, not with 'modern' development and industrialization – and not with the ideology about management and development their text exemplifies. A binary is constructed in which the management and organizational systems in the 'premodern', 'pre-industrialized' are represented as 'primitive' and deficient relative to the West's modern and effective systems. Thus such a 'primitive' system is held to be what is expected in Egypt (Harbison & Ibrahim, 1958; Harbison & Myers, 1959). Such disparagement even extends to representations of European management where it is suggested that: 'Some of the German owner-managers are still convinced that they are born to rule their enterprises and that their authority is based upon a kind of natural law rather than upon their function in the organization' (Hartmann, 1959). French and Italian 'patrimonial management' are similarly castigated.

The confrontation of the modern with the premodern is often put in terms of a trenchant clash of values:

> The logic of the industrialization process requires that selection and promotion be made on the basis of ability and competence. It demands loyalty to the enterprise and to the work group... and to a

nationalist aspiration rather than to the extended family as such (Kerr et al., 1960: 92).

The transference of allegiance from extended family to nation is note-worthy here. It is further argued that management, as conceived of by Kerr and colleagues, is a clear authority structure that will supplant existing forms: 'Acceptance by workers of this role for management typically means a substitution of one authority for another in the tran-sition to industrialization. Management of the enterprise tends to displace the head of the village family, the tribal chief, or the commu-nal leader as the authority which prescribes the duties, obligations, rewards, and punishments of workers at the work place' (ibid: 155).

In addition to these macro-level transformations, changes wrought by industrialization at the more micro- or individual-level are also out-lined in terms of the shaping of 'Industrial Man'. The changes envis-aged within the 'culture of industrialism' have resonance with the shifts along the pattern variables of cultural values of Parsons (1951, 1967). It is also asserted that industrialization induces new work regimes that make demands upon employees: on their behaviours, but also on their values, attitudes and relationships. Employees in indus-trializing contexts must learn to accede to the industrial regime and its demands on place and time. They must be prepared to go to the factory and submit to the regimen of time and order demanded (see for example Ashton, 1948). They must submit to the routines and repetitions of industrial production and adhere to a new authority structure constituted by the hierarchy of impersonal and professional management.

It is acknowledged that these are significant changes and likely to generate a reaction from workers: 'Industrialization, whatever the source, characteristically redesigns and reshapes its human raw mater-ials. The drastic changes in human beings and their relationships required to achieve a settled industrial work force have been made only with significant reactions from the workers-in-process' (Kerr et al., 1960: 199). Protest diminishes as increasing levels of worker 'commit-ment' manifest themselves, and because of the inherent seductions of industrialization at both the societal and individual level – thus, industrialization:

Has spread around the world primarily on account of the greater positive attractions of industrialization, despite the dislocations and readjustments for emerging workers. Industrialization has become a prime objective of nationalist movements and political parties; it is often requisite to national survival. The potential benefits to the individual worker nearly everywhere appear to transcend the negative consequences of industrialization (ibid: 219).

Furthermore, protest may become institutionalized through various forms of collectivized labour, but in variable ways. In the envisaged pluralist society of Kerr et al., worker protest is to be expected and can be accommodated – managed as just another manifestation of the operations of markets. In pluralist, and idealized societies, like the US, organized labour organizations become mildly reformist in their ideology. It is even suggested that the seeds of class conflict wane as industrialization develops: 'The road to industrialization is paved less with class warfare and more with class alliances' (ibid: 226).

Education plays a vital role in industrialization and again there are universal demands. One prime imperative is to ensure an adequate supply of the managerial elite deemed necessary to drive industrialization. This means gearing up education, especially tertiary education, to ensure such a supply, as well as the effective training and development of managerial and professional competences. Indeed, it is argued that such demands take precedence even over basic levels of literacy:

> A substantial proportion of the community must be literate in any progressing society, but industrialization does not require at the outset that the majority of peasants, factory workers, porters, or servants have the rudiments of an education... Resources need to be invested in appropriate institutions of higher education even at the expense of some delay in providing universal general education (Harbison & Myers, 1959: 107).

On this logic, education is a societal investment associated with the imperatives of industrial development; it should not be conceived as a right for all members of society, and a rational calculation does not support the idea that basic education of the masses is preferable to the professional education of a small managerial elite. In their postscript to the 2nd edition, Kerr et al. (1973) suggest that one of the failures of some industrializing countries is that of investing inappropriately in education.

The message is clear and stark. The logic of industrialization is an imperative impelling society along a uniform trajectory, one that alters, displaces or dismantles a range of key structures, relationships, processes, values and other attributes of 'traditional' society. In order for industrialization to succeed, societies must embrace a range of new forms that, in sum, constitute the 'culture of industrialization', which has the following characteristics:

> (a) a nuclear family system which tends to accentuate individual incentives to work, save, and invest; (b) a relatively open social structure which encourages equality of treatment and advancement on the basis of ability; (c) religious and ethical values which are favourable to economic gain and growth, innovations and scientific change; (d) a legal system which encourages economic growth through general protection of individual and property rights from arbitrary or capricious rule; – and (e) a strong central governmental organization and the sense of being a nation which can play a decisive role in economic development (ibid: 105).

Once again, the discourse here engages in the construction of binaries in which the West is valorized whilst its Other is disparaged. Second, the discourse also trades in the tropes of lack and deficiency when representing the Other. Third, the positively positioned 'culture of industrialism' is presented in abstract and universalistic terms, in ways that efface its obvious provincial nature – its location within the ideology, interests and motives of the West.

As noted earlier, the industrialization thesis also rests upon a form of technological imperative (see Theodorson, 1953: 481). In some ways this is the force that drives many of the other changes. It is the technologies of production that frame common modes of working and hence common modes of management and organization. As Kerr et al. (1960: 292) state: '(...) the iron hand of technology tends to create relative uniformity in job structure, compensation differentials and technical training'. There is a form of technological determinism that demands a universal response. Two key figures also instrumental in shaping the emerging field of ICCM, Farmer and Richman (1965: 41),[4] argue in a similar vein that: 'There are only a limited number of rational ways to make steel and a country does not get output in this sector by using prayer rugs, doctrinaire slogans, or wishful thinking'. These are derogatory comments about the failings of traditional ways that denigrate the Other whilst claiming the veracity and utility of the Western approach.

The argument supposes that *techné* – as Jamieson (1980) has it – contains necessary requirements for efficiency and that this value becomes both the rationale and the justification for all manner of changes under the umbrella of industrialization. Efficiency becomes the ideology that demands obedience to the demands of capital, the subservience to the dictates of industrialized work regimes, and the erosion and suppression of traditional systems of knowledge and organization. But as Jamieson (1980: 4) points out, there is no inherent logic underwriting technology and the value of, and demand for, efficiency is not embedded in technology. Instead, it comes from the capitalist and is embedded in the values, language and ideology of capitalism.

Kerr and colleagues place great emphasis on the role of elites in economic development and industrialization. Critical analyses of the processes of decolonization and nationalism have also drawn attention to the role of indigenous elites (Guha & Spivak, 1988; Ngugi, 1983; Werbner & Ranger, 1996). For some, indigenous elites have simply reoccupied the structures of colonialism and acted in ways that sustain the asymmetrical relationships between themselves and the oppressed mass of the population that had characterized the colonial period. For others 'Third World' nationalism exhibits its own character and is not a mere replication of Western versions (Chatterjee, 1993). Kerr and colleagues argue that the radical, sometimes violent changes accompanying industrialization need to be introduced and steered by powerful elites either within the society, or external to it, be those elites: 'the colonial company, the indigenous entrepreneur, the government agency, the military unit' (Kerr et al., 1960: 57). They acknowledge that such changes will encounter points of resistance, but these are disparagingly referred to as 'static' minorities such as aristocrats, landowners and 'medicine men'! (ibid: 58). Adding to the rhetoric of inevitability, it is argued that such resistant groups can delay the process and affect its timing and location, 'but they cannot prevent the transformation in the long run' (ibid: 58).

The elites are classified as 'ideal types' and enumerated thus: the middle class, dynastic leaders, colonial administrators, revolutionary intellectuals, nationalist leaders. In the US, it is argued, it is the 'middle class' elite that is dominant and that situation is described in such a way as to suggest that this elite, their mode of pursuing industrialization, and the sociopolitical context that surrounds them, is the preferred model for economic development and industrialization. Change brought about by a middle-class elite is depicted as gradualist, nonviolent, pragmatic and stable. Further, middle class ideology is described as 'economically individualistic and politically egalitarian' (ibid: 61) thereby mirroring the US' espoused ideology and values. There is a presumed morality underpinning individualism, which has it that each person has a responsibility to make the best of his/her opportunities. The pursuit of self-interest within a framework of the rule of law is the legitimized animus for the society in which the middle class rule. A level of conflict and dissent is permitted, indeed seen as inevitable, but contained within a variety of societal and institutional mechanisms – a Web of Rules – but ultimately contained by 'reason'.

The middle class elite is closely related and sometimes a virtual proxy for a managerial class and this aligns very closely with the form of managerialism and managerialist imperative so central to the industrialization thesis. Harbison and Myers set out their stall at the outset, asserting in the *Preface* that: 'The purpose of this study is to trace the logic of management development as related to the processes of industrial growth' (1959: vii). There is a dual, and mutually reinforcing, imperative embedded in the thesis. On the one hand, it is argued that there is a uniform and inevitable logic driving managerial development and that this form of management development is a prerequisite for industrialization to be pursued effectively. Management is conceptualized as a three factored construct: as an economic resource or factor of production that must be accumulated and productively put to work; as a system of authority with inevitable but legitimated power asymmetries; and as an elite or class within society, one that assumes increased prominence as industrial development matures.

On the other hand it is argued that as industrialization develops there is an imperative requirement for management to develop. This involves both the development of a substantial cadre of managers that accord with a specified ideal that is described as 'modern' and 'professional'. It is a model of management directly informed by that prescribed and emergent within the US economy (associated with Drucker, Simon, McGregor noted earlier). Marshalling these ideas, Kerr and colleagues construct a discourse about management – as a conceptual construction and as a prescriptive practice – that is distinctive, particularistic and ultimately ethnocentric. Harbison and Myers (1959: 38) specifically argue for the necessity of management for industrial and economic development and that an 'advanced society' is distinguished from a lesser one by its more intensive use of managerial resources. It is further argued that economic progress is made possible by the substitution of labour by capital and management. Therefore, it is argued, 'the accumulation and productive employment of high-level managerial resources, like the accumulation and productive investment of capital, is a universal imperative in the industrialization process' (ibid). Whilst the development of management will exhibit variance in different parts of the world, primarily under the mediating influence of different dominant elites, it is a US model being normatively prescribed and upon which other systems will converge.

Normative convergence

It is apparent from the above discussion that the logic of industrialization is presumed to propel nations on a particular trajectory of economic change that leads to a common mode of economic and social order. It is this common trajectory that is the essence of what has been labelled the 'convergence hypothesis' (Webber, 1969). The question is: what is it that is being converged upon? Part of the answer, as provided by Kerr and colleagues, is convergence to a general socioeconomic order which they sometimes label as 'industrial pluralism' and which is characterized by 'an open and mobile society, an educated and technocratic workforce, a pluralistic set of organized interest groups, a reduced level of industrial conflict, and increasing government regulation of the labor market' (Kaufman, 2005: 413–414). This is important, since it makes clear that industrialization is much more than the pursuit of particular technical or production solutions.

As has been made clear in the above, the technological imperative might be a key driver, but industrialization also involves the development and deployment of a certain mode of management, the reconstitution of employment relationships and the restructuring of organizational forms. These in turn impact upon structures and relations in the wider social formation; for instance, reconfiguring authority structures and familistic relations. But changes at the individual level also occur as the logic of industrialization requires people to acquiesce to the demands of the new economic and organizational order and accept the new regimes of work, including expectations of locations in time and space. These, together with the more macro-changes, impact upon people and precipitate a shift in values and attitudes. Such shifts have been explicated in terms of the Parsonian pattern variables, as Theodorson (1953: 481) states: 'The reorganization of society (from non-industrial to industrial) can be analysed in terms of four of Parsons's pattern variables'.

The logic of industrialization includes a shift in the normative framework constituting order in a society, or more specifically, a shift in the value preferences of people that constitute the patterning of relational institutions within the social formation. Thus, under the pressures of industrialization, people will be expected to move in the following manner: (a) from affectivity, and the choice to pursue immediate gratification, towards greater affective-neutrality and to sublimate and defer immediate gratification in favour of wider moral and social interests. One might recast this as an increase towards the disciplining of the self; (b) from collectivism to greater individualism: thus people, in deciding how to act, have greater recourse to an internal sense of self, and the prime source of reference is the individual self rather than some external collective (such as the family). Furthermore, private self-interest comes to take precedence over alignment and allegiance to collective interest; (c) from particularism towards greater universalism: wherein the standards by which behaviours and actions are defined and judged as appropriate and 'right' are derived from a set of abstract, universal forms that are invariant in their relevance and application versus derived from the particularities of specific behaviours embedded in specific relationships within specific times and locations. In other words universal rule systems come to override the obligations to particular relationships (d) a shift in the modality of the social object from an ascription orientation to an achievement orientation. In the former, social value and status accrues from an ascribed role derived from personal qualities or attributes, including one's inherited characteristics, traits and status or location in the social system. Under an achievement orientation, a position in the social system is secured through achieving performance standards or outcomes valued in the society; (e) finally, from diffuseness to increased specificity with respect to roles and relationships. Under a diffuseness orientation, a person's social contacts and obligations are broad and extend beyond the specific obligations pertaining to any specific role and the relationships it engenders. Under specificity orientation, behaviours and obligations are narrow and are circumscribed by the particular role that is currently engaged and the attendant relationship: roles and relationships become compartmentalized and confined to particular contexts.

Thus, in modern, industrial or bureaucratic organizations, the obligations of a subordinate to a superior are narrow and specific and are circumscribed by the particular rule system of the organization – they do not extend outside of those bounds into, say, the private, non-worklife of the individual. In general, industrialization is presumed to involve a shift from more expressive to more rationally and functionally instrumental modes of orientation, or as Theodorson puts it: 'The thesis advanced here is that an increase in universalism, achievement, suppression of immediate emotional release (affective neutrality) and specificity all accompany industrialization in the long run' (1953: 481).

The reliance on Parsons is significant both because of the functionalist commitments he exemplifies, which become embedded in the emerging ICCM discourse and persist down to the present, and for instigating a view of culture in terms of value dimensions as analytic categories. They are apparent, as indicated earlier, in most of the leading attempts to discuss and/or measure and dimensionalize culture in MOS/ICCM. However, a difference lies in the fact that scholars like Hofstede used his dimensionalization of cultural values to identify and discuss cultural differentiation, whereas Kerr et al. invoke Parsons to suggest a convergence of value orientations and the erosion of difference.

The convergence thesis has emerged at various times in ICCM since its appearance with Kerr and colleagues. One important related perspective for example was the so-called 'culture-free hypothesis' originally propounded by Hickson et al. (1974). It assumed that the contingencies of organization design and structure (such as technology, size) would exhibit a common shaping imperative on organizations that would override local cultural environment and result in organizational structural features and designs of great commonality, signalling universal properties. The contingency factors themselves are culturally invariant, it is argued, and hence universal in their effects. It is a position that has claimed to have empirical support from meta-analysis (for example Miller, 1987). This is not to say they have not been contested. From the outset the culture-free hypothesis was disputed by those for example arguing from a societal effects or embeddedness position (Maurice, 1976; Sorge, 1991).

Conclusion

In this chapter we have revealed the very particular set of conditions of the immediate post-World War Two period that helped enable, determine and shape the emerging discourse of ICCM. These included the rapid expansion of US international business, the Cold War and strategies to counter Soviet incursions and the spread of socialism, and the emergence of nations following processes of decolonization. Management theory more widely was only just consolidating and naturally ICCM drew on this. Embedded in both was a particular ideological bend. As Landau (2006: 637) says of management discourse, it: '[...] appropriated Cold War ideological concepts and national myths and translated them into rational-instrumental terms'. ICCM's deep imbrication with the Cold War was facilitated by the The Ford Foundation's sponsorship and supporting of its activities such as the I-USPLED project. We do not have to assume intentionality on the part of ICCM scholars for their involvement in these networks related to the commercial-industrial-military complex to be consequential.

The key texts produced by Kerr and colleagues as part of the I-USLPED project were comprehensive and influential, and gave clear expression to expectations about management development and industrialization processes around the world. But they were clearly operating under the assumption that the drive to do so would emanate from the US. The very conceptions of modernization, development and industrialization were Western in tone and imbued with the interests, ideology and assumptions of the US. The texts promulgate not only a technical change process and describe an industrialization process; they advocate the necessary accompaniment of American values of democracy, liberalism and freedom and the newly emerged ideology of managerialism.

For some, this state of affairs continues through to the present time under the aegis of globalization, the subject of our next chapter.

6
Globalization and Multiculturalism

Introduction

> The context for international collaboration continues to change. In recent decades, the purposes of international organizational research have changed from spreading the post-second world war US business system (e.g. Harbison and Myers, 1959) to studies reflecting genuinely global interests (Peterson, 2001: 78).

To reiterate where we are, in Chapter 4 we argued that there is a historical debt to the colonial encounter within ICCM. Our field relies unwittingly on discourses of science, anthropology and earlier colonial commercial practices that were directly involved in the pursuit of formal European Empire. In Chapter 5, we looked at the changes to this complex of economic, political and military interests in the first half of the 20th century. We placed particular focus on the immediate post-World War Two period, when the US emerged as a world power enabled by a commercial-industrial complex. We demonstrated how selected foundational studies of ICCM were infused with the key contextual factors of the day, notably the Cold War and decolonization processes. This final chapter of Part II moves our temporal frame forward to the latter quarter of the 20th century. Whilst the two decades after World War Two were dominated by the institutional practices of modernization, industrialization and development, it might be said that a new paradigm for economic and cultural life emerged over the last three decades of last century: that of globalization. What is the nature of economic and cultural life under globalization? What, if anything, has changed or remained the same? And what implications might it have for our historicizing account of ICCM?

The kinds of social change associated with, and often attributed to, the phenomenon of globalization cut across economic, political, and cultural domains, and are typically considered to be profound, confusing and contradictory. Friedman (1994: 233) describes an 'era of disorder, even of increasing disorder' in the global system since the 1970s, one in which the relative stabilities of the geopolitical system associated with the Cold War, US hegemony and the underdevelopment of the majority of the world's nations via modernization theory have come undone. These changes have been mirrored in the discourse of the social scientific academy. Carl Pletsch (1981, outlined in Kelly, 1999) describes the Western social sciences research of the 1950s through to 1975 as organized predominantly around modernization theory, and the work of critics and advocates alike. Pletsch predicted the demise of modernization theory in consonance with the transformations witnessed in the wider social sphere. Kelly (1999: 242) argues that since Pletsch's prediction:

> Not one but two alternative conceptual umbrellas have been proposed with both the potential breadth of reference and the conceptual simplicity ... necessary to be new transdisciplinary paradigms. Both are imbricated with changes in the social world, including the end of the cold war, but neither, as yet, has been established institutionally: I refer of course to postmodernism on the one hand, and globalization theory on the other.

We would argue that in the ten years since Kelly's quote, globalization can perhaps be viewed to have been thoroughly institutionalized. In the social sciences, globalization has had profound consequences not only in terms of stimulating new research topics, but as a context and rationale for the organization and provision of research support by funding bodies.

On the surface, these developments are highly propitious for ICCM given its substantive focus on culture, diversity, MNCs and global capital. However, as noted by Banerjee et al. (2009), much management scholarship lacks a serious and critical questioning of the dimensions and implications of globalization. In this chapter, we draw upon concepts from the interdisciplinary literature on globalization, notably those inflected by a postcolonial frame of reference,[1] to present a critical account of the changes as well as the continuities associated with economic and cultural processes of globalization. In disputing Peterson's claim above that international organizational research reflects 'genuinely global interests', we shall argue that the contemporary realities of globalization, and the continued and mutating neo-colonial and imperial economic and cultural formations involved, are overlooked and poorly understood in ICCM discourse. These formations present a challenge to future ICCM scholarship to recognize a more politicized view of one of its core concepts. The chapter is organized into three key sections. In the first section, we provide a selective discussion and explanation of our use of the term globalization. In the following two sections, we focus on the changes and continuities indexed by globalization *vis-à-vis* earlier periods in the economic and cultural spheres respectively.

Historicizing and politicizing globalization

According to Burawoy (2000: 338): 'Globalization studies are (...) a growth industry in the humanities and social sciences as well as in the mass media'. As a discourse, globalization is ubiquitous across corporate, government and civil society spheres and has even crept into everyday language use. Despite, or perhaps because of this proliferating discourse, the concept and meanings attributed to globalization display terminological contradiction and confusion. Scholte (2000) argues that this confusion pertains to multiple areas of discourse about globalization: how it is defined and measured; its chronology and causes; and its implications for social structure across economic, political, social, cultural and environmental domains. He notes ascerbically: 'In spite of a deluge of publications on the subject, our analyses of globalization tend to remain conceptually inexact, empirically thin, historically and culturally illiterate, normatively shallow and politically naïve' (Scholte, 2000: 1). The uninspected assumption that globalization is an objective and an inevitable reality is a source for considerable critique. Cameron and Palan (2004: 30) refer to this assumption in terms of a 'globalization as truth' approach, where the term is viewed as 'referring directly to real, concrete phenomena which have led or will inevitably lead towards the creation of a world characterized by the dominance of political and economic systems constituted on a global scale'. Furthermore, Rizvi notes that:

> (...) much of the recent theorization of globalization assumes it to be an objective self-evident entity, and does not attend sufficiently to the task of historicizing it, pointing to the hegemonic role it plays in organizing a particular way of interpreting the world.

Globalization is often reified, ascribed a range of universal character-istics (2007: 256).

Rizvi's comments on the social scientific treatment of globalization resonate with many critical commentaries on the state of globalization scholarship in MOS, including Banerjee et al.'s (2009) noted earlier. They suggest (2009: 187) that: 'few management scholars have ques-tioned what globalization itself is constitutive of or constituted by, let alone explored the imperial formations of globalization'. Such lack of critical imagination has the effect of turning scholarly attention away from the manner in which the discourse of globalization itself has con-stitutive effects on global relations in a postcolonial world. And when viewed as an inevitable phenomenon, it has the further effect of ren-dering potentially unimaginable radical disjunctures and alternatives to the current economic and cultural status quo (Hirst & Thompson, 1998).

At this juncture, it is important to clarify our own use of the term 'globalization'. First, we are referring to the particular version of global-ization associated with neo-liberalism. Second, we take the view that the distinctiveness of the current period of (Western) history lies in the 'increasing transnationalization of economic and cultural life' (Robins, 1997: 12), and the emergence and prevalence of 'supraterritoriality'. Burawoy (2000) notes that sceptics typically argue that the period 1870–1914 provides an earlier, and more appropriate example, of glob-alization, with its characteristically high levels of international trade *inter alia*. We share Burawoy's view that this period is better charac-terized as one of the internationalization, rather than globalization, of capitalism, with 80 per cent of production intended for domestic con-sumption and the state exhibiting a strong power over economic and political relations.

According to Scholte (2000), there has been a greatly accelerated rise of supraterritoriality since the 1960s involving a 'major reconfiguration of social geography' (2000: 5). This distinctive theme is identified by Burawoy (2000: 4) as common to the major sociological treatises on globalization over the last two decades (Harvey, Giddens, Castells) and signifying 'the recomposition of time and space – displacement, com-pression, distanciation, and even dissolution'. Scholte (2000) argues that the growth of supraterritorial spaces involves dynamics of de-territorialization and re-territorialization that have facilitated the emer-gence of: new forms of capitalist production – that overcome national boundaries and achieve world-scale advantages; multilayered and more diffuse governance; greater pluralism in the construction of community; increased questioning of rationalist knowledge. The workings of globalization thus cut across multiple domains that are associated with the activities and actions of a number of interconnected social actors. In this regard, Banerjee and Linstead (2001: 689) observe that:

> Today, international institutions and transnational corporations are writing the rules of globalization. Global political changes often involve coercion (the various trade embargoes orchestrated by western powers), surveillance (as evidenced by several World Bank and IMF policies), legitimacy (as offered by the World Trade Organization) and authority (granting of 'most favoured nation' status by the United States).

On the one hand then, globalization is a multiplicity of processes that form part of a complex circuitry that transcends the different varieties of capitalism, and contains many linkages, feedback loops, and key nodes in New York, London, Tokyo, Singapore, and Washington amongst others (Banerjee et al., 2009). Institutions and agencies such as TNCs, states, global organizations such as the UN, World Bank, IMF, WTO, the G8 and NGOs play a key role, with their relations located anywhere on a continuum from collaboration to mutual conflict (ibid). As Levy (2008) notes in his conceptual essay on global production networks, these institutions and actors can be considered an example of a 'historical bloc' (*pace* Gramsci, 1971), in which tensions but also stabilities in their relations characterize international political economy. Levy (2008: 951) describes how this historical bloc 'sustains its position through the coercive authority of the state, dominance in the economic realm, and the consensual legitimacy of civil society', a statement that casts light on the political and uneven nature of globalizing processes.

Finally, and relatedly, we view globalization as a set of processes that involve both change and social innovation (Robins, 1997), as well as continuities, of an uneven nature. A simple example is contained in Scholte's reference to multilayered forms of governance, which suggest that the nation-state is neither obsolete (as suggested by Ohmae, 1995) nor omnipotent in terms of regulating the activities of members of the historical bloc. With regard to technology, moreover: 'it is preferable to say, not that the new technologies are overcoming spatial constraints, but, rather, that they are changing the basis on which global corporations relate to place and territory' (Robins, 1997: 25). The new social geography of globalization does not then mean an 'end' to place-specific, or territorially-bounded social action (as if that were possible); it means, not so simply, a complex reconfiguration of it.

In terms of inequities, Scholte (2000) provides a balanced view of the positive and negative outcomes of globalization in the spheres of human security, justice and democracy cautioning that certain injustices have flowed 'from the policies that we have applied to globalization rather than to globalization per se' (2000: 6). He points, for example, to: class and country stratification (for instance, the continuation of the 'North/South' divide); stratified access to global spaces (for instance, the concentration of global communications on professional and propertied classes, countries of the North, urban dwellers, young); the predominance of white men in the management of global organizations; the decline of the redistributive state; and resistance to arbitrary hierarchies through global social movements *inter alia*. He argues that the losers from the new international division of labour are the poor, women, children, and those in rural areas, that is, those with typically less access to modes of mobility, or, those that migrate to low-paid jobs in richer countries.

The extent to which one agrees with the enumeration of these pros and cons above depends, like all things, on one's vantage point. Burawoy (2000) outlines three perspectives on globalization: the sceptic; the radical; and the perspectivalist. According to Burawoy, sceptics see globalization as hype, or 'pure ideology' and point to earlier periods in time as displaying more of the characteristics of globalization. As for radicals, globalization is real and with dramatic consequences; ideology is an expression of underlying reality rather than hype. Burawoy argues that: 'Radicals and sceptics suffer from two common defects: a simplistic view of ideology and a thin conception of history' (2000: 314). In terms of ideology, he wants sceptics to realize that ideologies have their power because they are rooted in everyday life and speak to lived experience. As for radicals, Burawoy argues that they render ideology problematically epiphenomenal, and singular. He notes how a constellation of ideologies associated with globalization becomes a terrain of struggle in everyday life, not a singular expression of false consciousness. Ideology is neither just mystification nor a simple reflection of reality according to Burawoy. Moreover, in terms of history, both radicals and sceptics commit the fallacy of globalism. That is to say, writing history by postulating 'changes or continuities at the global level that are presumed to imprint themselves on the local level' (ibid: 343). He notes that there is no such isomorphism of the global and the local; at both levels, movement is manifold, multiple, combined and uneven and unpredictable.

Burawoy finds a way forward in conceptualizing globalization in the work of Hall who distinguished between 'global imperialism' (GI) and the 'global postmodern' (GP). Whilst the latter refers to the decentred world of American mass culture, the former refers to the era of Empire and British domination where nations were organized in a hierarchy of domination. Hall argues that, in contrast to GI, there is no such totalizing logic in the global postmodern, instead flexible accumulation, more relations above and below the state, and hybrid and fragile cultural identities. However, Hall also notes that whilst the old economic forms, political regimes and cultural identities of GI are being displaced, they have not completely disappeared. Based upon this insight, Burawoy calls for an understanding of globalization as somewhere between the emergence of GP and the displacement of GI. Burawoy refers to 'globalization in transition', and notes multiple and uneven modalities of displacement and thus 'scattered hegemonies' (ibid: 349).

We further unpack the economic and cultural nature of these displacements in the following two sections. In the next section, we reinterpret globalization through a political economy lens and draw on a number of sources that explicitly use PCT in order to interrogate critically the interaction of political/governmental and economic/corporate interests of production.

Contemporary international political economy

(...) notions of globalization are inextricably linked with the continued development of First World economies, creating new forms of colonial control in the so-called 'postcolonial' era. Thus, globalization becomes the new global colonialism, based on the historical structure of capitalism and is a process that executes the objectives of colonialism with greater efficiency and rationalism (Banerjee & Linstead, 2001: 683).

In Chapter 5, we noted how modernization theory became a driving force for both international business scholarship and formed a key discourse for the commercial-military complex of the United States in the post-World War Two era. Modernization theory institutionalized the classification of first, second and third worlds, which enabled judgements to be made regarding how well developed a particular society was. As Kelly (1999: 42) describes: 'General laws of human behaviour were thought to be visible especially in the first world, where things and people were most developed and unconstrained by either ideology (as in the second world) or tradition or culture (as in the third). The third was destined to modernize, and become either more like the first world, or entrapped in ideology by the second'. Appropriate interventions into the 'development' of other nations could be justified on the basis of these comparisons, with the goal of convergence towards a common economic and political system desired by a US-led world order.

A simultaneous body of work, critical of the tenets and practices of modernization theory and its neo-colonial relations, emerged labelled dependency theory (Andre Gunter Frank), or underdevelopment theory. As Hoogvelt (2001) notes, dependency theory had roots in classical theories of imperialism (for instance Lenin) and a concern to articulate the problematic effects of imperialism, as pursued notably via modernization. Hoogvelt (2001: 38) explains that:

> The impetus for the postwar dependency perspective was the perceived need to critique bourgeois modernization theory. Dependency theory concentrated on locating the cause of backwardness of Third World countries (initially, more especially Latin America), within the dynamic and contradictory growth of the world capitalist system. (...) The essence of the dependency theory is the contention that, as a result of penetration by colonial capital, a distorted structure of economy and society had been created in the colonial countries which would reproduce overall economic stagnation and extreme pauperization of the masses for all time.

At an economic level, this distorted structure involved the subordination of TW economies to the structure of advanced capitalist countries, and an associated dependency on external markets for both capital and technology. At a societal level, a class alliance emerged between foreign capital and comprador (a term referring to mercantile and landed elites). A distorted internal class structure emerged in TW societies where a small elite dominated, whose economic fortunes became entwined with advanced capitalist states, and the reproduction of patterns of social inequality.

Dependency theory should be appropriately located as an expression of a world-systems perspective on international political economy, introduced earlier in Chapter 1. Here we noted Wallerstein's (1974) argument that the capitalist world system 'underdeveloped' economies, rendering them dependent, exploited but crucially vital to the fortunes of the capitalist core. Ashcroft et al. (2000) describe how dependency analyses encouraged Third World countries to break with this system, contributing to the development of Third Worldist perspectives on trade and political action.

According to Hoogvelt (2001), by the mid-1970s, demands for changes to extant economic and social arrangements by Third World and other critics were rendered obsolete by the radical structural changes to the world system. Hoogvelt's neo-Marxist analysis posits that the transformation of global structural arrangements at this time was an outcome of the necessary adjustments to the internal contradictions of the capitalist system. Hoogvelt describes how:

> a new stage of capitalism is fermenting in the core of the system, one in which the geographic core-periphery polarization is being replaced by a *social* core-periphery divide that cuts across territorial boundaries and geographic regions (...) the new global configuration drives a *politics of exclusion*, contrasted with the politics of incorporation (and 'developmentalism' in the broadest sense) that marked previous periods of capitalist expansion (2001: 64–65, italics added).

The kind of world system imagined by Wallerstein, in which an organized hierarchy of capitalist economic and social relations relied on the integration of developing nations into the system, was no longer appropriate. Instead, as Hoogvelt argues, a politics of exclusion replaces this politics of incorporation. Continuing her materialist analysis, she argues that a profound change in capitalist modes of accumulation – from 'expansion' to 'involution' – has effected this change in political economy. By involution, Hoogvelt presents as evidence economic data that illustrates the increasing concentration of economic activity within the reconstructed core of the world system during and subsequent to the 1970s. These changes overlapped with the period 'that was still theorized and institutionalized as a period of "development" of the "Third World" as a unitary category' (ibid: 66). The status of certain TW and peripheral economies and societies had changed from one of structural exploitation to structural irrelevance.

At this point in her argument, Hoogvelt explicitly draws upon postcolonial discourse to characterize and illuminate the new and variegated forms of exclusion that emerged and exist today. She highlights the fact that these forms of exclusion continue a historical path or

tradition rooted in previous forms of colonial and neo-colonial economic development. In this regard, she provides evidence of Hall's
notion of 'globalization in transition' between GI and GP, and the existence of scattered hegemonies. She talks of different kinds of postcolonial condition, or different 'postcolonial formations' (as she
calls them) in four zones: Sub-Saharan Africa; Islamic revolutions; the
developmental states of East Asia; postdevelopment in Latin America.
Hoogvelt is careful to note that whilst she talks about 'zones', she
wants us not to understand them in unnecessarily rigid or homogeneous ways. There is 'a certain fluidity and ambiguity between the
area-referential emphasis and the subject-positional one' (ibid: 171),
with locally-specific contestations of the postcolonial condition and
points of resistance to imperial formations.

For Sub-Saharan Africa, she argues that the peripheralizing consequences of globalization have gone furthest: debt, structural adjustment, the integration of elites into the world economy and the
replacement of programmes of development and incorporation with
the 'management of exclusion' have wrought terrible effects here. The
other three zones instantiate different kinds of postcolonial formation.
In militant Islam, globalization and modernity have been denied, as
suspicions of a neo-colonial developmentalism met a tradition of
Islamic cultural renewal. In the developmental states of East Asia,
Hoogvelt describes a more enthusiastic response to globalization,
whilst in Latin America, the articulation of a postdevelopment ethos
based on liberation is furthest developed. She suggests that this ethos
differs from antidevelopment sentiments in so far as it does not deny
globalization or modernity; rather it tries to find ways to accommodate
it in civil society. In sum:

> The *anti-developmentalism* of militant Islam is different in its
> origins and expression from both the *management of exclusion*
> in Sub-Saharan Africa and the *postdevelopment* response in Latin
> America (ibid: 172, italics in original).

What these different postcolonial formations manifest are 'hybrid
forms of struggle and local experimentations with alternative social and
economic organization' (ibid). Hoogvelt's argument can be extended
to examine national differences within these zones in terms of their
'modalities of displacement' (Burawoy, 2000). Within Africa, we could
point to the very different trajectories of the Sudan and South Africa;
within Asia, between Singapore and Malaysia; and also Australia's

attempts to assert its role as an Asian nation rather than one tied to the aftermath of formal British rule (though the Queen is still Head of State in Australia.)

In a simultaneously fascinating but disturbing article that extends Hoogvelt's account, Banerjee (2008) places death, violence and the military centre stage of contemporary international political economy. The organization of military forces, and the presence of violence and death in the pursuit of profit, has a long historical record. As we noted in Chapter 4, for instance, the corporate colonialism of the East India Company and the management and organization of slavery involved physical abuse, death and the dispossession of land. Banerjee refers to the contemporary articulation of 'commerce and the sword' as necro-capitalism, which he defines as 'contemporary forms of organizational accumulation that involve dispossession and the subjugation of life to the power of death' (2008: 1541). Necrocapitalism is a new form of imperialism in the postcolonial era that takes shape between different actors, notably TNCs, states and local elites, in varying contexts and via a number of different machinations of power (institutional, economic and discursive).

At the centrepiece of Banerjee's argument is Agamben's concept of 'states of exception' – contexts where the application of law is suspended but where law remains in place, and thus torture and death can occur.[2] Historically speaking, Banerjee points out (*pace* Mbembe) that the colony was a permanent state of exception in which sovereignty was exercised outside the confines of the law. Banerjee argues that these states of exception are created by neo-liberal policies – thus 'neoliberalism by exception' (ibid: 1546) – and pursued by the different actors in the historical bloc noted earlier. Moreover, he argues that they exist in both former colonies as well as the West (as the case of illegal immigrants and refugee populations in metropolitan centres illustrates). According to Banerjee, necrocapitalist practices are highly efficient modes for the accomplishment of imperialist goals, or, to use his words, 'an imperialism that has learned to "manage things better"' (ibid: 1546). Banerjee gives a number of examples. In South East Asia (*pace* Ong, 2006) for instance, he describes how several Asian Tiger Economies can be interpreted to have 'gone global' through the use of political strategy and military repression, with problematic consequences for the local population. He also describes the nexus of economic interests and military power in Iraq, for instance through the award of reconstruction projects to the MNC Halliburton. Furthermore, here, and in earlier articles (for example 2001), Banerjee shows how conflicts over the control and extraction of natural resources in developing countries have involved necrocapitalist practices.

In conclusion, these postcolonial sources (Hoogvelt and Banerjee) suggest four important insights: first, that the contemporary and reconfigured commercial-political-military complex uses economic 'management by exclusion' and a political economy of 'necrocapitalism' in the pursuit of its varied interests; second, that neo-colonial structures continue and new imperial formations have emerged that form the basis for such exclusions; third, that they highlight multiple and differentiated forms of contemporary postcolonialities; fourth, that they point to continuing forms of power asymmetry, military power and death in the pursuit of economic goals. In short, concepts of imperialism and colonialism continue to have a valuable role in describing and politicizing contemporary global economic and political relations. The same might also be said of cultural processes of globalization to which we turn next.

Cultural globalization and multiculturalism

Appadurai (1990: 295) argues that 'the central problem of today's global interaction is the tension between cultural homogenization and cultural heterogenization'. In this section we begin by exploring some of the paradoxical developments in the relationship between so-called global and local cultures as captured in Appadurai's quote. We use this material as a backdrop for a critical discussion of the discourse of multiculturalism that has been mobilized by states and organizations alike to 'respond' to the cultural demands of globalization.

Global and local culture

Homogenization versions of cultural globalization can be found positively articulated in ideas such as McLuhan's 'global village', and popular cultural and marketing representations of an interconnected world in which a 'common humanity' is purported to bridge cultural differences. Cameron and Palan (2004) refer to these notions as examples of 'cosmopolitan democracy'. A more negative version of cultural homogenization is articulated in notions of globalization as Westernization or Americanization, which typically overlap with a global commoditization thesis. Here the spread of American culture via commodities and brands such as Coca-Cola, Starbucks or McDonald's, news media such as CNN, and popular cultural forms such as movies and soap operas, is viewed as a corrosive influence on local cultures. Images of African or Rainforest Indian tribes wearing Nike caps come to mind here.

Critiques of these variants of the homogenization thesis are well-rehearsed across a number of disciplines. For one, Featherstone (1993: 169) argues that the result of the globalization of cultural processes is an awareness of more cultural particularities: '... one paradoxical consequence of the process of globalization, the awareness of the finitude and boundedness of the planet and humanity, is not to produce homogeneity but to familiarize us with greater diversity, the extensive range of local culture'. Apart from a growing awareness of difference as well as interdependence, there is considerable evidence for the continuation of expressions of cultural difference and local particularity, for instance in the area of food consumption. Moreover, the cultural uncertainties associated with globalization have, according to some claims (Meyer & Geschiere, 1999), created a need for many individuals and communities to search for fixed identities, often 'retreating' into perceived forms of cultural authenticity. Such a retreat can lead to a 'hardening' of cultural contrasts, which shore up the expression of local identities, as well as the creation of new kinds of opposition.

Further evidence for heterogeneity lies in the ways in which the elements that move or travel via processes of cultural globalization – objects, media images, brands and so on – become indigenized, and domesticated in local cultural contexts and used to mark communal, parochial identities. Meyer and Geschiere (1999), for instance, present anthropological evidence that in parts of Africa, the accumulation of Western goods is viewed as witchcraft and a way to distinguish trustworthy and untrustworthy people. The concept of hybridization is used to denote the processes in which elements from home and foreign cultures are intertwined and mixed to create new cultural forms. Caldwell's (2004) study of McDonald's in Russia (one of many similar anthropological studies) demonstrates the 'nashification' of this global brand. Her ethnographic study revealed the manner in which certain elements of the McDonald's offering (such as the burger) make their way into indigenous Russian culture and how McDonald's outlets were used for locally-specific cultural purposes (including bathing and socialization). By the same token, however, Caldwell shows how McDonald's itself was changed by the intercultural encounter, adapting its cultural articulation to speak to Russian concepts of home, trust and pride. Anthropologist Richard Wilk's (1995) concept of 'structures of common difference' neatly captures the global/local cultural dynamics at work here. According to this concept, there exist common templates for the global flow of culture (so, brands, media etc) but their articulation and content demonstrates considerable diversity. In this sense, it is possible to hold together the global and the local in a relational fashion. Appadurai sums it up as follows: 'the central feature of global culture today is the politics of the mutual effect of sameness and difference to cannibalize one another and thus to proclaim their successful hijacking of the twin Enlightenment ideas of the triumphantly universal and the resiliently particular' (1990: 307–308).

The implications of these kinds of paradoxes as associated with globalization are profound for the study and conceptualization of culture. For one, they impel us to give up on fixed and essential notions of culture tightly sealed around the boundaries of the nation-state, and to work with a fluid notion that highlights the making and unmaking of new localities (Meyer & Geschiere, 1999). They also suggest that we need to give up on the view of a world that is comprised of a conglomerate of separate and internally homogeneous cultures. As Meyer and Geschiere (1999: 4) state: 'Far from celebrating globalization merely in terms of a creative blending of different, pre-existing cultural traditions, [we need to] ... try to unravel the politics of the making and unmaking of boundaries, localities and "cultures" in particular power constellations'.

The work of anthropologist Appadurai (1990) is, to a large degree, helpful in this respect. He describes global cultural flow through the concept of five different and interacting 'scapes' – ethnoscapes, mediascapes, technoscapes, finanscapes, ideoscapes. These are not objective entities, but perspectival constructs that reflect the particular historical, linguistic, political and other contexts of various social actors. He argues that this discourse of scapes should replace the vocabulary of world systems and dependency theory, especially its purported dualisms (core and periphery, old and new, first and third world, north and south and so on).[3] Instead, these so-called scapes form parts of a cultural whole constructed by different people in different places. But these are no 'smooth' cultural wholes. Instead, Appadurai insists that the global cultural economy is characterized by a series of disjunctures, primarily associated with the cultural politics of de-territorialization. As a result of these disjunctures, multiple forms of affiliation to global culture are possible, as noted by Featherstone (1993), ranging from reimmersion in local culture and the 'rediscovery' of ethnicity, and instances of problematic acculturation by new migrants to FW contexts, to cosmopolitan bonds and attitudes associated with (but not guaranteed by) greater levels of intercultural contact. These divergent cultural affiliations are, of course, patterned by socioeconomic circumstance, and the new global division of labour.

The nation-state

For the nation-state, the challenges of these multiple and conflicting forms of cultural identification on a translocal scale are profound, since they point to the undermining, or even decoupling, of the links between nations and states. Whilst Scholte (2000) presents evidence for the latter point, he also points out that nationhood continues to act as a primary frame for the collective solidarity of many. According to Featherstone (1993), in modernity, national cultures usually emerged alongside state formation processes and were attempts by political elites to get rid of ethnic and regional differences that would enable better social control. Modernization can therefore be interpreted as the containment of difference and, in the context of the modern nation-state system, a response to the pressure 'to develop a coherent cultural identity' (Featherstone, 1993: 173). The disjunctive global cultural economy has forced a reimagination of this idea of national cultural identity. Appadurai (1990: 304) expresses it thus:

> (...) whilst nations (or more properly groups with ideas about nationhood) seek to capture or co-opt states and state power, states simultaneously seek to capture and monopolize ideas about nationhood. In general, separatist, transnational movements (...) exemplify nations in search of states (...). States, on the other hand, are everywhere seeking to monopolize the moral resources of community, either by flatly claiming perfect coevality between nation and state or by systematically museumizing and representing all the groups with them in a variety of heritage politics that seems remarkably uniform throughout the world. (...) Typically, contemporary nation-states do this by exercising taxonomical control over difference; by creating various kinds of international spectacle to domesticate difference; and by seducing small groups with the fantasy of self-display on some sort of global or cosmopolitan stage. (...) state and nation are at each other's throats, and the hyphen that links them is now less an icon of conjuncture than an index of disjuncture.

The emergence of state nations, ethnonations, regionations, and transworld nations (Scholte, 2000) is an outcome of such dynamics, as is an important paradox of ethnic politics also noted by Appadurai. He talks of the manner in which 'primordia, (whether of language or skin colour or neighbourhood or kinship) have become globalized. That is, sentiments whose greatest force is in their ability to ignite intimacy into a political sentiment and turn locality into a staging ground for identity, have become spread over vast and irregular spaces, as groups move, yet stay linked to one another through sophisticated media capabilities' (ibid: 306). A parallel development is that states have faced the need to tolerate a greater diversity within their boundaries and to reconstitute their collective identities 'along pluralistic and multi-cultural lines which take into account regional and subnational cultures' (Featherstone, 1993: 179). State-sponsored multiculturalism is 'a complex discourse of cultural pluralism, inclusion and equity found within liberal/humanist ideologies of various types, as well as existing policy structures of some Western settler nations like Australia and Canada' (Carter, 2006: 681). We return to the discourse of multiculturalism later in the chapter.

In addition to the cultural complexities within nation-states, a further set of reconfigurations is also taking place in the geopolitical relations between nation-states. The systemic disorder identified by Friedman (1994) relates to the changing position of the US and its allies in the global cultural hierarchy between the earlier and later decades of the second half of the 20th century. In this regard, the Americanization thesis of globalization and the discourse of modernization were intimately connected as rhetorical artefacts of the two decades after World War Two. The Americanization thesis critiqued a global cultural hierarchy in which the US was dominant and able to spread its hegemonic culture into other parts of the world. Critics viewed American culture as a corrosive force for other cultures as they became drawn into a US-modelled modernity. Both supporters and critics of this modernizing/Americanizing view of global relations fall into the same trap. First, they adopt a US-centred point of view, with the critics of Americanization typically overlooking the existence of other, and multiple, forms of cultural domination in the world. As Appadurai puts it: 'for polities of smaller scale, there is always a fear of cultural absorption by polities of larger scale, especially those that are nearby'. He points to Japanization as a concern for Koreans, and Russianization as a concern for Georgians as two instances. Furthermore, Americanization and modernization theses often assume that the spread of American models and values has been and continues to be successful and with little or no resistance, and/or that the US has itself not experienced the challenges of other cultures. Both assumptions are infelicitous.

The reordering of the global cultural hierarchy in the last three decades has had significant implications for the linear trajectories of history that underpinned modernization and colonialism. As Featherstone notes:

> The perception of history as an unending linear process of the unification of the world with Europe at the centre in the nineteenth century and the United States at the centre in the twentieth century, has become harder to sustain with the beginnings of a shift in the global balance of power away from the West. Hence, in the late twentieth century, there is increasingly the recognition that the non-Western world has histories of its own (...) The sense that there are plural histories to the world, that there are diverse cultures and particularities that were excluded from Western modernity's project, but now surface to the extent that they cast doubts on the viability of the project, is one particular outcome of the current phase of globalization (1993: 171–172).

The key example here, as Featherstone notes, is Japan in the 1980s, not just because it was 'outmodernizing' the West in economic terms during that time, but also because the Japanese articulated theories of world history that disputed the placing of Japan on the Western metanarrative of 'premodern, modern and postmodern'. Morley and Robins (1992), for instance, discuss the considerable anxiety and distress caused by the success of Japan in the US in their essay on techno-Orientalism. At this point in history, not only were Japan's leading corporations eroding US and European market shares and setting up factories in their backyards, there were fears, or more accurately fantasies (to use Morley and Robins' terminology), about the pernicious cultural impact of Japan in particular on the American way of life. Morley and Robins survey numerous press commentaries from the 1980s that positioned Japan as a threat, an alien culture, complex and ambiguous in the Western imagination, working behind the scenes in a 'chameleon-like' fashion to erode the economic and cultural values of America, slowly but surely. Morley and Robins describe how the broader cultural theme here was one where Western modernity was being brought into question, and gesturing to a shift from 'Coca-colonization to sake imperialism' (Morley & Robins, 1992: 139).

They describe how these fears were projected into popular culture through a discourse of techno-Orientalism, essentially the 'grafting' of Orientalist binaries onto various media and cultural products such as the Mutant Ninja Turtles or computer games. This discourse produced problematic images of Japanese culture and a strain of racism that reinforced views of the Japanese as being like their technologies: cold and machine-like. Morley and Robins conclude that: 'There is something profoundly disturbing in this Techno-Orientalism. Following Castoriadis, we have suggested that western xenophobia and racism are motivated by the apparent incapacity of a culture to constitute itself without excluding, devaluing and then hating the Other' (1992: 155).

But what happens when it is no longer possible to keep the Other in subordinate place, Morley and Robins ask: 'Japan has now become modern to the degree of seeming postmodern, and it is its future that now seems to be the measure for all cultures. And, thereby, the basis of western identity is called into question' (ibid: 141). It was no longer Europe or the US that was the key site of modernity; Japanese technological superiority suggested that they were the vanguards of postmodernity, an even more advanced stage of history. Here the non-West was reclaiming a subjectivity lost by the kinds of Orientalism that excluded them from history (as defined in Eurocentic narratives). Japan has destabilized the West/East modern/premodern binaries – Japan should be premodern or at least non-modern, not postmodern. This ability of Japan to express its own history and subjectivity was facilitated by 'nihonjinron' discourses of Japaneseness, a brand of cultural nationalism that assumed Japanese superiority and uniqueness over other civilizations.

As Featherstone (1993) suggests, it would be fallacious to assume that changes with globalization necessarily mean a 'flattening out' of global cultural power differentials. It is perhaps better seen as a reconfiguration of the geopolitical hegemony, one in which the US has been slowly losing its grip. Just because power is shifting from the Western bloc does not guarantee that the TW will necessarily benefit. He suggests that there may be new sources of globalizing and universalizing images with associated problems. Following the success of Japan, one wonders what the current impact of China will be in terms of reordering this hegemony.

Multiculturalism

> The different centres of 'calculation' ... that make up the cultural circuit of capitalism can perhaps best be thought of as shifting 'assemblages' of governmental power, made more powerful by their strictly temporary descriptions and attributions (Olds & Thrift, 2005: 199).

In this sub-section we look selectively at what happens to notions of cultural diversity when they enter particular 'centres of calculation' and become subject to their assemblages of governmental power. We ask: when this diversity is encoded in the discourse of multiculturalism, what happens as it is taken up by certain actors in the international political economy to address economic and/or political imperatives and interests? In other words, how is cultural knowledge put to use in the service of capital accumulation/political sovereignty in the era of globalization, and what are its implications in different postcolonial contexts?

The concept of the cultural circuit of capital (Olds & Thrift, 2005) is a useful one for holding together a view of cultural globalization, not just as the flow and manipulation of a multitude of different cultural knowledges by global actors, but as a process in which economic and culture spheres intertwine and become mutually constitutive. Resonating with views in the emerging stream of work on 'cultural economy' (Du Gay & Pryke, 2002), the cultural circuit of capital views the 'economic', 'cultural' and 'the political' not as separate spheres, but mutually imbricated ones. Multiculturalism is thus potentially as much a cultural and political discourse as it is an economic one.

In recent decades, business and management knowledge, and the manner in which it encodes and normalizes particular understandings of cultural diversity, have become important players in this circuit. Olds and Thrift (2005: 201) argue that since the 1960s there has been a 'link up of a series of institutions to produce and disseminate business knowledge. In particular, this circuit arises from the concentration of three different institutions – management consultants, management gurus and especially business schools – all surrounded by the constant presence of the media'. Banerjee et al. (2009) make a similar point, though they refer to the emergence of a new 'business-consulting complex' in recent years, which they define as an amalgam of a global management ideas industry (selling discontinuous innovation and the merits of consultancy), the 'global' MBA (with its American educational model) and global accounting firms. They also point to the role of accrediting bodies such as AACSB and EQUIS in spreading the complex's hegemonic influence. Common to both Olds and Thrift and Banerjee et al. is an assertion that these institutions, and the knowledges they promulgate, have potential normalizing and disciplinary effects on human subjects. We can demonstrate this at state and organizational levels.

First, Olds and Thrift (2005) illuminate their own concept with reference to one particular node in the cultural circuit of capital – business schools – and in one particular postcolonial context: Singapore. They give an account of Singapore's attempts in recent years to position itself as a leading force in the contemporary knowledge economy through the creation of a so-called 'global schoolhouse' for business and management in the Asia Pacific region. Or, to use Olds and Thrift's terms, a 'laboratory for the corporate interests of both the cultural circuit of capital and the state' (2005: 200). They argue that the Singaporean strategy is one that several other postcolonial states, notably Malaysia and India, have engaged in order to foster economic modernization. The goals of this radical and state-planned socioeconomic transformation were captured in its Economic Development Board's 'Industry 21 strategy', in which was expressed the goal to transform the city-state into a global hub that would provide technological and innovative advantage for organizations located there. The development of a world-class education sector was deemed to be vital to achieving these goals, and a strategy was put in place to create a global education hub that could train students to work in such organizations. Primarily the strategy involved the creation of partnerships and a variety of other alliances and relationships with elite, foreign institutions that would attract students from the Asia Pacific area. In terms of business schools, this meant INSEAD, Wharton, Chicago, and Cornell's hospitality school.

In this case, the cultural circuit of capital has been aligned with the Singaporean state in at least two ways. First, these state interventions ultimately aimed to facilitate the mass production of knowledgeable and enterprising subjects in Singapore. This is governmentality on a grand scheme (also noted by Chio, 2005 in her study of Malaysia) – the production of new subject-citizens who would come to see themselves, and their education, knowledge and skills, as economic assets. As Olds and Thrift note, the small scale and governmental particularity of Singapore renders it a place where state actions can directly input into the everyday work behaviour and non-work life of its citizens in ways that are not available to other states. Second, and in relation to multiculturalism, Singapore's cosmopolitan nature was played up by the EDB to attract elite institutions to its shores (along with other financial and fiscal incentives of course). To align state and commercial interests, Olds and Thrift describe how the Singaporean government had to walk the difficult line of simultaneously respecting ethnic differences in its societal culture, whilst also seeking to 'minimize' them to avoid causing concern to investors.

A number of scholars have commented on the manner in which multiculturalism is deployed by governments, and often those of postcolonial nations (for instance Australia, Canada, New Zealand, US, UK), to organize and manage their internal diversity such that it does not 'interfere' with the everyday business of society (Banerjee & Linstead, 2001; Carter, 2006). Typically, multiculturalism is manifest in 'celebratory' governmental and popular discourses, and the superficial and aesthetic appeals of advertisements (think United Colors of Benetton) and consumer products (new ranges of ethnic foods, ethnic chic in clothing and furniture and so on). Fish (1997) famously refers to the latter as 'boutique multiculturalism' associated with ethnic restaurants and weekend jazz – a kind of 'radical chic'.

Rather than a 'celebration' of difference, an alternative conceptualization of multiculturalism as state policy is one of management and control of 'the culturally and ethnically diverse'. Banerjee and Linstead (2001) demonstrate that elements of social control are barely hidden in recent Australian government discourse on multiculturalism, illuminating limits to what can be expressed and experienced as an ethnic identity in Australia. There are, therefore, acceptable and unacceptable forms of multiculturalism, the former tied to the preservation of the interests of elite segments of society, the latter in requirement of management and control. They suggest that 'the possibility of multiple structures and multiple institutions serving multiple cultures is a real fear for governments' (Banerjee & Linstead, 2001: 704), one that plays with fears of cultural disintegration brought about by multiple, conflicting cultures. They go on to introduce Radhakrishnan's (1996) critique of the cultural category of 'ethnicity' and the problematic epistemological issues of which it speaks. The argument here is that multiculturalism can never truly or effectively embrace diversity, since its deployment as a totalizing category 'normalizes different histories of a variety of minority groups and constructs a category that is opposed to the mainstream – positioning it as an *alien* category. Thus, ethnicity is maintained "by the paranoia of the dominant culture as eternally illicit, transgressive, and lawless"' (Radhakrishnan, 1996, in Banerjee & Linstead, 2001: 706).

If we move from governments and states, to organizations and corporations, a well-established canon of work on managing diversity in the workplace echoes these foundational criticisms of multiculturalism. Cultural diversity, it barely needs to be said, is seen as something that organizations can handle, organize, bring under control, through a number of different interventions (usually HRM and HRD-related) that can ultimately contribute to business objectives. These interventions, ranging from diversity audits, awareness raising seminars, cross-cultural and linguistic training, videos and reading material, have spawned what Jack and Lorbiecki (2003) called a 'cross-cultural training industry'.

Diversity management originated in the United States and has since been applied in a range of private, public and government organizations and national contexts with some enthusiasm over the last two decades. The discourse of 'managing' diversity marked a significant change from the earlier term of 'valuing' diversity, and initial affirmative action programmes, in the US (Omanovic, 2006). Valuing diversity indexed acceptance, tolerance and an awareness and encouragement of the benefits that diverse members of organizations could bring. Ultimately this would morph into the 'business case' view of diversity. Accordingly, monocultural organizations were viewed as no longer effective in today's global market. Multiculturalist transformation was needed since it would enhance productivity, decision-making and understandings of diverse customers (so the argument goes). Contained in articles such as 'Diversify for dollars' (Segal, 1997) and 'Diversity: a bottomline issue' (Owens, 1997), such economic discourse has become predominant and used to legitimize organizational scrutiny of employers' responses to difference, suggesting there were ways to change them if deemed 'inappropriate'. In this sense, diversity management became programmable, as it could be incorporated into the routines and procedures of human resource management.

Once again, however, this positive discourse can be seen to hide or distort many of the unsavoury realities of cultural diversity in organizations. In this regard, Prasad and Mills (1997: 3) described the various 'shadows' of diversity management, that is to say, 'the serious dimensions of difference in organizations' associated with gender conflicts, racial tensions and cultural frictions that the literature on diversity and multiculturalism fails to address. They note several: to start, the fact that what constitutes workplace diversity will differ depending on the particular social group one asks; antagonism and backlash, especially in the form of white rage; resistance to acculturation; and the criticism that diversity management is all hype with little discernible, positive impact on minority groups, leading to continued frustration and little real organizational change (also noted by Hoobler, 2005).

A key criticism of DM discourse concerns how and who we define to be different. Litvin (1997), in her discourse analysis of the conceptualization of diverse workforce in a sample of OB textbooks, illustrates the essentialist assumptions found in conceptualizations of difference. 'The acquisition of knowledge about groups exotically, essentially and immutably different from one's own is prescribed as an effective strategy for managing diversity' (Litvin, 1997: 187). But as she goes on to argue, nothing is less obvious than who exactly is a 'member' of these groups. She asks what criteria might be used to determine whether an individual is to be classified amongst 'the elderly' or belonging to a specific racial group. Furthermore, the oft-noted lack of organizational change to emanate from DM initiatives serves to continue the prevalence of monoculturalism in most large organizations and, consequently, the continued existence of varying forms of inequality.

Blommaert and Verscheuren (1998) argue that in effect, debates on diversity, though couched in the language of tolerance, are really about managing the negative effects of undiverted and unaccepted diversity, but from the point of view of the most economically and politically privileged segments of society who are, in the US and the UK (initial leaders in DM), traditionally members of the white, male and non-disabled dominant group. As Cavanaugh (1997: 18–19) points out 'work-place diversity programs may well serve to solidify the dominance, or hegemonic control, of organizations by white males'. Oseen (1997) suggests that the problem lies in linguistic practices surrounding diversity discourse. She argues that, unwittingly, 'difference' in diversity management initiatives is subtly encoded to mean both 'other than' as well as 'less than', a function of the hierarchical of language in which one side of an opposition (the same) is privileged over the other (the different).

Provocatively, Fish (1997) argues that multiculturalism does not exist! He is not denying the 'empirical reality' of cultural diversity and the associated challenges of racism or hate speech. Instead, the problem is conceptual. On the one hand, 'the boutique multiculturalist resists the force of culture he [sic] appreciates at precisely the point at which it matters most to its strongly committed members [...] and cannot take seriously the core values of the cultures he tolerates. The reason he cannot is that he does not see those values as truly "core" but as overlays on a substratum of essential humanity' (Fish, 1997: 379). To give an example, Fish talks about the boutique multiculturalist who will enjoy rap music and soul-food restaurants but become troubled by affirmative action or an Afrocentrist teaching curriculum. Fish identifies a similar problem with strong multiculturalism, that is a politics of difference that demands a deep (rather than shallow) respect and appreciation of cultures and their core. The key principle here is tolerance (rather than support of a putative universal humanity) but, he notes, the problem lies in the fact that 'sooner or later the culture whose core values you are tolerating will reveal itself to be intolerant at the same core' (ibid: 383) thus compromising the tolerance of the strong multiculturalist. Fish argues that, in the end, strong multiculturalism is simply a deeper example of its boutique relation, and that neither can adequately deal with difference rendering the concept 'impossible'.[4]

> The boutique multiculturalist does not take difference seriously because its marks ... are for him matters of lifestyle (...), and as such they should not be allowed to overwhelm the substratum of rationality that makes us all brothers under the skin. The strong multiculturalist takes difference so seriously as a general principle that he cannot take any *particular* difference seriously, cannot allow its imperatives their full realization in a political program, for their full realization would inevitably involve the suppression of difference (ibid: 384).

Conclusion

We started this chapter with, to our minds, Peterson's rather optimistic claim that international organizational research had shifted from propagating the interests of the US business system in the 1950s and 1960s, to embedding global concerns in more recent concerns. Our goal in this chapter has been to describe certain elements of the historically evolving political-commercial-military complex under globalization, and its implications for ICCM. We have illustrated how significant forms of disjuncture in global and local cultures, and in international political economy, in the last three decades have produced new but still problematic imperial and postcolonial forms of socioeconomic and cultural exclusion. In the domain of international political economy, we deployed Hoogvelt's concept of 'management by exclusion' and Banerjee's 'necrocapitalism' to illustrate. As for the contemporary global cultural hierarchy, we illustrated the tensions and uncertainties associated with changes to the established order under modernity, and the manner in which multiculturalism, when propagated through various state – and organizationally – sponsored projects and initiatives functioned in a cultural circuit of capital to produce new forms of social and cultural control. ICCM therefore needs to grasp these continuous as well as innovative forms of neo-colonial and imperial domination that temper and reconfigure Peterson's assessment.

In the next section of the book, we pursue our analysis of the cultural domain in which practices of inclusion and exclusion, similar to those associated with diversity management, can be deemed an essential and worrisome part of ICCM. We do this through a close reading of core ICCM texts.

Part III

Strategies of Appropriation in ICCM

7
Representational Strategies One: Orientalism and Othering

Introduction

In Part I of the book, we set out our domain of interrogation and specified the contours of its topography. We sought to explicate the current location of that domain in terms of its contextual, quantitative and qualitative parochialisms. In these respects, we identified and critiqued the limited and limiting paradigmatic location of most ICCM research, the hegemonic practices and institutional structure by which its orthodoxy is sustained, and the resultant commitments and omissions. In the second part of the book, we examined the historical conditions in which science, anthropology and colonial commerce, key knowledge systems and material practices for the later development of ICCM, emerged. Our examination revealed the foundational significance of the colonial encounter, and thus the colonial legacies of ICCM as a modernist project, as well as the future configurations of these knowledge systems and material practices in the post-World War Two discourses of modernization, industrialization, development and globalization.

In this part of the book we move to a micro-level of analysis concerned with how this legacy and hegemony is manifest and reproduced by the representational practices and textual strategies of academic study in IB and ICCM. We do so primarily through a Saidian-inspired neo-colonial discourse analysis (prefaced in Chapter 1) of a series of texts that have been central to the canon of ICCM from the 1950s to today. This analysis spans the next two chapters. Whilst Chapter 6 focuses on selected texts from the 1950s to the 1970s, Chapter 7 picks up from the 1980s through to the present day. This analysis will reveal the problematic deployment of binary structures of representation by certain leading ICCM scholars that enable a routine and persistent trade in universalisms, essentialisms, exoticisms and appropriations of Others. Our analysis of these binary structures is part of our strategy of 'strategic essentialism' (Spivak, 1987) and a necessary condition for critique. That is to say, we recognize that the relationship between both sides of the binary (such as colonizer – colonized) is not unilinear, passive or homogeneous. Rather, the mode of domination associated with binaries of West-Rest, centre-periphery and so on is sustained by the effacement of the hybrid cultural forms that characterize the interactive and heterogeneous relationships between both sides of the binary. In Chapter 9 we explore a variety of modes of hybridization and engagement that co-exist but are effaced from the same canon of ICCM that has developed since the 1960s. Our analysis thus offers a reconfigured understanding of ICCM not as the study of similarities and differences between national business systems or culturally-based work-related values, but as an exercise in the politics of alterity.

Before we proceed with that discussion, it is appropriate to comment briefly on the nature and selection of texts (see Table 7.1). First, the texts we have chosen are instances of different but related academic genres, ranging from quasi-research monographs in the form of edited collections on comparative management (such as Weinshall, 1977) and practitioner-orientated texts on understanding national cultural differences (such as Lewis, 2006), to the kinds of student textbooks that are typically prescribed in undergraduate and/or postgraduate courses on international management (such as Mead, 1994). Whilst all share a common goal of imparting knowledge about culture and its impact on management and organization, there are generic and structural differences between them. In part these differences reflect developments in English-language academic writing and publishing in the post-World

Table 7.1   ICCM Texts Analysed

Harbison & Myers, 1959
Kerr et al., 1960
Farmer & Richman, 1965
Haire, Ghiselli & Porter, 1966
Weinshall, 1977
Harris & Moran, 1979
Nath, 1988
Ronen, 1986
Hickson & Pugh, 1995
Mead, 1994
Hodgetts & Luthans, 2002
Lewis, 2006

War Two period, notably the emergence of the glossy textbook crit-iqued in Chapter 3. Whilst acknowledging these differences, all the texts chosen express an explicit pedagogical goal not only to inform and raise awareness of cultural issues amongst their readers (students predominantly, also practitioners), but also to affect their audiences' future behaviour in managerial contexts with cross-cultural elements.

Our choice of these explicitly pedagogical texts, as opposed to journal articles, lies in our concern with the potential subjectifying effects that these texts carry. There are qualitative and quantitative elements to this claim. In terms of the former, the texts are a crystallization of contem-poraneous theory, conceptualizations and research in the field, and carry the orientations and values embedded therein. As texts that aim to culti-vate a particular kind of cross-cultural sensitivity amongst their readers, who are either already embedded within the world of work, or strive to achieve high status managerial jobs within it, they also contain subject-ifying effects amongst an occupational group with potentially consider-able impact on the lives of others.

A quantitative dimension can be added, which relates to the wide cir-culation of these texts. We selected texts on the basis: (i) that they are influential in the field – partly a subjective judgement, partly an adjudica-tion made as a result of the following criteria; (ii) of the success of the text in terms of sales, editions and adoptions; (iii) of reputation and citations. In addition to the texts chosen, we have examined many others across the time frame as part of the research process and are reasonably confident that analysis of most of those others would not have revealed anything substantively different. Again this is a subjective judgement. The subjectifying potential of these texts is multiplied then by their wide-spread circulation amongst the large and ever-increasing number of stu-dents taking business or management degrees, noted in Chapter 3. Our view, as articulated more fully in Chapter 10, is that to transform the nature of future ICCM scholarship, an important starting point lies in a re-evaluation of what the next generation of scholars will read and understand about culture. With these points in mind, we now turn to a discussion of the politics of representation and the ideology of represen-tationalism, before briefly reintroducing Said's work and then moving on to the analysis of representational practices.

Representationalism and the properties of representation

Whereas the politics of representation have been very much at the core of postcolonial studies, ICCM – along with much of MOS – has mostly remained neglectful of the issues. This is not the case in other fields and disciplines such as anthropology, cultural studies and literature studies. ICCM has assumed a naïve posture that sees the language it deploys as transparent, innocent, neutral, universal and non-problematic. It is a non-reflexive and uncritical posture that enables the ICCM scholar to assume the authority to speak for and about others. This is in contrast with some critical areas of management and organization studies where there has been concern about the politics of signification and the problematics of representational practice (for example Jeffcutt, 1994; Linstead, 2003; Rhodes, 2001; Westwood & Linstead, 2001).

Postcolonial theorists have given close scrutiny to multitudinous forms of representation, most often with the intent of revealing the implications of those representations for producing and reproducing the power inequalities that have persisted through the colonial era and into the conditions of postcoloniality (notably Bhabha, 1994; Said, 1978; Spivak, 1988). Such work can be considered part of the genre of colonial discourse analysis. The insistence on the question of representation matches the turn within postmodern philosophy and its predecessors – for example Heidegger – away from the notion that there is a clear presence delivered with transparency through language and that what matters is the seeking of ever more 'truthful' or 'real' representations. In contrast, Said (1978: 21), significantly influenced by Foucault, argues that: 'In any instance of at least written language, there is no such thing as a delivered presence, but a re-presence, or a representation'. He naturally relates this to the focus of his investigation, the representation of the 'Orient' in various Western discourses. He argues that any representation – any written statement or other signification – of that which comes to be labelled the 'Orient' actually has little to do with anything that might be taken ontologically as the Orient. On the contrary, he insists such representations are 'a presence to the reader by virtue of its having excluded, displaced, made supererogatory any such real thing as "the Orient"' (ibid).

We might note immediately that such an ontological and epistemological position is at odds with the realism and objectivity paradigmatically prevalent within MOS and ICCM's structural-functional orthodoxy. Some scholars, such as Chia (1996), would castigate this orthodoxy as a form of 'representationalism', a position driven by an ontological belief that theories are able to represent reality fully and accurately, in some direct, unmediated form. It is precisely this belief, among other things, that poststructuralism has sought to undermine and certainly something Said's work assaults. Like Foucault, Said is concerned about the erasure of power and power effects in represent-ationalism. Any assertion of the truth-value or knowledge status of a representation is an act of displacement and exclusion in which alter-native claims are pushed aside, sublimated, marginalized or silenced. Modernist, positivistic science in its assertions of objectivity, universality and neutrality denies or eschews this power and politics. Representation is an appropriation, a 'laying hold and grasping' (Heidegger, 1977: 149) and can be considered an act of violence; carving out a singular relation between signifier and signified, pushing a singular meaning and erasing or moving aside alternatives.

Kwek talks about the property of *proprietorship* possessed by repres-entation – one of a number of representational elements he articulates (2003: 126–127) in his neat précis of key poststructuralist insights into language. The first property Kwek refers to as *circularity*, whereby representation both draws together and holds apart: both signifies something other than itself, signifies that it is not what it represents, but at the same time is held to be constitutive of that which it repre-sents. The ideology of representationalism rests, to a degree, in the proclamation of the latter and the effacement of the former. It can only do so by acts of *containment* – the second of Kwek's properties. Containment is the inclusion/exclusion practice of representation in which the singular integrity of a particular representation is asserted and differentiated from others and other possibilities. That is to say, containment constructs a boundary that clarifies and fixes same/different, and through which it includes some particular meanings whilst excluding others. Next, representation brings forth something for us to apprehend – objects and ideas that we can work on/with. It creates a *presence* of that, which at the same time, remains absent. It also *substitutes* for that which is never really present, substitutes for the object/event that it seeks to represent. In that sense, representation is always in fact a *re-presentation* of an object – the object itself remain-ing absent and *displaced,* an ever present *absence* always implied by presence.

Further, and of critical importance for Said and our project, is that *essentialization* is a core property of representation. Representation works to make available to us simplified and reduced categories of the objects/events in the world. It de-differentiates and offers up categories that smooth over differences and constitute sameness. All the unique, individuated and singular things in the world are gathered up into rep-resentable categories, unities and similarities that provide an economy of signification that facilitates our apprehension, appropriation and control. There is an inescapable *reduction* in essentialization through which individual uniqueness and particular features not required by the particular representation are effaced and lost.

The reduction participates in the construction of the boundary of exclusion/inclusion and separates the present from the absent. But, as we have noted, the excluded and the absent remain – they cannot be fully removed and hidden (Prakash, 1999). The very act of representation gestures to that which is absent and excluded, indeed, depends upon them. The ideology of representationalism, however, works to mask this and to pretend that there is *transparency* and equivalence. These dynamics of language can be captured in the idea of a 'politics of alterity', and related further to Said's discursive framework in *Orientalism*.

As Sardar (1999: 19) says of Orientalism in general, it has always been characterized by 'wilful misunderstanding and knowledgeable ignorance' since 'Orientalism is composed of what the West wishes to know, not of what can be known'. Indeed, Sardar goes so far as to say that essential to the Orientalist project is 'the desire not to know' (ibid: 4). It is a wilful ignorance in which representations are not designed or intended to deliver a truthful and accurate representation of the East/Other but rather 'as instruments to "contain" and "manage" these [other] cultures and civilisations' (ibid). Most importantly, as both he and Said argue, Orientalist representations are about the West itself. This aspect of the politics of alterity defines the Other (in negative and inferior terms) and in the same movement defines the Self (in positive and superior terms), the former is thus 'less than' rather than just 'different to' the latter. We refer to this as a 'Manichean structure' of imperial ideology (Ashcroft et al., 2000), separating Self and Other into categories of 'good' and 'evil', thereby valorizing the Self and castigating the Other.

The non-West, like 'the Orient', is often represented in ways that conform to Kwek's (2003) properties of representation, particularly those of essentialization, containment, circularity and displacement. We illuminate these properties in our analysis of the chosen texts below.

Orientalism and essentialism in the discourse of ICCM

Orientalism as discourse, institution and practice is not dead (Sardar, 1999). We shall show that it is present in the central texts of ICCM and that it has continued to be so from its inception as an academic discourse in the 1950s until today, even though the strategies of representation and their obvious reliance on Orientalist tropes might have altered. For the sake of convenience, we start in this chapter with the texts of the I-USPLED, moving through to examine some core texts from the 1960s and 1970s. In the next chapter we continue the journey, looking at a set of texts from the 1980s through to the 2000s. We reveal how a canon emerged within ICCM that sedimented certain representational practices that contain an Orientalist echo and sustain a Western hegemony that universalizes, appropriates and essentializes. You will note that our illustrations pertain to studies of multiple nations, including comparative work on the US and Europe. The latter we use as examples of gross stereotyping and essentialism within a context of cultural imperialism rather than neo-colonialism.

Industrialization and its essentialisms

We have already encountered some of the essentializing, universalizing and Orientalist representational strategies within the ICCM corpus when we examined the modernization/industrialization/development discourse(s) embedded in the work of Kerr and colleagues associated with the I-USPLED project in Chapter 5. The central texts of Harbison and Myers (1959) and Kerr et al. (1960) are projects designed to represent the non-Western[1] world to the West, or more specifically to the US. The non-Western world is constructed through these texts and represented in them in ways that make it accessible and comprehensible to the West so that the West is better able to formulate its international economic and business strategies. To achieve this, the representations need only to function as enabling devices for Western actors. They do not need to be accurate representations of the non-West. In this and other ways, we argue, these texts can be considered as exhibiting a variant of Orientalism.

The texts are certainly replete with essentializing representations. The following are just a few simple examples: references to *Indian, German* and *Chilean* 'authoritarianism' and 'paternalism', *British* 'aristocratic values', the low levels of 'trust' among *Italians*, and the 'unquestioning loyalty' of the *Japanese*. The non-US world's management and business practices are also diminished in a variety of ways. For instance in Kerr et al., leadership is disparaged: 'In India today there are examples of this "benevolent paternalism", based on an apparent willingness of the employee to accept a dependent status and of the manager to play the role of a wise father' (1960: 151). Indeed, paternalistic management was seen to be prevalent not only in India, but also in Japan, France and Italy. French family businesses are held to place '(...) inordinate stress on safety and security. It fears change and is unwilling to borrow for fear that the lender, whether individual or bank, will gain a foothold in the enterprise. As a result, the firm prefers to enjoy its own little market' (ibid). Note the use of terms such as 'inordinate', 'fear' and 'fears change'. Paternalistic management/leadership is contrasted with the professional impersonalism of 'modern' management in the US and positioned as inferior and unsustainable in a modern industrialized economy. The text also performs a typical Orientalist practice by tying the management/organizational practices of the non-US to the past, and to ineffectiveness or failure. Hence, Italian familistic capitalism, for example, is held responsible for the retardation of industrial growth in that country.

Similarly, Harbison and Myers (1959), in their construction of the triumvirate modernization/industrialization/development discourse, position anything that cannot be positively located within that discursive frame as backward, anachronistic, deficient, regressive and flawed. Premodern, preindustrial management and organization systems are held to be ineffective and inefficient and to rest upon 'illogical and non-productive activities' (Harbison & Myers, 1959: 33). Such a critique is not confined to the developing or Third World but to all nations and economies that are not as 'advanced' on the modernization/industrialization/development path as the US. Thus, referring to the management and organization systems of France, they say that business leaders and owners seek family maintenance and reputation rather than the purely financial goals appropriate to the 'modern' corporation and rational markets.

Essentializing practices are abundant throughout the ICCM and comparative management oeuvre and it is a reductive representational practice in Kwek's (2003) terms, as we have noted. That is, it constructs categorizations that smooth out differences and erase uniqueness – it reduces difference to the 'regime of the Same' (Bhabha, 1994). It does so by pretending to apprehend in a single categorical label that which is presumed to be essential to all cases and which might be taken to be subject to that category. Any qualities, attributes, features or characteristics of persons/objects not identified with the essential are overlooked and remain absent from the representation. That which is thereby lost remains hidden through sustained ideological work which repeats and re-presents the essentialization, reifying it and leading us to forget the absent in the (re)-presented. Thus, as with Harbison and Myers, one might represent 'loyalty' as an essential cultural characteristic of Japanese and hence all Japanese are represented by that characteristic, allowing statements such as 'the Japanese are loyal' to be constructed and to pass as sensible across a whole range of organizational (and other) situations. Or it might be that Germans are essentialized as 'authoritarian' such that all the actual variation and individuation among German people is smoothed out and homogenized under the weight of this particular representation. The reductive, shorthand is apparent in these forms of representation – we could go on endlessly with statements of the form 'the African is...', 'the Vietnamese are...', 'the Arabs are...'.

Part of the difficulty here is that such representational strategies are so embedded in our knowledge systems that we take them for granted and typically do not consider them to be problematical. Indeed, Smart (1996: 183) argues that there is a preoccupation in Western modes of reasoning and analysis with 'disclosing an assumed underlying essence'. Essentializing on the basis of culture is a modern form of this tendency. Thomas (1994) sees anthropological typification as a marker of modernity and notes how culture has superseded race as the essentializing typification. As he says: 'Each of these concepts [race, nation, culture] privileges differences – understood at different moments primarily in temperamental, physical and now cultural terms – and rendered the essentialized entities through an array of attributes that are supposedly peculiar to them' (Thomas, 1994: 89). In the discourse of ICCM it is this essentialization *via* culture (rather than race or ethnicity) that became prominent, even at its inception in the 1950s but also repeatedly through subsequent decades.

The nineteen-sixties

Farmer and Richman, 1965

Farmer and Richman were significant figures in the emergence of ICCM and provided a model to guide future theory and research in comparative management studies (Farmer & Richman, 1965). In their model, culture was positioned as a core variable accounting for differences in management and organization practice. Despite the emphasis on culture and difference, elements of universalism and technological determinism remain in their work related to a view of rationalism as the prime mover for modern business and management. The following quote (also presented earlier) is indicative of the interplay of these motifs that are apparent throughout the text: 'There are only a limited number of rational ways to make steel and a country does not get output in this sector by using prayer rugs, doctrinaire slogans, or wishful thinking' (Farmer & Richman,

1965: 41). The technological determinism and rationalism echo Kerr et al.'s thesis and their modernism-industrialization-development discourse. Farmer and Richman concur with Kerr et al. that economic growth through industrial productivity is the only rational way forward for all nations and that all nations will aspire to such a trajectory; thus the same universalism of motive and method. Their work is also infused with references to the primitive and the illogical when talking about management in non-Western contexts and relating this to the failings of traditional patriarchal systems. For example, they castigate Japan's organizational regimes as being mired in feudalism, paternalism and familialism. Even European regimes are not exempt from such representations.

In all this work there is a frequent conflation of business, economics and politics. In Kerr et al. there is a clear presumed alignment between economic development and the values of a liberal, democratic society with a developed middle class and a civil society. Kolde (1968: 8–10), in Farmer's (1968) collection of papers on *International Management*, divides the world into the 'Industrial West', the 'Sub-industrial South' and the 'Communist East'.[2] The Industrial West (which includes Australasia, South Africa and Japan) is held to be uniformly guided by an economic philosophy characterized by 'private property, free enterprise and open competition' and politically by the principles of 'representative government, democratic process and the rule of law' (ibid). This is, in turn, all held to be shaped by 'Western culture' (although, as becomes common, Japan has to be considered an exception). There is no reflection on the sociopolitical context of apartheid South Africa and its inclusion in this scheme, yet alone on the drastic reductionism it involves. Furthermore, as with all Orientalist practice, the representations are constructed in antagonistic binaries. The representations of the Industrial West noted above are contrasted with the autocratic dictatorship of the Communist East. The Sub-industrial or 'underdeveloped' sector is characterized by lack and negative absence, having 'no basic doctrine or economic philosophy of its own' (ibid). Such a Manichean manoeuvre is typical of Orientalist discourse and of the reductionist levelling of difference and individual uniqueness. The whole of Central and South America, Southern Asia, most of Oceania, and all but the tip of Africa are held to be devoid of any independent, indigenous approach to economic matters. Furthermore, politically they are characterized by 'pseudo-democracies and outright personal dictatorships' (ibid). Kolde acknowledges some differentiation, noting that the political systems of India, Pakistan and the Philippines are 'exceptions to prove the generalization' (ibid), but even then European provenance is noted.

Part of the machinery for economic development and success in the West is held to reside in the institutions of economic integration forged through such mechanisms as GATT, the European 'Common Market' and other trade 'liberalization' tools. Such integration failed to materialize in Africa and Asia it is argued, with any such attempts being 'drowned in the violent tides of nationalistic, racial, and tribal conflicts which have beset the ex-colonial societies' (ibid: 14). Again there is no reflection on the violence through which the colonial powers imposed their economic and political will on the rest of the world, enabling the construction of the very model of economic success that it is now insisted the rest of the world emulate. It is asserted that the 'developing world' is united in its desire to industrialize and grow economically. There is a warning though, not to embrace the interventionist accelerations offered by the Soviet bloc. Indeed, Kolde composes the same type of intersections between economic and social development, politics, business and the 'Soviet threat' as Kerr and others (such as Fenn 1957). He depicts the 'Communist orbit' as presenting both 'political aggression' and 'economic imperialism', saying that: 'Through its example and propaganda, the bloc presents a frontal attack to the free enterprise system as such' (ibid: 32). He interprets the developed world as having constructed a socioeconomic system that is a 'volatile mix' of capitalism based on free enterprise alongside communist-inspired state intervention and nationalization. He argues that free enterprise must recognize and learn to function in such a situation or run the risk of being considered inappropriate and antithetical to the interests of developing nations, thereby pushing them towards communism or socialism. Adapting to the realities of a hybrid system is the only real choice 'short of armed force and reinstitution of the colonialist system' (ibid: 24). The adoption by developing nations of non-aligned positions is portrayed by Kolde as a manipulative, 'mock neutral' one designed to optimize economic aid and economic concessions!

There is another thread in the emerging ICCM discourse that was apparent in Kerr et al. that is also present in Farmer (1968). This concerns the required changes that accompany industrialization and modernization, not just in terms of organization and management, but also in terms of the demands of work regimes, and ultimately in the value orientations, attitudes and behaviours of people. Lowe (1968: 58) argues that people in developing countries need to adapt to the new work regimes of the modern enterprise and drop their old methods and practices. This is an imperative if the productivity and economic gains are to be realized – 'there is no alternative' he says (ibid). Lowe adds that to pursue the 'new, strange and revolutionary standards and practices' (ibid), self-discipline, motivation and financial integrity are required. The risible implication that such things were completely absent in all these societies prior to any industrialization process is not acknowledged. It is apparent, however, that quite specific versions of these three characteristics is what is intended. Thus self-discipline is equated to the capacity to stand on a production line under surveillance for eight hours a day – a level of self-discipline beyond most people in developing countries Lowe avers.

Haire, Ghiselli and Porter, 1966

A somewhat different, but still influential, text that appeared in the mid-1960s was Haire, Ghiselli and Porter's (1966) *Managerial Thinking: An International Study*. It reports a large empirical survey of managerial attitudes across 14 countries and is a monograph. We have included it because of its impact and because it was one of the first detailed, expressly cross-cultural empirical studies. They surveyed 3641 managers at all levels regarding work goal importance, motivational needs, aspects of management style and control, and conceptions of the management role. The text largely consists of the reporting of this study and its results. It needs to be noted that the theoretical foundations, constructs, and methods were all developed in and are a reflection of US conceptions of management and research. For example, the measures of motivational needs are an adaptation of Maslow's model. The attitudes collected are aggregated at the country level and subjected to statistical analysis, but there is a tendency to go further and to aggregate at a presumed 'regional' level. Thus the authors talk about the 'block of four Nordic countries' and the 'block of four Latin countries' (Haire et al., 1966: 26). Such a conflation allows them to assert that both these blocks exhibit similarities, for example in showing 'similar patterns of clearly negative views of individuals' capacities for leadership and initiative' (ibid: 26). Such clustering sets a trend that has persisted in the field.

Throughout, it is 'modern', US-based management attitudes and practices that are the standard against which those of other countries are judged. Once again, there is a Manichean ordering typical of Orientalist texts wherein the West – the US specifically – is represented as modern, effective, democratic, developed and progressive, in a positive matrix of attributes against which others are contrasted. The reported differences are held to be the result of a mixture of culture and tradition. For example, it is argued that: 'The highly formal (and formerly feudalistic) structure of traditions which tend to exist in Japanese society would suggest that a business executive in that country would believe in a relatively narrow distribution of capacity for initiative and leadership on the part of the average individual' (ibid: 21). Similarly, a German manager 'living in a society with a rather strong authoritarian tradition, would be far less likely to advocate participation' (ibid). Relatedly, German 'traditions' are held to lead them to prefer directing over persuading, or to see little difference between them (ibid: 50, 56). This is not only essentialist, but highly selective. One wonders if speculation about the history of slavery in the US would reveal an impact on contemporary attitudes about managing and employer-employee relations.

The authors have recourse to rather tortuous remedial construals when the findings are not in conformance with expectations (one might even say 'stereotypes'). For example, contrary to expectations, Japan scored second highest in terms of holding a 'democratic-type' view of the average person's capacities. Confronted with this 'anomaly' the authors say:

> The meaning of this finding is not immediately obvious. One possible explanation is that the Japanese managers, more than the other groups of managers in our sample, had a strong motivation to try to 'please' the American researchers by giving them the response they thought the Americans wanted...It is also possible that because of their past traditions the Japanese, especially those managers sent to executive development programs, have a tendency to overreact to participative, democratic-oriented ideas and practices (ibid: 30).

Thus, whereas in most instances the responses of people are taken as valid, when an anomalous result is found it is explained by some decidedly odd suppositions about the culture of the respondents and their presumed need to either 'please' the researchers or their 'overreaction' to something new to their cultural context. We discuss Haire et al.'s work further a little later in this chapter.

The nineteen-seventies

Interest in ICCM continued to grow into the 1970s as US business expansion and internationalization continued. Culturalist explanations of differences in international business and management continued to grow, though as we noted earlier, there was little discussion of what the culture concept actually was (Boyacigiller et al., 1996). The

1970s saw the emergence of Hofstede's massive empirical work with its measures of cultural value differences, though his impact largely came later following the publication of *Culture's Consequences* in 1980. We will focus here on two influential texts published during the 1970s: Weinshall's (1977) *Culture and Management* and Harris and Moran's (1979) *Managing Cultural Differences* that in different ways encapsulate the strengthening culturalist position in ICCM.

Weinshall, 1977

Weinshall's edited book was significant since it sought to collect some of the leading empirical and conceptual work on the relationship between culture and management at the time. It contains 15 chapters divided into four parts and draws on the work of leading scholars in the burgeoning fields of ICCM and IB. The first part is the introductory *Conceptualization of the Relation between Culture and Management*. Usefully for us, its opening chapter is a reprint of Richman's '*Significance of Cultural Variables*', which reprises the work by Richman and Farmer that we discussed earlier. Also included is Roberts's much cited overview and methodological critique of cross-cultural research and Webber's assessment of whether managerial and organizational behaviours are converging or diverging. Part two is called *The Cultural Framework: The Effects of Values, Beliefs and Manifest Behaviour on Management*, which is fairly self-explanatory. The first selection dates back to 1960 and is an extract from John Fairweather purporting to provide insights into the impact of culturally-informed values and beliefs on the interactions of US managers with those of other cultures. The second is an odd, somewhat tongue-in-cheek piece from *Harper's Magazine* on *How to do Business with a Frenchman* by Eggers. This is followed by a very different, more sober discussion of possible paradigmatic relationship orientations between West and East (in this instance broadly construed as capitalistic West and communist East) by Perlmutter. The final selection is a melange of empirical work and commentary on aspects of intercultural relations by Weinshall himself. Part three is *The Managerial Framework: Factors of the Decision-Making Process in Different Cultures*, which opens with an extract from Harbison and Myers (1959). This is followed by a piece by Carson offering insights from anthropology to inform cross-cultural management. Then there is a reprint of Sirota and Greenwood's large, international survey of work-related values. The final paper is another empirical study of the characteristics of CEOs from a range of European countries in comparison with the USA (de Bettignies & Evans). The final part of the book is *The Managerial*

Framework: The Effects of Size on the Managerial Structure, which is something of a misnomer since organizational size is really only considered
in one chapter. For example, the first paper is an excerpt from the
Haire, Ghiselli and Porter study of managerial values discussed above.
Equally, the second chapter is in two parts, containing two comparative studies by Heller and colleagues of English and US managerial
attitudes. It is the next paper that fits the section heading better.
It contains Hickson et al.'s influential culture-free hypothesis and
is based on US-UK comparative work on determinants of structural
variation. This work was part of the famous Aston studies, which were
foundational for contingency theory in organization studies. The book
concludes with another offering from Weinshall, which is again a
collage of previous work he had done on MNCs.

We included Weinshall's book for a number of reasons. First it is an
edited collection that brings together articles that were considered to
be among the most significant to date by the mid-1970s. It also serves
as a useful bridge chronologically since 40 per cent of the work
included was produced in the 1960s, the rest coming from the 1970s.
It further serves as a bridge since it reproduces work that we have
already included in our discussions, such as that of Harbison and Myers,
Farmer and Richman, and Haire et al.'s significant study, and alludes
to other work we touch upon, such as that by Webber, and Hickson
et al.'s culture-free hypothesis. In addition, this book was, once again,
successful and impactful: Weinshall revisited the idea and format with
an expanded alternate version (Weinshall, 1993).

A particularly pertinent link to our earlier discussion, notably of Fenn,
is the concern shown for Soviet expansionism in Perlmutter's contribution, which is preoccupied with East-West relations construed as an
ideological clash between the capitalistic West and the communist, or
Soviet, East. He is concerned at the macro-level with possible modes
of relationship between East and West and identifies four different
sets of assumptions about the relationship. He labels these assumption
sets as submergence theory, divergence theory, convergence theory, and
emergence theory, and they are held to be inferred from the policies
and practices of business leaders in the East and the West.

Submergence assumes that the ultimate aim of either side appears
to be the submergence of the other's political system – by military or
other means (Perlmutter, 1977: 142). As he notes, in game theory this
relationship is based on zero-sum premises, but further, it sees capitalism and communism as 'engaged in moral combat' (ibid). Divergence
and convergence are conceptions also considered by Webber in the

book. Divergence suggests that East and West are actually drifting further apart. Whilst Webber sees the forces for divergence mainly in cultural terms, Perlmutter sees them in ideological terms. Convergence, on the other hand, suggests the possibility of the two systems coming together, which for Perlmutter means the free market and communist style economies converging to a common pattern. Significantly, Perlmutter invokes the industrialization thesis to explain potential convergence saying that: 'the key idea of convergists is that industrialism imposes its own rules, which leads to uniformity between economies at similar stages of advancing economic development. Industrialization requires similar political, social and economic institutions, regardless of the ideological base' (ibid: 148). The arguments are very similar to the industrialization thesis of Kerr and colleagues, arguing that there will be common solutions to common national economic and industrial problems. Perlmutter raises the idea that there are many communisms, just as it has become fashionable to talk about varieties of capitalism (Amable, 2003; Clegg, Redding & Cartner, 1990; Coates, 2005; Hall & Soskice, 2001; Hamilton, 2006; Whitley, 1999). This implies, then, not so much a binary with a wide gulf, but a continuum with positions of adjacency. He references Rostow's (1960) thesis that Marxist sociopolitical systems are only viable in the earliest stages of industrialization and that economies will move more towards the US model, but also notes that there is considerable ethnocentrism in the convergence views expressed in the US.

Emergence theory depends upon the notion of 'trans-ideological dialogue', that is relationships that 'cut across and through ideologies (yet which do not claim to be "above" or "below" the ideologies, or "beyond", in the sense of better)' (ibid: 155). He basically argues that as interactions develop between nations and their business systems, interdependencies develop that transcend ideological differences. He identifies five arenas of interaction: international divisions of labour; worldwide market penetrations; the geocentric requirements of science and technology development; balance of payments manipulations; and sheer ideological diversity. He concludes by suggesting that 'different approaches to building a world economic system are becoming more apparent, and the interdependence of humanity more concretely felt, in the industrialization process which executives of multinational firms must manage... Now there may be a role for geocentrically orientated, trans-ideological industrial institutions' (ibid: 161). It is clear that these types of argument are a prolegomenon to a globalization thesis in many respects.

As noted above, Webber also discusses the convergence/divergence issue, not in terms of economic and political ideology, but simply in terms of management systems and philosophy. He begins by citing Maslow's needs theory, implying that it has some universality but also that: '(...) Some of the more somnolent societies have not yet started to climb this ladder [Maslow's needs hierarchy], but eventually they too will set out on what is a never-ending quest. Increasingly, mankind is becoming united in the belief that economic growth is vital for satisfaction of the full range of human needs' (Webber, 1977: 39). He goes on to argue, along with Kerr and colleagues, that it is a common economic orientation and goal that drives societies along a common path and towards convergence. He maintains that the argument for convergence is strongest in terms of economic structure, and the relationship of man to machine, thereby invoking a similar technological determinism as witnessed in Kerr et al. Indeed, Webber argues that, like the language of mathematics, technology is universal and goes on to say: 'by obeying the laws of reason and science, men of varying cultural and ideological positions presumably can agree on the best machine design or most desirable production system. For the most part, this technology is Western' (ibid: 40). Of note is how he invokes the discourses of science and reason here, both weighty discourses within modernity, and aligns them squarely with the West. He also, as with Perlmutter and Kerr, maintains that it is the imperative of industrialization itself that explains convergence.

However, Webber also identifies forces sustaining differences in management systems and philosophy – divergent forces – principally in terms of time, natural resources, geography and 'most important', culture. Again, as with Kerr, industrialization and technology bring social structural changes that result in less autocratic arrangements, the triumph of achievement over ascription, the replacement of class structures by occupational structures, and more social mobility. Also echoing Perlmutter, he asserts that the convergence argument presumes that pragmatism becomes the 'leading ideology', saying that: 'Most managers, owners, politicians and customers want efficiency. Hindering ideologies, beliefs and dogmas surrender to economic pragmatism' (ibid: 45). We also see the support for the emergence of managerialism in the suggestion that professional management and technical specialists are necessary to run a modern organization. Webber concludes by saying that: 'For a long time at the least, cultural factors will exert a strong and differentiating influence upon managerial philosophy and practice: less on technological and production decisions, less on the relations of man and job, less on the firm's relationship to its customers and society; but more on the methods of motivation, patterns of communication and styles of leadership' (ibid: 54). We see in Webber a repeated affirmation of the industrialization thesis and support for managerialism.

One entry in Weinshall's book is somewhat curious, and intellectually and stylistically at odds with the more sober academic contributions. This is the chapter by Eggers entitled *How To Do Business with a Frenchman* reprinted from *Harper's Magazine*. Although Weinshall acknowledges that this presentation of differences between French and American business people is in a 'light vein', its intent in the book seems serious. In fact, the chapter centres on a whole series of stereotypes and rather crude essentialisms. Eggers offers 12 'laws' purportedly dealing with the basic differences between an American businessman and his French counterpart, which we reproduce in a modified form without commentary, letting them speak for themselves.

1. Whereas the American tries to think in a straight line, the Frenchman insists on thinking in a circle... The American mistrusts complex things and tends to oversimplify. The Frenchman...mistrusts simple things and tends to overcomplicate.
2. A French businessman mistrusts the very things in which an American businessman has the most confidence.
3. An American executive tends to forget what he said in a letter. A Frenchman never forgets what he's purposely left out.
4. An American will probably lose his typical enthusiasm for a project before a Frenchman gets over his typical reservations.
5. A French company prepares its balance sheet and profit and loss statement not to show its stockholders how much money it has made, but to show the tax authorities how little.
6. A Frenchman's thoughts are packaged in small and more specific sizes than Americans... This is due partly to the metric system and partly to the fact that the French economy is only 13 per cent the size of the American economy.
7. To a Frenchman, economic prosperity is a series of non-durable pledges of lasting value. To an American, prosperity is a tangible product with constant model changes.
8. A Frenchman feels ill at ease with anything mechanical as an American does with a domestic servant.
9. An American businessman treats his company like a wife: a Frenchman treats each of his companies like a mistress.
10. The word 'immoral' in English refers to what people do; in French it can apply to what companies do.

11. When a Frenchman is polite he is very, very polite and when he's rude, he is very, very French.
12. To the Frenchman a business career is usually a means to an end. To an American it is often an end in itself. (Eggers, 1977: 136–139)

That this is deemed appropriate in Weinshall's text speaks volumes for the status of the stereotype in MOS/ICCM at that time.

In contrast to Eggers', the Sirota and Greenwood (1977) study is more serious and made a significant impact. The study is explicitly presented in the context of pragmatically seeking to help US MNCs in their operations overseas. The study is in fact based on a single US multinational corporation and it is likely that US company values and preferences had been inculcated in the employees and therefore the subjects of the research. In many ways, the study and its methods are similar to those adopted by Hofstede and have perhaps become paradigmatic for an idealized approach in cross-cultural research in the field. It involved a survey related to work goals among sales, technical, and service employees, administered across 46 countries.[3] The research design, particularly the use of employees from one US multinational, may be of significance for the findings since the main findings show a 'remarkable similarity in the goals of workers around the world' (Sirota & Greenwood, 1977: 263). It is noticeable that despite the similarity, the authors seek out clusters, and this clustering compulsion had become very much part of the orthodoxy in ICCM by this point in time. There are some apparent oddities in the clustering; for example the so-called Anglo cluster rather inexplicably includes Austria, Switzerland and India. The northern Europe cluster includes Denmark, Finland and Norway, but Sweden is classified as an independent, as are Brazil, Germany, Israel, Japan and Venezuela – the first and last of these failing to load with other Latin countries. The goals explored in the research are conceptually drawn from Maslow's work and the methods are typical of questionnaire survey work. The authors conclude that the 'research data do tend to support the current models of human motivation developed by industrial social psychologists' (ibid: 275) – yet another universalistic claim. There is little reflection on the possibility that the theory, constructs and methods are all a reflection of the cultural and ideological inclinations on the very US researchers responsible for those models, although it is acknowledged that the emphasis on autonomy may reflect the theorists' own goals. But this is seen to derive from their professional environments, not wider cultural and ideological locations.

The Haire, Ghiselli and Porter paper is similarly perceived as influential and has been widely cited. Since we have discussed this work in an earlier section we will not devote much space to it here. We would note that again, like the Sirota and Greenwood study, this is a large questionnaire survey study of managers across numerous countries,[4] so paradigmatic for the large-scale survey work that becomes the ideal within the field. We also note that, reflecting the self-referentiality of the field at this point, the authors cite and relate their work to Harbison and Myers' study. Interestingly, although they recognize that reference to a Democratic-Autocratic focus on leadership is hackneyed, they still deploy it and relate it to Harbison and Myers and their use of a dictatorial/autocratic to democratic/participative dimension. This signifies an established and much-used Orientalist binary explored by Said and others. The leadership measure incorporates four elements that are clear reflections of US managerial ideology: (a) the belief in the individual's innate capacity for initiative and leadership; (b) belief in sharing information and objectives; (c) belief in participative arrangement, and (d) belief in internal control rather than external control. It is notable that the authors equate the notion of peoples' innate capacity for initiative and leadership with the core US ideology that all men (sic) are created equal even though these are not at all the same thing. Further, the authors maintain that elements b, c, and d 'follow logically from the first item'. They are then somewhat surprised that managers from other cultures do not endorse this structure and these values, and they suggest that alternatives represent a different 'psychological pattern' that somehow deviates from the logical.

We note with interest however that on page 299 they reflect that 'it is at least possible that this result is the effect of the partial digestion of 15 years of exhortation by the group-orientated consultants and professors of management', and then, quite frankly: 'our text books and lectures may have exported a new concept of management which rests on a concept of man that is less accepted abroad' (ibid: 301–302). They argue too that the results do not fully match those of Harbison and Myers and partially challenge the industrialization imperative, maintaining that the shift to more participative management does not neatly follow the stages of industrialization. They even intimate that the relationship between industrialization and leadership/authority shows up because most of the previous scholars had backgrounds in economics and this leads to a downplaying of cultural factors. In general, Haire and colleagues pursue a culturalist argument against forms of economic determinism particularly with respect to the deep cultural traditions in forming attitudes towards control and authority.

The chapter contributed by Hickson and colleagues is a reprint of their essay 'The Culture-Free Context of Organization Structure: a Trinational Comparison', published in *Sociology*, 1974. This is a paper and a position that emerged from the growing contingency theory perspective associated strongly with the Aston studies group in the UK. It is again an influential and much cited paper. It begins from quite a different position from the culturalist papers in this collection and indeed is expressly in opposition to the attitudinal and normative aspects of organizational behaviour that Hickson et al. see as prevalent in other research. They note that the universalistic presumptions of management and organization theory have led to a neglect of the organizational level in cross-national research. Their focus is upon the characteristics of organizations *per se* and how contingent factors that impinge upon organizations shape them and the behaviours within them. It is the non-cultural factors of organization size, ownership, technology and field of operation (Hickson et al., 1977: 356) and their effect on organization structuring that they pursue, as opposed to cultural factors. The hypothesis is that the relationship between these contingency factors and organization structure will be relatively stable between societies, expressed formally as: 'Relationships between the structural characteristics of work organizations and variables or relational context will be stable across societies' (Hickson et al., 1977: 360).

They further state that this hypothesis 'rests on the theory that there are imperatives, or "causal" relationships, from the resources of "customers", of employees, of materials and finance etc., and of operating technology of an organization, to its structure, which take effect in surrounding societal differences' (ibid). They report a study testing this hypothesis involving 70 matched manufacturing organizations in the USA, Britain and Canada using standard measures of structure developed by the Aston group. The broad findings say that the pattern of relationships between the variables is the same in all countries, although they allow for variation in terms of detail. Thus, for example, they assert that as organizations increase in size, that has an imperative and determinable effect on structural form. They therefore assert that the culture-free hypothesis is affirmed, although they acknowledge only at this point that the data is derived from three Anglo-Saxon societies and further studies are needed. The culture-free hypothesis is frequently reasserted by contingency theorists and others who doubt the culture argument. Of most significance is that this paper is a reflection of the structural functionalism and positivism that came to dominate the field, as well as the fact that the whole theoretical frame and the assumptions upon which it rests, as well as the methods and measures, were all developed in the West. The approach and the related 'culture-free' hypothesis inevitably add to the presumptions of universalism and indeed is how the approach has been incorporated and embedded in MOS and ICCM.

The final chapter is another contribution from Weinshall and is a discussion of the role and impact of MNCs. In many respects it echoes the industrialization thesis in suggesting that MNCs are an inevitable consequence of the evolution of organizational forms. A central point he makes is that the power and influence of MNCs as they grow is exceeding that of nation-states in some areas, reprising Perlmutter's earlier arguments. He seems to see this as both inevitable and welcome. As he says: 'I believe this is a development for the better in terms of the true interests, desires and well-being of individuals and groups throughout the world' (Weinshall, 1977: 385). He also relates the emergence of the MNC with the demise of colonialism: 'It could well be that, with the loss of its colonial outlets, the international company lost its sense of national affiliation' (ibid: 393). The assumption by MNCs of some of the roles traditionally performed by nation-states has some significant consequences Weinshall argues. We feel some are worth repeating here:

1. The multinational corporations constitute barriers to war.
2. They move technology, capital, know-how and more advanced standards of living from the developed to the developing areas of the world, helping bridge existing economic gaps.
3. They carry with them the most advanced managerial concepts and techniques.
4. They induce less advanced nation states, through their mere presence, to change their cultural environments (ibid: 404).

These are all clearly highly contentious assertions and are much contested in current antiglobalization arguments (as discussed in Chapter 6). The last consequence pictures MNCs as 'change agents' whose mere presence in the country is a force for transformation: indeed they are seen as 'the most powerful carriers of the convergence of cultures' (ibid: 409). Such changes, it seems, are only viewed positively by Weinshall, and this of course relates to the second point above, which represents a most sanitized and blinkered view of globalization. He is maintaining that the MNC helps to bridge the gap between rich and poor around the world, but there is no reflection on the fact that MNCs in fact depend upon and exploit precisely such gaps. The first statement above is somewhat shocking in view of some MNC's and international capital's involvement in the global arms business (as noted by Banerjee, 2008). His rationale for the statement rests on the notion that the transnational involvement of MNCs means that it is not in their interest for war and conflict between the nations within which they have business operations and dealings. This is a simplistic and naïve view of the intersection of geopolitics, international strategy, the military, and business – the type of intersection we noted in the last chapter. Weinshall's conclusion is a good way to end this discussion of his book:

> It is shown that on such matters as ensuring peace and understand-ing between nations, bridging the gap between the rich and poor parts of the world, transfer of technologies and managerial practices, convergence of cultures to developments in technology and the rise in standard of living, etc. – the beneficial contributions of the multi-national corporations outweighs, to a large extent, those of the nation states (ibid: 427–428).

Harris and Moran, 1979

The appearance of Harris and Moran's (1979) text is important since: it was a more popularist text than many that had preceded it, being more expressly aimed at a broader, non-academic readership; it explicitly sought to offer guidance to the international manager in functioning in a cross-cultural environment; and finally, it was successful, popular and presumably influential. The popularity of the text is attested to by its sales and by the fact that it has now gone into its seventh edition[5] (Moran, Harris & Moran, 2007).

Harris and Moran structure the book as follows. The first section details the orientation, skills and competencies of the 'new' multi-national manager (and it is really US managers they are addressing), and identifying the need for such managers to be cosmopolitan, inter-cultural communicators, cultural transmitters and change agents. The last is significant since the authors expect international managers to be change agents within the foreign settings in which they work. Change is not limited to innovation or the introduction of new work methods, but extends into the 'community' as a force for general development (Harris & Moran, 1979: 29). Note how this repeats the arguments of Harbison and Myers as well as those of Perlmutter and others in the Weinshall text.

The next section deals with the 'cultural impact of international man-agement'. Harris and Moran first define and outline the content and parameters of culture, which are conceptualized in systems terms with eight sub-systems that shape/constitute culture: kinship, religion, education, economy, politics, association, health and recreation. However, they fail to theorize the relationship and interdependencies between these sub-systems. The book moves on in this section to discuss the influence of culture on managing international business relations and they make explicit use of Kluckhohn and Strodtbeck's cultural problems framework. A discussion of culture shock and the management of organizational culture follow this. The next section is again very practical and considers the issues surrounding expatriate management, discussing cross-cultural training and overseas deployment. The final section of the book is of most concern to us since it presents a series of cases and discussions of the cross-cultural issues held to pertain when working in different parts of the world – from a US perspective. Thus, separate chapters deal with working in England and Ireland, Japan, the People's Republic of China, the Middle East[6] as well as within 'American Areas'[7] and sub-cultures within the USA. A chapter precedes this that provides an orientation to a mode of 'analysis' for examining 'cultural themes and patterns' in different locations by looking at examples from Africa, Europe (France), the Middle East (Saudi Arabia), the Eastern European Bloc, and Latin America.

To provide a flavour of this last chapter, themes identified for 'doing business in France' include idealism, social structure and status, trust and respect, personal characteristics, humour and style of conversation. Then, in relation to the first of these they say: 'The French tend to believe that the basic truths on which life is based derive from principles and immutable or universal laws' (ibid: 219). In talking about 'trust and respect' they offer a simple comparison with the US: 'A Frenchman trusts a person according to inner evaluation of the personality. An American trusts a person according to past achievements and upon other people's recognition, and ranking of that person' (ibid: 221). Regarding 'personal characteristics' they maintain that 'French people are friendly, humorous, and sardonic…Americans need to be liked. French people do not' (ibid: 221). These are clearly gross generalizations, not to say simplistic stereotypes. The book is, in fact, replete with essentializing representations of this type in relation to each of the cultures/countries/areas considered.

To illustrate further this essentialist torrent, we might usefully focus on what they say about Africa and 'The Middle East'. The first thing to note is that Africa is undifferentiated and groundlessly homogenized. Indeed, the authors maintain that the cultural factors they identify 'apply in general, but with appropriate changes, to all nations in Black

Africa' (ibid: 213). In terms of the Middle East, the authors talk expressly about Saudi Arabia and Iran,[8] but also make statements about 'Arabs' in general. Below is just a selection of essentializing statements about Africa and the Middle East:

> In Africa, time is viewed as flexible, not rigid or segmented. People come first, then time. Anyone in a hurry is viewed with suspicion and distrust. (ibid: 216)

> If a foreigner appears too task-oriented, the African counterpart interprets it as planned foul play. If hurried through business negotiations, the African suspects cheating. (ibid: 218)

> Africa is a high-context culture. In the communication process, most of the meaning is not from the words, but is internalized in the person. (ibid: 219)

> Arabs love the spoken word, tend to ramble and don't get to the point quickly. (ibid: 227)

> To an Arab, a mere yes/no means 'maybe' or even the opposite. (ibid: 217)

> Arabs are very emotional people and are easily outraged by even slight provocations. Don't regard these emotional displays as having serious implications for a relationship with an Arab and don't feel you have to act calmly 100% of the time yourself. (ibid: 228)

> Arab time sense is different than the Western time sense and they lose track of it. (ibid: 337)

There is quite a focus on so-called 'business etiquette' and guidance on appropriate behaviours in different cultural contexts. This approach has become a business in its own right, with a rash of books, videos and other things offering guides to doing business in all manner of locations (for example Brake, Walker & Walker, 1994; de Mente, 2004; Martin & Chaney, 2008; Morrison, Conaway & Borden, 1994; Sabath, 1998, 1999). In their text, Harris and Moran use the device of cross-cultural scenarios with optional responses as a learning tool. Through these students can learn to 'manage' difference.

By this point, we can see the beginnings of the formation of a canon of work in ICCM. In the next chapter, we unpack this claim, and illustrate that, despite the growing amount of published work on ICCM issues, similar representational problems of essentialization, exoticization and Orientalism continue through the 1980s to the present-day.

8
Representational Strategies Two: Establishing a Canon

Introduction

By the time we enter the 1980s, ICCM has become a significant sub-discipline within MOS, significant enough to suggest that something approaching a canon had emerged. By canon, we refer to: a) a set of core texts that are considered valid and referential within the field, and taken as (virtually) axiomatically central to it; b) a body of knowledge, methods and principles that are held to be valid and taken as a guiding frame for activity within the field; c) as a result of the preceding two, a set of boundaries that can be used to delimit or demarcate the field. The canon is built on the foundations established by Kerr and colleagues as well as other foundational figures such as Richman, Farmer, Haire, Abegglen, McClelland and others. However, it begins to coalesce more visibly and institutionally around the work of Hofstede following the publication of *Culture's Consequences* in 1980. This represented a watershed (Boyacigiller et al., 1996); indeed for some, it is taken as the birth of cross-cultural management as a *bone fide* empirical field of study. We elect, however, not to focus directly on the Hofstede text here, principally because it is already so well known and has received more than adequate critical treatment in the literature (for example Ailon, 2008; Dorfman & Howell, 1988; Fougere & Moulettes, 2006; Kirkman, Lowe & Gibson, 2006; McSweeney, 2002; Søndergaard, 1994; Triandis, 1982).

In this chapter we trace the development of this canon through the 1980s, 1990s and into the 2000s. We note the persistence of some of the strategies documented in the last chapter, as well as some nuanced differences in the representation of the Other. Although there are shifts in tone and focus over time, what our analysis reveals is the continued

essentialist, ethnocentric, universalistic and stereotypical representations of Others as the Western-dominated ICCM discourse develops.
The institutional framework proceeds to consolidate around a clear
North Atlantic axis with large parts of the world – Africa, Latin America
and the Middle East perhaps most notably – continuing to be largely
ignored or marginalized. Within the discourse, a canon of works is self-
referentially embedded, providing an additional boundary-forming
structure and set of practices. Moreover, orthodox paradigmatic commitments of the field, in terms of ontology, epistemology, methodology, ideology and ethics, become further entrenched.

The nineteen eighties

Culture, as an explanatory variable and point of analytic focus, significantly expanded its place in the discourse during the 1980s. There was
a strong culturalist tendency, not only in the focus on the cultural
influence or determination of differences in management as exemplified
by Hofstede and others (for instance Adler, 1986; Kelley & Worthley,
1981; Negandhi, 1983; Triandis, 1982), but also in the elevation of organizational culture as a significant variable in organizational performance
and differentiation and, to a lesser extent, in the emergent focus on intercultural interaction. Hofstede notwithstanding, two of the most influential textbooks in the field at the time were Ragu Nath's (1988) edited
collection *Comparative Management: A Regional View* and Simcha Ronen's
(1986) more empirically-grounded *Comparative and Multinational Management*. Both were core texts in the growing field of comparative management, and significant attempts to draw together the extant field to that
point: one (Nath) through an edited collection, the other (Ronen) through
a summary, synthesis and commentary on (mainly) empirical comparative work. It is to these texts that we apply an interrogative reading here.

Ronen, 1986

Ronen's book is a textbook aimed at students and practitioners, but
reports extensively on and synthesizes current research in ICCM. Ronen's
aim in writing the book was to: 'heighten the awareness of managers
and students... to the complexity of operating in other cultures and in
unfamiliar nations. The book provides a framework for understanding
individuals' cultural differences and the implications of such differences in forming managerial policies' (1986: vii–viii). However, whilst he
reviews earlier frameworks, there is no clear indication of what his 'framework' is. What is offered is a review and synthesis of research and theory

pertaining to cultural differences relevant to international management, focusing on the issues of communication and interpersonal relations, employee attitudes and motivation, and managerial behaviour
and leadership style. It is an expressly culturalist and strongly psycho-
logistic perspective. The vexed issue of convergence or divergence is
also addressed. The book begins with *Historical Perspective of International
Management* as part of seeking to establish a background context for the
review and synthesis. The first part of the book includes an overview of
culture and cultural difference and a chapter on methodological issues.
Part two is entitled *Attitudinal and Behavioural Differences*. It incorporates
Chapters 4 through to 7, and examines the differences and similarities in
managerial and organizational attitudes and behaviours deemed to be
influenced by culture. There are chapters on communication and interpersonal relations, employee attitudes and motivation, managerial behaviour and leadership style, as well as on convergence/divergence issues. It
is this part of the book that is of most interest, but we begin with a brief
discussion of some issues arising from part one.

What is noticeable in the historical perspective of part one is its
limited scope, and its Eurocentric biases. In the brief preface to the
chapter, Ronen does acknowledge that the Egyptians, Phoenicians and
Greeks engaged in international trade and business in other cultures,
but after that the focus is almost entirely European. He makes use of
Robinson's (1978) classification of the history of international business
into four eras across the timeframe 1500 to 1970: the commercial era
(1500–1850); the explorative era (1850–1914); the concessionary era
(1914–1945); and the national era (1945–1970). One can already sense
the Eurocentric flavour of this categorization; indeed Ronen states
quite boldly that international business in all eras was almost entirely
a Western phenomenon (ibid: 4). Given that he has mentioned Egypt,
the Phoenicians and Greece, and could have mentioned China, India
and a whole range of other highly organized and managed societies, to
begin the discussion of international management practice with Christopher Columbus is a reflection of a profound Eurocentric bias right
from the outset. And in a massive gloss of colonial engagement, Ronen
simply notes that 'European countries initially preserved their colonies'
traditional political institutions, but these institutions became more
and more dependent on foreign rule' (ibid: 5). In an echo of the Harbison
and Myers's thesis, Ronen maintains that the encroachments of Western business and organizational practices into other cultures dissolved
both traditional political systems and cultural values, replacing them
with Western equivalents.

Most time is devoted to the national era, with initial attention paid to the emerging nationalist movements around the world. Ronen identifies what he takes to be two new influential factors, the first of which is the emergence of 'locally responsible' political leaders and the availability of alternative sources of capital and technical skills; the latter, a reference to Cold War polarization and the support from the Soviet bloc for developing countries. Much of the rest of the section deals with the growth and internationalization of US business firms through the 1950s and 1960s and the degree of disenchantment and disinvestment in the 1970s. Moving forward, the 1980s is seen as offering fresh growth and new challenges, and it is the expected increase in cross-cultural engagements that necessitates more cross-cultural research and provides justification for the rest of the book.

The second chapter, entitled *Cultural and National Perspectives*, seeks to draw a parallel between comparative management studies and anthropology. Again drawing on Robinson (1978), Ronen suggests three approaches open to comparative management: a universalistic approach, presupposing few important differences across cultures in terms of management behaviour; an economic cluster approach exploring similarities and difference at the economic system level; and a cultural cluster approach presuming differences in behaviours and attitudes across cultures and their relationship to management and organizational behaviour. It is clear that Ronen favours the last, which he discusses in terms of a 'value systems' approach, citing the work of Kluckhohn and Strodtbeck, Vernon, Morris, and Rockeach. He also makes reference to a broader systems approach, and interestingly draws upon a systems framework from Harris and Moran (1979).[1]

The issues in Ronen's text of most concern to us are contained in part two: *Attitudinal and Behavioural Differences*. As with so many others, Ronen acknowledges at the outset the dangers and risks of stereotyping and ethnocentrism. However, although perhaps more careful and guarded than some, he still produces some stereotypical and ethnocentric representations. Indeed, we have already noted that the whole book is set up from a Eurocentric point of view. There are numerous examples of stereotypes and essentialisms dotted throughout the text. For example, he makes reference to 'Orientals' and their bowing behaviour, at the same time making the incorrect statement that bowing is culturally distinctive and has no counterpart in Western culture (ibid: 102). Still in the communication area and discussing goal orientation, Ronen quotes Samovar et al. (1981: 94, in Ronen, 1986: 107):[2]

> Westerners tend to believe that through their deeds and acts they can cause things to happen. Eastern people may be more content with waiting for events to happen rather than trying to cause their occurrence. While Western people are prone to actively pursue truth, many Easterners more commonly share the view that truth will present itself when the time is appropriate. How different views toward world and activity manifest themselves in different cultures is reflected in the following anecdote:
> If you ask a Hindu why he got only ten bags of corn from his land while nearby farmers got much more he would say it was the wish of God. An American farmer's answer to the same question would be: 'Hell, I didn't work hard enough.'
> The Hindu's explanation that it was God's wish is indicative of a passive activity orientation. And the American's perception of not having worked hard enough reflects a maximum doing activity orientation.

What is interesting here, the essentializing notwithstanding, is that this difference is glossed in the text as a difference in psychology, rather than, say, religious belief or ontologies, epistemologies, or metaphysics.

In talking about training for intercultural communication, Ronen cites Moran and Harris (1982) in pointing out that many communication training methods have been developed according to American priorities and assumptions about other cultures and that this is neither 'acceptable' nor 'realistic' (Ronen, 1986: 112–113). Ronen goes on to reproduce statements from Moran and Harris containing essentialisms and Orientalist representations. These include:

> Middle Easterners are generally very temperamental, and therefore they try to avoid arguments. Once there is an argument, it tends to be heated because each one in the discussion wants to be right;
> The management style in the Middle East tends to be much more authoritative than in the United States. This is a cultural characteristic...;
> Middle Easterners are introverted and shy until the mutual trust is built...
> (Moran and Harris, 1982, cited in Ronen, 1986: 113–114).[3]

In terms of drawing on and consolidating the canon in ICCM, we have already noted some elements to which Ronen refers. For instance, in his discussion of achievement he draws primarily on the work of McClelland. McClelland pursued an argument that culture influences attitudes and orientations towards achievement, and that across a given culture this impacts upon economic development. Ronen reproduces this argument together with its supposed relationship to religion and specifically the facilitation of an achievement orientation through the Protestant work ethic. He also offers a misinterpretation of McClelland when he implies that economic growth is simply a function of the presence of a high need for achievement within a given society, and that if two countries have the same level of achievement need, they will have the same level of economic development (ibid: 153). Further citations and discussions associated with emergent canon formation relate to Barrett and Bass (1976) on work motivation, The Meaning of Work research project (England, 1986; The Meaning of Work International Research Team, 1987) and, of course, Hofstede (1980). Indeed, Ronen allocates a significant amount of space to Hofstede's work, which concludes the discussion of attitudes and motivation. He seems appreciative of Hofstede's major empirical work, reporting it fully and with little critical comment. He offers a series of brief country overviews, which are designed to give 'the reader a flavour of the country specific characteristics identified in Hofstede's work' (ibid: 179–182). There are some noted essentialisms in this presentation and we quote a sample here:

> Australia: This country is moralistic
> Turkey: Emphasis in Turkey is on revealed truths
> France: In France there is strong emphasis on logic and rationality
> Italy: Italians are willing to accept affection and warmth but are high on masculinity
> Latin America: Rapid decision-making, little conscious planning, reliance on intuition, and emotional judgments are dominant
> The Netherlands: The Dutch are concerned with expertness and duty
> India: India is autocratic and paternalistic... the people are concerned with rules and emphasize patience and modesty; concomitantly they are low in risk tolerance and de-emphasize pleasure (ibid: 180–182).

One has the feeling of reading the contents of a fortune cookie!

Ronen devotes four pages to the issue of work motivation in developing nations. The implication is that developing countries represent a special case, an exception. However, and ignoring the homogenization and lack of differentiation contained in his use of the label 'developing nations' for a moment, Ronen's cultural analysis offers no analysis or comment on possible materialist explanations, nor on issues of systemic inequality and exploitation. Rather he argues that extant motivation theories are developed in the industrialized West and may not be applicable to developing contexts. This is an odd line since he barely questioned the relevance of such theories to other parts of the developed world outside of the North Atlantic where they were developed. One culturalist argument that he invokes is via Kanungo's (1983) study of worker alienation, in which he questions the applicability of Western theory and intervention strategies by arguing that they rest upon Western 'individualistic' value orientations not present in many Third World countries. Ronen notes that, despite relative neglect, there have been some studies of motivation in developing contexts and they lead him to conclude that 'work motivation [in these contexts] can be attributed to culture strength (lack of dilution by other cultures), as well as to the level of industrialization' (ibid: 183). Again citing Kanungo (1983), it is suggested that Eastern and Western cultures differ in socialization practices and that in the West they inculcate the values of individualism, autonomy and personal achievement. This contrasts with the collectivism and salience of security and social needs induced by Eastern socialization.

The problem here is that the terms and language deployed are already beholden to Western theory – principally via Maslow and McClelland. It is further argued, this time citing Orpen's (1978) study of black employees in South Africa, that work itself does not have the same meaning in developing and traditional cultural contexts compared to the West where the Protestant work ethic is held to have shaped work attitudes. We view this as a tendency for Ronen to use unwarranted assertions and generalizations about culture, cultural differences and their presumed effects.

Citing another study of motivation outside the West, this time Redding and Martyn-Johns' (1979) study of culture, cognition and motivation in Southeast Asia, it is again argued that 'Oriental' cultures do not cultivate individualistic values and hence employees are more 'susceptible to authority and formal control'. It should be noted that Redding and Martyn-Johns go further than suggesting cross-cultural values differences by arguing for differences in cognitive processes. Ronen appears to be trying to argue that cultural traditions have a bigger impact on work attitudes and motivation than the degree of Westernization or stage of industrialization, although he acknowledges that the infiltration of Western values and the industrialization process do change attitudes. Indeed, in developing countries, he sees the conflict between traditional values and the forces of modernity and industrialization as a dynamic shaping work values and motivation. In general, then, Ronen's analysis seems to be broadly supportive of the industrialization thesis. Traditional cultural values continue to be influential but are subject to erosion as industrialization and Westernization strengthen.

The next issue Ronen turns to is managerial behaviour and leadership style. In terms of the canon, he immediately acknowledges Harbison and Myers (1959) and, in affirmation of our analysis, sees them as responsible for the 'initial studies in modern comparative management' (ibid: 187). He also immediately cites Farmer and Richman's (1965) model and, furthermore, acknowledges that the cross-cultural study of leadership began with the Haire, Ghiselli and Porter (1966) study discussed earlier. In discussing leadership, Ronen maintains that it is a universal phenomenon, but that the enactment of leadership style is not the same around the world. The first determinants of leadership discussed are values, and he cites England's work (for instance England et al., 1974). Since that work revealed managers around the world widely supporting pragmatic values, the possibility of an international management that transcends local national cultures and centred on the values of pragmatism is mooted. The expansion of the Western management model, and in particular of management education based on the model, encourages that possibility. He also discusses the impact of beliefs on leadership style. The belief in the US that people can intervene in the environment and determine outcomes is presented as an example, as is the supposed finding that Indian managers are cynical and need to compromise ethics and morals to get things done (citing Smith and Thomas, 1972). Needs and need strength are also seen to influence leadership and here again Maslow and McClelland are cited.[4]

He next attends to cognitive processes, again drawing on the Redding and Martyn-Johns's (1979) study, which proposes differences in cognitive processes between cultures. Both Redding and Martyn-Johns, and Maruyama (1974) maintain that Western cultures are characterized by a 'unidirectional causal paradigm', whilst 'Oriental' society is characterized by a 'mutual causal paradigm' (ibid: 210). It is a fundamental difference said to indicate broadly that Oriental cultures have a 'less differentiated view of reality' than Western cultures. It is described as a paradigmatic difference that reflects variations in approach to science, cosmology, ideology, philosophy, ethics, religion, decision processes, logic, perception, knowledge, and analysis. These are captured in a table (see Table 8.1) that again constitutes East and West through binary differences.

These are sharp and weighty differences exhibited in Table 8.1 that rest on gross essentialisms and little is offered to support or justify them. Many are grand gestures, such as that of presumed cosmological differences.

Table 8.1 Oriental and Occidental Paradigmatic Differences

	Unidirectional causal paradigm – Occidental	**Mutual causal paradigm – Oriental**
Science	Traditional cause-and-effect model	Post-Shannon information theory
Cosmology	Predetermined universe	Self-generating and self-organizing universe
Ideology	Authoritarian	Co-operative
Philosophy	Universalism	Network
Ethics	Competitive	Symbiotic
Religion	Monotheism	Polytheistic
Logic	Deductive axiomatic	Complementary
Perception	Categorical	Contextual
Knowledge	Belief in one truth	Polyocular

Source: Adapted from Ronen, 1986: 211, citing Redding and Martyn-Johns, 1979, p. 110.

Others are generalized to the point of inaccuracy, thus monotheism and polytheism. Some are atypical, such as suggesting that the West's ideology is authoritarian while Oriental is co-operative, whilst still others are inexplicable, for example the contrasting of the 'philosophy' of universalism with that of 'network', whatever that might mean. Still referencing Maruyama and Redding and Martyn-Johns, it is further suggested that Oriental cognitions are less abstract and lead to a less differentiated view of reality than in Western culture. As Ronen notes: 'These authors suggest that as a managerial activity, organizing is difficult in Oriental cultures because abstract thinking is not very natural for people in the Orient' (ibid: 210). Redding has gone on to construct a whole picture of overseas Chinese management and business characterized by such things as low formalization, personalism, flexible structures, in the absence of formal planning (Redding, 1990). Whilst Redding's is a sympathetic and thoughtful account of Chinese management practice, it has been criticized from an indigenous perspective and for objectifying the Other (Xu, 2008).

Moving on, Ronen's discussion of convergence and divergence draws upon Webber's formulation we discussed in the last chapter. Ronen's way of tackling the issue is to draw upon his favourite clustering method and to interpret convergence/divergence in terms of relations between cultures within a cluster space. He offers a reanalysis of eight comparative studies through cluster analysis. In terms of establishing the canon, studies include those by Sirota and Greenwood; Haire, Ghiselli and Porter; Hofstede (two studies); Redding, as well as one by himself together with Kraut (Ronen & Kraut, 1977). The results of the cluster analysis matter less for our purposes than the rationale and mode of presentation. The main rationale is to provide a picture of the world that enables 'the subdivision of international populations of employees on the basis of their work values and attitudes to explore forces underlying the various subgroups' (ibid: 254). Broadly, the analysis suggests that three interdependent dimensions – geography, language and religion – underlie the clusters. Ronen also suggests, gesturing to the industrialization thesis, that level of technology and corresponding levels of development impact managerial style and attitudes and thereby clustering. A further impact on clusters is colonization, and the analysis reflects this to some extent.

The following clusters emerge from the analysis: the Anglo cluster, the Nordic cluster, the Germanic cluster, the Latin European cluster, the Latin American cluster, the Far Eastern cluster, the Arab cluster, and the Near Eastern cluster. Four countries failed to cluster and are labelled as independent: Brazil, Japan, India, and Israel. There is nothing very surprising in these clusters or that managerial values and attitudes should show some similarity within clusters and differences across clusters. The question is what really is to be gained by generating such clusters that simply move us further away from understanding the particular, local specificities, and their relational qualities to the 'global' that drive organizational behaviour. As we go on to note in Chapter 10 in regard to global ethnography, we need to understand cultures in circulation, not cultures as bound either in the rigid terms of the nation-state or the arbitrary borders of the country cluster. Clearly examining similarities and differences is central to comparative studies, but two things are at issue: that there is a poverty of knowledge and understanding of the localized, emic level and so any comparisons tend to be gross and superficial; and that there is a tendency to reproduce crude essentialisms and stereotypes of the type that we have revealed in this and the preceding chapter. In sum, Ronen's text is a scholarly one that summarizes and builds on extant research in ICCM. Its scholarly and sober approach does not, however, result in the avoidance of essentialist, Orientalist or even exoticized representations. Moreover, what we also see in Ronen is the use of a number of key resources that aid in the further sedimentation of a canon in ICCM, a canon that begins to operate as an almost axiomatic authoritative resource and justification.

Nath, 1988

The Nath text (1988) consists of a frame-setting introduction by Nath followed by six contributed chapters on management in North America (Allen, Miller & Nath), Japan (Namiki & Sethi), Europe (Banai & Levicki), China (Tung), Africa (Kiggundu), and Latin America (Quezada & Boyce). Nath joins with Sadhu to offer a concluding discussion. What is notable is the apparent diversity and international nature of the contributors. In the preface, Nath cites this as a distinctive feature of the book and maintains that in the process of developing the book 'scholars were selected to write chapters on particular regions or countries based on the dual criteria of their knowledge-based expertise and cultural sensitivity. Therefore, the various authors of this book constitute a truly cross-cultural team of scholars' (Nath, 1988: xiv). However, at the time the book was written, all were working in North American universities.[5] Furthermore, almost all had received their PhDs in the US, Canada or England.[6] This attempt to internationalize the text and its content is indeed laudable, but the question remains as to the extent to which the institutional location and perhaps intellectual embeddedness of these academics permit any critical distance from mainstream Western knowledge systems.

Such doubts are amplified to some extent by the approach taken and the content of the text. For example, in the opening chapter, Nath offers an overview that has its provenance entirely located in the orthodoxies of the Western academy. The framework he offers draws on that bastion of US organization and management theory – open systems theory. It considers the 'environmental system', which is composed of a number of sub-systems, including the 'cultural milieu', the sociopolitical context, and the economic (sub)system. This environmental system interacts with a second system, that of business and management comprised of *inter alia,* organization structure, human resource management, union management relations and organizational processes. Each geographic location in the text is considered (albeit somewhat loosely) in terms of this frame.

Furthermore, the text appeared in the aftermath of the publication of Hofstede's work (Hofstede, 1980) and his dimensional analysis is utilized as the main device for discussing the cultural sub-system in each location. Each chapter has a fairly extensive section positioning the country/region at issue in Hofstede's cultural dimensional terms. There is even speculation about the dimensional location of those nations that, at that time, had not been measured by the Hofstede instrument. Thus, it is suggested by Tung (1988) that China is different from Hong Kong and Taiwan (for which there *were* Hofstede scores) and so she 'hypothesizes' China's dimensional location in the absence of empirical measures. Later Kiggundu similarly 'hypothesizes' that 'most African countries would be associated with high collectivism, high power distance, high uncertainty avoidance, and high femininity' (Kiggundu, 1988: 173). Hence, Hofstede's conceptualization and measurement of culture becomes the organizing frame for discussions of culture and their relationship to management and organizational behaviour. The discussion of the cultural milieu in Europe draws upon the classic Kluckhohn and Strodtbeck (1961) cultural problems/dimensions to consider cultural differences (Banai & Levicki, 1988: 121–122). This leads to some rather crude generalizations, for example:

> Human nature in both the communist and non-communist sectors may be regarded as mixed in nature... in Europe it always has been assumed that people are a mixed bag of both good and bad. (121)
> Time horizons throughout Europe tend to be spread on a continuum from the past into the present. (122)

The Kluckhohn and Strodtbeck schema is, of course, a primary theoretical resource for Hofstede and was influential at the emergence of ICCM, as we discussed in Chapter 3.

As is typical, the more pronounced Orientalist statements in Nath's text tend to be made with respect to Africa and to a lesser extent Latin America. The first thing to note is that there is again a failure to differentiate Africa and treat its cultural and other diversities analytically. Kiggundu, who is responsible for the chapter, does, of course, acknowledge cultural diversity, note that it is not a unified region, and suggest likely differences on each of the sub-systems that the framework deals with. However, the diversity he notes becomes a mere 'context' against which the discussion of 'the management process in Africa takes place' (Kiggundu, 1988: 170) and he goes on to make many generalizing statements, in effect treating Africa as an undifferentiated and homogenous entity. Despite the caveats, he is happy to adopt the Hofstede schema and to then talk about the 'African cultural milieu' (ibid: 171), speculating on 'Africa's' Hofstedean dimensional location. It is in this uncritical, taken-for-granted and increasingly routine invocation of Hofstede that begins to sediment part of a canon for ICCM.

Furthermore, he tends to make statements about 'African' management and organization systems and practices that are presented so as to appear to be unique to Africa, but are so broad and general that they could have been said about almost any management and organization system. For example, he says that: 'Management has the power, the controls, the authority, and the rewards and punishments. The workers are expected to do their work and obey management's instructions and directives' (ibid: 223). Somehow this power disparity is seen as peculiar to Africa. It is then associated with fear among the workers:

> In these organizations, one detects various sources of fear including fear of punishment, fear of losing one's job, fear of victimization, and fear of fear. There is a generalized sense of helplessness – of not being in control of one's destiny (ibid).

In another example, Kiggundu suggests that people in Africa do not display organizational commitment, only stay in jobs for personal, social or family reasons and are motivated by individual rather than organizational goals. Again, the idea that such an orientation is unique to Africa is risible. These are classic Orientalist tropes that serve to diminish the African worker, to position them as out of alignment with the modern organization and its practices, as backward and somehow dysfunctional. There is also the classic Orientalist trope about stagnation. Kiggundu asserts that in Africa, innovation, risk-taking and entrepreneurship are discouraged and weak – and this is related to Hofstedean collectivism – but it is also related to an inability or unwillingness to change: 'There is little support for change even when the status quo in these organizations is unsatisfactory' (ibid: 224).

Similar modes of representation are deployed with respect to Latin America. It too is spoken of *en masse*; its localized variability and diversity erased in favour of a presumed homogeneity. Whilst the contributors here, Quezada and Boyce, again acknowledge cultural diversity – much of which they attribute to colonial legacies – they move on to talk in generalizing terms of a 'Latin American management'. It too is represented via Hofstede's dimensions, leading to the same types of essentialisms as noted above. For example, they say that: 'persons in Latin America feel comparatively less comfortable in situations of uncertainty and ambiguity' (Quezada & Boyce, 1988: 247). Workers are also again represented as rather quiescent dupes who are obedient, 'usually doing only what they are told – no more, no less' (ibid: 264). Again too, they are held to exist in a state of fear – although the authors admit this observation is based on a visit to a single factory in Mexico!

There are numerous other instances of ethnocentrism and essential-izing in the book, but we have perhaps signalled enough to make clear that the representational practices of ICCM that we began to map in the last chapter, and in Ronen, continue into the 1980s. This is despite an apparently international set of contributors, increasing recognition of such issues in a growing postcolonial literature and a profound reflexive challenge to methods of representing the Other in fields such as anthropology around this time (Geertz, 1983; Marcus & Fischer, 1986). We move on now to consider the next decade and two more influential ICCM texts.

The nineteen nineties

By the late 1980s and early 1990s, virtually every business school in the US and many elsewhere had given focus to international business and management and many had departments or programmes dedi-cated to the sub-field. The Centers for International Business Education and Research (CIBERs) were established by Congress in 1988 with

Table 8.2   Core ICCM Texts into the 1990s

Author	Title	Date of 1st Edition
Lane and DiStefano	*International Management Behaviour*	1988
Adler	*International Dimensions of Organizational Behaviour*	1986
Luthans and Hodgetts	*International Management*	1990
Beamish et al.	*International Management*	1991
Mead	*International Management: Cross Cultural Dimensions*	1994
Deresky	*International Management: Managing Across Borders and Cultures*	1993
Hickson & Pugh	*Management Worldwide: The Impact of Societal Culture on Organizations around the Globe*	1995
Fatehi	*International Management: A Cross Cultural Approach*	1996

the express aim of increasing the 'nation's capacity for international understanding and competitiveness' (CIBER, 2008). It is a network of US universities with a particular interest and designated centre for IB research and teaching and a stated aim of linking 'the manpower and technological needs of the United States business community with the international education, language training, and research capacities of universities across the country' (CIBERWeb, 2008). This expansion of interest resulted in a growth in the number of texts devoted to these issues, as shown in Table 8.2.

In this section, we have selected two of these texts: Hickson and Pugh's (1995) *Management Worldwide*, and Mead's (1994, 1998) *International Management*. Both are successful and popular texts, and both this time have a European, and more specifically UK, connection. We will have cause to discuss some of the later editions of the other texts noted in the next section.

Hickson and Pugh, 1995

The Hickson and Pugh text is a global 'how to' book, offering accounts of distinctive approaches to management around the world and how to cope with them. The default audience is the Western manager, and the text exhibits a number of essentialisms and cultural stereotyping, as well as the universalistic and ethnocentric tendencies of earlier periods. By this time certain notions have, through repetition, become cemented in the discourse as accepted ways of representing nations or cultures. One of these is the presumed relationship-orientation and familism of certain cultures within Asia and Latin America.[7] These cultural orientations are presumed to take form in the need to develop trust and establish a relationship orientation in business relationships before substantive matters are addressed. This motif is found repeatedly in the literature, and none more so than with respect to Chinese business systems (in particular the Nanyang, or overseas Chinese in South East Asia) (for instance Chen, 1995; Putti, 1991; Redding, 1990). A version of it is explicit early on in Hickson and Pugh:

> Where there is high familism, full trust is concentrated within family relationships and runs beyond them only where personal relationships have been built up, face to face. Hence the greater time and trouble expended upon entertaining and on lengthy getting-to-know-you conversations, preliminary to business talks in Arabia and

Asia, than in the West. Though, even in the West the dilatory niceties in Britain or in France may frustrate an American who wants to get down to business faster still (1995: 28).

Another feature of this motif is the notion that personalism and relationship quality substitute for impersonalism and contracturalism. In other words in relationship-oriented, or what, following Hofstede, are sometimes called 'collectivist' societies, the quality of established personal relationships is the guarantee underpinning business transactions and formal contracts are seen as unnecessary.

The reference to Hofstede is not incidental. His schema once again features strongly throughout Hickson and Pugh. Indeed, there is even the explicit linking in Hickson and Pugh of cultural dimensional profiles to economic growth so apparent in Hofstede's work with Bond on the fifth dimension 'Confucian Dynamism' (Bond & Hofstede, 1989; Hofstede & Bond, 1988). This is evident in the discussion of Sweden, where its Hofstedean cultural profile is held to have 'produced, in the second half of the twentieth century, an economically successful country' (ibid: 108). Elsewhere the dimensions are also represented as causative. For example, the paternalism and personalism of small Chinese businesses is held to be the result of high power distance and collectivism. Elsewhere the dimensions are typically invoked individually. The dimension of uncertainty avoidance, for example, is used in the following illustration, which also plays to existing cultural stereotypes about the featured cultures:

> Another way of fending off uncertainty, as well as by working hard, is through orderliness...In Germany, for example, the rules tend to be abided by and things work as intended, whereas in another fairly uncertainty-avoiding country, Brazil, the rules tend to be treated lightly (ibid: 37).

In relation to time orientations, one is told that: 'Older societies, such as the British, the Indian and the Chinese, are past-oriented and have tended to be conservative in management and slow to change' (ibid: 38). Such statements are unpalatable, not least, for example, in view of the extraordinary level and rate of change witnessed in China since the late 1970s.[8] We also see the typical Orientalist trope of cultural stagnation and regression here, especially when, again, the contrast is with a vital and progressive Other

– in this case, the US. The following are examples of reworking this trope:

> In a future-oriented culture there is a comparative optimism that things can be changed for the better. Americans have long been held up as the prime example of this, being more forward-looking than any of the European or African nations from which they originate (ibid: 39, see also pp. 60–61).

> Americans value time especially highly and are said to want an answer before their French opposite numbers have finished considering the question (ibid).

The English are represented as traditional, risk-averse, conservative and 'wary of the future' (ibid: 58). Even Canadian management is distinguished from that of the US and is held to be more like the English – 'conservative and perhaps considerate' (ibid: 68).

Later in the book, the analysis of Chinese management and organization is represented through an odd melange of references to communism/statism, traditional or ancient culture, and Hofstedean dimensions. There is the by now familiar tendency to homogenize. Little is done to differentiate the 'mainland' Chinese from the Chinese in the diaspora around South East Asia and beyond. It makes for a superficial and confusing analysis and one that leads unsurprisingly to typical Orientalist representations. All the usual suspects are there from the iron rice bowl, to *guanxi*, through to harmony and personalism (see ibid: 167–171). For example, a presumed and essentialist 'personalism' is deployed to explain low levels of organizational formalization and that in negotiations the 'Chinese' constrain their 'emotional self expression' (ibid: 168). There is a similar representational practice with respect to Japan. The reader is presented with a brief array of cultural stereotypes: respect for age and status (ibid: 175), collectivism and relationship-orientation (ibid: 176), and patience and long-term time orientation (ibid), and these are used as if they explained the behaviour of all Japanese people.

The Orientalist trope of representing most non-Western (or more accurately in this case, non-US) power and leadership as authoritarian and autocratic, contrasted with a more benign and democratic mode in the West, features here too and throughout the text. It is illustrated in the discussion of African, Arab and Indian cultures. For example, it is suggested that 'Egyptian managers, in an upward-looking, high power distance Arab culture, are unlikely to find it easy to delegate authority, or to be flexible in executing decisions or to respond well to criticism' (ibid: 214).[9] Indian management is similarly represented and again the cause of its current 'imperious' form is held to reside in long-standing traditions:

> Indian management inherits a long history of aloof, imperious rule. It is inclined to maintain tight control at the top and to minimize delegation, even in larger organizations at a size which usually prompts Western managements to decentralize. Managers value status and power comparatively highly, in patriarchal tradition where this is naturally so (ibid: 243).

The Orientalist practice of suggesting stagnation in traditions and of unchangeable nature is very apparent again. There are other subtle disparagements of Indian culture and management too. On page 243, it is argued that Indian managers evaluate actions and performance in a 'moralistic' manner, as much as in terms of efficiency, and that traditional and paternalistic values provide the basis for a moral component in management action that, however, erodes efficiency. The Orientalist trope of the irrationality of the Other is implied here, but is even more apparent a couple of pages later when it is stated that 'whilst managers may talk in the same ostensibly rational managerial language as is spoken by managers worldwide (sic), they may act in a more emotive manner which goes deeper' (ibid: 245).

With respect to Africa, we once again find an unwarranted homogenization such that the authors do not discuss individual countries, just an undifferentiated 'Sub-Saharan Africa'. This region in its entirety is, broadly speaking, disparaged as organizationally and managerially incompetent. For example, on page 235, Hickson and Pugh assert that: 'The strain on the high echelons contributes to the lack of success in managing large-scale, complex projects and organizations, which are beyond the capacity of those at the top to oversee and control... Their in-trays overflow and they cannot attend to it all'. The Hickson and Pugh text, whilst reporting academic research, is popularist in tone and certainly reverts to the stereotype alarmingly. It also cements the trade in some common representations that are by now coming to have a taken-for-granted quality, for example around the notion of collectivism and personalism in Asia and beyond and what that means for business relations and organizational behaviour.

Mead, 1998

Mead's *International Management: Cross Cultural Dimensions* was first published in 1994, but the analysis here is from the second edition of

1998. We chose it, in part, because Mead is a UK academic and we wanted some balance to the US representation of the field. As the title suggests, the text has a broadly culturalist orientation and this is reflected heavily in the cultural frameworks he discusses in Chapter 3 as the basis for 'comparing cultures', including Kluckhohn and Strodtbeck's (1961) basic cultural orientations. Despite being UK-located, the discussion of these orientations is, right from the outset, put in terms of using the US as the yardstick. The text then deals with Hall's (1976) treatment of high-and low-context cultures before moving through Laurent's (1983) early work on comparative managers to focus on Hofstede's dimensions, the last taking up almost half the chapter. The rest of the book deals with a range of managerial issues and the implications of culture for the way they are approached. It includes chapters on motivation, negotiations, organizational structure and change, as well as others devoted to managing a cross- or multinational organization. The account is functionalist – in the sense that the study of culture is advocated for managers of organizations so that they can 'explain and predict the behaviour of its members' (1998: 1, see also p. 6).

The use of the above culturalist resources provides plenty of scope for reproducing essentialist representations. Thus, to begin, on page 24, Mead states that: 'Mainstream United States culture is optimistic insofar that any achievement is thought possible if worked for, and humanity is ultimately perfectable'. A page later the presumed time orientation and relationship to the environment of US culture is reflected upon: 'Americans tend to believe that a better future can be planned and controlled'. Then the typical contrastive Other, the Arabic world, is presented. Arab culture is represented as 'fatalistic towards attempts to change the world. Humanity can do little on its own to achieve success or avert disaster'. Other stereotypes and essentialisms are pervasive, for example on page 58: 'Japanese have a relatively low intolerance of uncertainty'.

One of the noticeable issues with this text is the strategy of using essentialisms to critique essentialisms. Despite making almost canonical use of Hofstede's dimensions, Mead does offer some criticisms by pointing to variations in manifestations of the dimensions. One example is from Thailand where it is asserted (following Brummelhuis, 1984) that a form of individualism exists, despite Hofstede reporting Thailand as a collectivist culture. Mead argues that the Thai concept of individualism needs to be interpreted in terms of avoidance and distrust of authority, and comments that: 'The individual's preoccupation is not so much with self-realization and autonomy as with adaptation to the social or cosmological environment' (ibid: 44–45). The point we are making here is that Mead's criticism of Hofstede's dimensionalizing is made by invoking yet another essentialism about Thai people and culture.

Again with reference to Hofstede, Mead also reproduces the rather spurious links between dimensional location and economic development and performance we witnessed in Hickson and Pugh. Mead repeats this by stating that: 'A general correlation occurs between wealth and individualism... the wealthier countries tend to be more individualist and the poorer more collectivist' (ibid: 443–444). Such relationships are heavily historically dependent and not well theorized. Apart from this presumed relationship between individualism and wealth/economic success, Hofstede had more particularly pursued the relationship with respect to the fifth dimension he co-developed with Michael Bond, which originally was labelled 'Confucian Dynamism', but subsequently renamed 'Long Term Orientation'. Again simple correlations between GDP growth and dimension scores for a range of countries purport to show the link. Theoretically strained at best, a different time series puts the whole relationship under pressure and certainly the relationship has been subject to criticism (McSweeney, 2002; Yeh & Lawrence, 1995).

Another notable aspect of Mead's text is that, perhaps reflecting changes in the discourse by the 1990s, Mead is somewhat reflexive about the colonial legacy that colours international management, not something apparent in earlier works. He argues that international managers cannot 'expect to force-fit members of another culture into his/her own cultural norms' (ibid: 16) and then goes on:

> The history of colonialism shows that the great powers making repeated attempts to enforce their value systems upon others eventually failed. The organization that attempts to impose its behavioural norms upon unwilling employees from another culture faces an uphill battle (ibid: 17).

Interestingly, he is at pains to point out that this is not a moral imperative but a practical expediency. Later, during an odd discussion of Saudi Arabia and the first Gulf War, he also says: 'Invasions by Western colonialists profoundly influenced cultures in the less-developed economies during the nineteenth century. But the significance of these changes was unclear to contemporary observers – and may still be unclear today' (ibid: 59). However, Mead is not at all impelled to embark upon any kind of postcolonial theorization to examine and clarify such effects.

Despite the recognition of cultural variability and the possibilities of cultural change, the text still tends to engage in Western-centred universalism. The international manager, regardless of context and location, is held to practice 'standard management roles' (ibid: 11). Mead draws on Mintzberg's classic description of managerial roles to present this etic view of the management task. Culture is held to bring mere nuances in the exercising of these universalistic roles. Another feature, one common to most of these culturalist texts, is the de-politicization and the disembedding of behaviour from a full historical, sociopolitical and ideological context. The focus on culture and its impact causes a negation of other factors in shaping organizational identities, values and behaviour. This is signalled at the start of the book when Mead tells us that: 'This book shows why the international manager needs to understand NATIONAL CULTURE. National culture influences how managers and employees make decisions and interpret their roles' (ibid: 3). This 'bolding' of 'NATIONAL CULTURE' eschews any consideration of nation as a sociopolitical, economic or ideological construction, or any inkling of how such things might influence organizational behaviour. There is an interesting illustration of this depoliticization through cultural focus later on when talking about female employment in Japan. The text asserts that:

> After marriage, most Japanese females are still expected to stay at home and rear children, and this usually means giving up their careers...Given this cultural trait, it is rational that Japanese companies should hesitate to recruit and train unmarried women to managerial posts when they are likely to quit the job on marrying (ibid: 56).

There are a number of important issues embodied by this quote. The obvious one is the attempted justification of gendered organizational practices by suggesting that the requirement for women to take up child rearing responsibilities legitimizes inequitable employment practices. The situation is argued to provide 'rational' grounds for companies not to employ women in managerial roles – even when they are single. But what is also of note is that it is culture that is held to be responsible for this state of affairs. The take-up of the child rearing role is held to be a 'cultural trait' and particular employment practices follow from that; there is no discussion of the material, economic, historical, political conditions that could be analysed to explain this situation let alone any reference to gender politics or systems of patriarchy.

The text does go on to suggest that external factors (notably economic) had influenced the opportunities for women in the economy – but then when the environment altered again (for example the economic crisis of the mid-1990s) things reverted to their earlier position due, it is maintained, to the force of the underlying culture. So culture remains supreme as the determining mechanism.

There is a classic exhibition of Orientalism on page 67 when Mead comments on Islam and states that: 'Islam teaches that language has divine origins, is precise, and so no useful distinction can be drawn between the dictionary definition of a word and its significance'. He suggests that this view leads, amongst other things, to a dependence on rote learning in schools and even universities. Whilst the Koran may be considered as divinely given, it is patently wrong to assert that this equates to a general view of language as consisting of single, fixed and unitary meanings. This is an Orientalist travesty that plays on an Orientalist stultification trope. As the respected Islamists Murata and Chittick tell us 'Muslims have disagreed over the exact interpretation of Koranic verses as much as followers of other religions have disagreed over their own scriptures. One of the sources of the richness of Islamic intellectual history is the variety of interpretations provided for the same verses' (Murata & Chittick, 1994: vii). They also note that Muslims will often cite the Prophet as saying that every verse in the Koran has seven meanings and remind us that:

> The language of the Koran is synthetic and imaginistic – each word has a richness having to do with the special genius of the Arabic language. People naturally understand different meanings from the same verse (ibid).

In sum, the 1980s witnessed a continuation and a deepening of ICCM's distorted and distorting representational practices and a genuine sedimentation of certain key texts into the canon, with Hofstede increasingly occupying a central location in that. We move towards the present now with a consideration of two texts from the 21st century. The situation does not alter appreciably.

Into the twenty-first century

The texts analysed in this section are in fact later editions of texts published in the decades preceding. This is a deliberate strategy on our part to reflect the development of an ICCM canon, in which the production of new editions of key successful texts plays an important role.

Pedagogically the field is now dominated by a handful of key texts, most of which are in multiple edition mode, a feature of the institutional environment discussed in Chapter 3. The two texts under primary consideration are: Hodgetts and Luthans' (2002, 5th edition) *International Management: Culture, Strategy and Behaviour* and Lewis' (2006) *When Cultures Collide: Managing Successfully Across Cultures*.

Hodgetts and Luthans, 2002

The Hodgetts and Luthans text has experienced consistently strong sales since its first edition appeared in hardback in 1990. It is now in its seventh edition (2008) and can be considered as a leading textbook on IM. It is squarely aimed at student populations within the US academic system where it has wide adoptions. We are taking the 2002, fifth edition which is divided into four parts: Environment (four chapters), Culture (four chapters), Strategy and Functions (four chapters) and Organizational Behaviour /Human Resource Management (five chapters). The text claims to adopt a 'Framework-Functions-Futures approach', which purports to offer a cultural framework that is then applied to a range of universalistic management functions. However, this framework is not really elaborated and seems to be merely a heuristic textual structuring device. The framework appears to be contained in the first two parts, which discuss the environmental context and the 'role of culture' respectively. The universalistic functions appear to be those covered in the remaining two parts of the book and include strategic planning, decision-making and controlling, motivation, leadership and human resource management.

The student textbook orientation notwithstanding, parts of this text have features akin to 'airport how to books' that deal with business etiquette and offer advice on how to behave in a range of locations. This is often very superficial and trades in stereotypes and ethnocentric readings. There are many examples; ranging from the understanding of Chinese names and name structures, to handshake protocols and business entertainment. Indeed, there is a whole section of the book that deals with 'business practices' in different countries/cultures, and each abounds with stereotypes and essentialisms – this despite their experience of the dangers of overgeneralizing and stereotyping (Hodgetts & Luthans, 2002: 160). We take a section on doing business in China as an illustration. In commenting on *guanxi* for instance, there is the typical Western move of repositioning a positive social practice as a negative, as judged from a Western purview, by seeing *guanxi* as a form of nepotism with all the negative weight that carries within the moral and social discourses of the West (ibid: 155). We are also told to 'never single out a Chinese and praise him or her for a particular quality, such as intelligence or kindness, because this may well embarrass the individual in the face of his or her peers' (ibid). The section on doing business in India contains similar simplifications and banalities such as 'when foreign business people entertain in India, the menu often is quite different from that back home' (ibid: 158) and offering suggestions regarding dress-code and non-verbal behaviours.

The section on 'Business with Arab Countries' again brings us to an encounter with the West's habitual Other and clear Orientalist practices. The text points firstly to the extent of the cultural difference, signalling the irreducible Otherness of Arabic culture. American business people and managers are then warned that they will typically find it 'extremely hard' to do business in Arab countries and that 'a number of Arab cultural characteristics can be cited for this difficulty' (ibid: 159–160). Among these cultural characteristics are orientations to time wherein we are informed that Arabs are 'fatalistic about time' – 'Arabs believe that Allah controls time, in contrast to Westerners, who believe that they control their own time' (ibid: 160). This 'cultural trait' is then used as an explanation for supposed Arab helplessness: 'This view helps to explain why some Middle Easterners take great satisfaction in appearing to be helpless. In fact, helplessness can be used as a source of power, for in this area of the world, the strong are resented and the weak compensated' (ibid). They offer the following example as rather bizarre evidence of this supposed cultural feature:

> In one Arab country, several public administrators of equal rank would take turns meeting in each other's offices for their weekly conferences, and the host would serve as chairman. After several months, one of the men had a mild heart attack. Upon his recovery, it was decided to hold meetings only in his office, in order not to inconvenience him. From then on, the man who had the heart attack became the permanent chairman of the conference. This individual appeared more helpless than the others, and his helplessness enabled him to increase his power (ibid: 160).

The Orientalist Manicheanism continues, with the authors presuming a cultural difference between Arabs and Americans based on emotionality and reasoning propensities. The authors state that 'Arabs often act based on emotion; in contrast, those in an Anglo culture are taught to act on logic'. This despite the historically documented and much commented on contribution of Arabs to the development of formal logic and mathematics, also noted in our Chapter 4 (such as Nasr & Leaman, 1996; Rahman, Gabbay & Van Bendegem, 2008; Walbridge, 2000).

The text also makes use of contrastive value tables that typically claim to compare the known value set of Americans with others. Hodgetts and Luthans even reproduce such a values table taken from the Harris and Moran text. At another point in the text they use Trompenaars' (1993) dimensions to contrast Japanese and US culture (ibid: 148). Such a form of referencing is present earlier when they make use of Hoecklin's (1995) *Managing Cultural Differences*, as if this were an authoritative source. For instance, they cite Hoecklin's discussions of cultural differences with respect to media advertising saying that 'Germans want advertising that is factual and rational; they fear being manipulated by "the hidden persuader"' (ibid: 98). The French, they say, again via Hoecklin, 'avoid reasoning or logic. Their advertising is predominantly emotional, dramatic, and symbolic', whilst the British 'value laughter above all else' (ibid: 98–99). They also reproduce a table from Hoecklin in which she makes use of Trompenaars' dimensions to offer guidance in the construction of marketing messages, so there is a double level of referencing into what appears to have become the popularist canon of ICCM.

They also reference appreciatively the managerial values work of England and colleagues and Ronen's work on cultural clusters, maintaining that this work offers practical value to international managers. What the Hodgetts and Luthans text signals clearly though is that, by this point in time, textbooks reference and draw authoritatively on a nascent canon of work on international and comparative management, with Hofstede firmly at the centre. An examination of the book's index reveals that easily the two most cited authors are Hofstede and Trompenaars, closely followed by Hampden-Turner, mostly through his co-authorship with Trompenaars. Others frequently cited include Adler, Haire Ghiselli and Porter, Likert, Ronen and Tung.[10]

Lewis, 2006

Moving on, the Lewis text, *When Cultures Collide: Managing Successfully Across Cultures*, first published in 1996, is a 'how to' guide and is expressly aimed at the practitioner. The book is in its third edition (Lewis, 2006) – and it is to that edition that we will refer – and is a commercial success, having sold over 50,000 copies and been the selection for the US Book of the Month Club in 1997.[11] It is clearly a culturalist book and the author argues that the roots of national cultures are deep-seated, robust and consequential. With an informed understanding of such cultural roots we can, he argues confidently, 'foresee and calculate with a surprising degree of accuracy how others will react to our plans for them' (Lewis, 2006: xvi). A working knowledge of cultural differences, which the book offers to provide, gives international managers the means to avoid 'unpleasant surprises' and interact successfully with other nationalities. He talks in the preface about identifying 'national psychology and characteristics', trading in the outmoded notion of national character. Indeed, he acknowledges that identifying national characteristics is 'treading a minefield of inaccurate assessment and surprising exception' (ibid: xvii). Deliberately inverting common stereotypes, he goes on to suggest that there may well be 'excitable Finns, wooden Italians, cautious Americans and charismatic Japanese', but there are also national norms, such that, as he suggests, Italians are in general more loquacious than Finns. He also acknowledges the risk of stereotyping when he constructs generalizations and talks about the typical Italian, German, American and so on. However, this does not prevent him from engaging in the regime of the stereotype repeatedly and radically throughout the text. Interestingly, he does acknowledge that perhaps the greatest cultural divide is that based on gender, saying that 'it is quite possible that an Italian woman has a world outlook more similar to that of a German woman than to that of the male Italian' (ibid: xviii).

The book is organized into three parts. The first seeks to establish the grounds for cultural understanding, a key element of which is Lewis' LMR framework, on which more shortly. The second considers key issues in managing cross-culturally, leadership, motivation, teams and development, meeting styles and decision-making and negotiating behaviour. Part three is a practical guide to understanding and dealing with cultural difference by 'giving an in-depth analysis of the background and cultural characteristics of over 70 of the world's major countries and regions' (ibid: xx). Chapter 2 of the book, 'Cultural Conditioning', provides a basic introduction to the notion of culture and cultural formation. Both here, and in the acknowledgements, Lewis recognizes the debt to Hofstede. It is Hofstede's notion of culture as the collective programming of the mind that informs Lewis' discussion. The next chapter, 'Categorising Cultures', is a significant one in the book because there is an attempt to provide a framework for determining cultural differences. Lewis first makes reference to other such attempts noting again Hofstede's work, but also that of Hall, Trompenaars, Kluckhohn, Tonnies, and Huntington. Setting out his stall, Lewis declares the value of categorization in terms of the ability 'to predict a culture's behaviour, clarify why people did what they did, avoid giving offence, search for some kind of unity, standardize policies, and perceive neatness and *Ordnung'* (ibid: 28).

Lewis develops a three-part framework in which cultures are considered as either multiactive, linear active, or reactive. There is very little definitional explanation of these types or categories. He prefers to explain them by story and anecdote. However, they have very much to do with communication and interactional style. Briefly, people in linear-active cultures prefer to do one thing at a time and in a sequential manner. They focus on the particular task or activity at hand at that point in time and will not seek to multitask. They divide time into discrete periods and activities fit into those periods. Multi-active cultures, on the other hand, are characterized by flexibility, by the ability and willingness to view time flexibly in relation to tasks and to undertake more than one task within a given time period. As Lewis says: 'Multi-active people are not very interested in schedules or punctuality... They consider reality to be more important than man-made appointments' (ibid: 30).

The allocation of country to category seems to be based upon some kind of questionnaire, but it is not made fully clear. Nonetheless, a table representing countries on the dimension linear active to multiactive is presented. Germans and Swiss are positioned as the most linear active, followed by white Anglo-Saxon Protestant Americans,[12] then Scandinavians and Austrians, followed by British, Canadians, New Zealanders, then Australians and South Africans. Around the mid-point on the 18 point scale are what he calls 'American subcultures', which he notes as Jewish, Italian, Polish in a very odd conflation. At the other extreme are firstly Latin Americans, then Arabs and Africans: note again, how these are all homogenized. Following these three groupings are Indians, Pakistanis (and he has 'etc' here, without explaining what that might be). Next come Spanish, southern Italians, 'Mediterranean peoples', followed by Polynesians, then Portuguese, and Russians and other Slavs, and Chileans as we head towards the middle of the scale again. A table is presented with long lists of characteristics purportedly relevant to each type, some 30 items per column. We do not propose to reproduce that here, but will give a selection (see Table 8.3).

Lewis illustrates reactive (or listening) cultures by representing them as people who 'rarely initiate action or discussion, preferring to listen to and establish the other's position first, then react to it and formulate their own' (ibid: 32). He positions Japan as the most reactive culture, followed by China, Taiwan, Singapore and Hong Kong, Finland, Korea,

Table 8.3 Elements of Lewis' LMR Framework

Linear-active	Multiactive	Reactive
Introvert	Extrovert	Introvert
Quiet	Talkative	Silent
Does one thing at a time	Does several things at the time	Reacts
Sticks to facts	Juggles facts	Statements are promises
Unemotional	Emotional	Quietly caring
Follows correct procedures	Pulls strings	Networks
Completes action chains	Completes human transactions	Reacts to partner
Confronts with logic	Confronts emotionally	Avoids confrontation

Source: Adapted from Lewis, 2006.

Turkey, Vietnam and Cambodia and Laos, Malaysia and Indonesia, and the Pacific Islands. He also has Sweden and Britain as occasionally reactive cultures. Another difference he draws is interaction style, suggesting that monologue is the preferred style in reactive cultures, whereas in linear active and multiactive, it is dialogue. It is argued that reactive cultures excel in 'subtle, non-verbal indications, which compensates for the absence of frequent interjections' (ibid: 37). A little later it is stated that reactive people have large reserves of energy, that they are economical in movement and effort, do not waste time reinventing the wheel, that they are seldom aggressive, and rarely aspire to leadership. This represents another set of gross generalizations and essentialisms for which the evidence is apparently purely anecdotal.

Lewis elaborates on the cultural types and in doing so produces a veritable plethora of Orientalist and essentialist representations. For example, he states that 'Latin Americans, Arabs, and Africans are multi-active in the extreme. They are excitable, emotional, very human, mostly non-affluent and often suffer from previous economic exploitation or cultural larceny. Turkey and Iran, with more Eastern culture intact, are furthest from the multi-active point' (ibid: 46). Such all-embracing and gross homogenizations are rare, even in this discursive terrain – all Latins, Africans and Arabs are 'excitable' and 'emotional'. The additional characteristic of 'humanness' is virtually inexplicable, whilst the invocation of economic deprivation and colonial exploitation is simplistic and out of place.

A graphic representation shows Belgium at the mid-point on the linear active – multiactive dimension, Canada at the mid-point of the linear-active – reactive dimension, and India at the mid-point of the multiactive – reactive dimension. Lewis argues that these positions are positive and productive for the nations concerned. He then somewhat inexplicably suggests that Canada, 'because of massive immigration and intelligent government cultural care, is the most multicultural country in the world' (ibid). He says of Indians that they are natural orators and communicators and have 'combined these natural skills and warmth with Eastern wisdom and courtesy' (ibid: 46–47). Then in talking about Singapore he suggests that Lee Kuan Yew exercised brilliant economic management, which is seen as result of 'combining his innate Confucianism with his degree from Cambridge', and succeeded in pushing Singaporeans to the borders of linear-activity in spite of their Chineseness! Then Koreans, whilst characterized by correctness and surface courtesy, 'actually suppress seething multi-active emotion, even tendencies towards violence, more than any other Asians. They frequently demonstrate explosive rage or unreliability *vis-à-vis* foreign partners or among themselves' (ibid: 47). He suggests that Indonesians and Filipinas have developed into cultural hybrids due to their extensive colonization – why hybridization should be more pronounced here than in other extensively colonized locations is not made clear. These are amongst some of the most excessive essentialisms in the literature.

In part three of the book, Lewis offers 'cross-cultural' advice on how to behave managerially in an enormous range of countries (70 plus). What is immediately noticeable in this part of the book is that even though the coverage of countries and regions is very extensive, there is one obvious lacuna. Yet again (sub-Saharan) Africa is homogenized into a single category and allocated a mere 13 pages; this despite countries within Central Asia,[13] so typically neglected, each given independent treatment; despite too the recognition by Lewis that the area is massive (three times the size of the US), is comprised of '48 different countries', and 'qualifies as the world's most culturally diverse continent' (ibid: 563). Oddly, and in an apparent contradiction, it is asserted in the very next paragraph that despite regional variations 'there is a firm, enduring underlay of African culture stretching all the way from the Sahara desert to the Cape of Good Hope' (ibid). Furthermore, in spite of acknowledging that its productive and cultural human history goes back at least as far as 7500 BCE, Lewis only devotes a single sentence to its pre-European engagement history. The devastating impact of colonization is acknowledged, although persisting industrial underdevelopment is attributed to 'geography [?] and political unrest' (ibid: 564). It is argued that the colonial experience has engendered an 'inferiority complex', although this has been 'offset' in the second half of the 20th century, it is suggested, by 'black supremacy in athletics' as well as the rise to prominence of certain African descendants. But reference is only made to *African-American* achievers: not one indigenous African is mentioned for his or her achievements – no African intellectual, writer, politician, scientist, artist or academic. A little later, the author strangely drops his insistence on the roots of a deep and persisting 'African' culture and reinvokes the colonial legacy and its cultural influence, referring to Francophone Africa and Anglophone Africa.

In terms of culture and cultural values, the essentialisms offered are abundant. As noted, despite reference to huge cultural variation within Africa, Lewis still feels able to talk of African values and to align them with his multiactive and reactive culture categorizations.

> Sub-Saharan Africans are warm, joyous, tolerant, often laid-back and have a great sense of humour (ibid: 566).
>
> No people are more colourful or exuberant (ibid).
>
> The African woman is charismatic, reliable and possesses great integrity (ibid: 567).
>
> (...) they are a very tactile people in terms of hugging and squeezing (ibid: 569).
>
> Africans are not renowned for their punctuality or any sense of urgency (ibid).
>
> Africans are courteous listeners who drink in information, though some repetition is advisable (ibid: 571).

Lewis also presents a list of 14 cultural aspects (they cannot all be considered values) without any additional commentary. These are, again, revealing and include: 'cooperation before competition', 'love of dance and music', 'fatalistic', 'theatrical', 'tribal ethics/morals (weakens state concept)', 'tendency towards consumption', 'respect for magic', 'fondness for the exotic' (ibid: 566). In talking about manners and taboos, the following observation is made: 'The Western appreciation of jazz music gives white people a certain feel for African cultural sensitivity, poetry and drive'. The section closes, as do all in this part of the book, with a boxed item on motivation[14] where we are encouraged to: 'talk loudly, clearly and slowly', 'evince sincerity; be cheerful and enthusiastic', 'evince sympathy', and avoid 'being patronising in any way' (ibid: 575) as well as to 'shed any hint of ex-colonial style'! (ibid: 574).

Lewis also deals with the 'Arab Countries' collectively, but then proceeds to explore them separately and discuss the differences between them. The opening, collective discussion, once again positions the Arab as the West's essential Other in the starkest of terms: 'Westerners and Arabs have very different views about what is right and wrong, good and evil, logical and illogical, acceptable and unacceptable. They live in two different worlds, each organized in its own manner' (ibid: 400). This gestures yet again to the longstanding Manichean binaries that have characterized Orientalist discourse. The Arab is positioned not only as irretrievably Other, but, the intimation is, as associated with the negative side of a string of elemental binaries. But note that in essentializing the Arab, he is also essentializing the West. Lewis then proceeds to present a list of 24 'cultural divergences' between Arabs and Westerners that lead each side to see 'certain things in a completely different light' (ibid). A number of these also echo or even reproduce typical Orientalist modes of representation. For example, the first one connotes the Orientalist trope of decline or stagnation: 'The West sees Arab society as one that is in decline, propped up temporarily by oil revenues' (ibid), although Lewis does concede earlier civilizational leadership and the expectation that this can be achieved again.

With respect to ethics and morality, there is a somewhat cryptic distinction: 'Westerners want to be fair, but just; Arabs want to be just, but flexible' (ibid). This is tantalizing, since what is meant by 'flexible' is left hanging and the full contrast remains implicit. Indeed, what is interesting here is that sometimes Lewis avoids the sharply contrastive binary in favour of something more elliptical, but the positive and negative weighting and the Orientalist echoes are not effaced through such a device. The section on Arab countries also displays some of the worst examples of cultural insensitivity masquerading as advice on cultural sensitivity. For example, we are advised that: 'If you handle a copy of the Koran, you should show it even more respect than a Japanese business card' (ibid: 404). Then there is this equating of Anglo-Saxon oaths with reference to Allah: 'Oaths are quite common in Arabic, so even if you slip in one of your less vehement ones when you get excited, it would not sound offensive to Arabs, who bring Allah into their arguments in almost every conversation' (ibid).

In another horrendous culturalist interpretation that also trivializes one of the most devastating politico-military acts of the past

50 years, Lewis, in talking about the need to talk loudly and clearly within Arabic culture, seeks to remind us that:

> (…) the Gulf War took place partly because President Bush [senior] spoke softly and Saddam [sic] did not believe that he meant what he said [about declaring war, etc] (ibid: 403).

In this chapter, our analysis of a selection of leading ICCM texts from the 1980s, 1990s, and 2000s has revealed the continued presence of the same essentialisms, exoticizations and Orientialist representational practices contained in texts in previous decades. More disturbingly, perhaps, these practices would seem to have become embedded in a canon of ICCM knowledge that has emerged from the 1980s through to the present. This chapter has demonstrated the development of this canon through practices of mutual citation and the replication of core frameworks (such as Hofstede's) amongst leading names in the field.

Whilst our analysis has prioritized and illustrated the problematic, and Manichean, structure of the binaries used in ICCM scholarship, there is more to a postcolonial textual analysis than this. As Frenkel and Shenhav (2006: 858) suggest: 'while it is politically important to consolidate and essentialize the struggle against colonialism and its aftermath, the use of a binary perspective masks the hybrid nature of both the colonial encounter and the postcolonial condition'. In the next chapter, we give attention to the varied forms of response to the Western hegemony in ICCM, including hybridization, appropriation and resistance.

9
Engagement, Hybridization and Resistance

Introduction

The preceding two chapters presented an analysis of a set of texts that form(-ed) part of an emergent canon of knowledge in ICCM. Our analysis illuminated a persistent series of ethnocentric, universalizing, essentializing and appropriating representational practices that very often rest upon and reproduce Orientalist tropes. The focus on Western and predominantly American texts may have conveyed the impression that the engagements with the Other in this corpus of work are unidirectional, homogeneous and monolithic and that the non-West has simply been a passive recipient of these practices and their effects. This is assuredly *not* the case. In what follows we give recognition to the fact that we are dealing with an *engagement*, an *interaction*, and not a unilateral relationship between centre and periphery. We therefore examine the nature and consequences of that engagement and the various modes of action/reaction that the non-Western Other, conceived as active agent, has adopted, or might adopt. Such actions/reactions might include *inter alia*: assertions of indigeneity; modes of hybridization; forms of mimicry; reappropriation and return; avoidance and isolationism; silence. In this chapter, we illuminate and provide a theoretical discussion of instances of these different responses to the representational practices of the Western centre, and thus consider their role in resisting, challenging, altering and/or subverting the cultural hegemony and the dominant power relations that support it. We turn first to theoretical matters.

Forms of engagement

There has long been recognition within postcolonial studies that the colonial relationship cannot meaningfully be considered as unidirectional and monolithic, nor viewed as a homogeneous project with invariant practices and effects (Dirks, 1992; Thomas, 1994). It is inappropriate to envisage the colonial encounter simply as one in which the 'powerful' encounters and dominates the 'powerless', or in which the colonizer has all the power and the colonized none. Or further, that the encounter was necessarily a zero sum game in which the colonizer intruded, exercised power and gained, while the colonized was quiescent and always lost. Indeed, despite[1] Said's reliance on a Foucauldian perspective, he has been accused of perpetuating such a one-sided view of colonialism (Bhabha, 1994). It may be argued that Said did not push enough on the interdependence and mutuality of the colonial encounter, choosing to prioritize focus on the realization of the Western self through the construction of the Other. Other scholars have emphasized that colonialism is the creator of *both* the colonizer and the colonized (Stoler, 1992). Indeed, Memmi clarified that the conditions of colonialism 'chained the colonizer and the colonized into an implacable dependence, moulded their respective characters and dictated their conduct' (1968: 45). A tendency to position the colonized as passive dupes and disempowered objects of colonial effects has thus been decried and the agency of the colonized restored (Gandhi, 1998; Parry, 1987).

Furthermore, the categories and binaries, such as East-West, have been interrogated and their boundaries radically reassessed. Such categories and the relationships between them are seen to contain within contestations about their meaning, and thus the grounds for resistance to, their potentially homogenizing and hegemonic positioning. Of course it can be argued, in defence of Said, for example, that such simplified binary constructions were a kind of strategic necessity to permit any type of critique, rather in the manner of Spivak's strategic essentialisms (Spivak, 1987). In regard to our book, this is how we wish to see our critique of the texts of ICCM in the preceding chapters.

Although the dynamic, heterogeneous and nuanced nature of colonial encounters has been increasingly acknowledged and theorized, its recognition has always been apparent in some parts of PCT. For example, the Martinican poet-theorist Glissant (1989) insists that flow characterizes all cross-cultural and colonial encounters, and that *métissage* or creolization is the ever-present identity forming processes in such encounters. As Dash (1989: xxviii) in his introduction to Glissant's *Carribean Discourses* states: 'Glissant sees the world... in terms of an intricate branching of communities, an infinite wandering across cultures, where triumphs are momentary and where adaptation and métissage (creolization) are the prevailing forces'. He is also opposed and seeks resistances to the totalizing language and historicism of the West, which tends towards singularity, linearity and progression as well as binary structures of difference.

A key challenge of this more nuanced view of the colonial encounter is to acknowledge the diversity and localized specificity of the colonial encounter. As Parry (1987) points out, there has infrequently been the construction of an unmediated or unrefracted locus of pure opposition. This is not to say that resistance has not been manifest, rather that it has been diverse, situated and often subtle and nuanced. Such strategies of resistance have included: denial, avoidance and disengagement; reappropriation, return and repositioning; mirroring imitation and hybridity. As Spivak has insisted, any postcolonial analysis must always be conducted in a 'persistent recognition of heterogeneity' (1987: 211).

It is crucial that we acknowledge these insights in our analysis of ICCM. Thus, whilst it is important to recognize and surface the Orientalist assumptions and tropes inscribed in the texts of MOS/ICCM, we also need to attend to the inevitable processes of hybridity inherent to colonial and neo-colonial practice, including the construction of such texts but so often masked by them (Frenkel & Shenhav, 2006). It is necessary to examine the full and varied nature of the engagement(s) engendered by ICCM as a discourse and set of practices and not to focus solely on Western representational practices. In so doing, we reflect more accurately the nature of any hegemony that contains challenges to its authority and, on occasion, necessary accommodations.

Local and context-specific modes of management and organization

Theorizing the 'local voice'

We have stated that ICCM as a formal academic discourse has its roots in the Western academy and Western epistemology, but we are certainly *not* suggesting that there has not been research, theorization and writing about management and organization outside of the Western academy. Rather, we are asserting that the Western academy has produced a discourse that has achieved a cultural hegemony and supporting institutional frame that effectively pushes work from the periphery out, so much so that often it becomes invisible. This situation is compounded by the citation regimes and circuits of self-referentiality in which the Western academy engages. However, and crucially, there is, if one looks, a significant amount of work that resides in the locales in which it is produced and never penetrates the discourses of the centre. Sometimes this work has deployed Western ideas and theories, sometimes it is more indigenously informed and constructed.

A significant feature of PCT is the call to recover, resurface and give voice to indigenous perspectives and accounts, particularly those that have been marginalized or silenced through colonial or neo-colonial practices. This has been especially frontal with respect to those marginalized and made subaltern by the historiography of the colonizers and/or an indigenous, but hegemonically held, bourgeois elite. These are issues addressed by the so-called subaltern studies – a mode of historical recovery and representation that, using the concept provided by Gramsci, began in India with Guha's *Subaltern Studies* series (see the initial series of five – Guha, 1982, 1983, 1984, 1985, 1987) and spread across the previously colonized world (see Chaturvedi, 2000 for a summary and update). The core problematic is that colonial and neo-colonial elites had constructed totalizing discourses that had covered, in this instance, India and represented it in a narrow and self-serving manner. India had not represented itself; indeed, as Guha (1982) laments, India as a nation had failed 'to come into its own'. These elites do not speak for India – they speak for their own interests and in so doing reproduce a neo-colonial discourse that creates subaltern positions for the masses and severely circumscribes positions of intelligibility from which India can be understood. These are discursive strategies and effects that have analogues across multiple colonial encounters and we would argue that includes the discourses of ICCM. In other words, ICCM has come to operate as a totalizing and hegemonic space that polices its boundaries and squeezes out or silences the articulations of Others. The silencing does not need to be malicious. It can be an artefact of neglect.

There is an additional problematic famously surfaced by Spivak (1985) with the question of 'can the subaltern speak?' Briefly, the problematic is, if the discourse (in the original context that related to the historiography of India) is so dominant and totalizing, what space remains for those excluded from the circuits of power and influence that the discourse serves to find a space for articulation? The subaltern is excluded from the circuits of power and has no access to the spaces for articulation within the dominant discourse. As Spivak (1985: 128) says 'in the context of colonial production, the subaltern has no history and cannot speak'. The only space of articulation that has legitimacy and efficacy resides in the totalizing colonial discourses – to not participate in those discourses is to be effectively silenced, to speak within them is to engage in processes of self-misrepresentation that collude with and reaffirm the colonial knowledge-power nexus. Guha and Spivak adopt a different strategy. Whilst suggesting that the colonized cannot simply circumvent the dominant Western historical discourse in order to speak, they assert that the only option is to reinterpret and open up that discourse to alternative readings and fresh positions of intelligibility (Guha, 1983; Guha & Spivak, 1988).

Participation in the ICCM discourse of the centre requires that what one has to say is in conformance with that discourse, in other words uses or engages with its theorization, modes of research and interests. This is reinforced, materialized and policed by the publishing regime. Quite simply, if one does not produce work that fits the orthodoxies of the discourse, the work does not get published and one's voice remains silent – at least in that discourse and among the language community who participate in it. This, of course, does not mean that people writing about management and organization from outside the centre and outside the dominant discourse are absolutely silenced; they may find spaces of articulation within their own locale and with respect to their own language groups.

We can point to work on management and organization that exists but has failed to penetrate the discourse of the centre, residing in the specific locales in which it was produced. There are multiple sites where one can locate such work, but for reasons of economy, we elect to illustrate with just one or two examples. Notions of flow, interpenetration, and hybridization are no more apparent than in the locale we first choose to 'reveal' (or rather 're-reveal'): texts on management and organization that have been invisible within the dominant Western discourse.

Values and interpretation

The very history of the Philippines reflects processes of continual flow and cultural interpenetration. Magellan claimed the islands for Spain in 1521 and they were governed by Spain until 1898. European immigration resulted in significant populations of 'criollos' and 'mestizoso' and there was extensive trade and other flows (Zaide & Zaide, 2004). The Spanish-American war resulted in Spain ceding the Philippines to the US in 1898, and it would not achieve independence from the US until 1946. The population of the Philippines is large (90 million) and diverse with high numbers of 'mestizoso' as well as a number of indigenous groups, plus immigrant components such as Chinese and Indonesian, and a significant cultural impact from the US. It can be suggested that organizations in the Philippines reflect this cultural melange and multiple flows, with vestiges of Spanish colonial admin-istrative and bureaucratic practices, US and Western style corporate practices, indigenous and immigrant businesses and so on.

In spite of this diversity, there have been attempts to articulate a Philippine or Filipino style of management and business practice. One example is the work of Andres (1981, 1985, 1989), which seeks to con-struct a distinctive management approach that, he argues, is consistent with, and resonant of, Filipino values. Whilst he acknowledges some general principles or goals of business and organization, such as the need for productivity, he suggests that these need to be contextualized. He asserts that there are factors unique to the Philippines – 'local climate and national characteristics' (1985: 27) – that irretrievably impact the pursuit of 'productivity'. His premise is that to manage in the Philippines is difficult because the Filipino is complex – 'one of the most com-plex creatures' (ibid: 3). Economic development (broadly construed and including social development), which is his aspiration, means under-standing the Filipino, and to do that, Andres argues, we need to 'under-stand Filipino values' (ibid). There is already a risk here of essentializing the Filipino, making clear that such practices are not the sole province of Western commentators, although Andres clearly recognizes diversity within the Philippines. We should also note that although he focuses on values and values alignment, he does comment too on the particular material conditions in his country and their bearing on what is feasible or desirable organizationally and managerially.

Andres attempts to articulate some core and persisting values and to relate those to organizational behaviour, examining both negative and positive consequences. For instance, he connects Filipino values broadly to pre-Hispanic familism and then discusses a series of more specific values, many of which have a link to familistic relations and processes. Central is the value of *pakikisama,* which equates to a sense of 'getting along together' (Soriano, 1991). Other values discussed include *hiya* (embarrassment, shyness), *amor propio* (self-esteem, face sensitivity), *utang na loob* (obligation, indebtedness), *bahala na* (I don't care).[2] Andres (ibid: 14) insists that the Filipino manager needs to adhere to three broad imperatives: 'relational (*pakikipagkapwa-tao*), emotional (*damdamin*), and moral (*karangalan*)' (ibid). In relation to the last, it is argued that a manager needs to be mindful of moral concerns in his/her decisions and courses of action, specifically ensuring adherence to the proper form of the Filipino values of *dangal* (honour), *puri* (modesty) and *utang-na loob* (sense of gratitude). Equally, it is maintained, a manager should avoid violation of these values, particularly being seen as unable to get along with others and socially inept (*walang pakikisama*), failing to meet mutual obligations, norms of reciprocity and displays of appropriate gratitude (*walang utang na loob*), or displaying a lack of propriety (*walang hiya*) (Jocano, 1981). Andres (1985) proceeds to discuss all manner of management tasks and activities, from leadership and decision making through human resource management issues to communication and conflict resolution, and seeks to align them with these supposed basic Filipino values. It needs to be noted that he does this in relation to Western management theory sources[3] seeking, in the end, a kind of accommodation of Filipino values to Western management theory and practice. Before and since Andres's texts, others have reiterated an account of a unique Filipino management approach through reference to a similar set of values (Hollnsteiner, 1965; Jocano, 1981; Soriano, 1991).

However, there is an important corrective to this mode of representation that points to the risks inherent in the intrusions of Western (social) science into other contexts. In a very thoughtful and scholarly piece, Enriquez (1988) challenges the account of Filipino values that appears to have become sedimented in Western and even local social science and is reproduced in texts like those of Andres. Enriquez begins his discussion by stating that:

> The colonial character of Philippine social science developed and written in the English language is particularly evident in studies on Philippine values. Unfortunately, the majority of said studies rely uncritically on a borrowed language, inapplicable alien categories of analysis, and token use of the resources of the local language and culture (Enriquez, 1988: 124).

He is not opposed to an external perspective on Philippine life and culture *per se*, acknowledging that there can be value in an outsider view. The problem comes when the outsider 'happens to come from a supposedly superior culture, a belief fostered by the colonial relationship' (ibid). In reference to a supposed Filipino view of time, for instance, he argues that there is really nothing distinctive about it except that 'colonized peoples tend to be characterised as inadequate approximations or imperfect copies of people from presumably better cultures. The superiority of the colonizer's way of handling time is implicitly assumed' (ibid: 125).

Enriquez argues that the representations of Filipino values in both local and international social science are flawed and only deal with values in a superficial manner. The fault lies, he maintains, in both method and epistemology. He suggests that the presumed knowledge of values rests mostly on a colonial perspective and is derived using the colonizer's language. All aspects of the research design from which such presumed knowledge is derived have typically been conducted in English. There are all manner of risks inherent in this, but of critical importance is that although certain values might be unearthed in the process, they invariably fail to 'relate the supposed values and patterns of behavior to indigenous ways of perceiving and categorising the said values' (ibid: 125). Enriquez sees the application of indigenous words to the result of these Western research processes as little more than a form of tokenism that merely adds:

> a measure of respectability to otherwise completely exogenous and imposed interpretations of the Filipino way, but still basically a disregard for the rich resource of the culture available in the language. The organization and logic of the value system from the indigenous perspective is unwittingly ignored and a borrowed Western perspective is imposed instead on the labels for values and behaviour patterns (ibid).

In other words, the approach is an example of an imposed interpretation grounded in Western knowledge systems and modes of understanding, and one that ignores the conceptual and theoretical resources in the indigenous context and embodied in the local language. He further argues that these decontextualized and surface representations are constructed to be consistent with colonizer interpretations and interests and 'serve to perpetuate the colonial status of the Filipino' (ibid: 126). In that sense they are yet another example of Orientalist practice. He points, for example, to the elevation of *utang na loob* as a central value, which when decontextualized and simply translated as a 'debt of gratitude', reinforces the colonial status of the 'Filipino mind', including inducing gratitude for foreign aid even when that has imperialistic overtones (Enriquez, 1977). He also argues, in line with an Orientalist reading, that such representations result in a distortion of Philippine reality, with negative consequences in terms of derived social policy, for example in education.

Enriquez further argues that a lack of in-depth understanding of Philippine culture and language leads to a misleading focus on superficial values and a failure to properly identify more basic and fundamental values. He suggests that the value of *pakiramdam* is a more basic value to which the three more surface values of *utang na loob, pakikisama* and *hiya* in fact all relate. *Pakiramdam* is a 'pivotal value...[and] an essential requisite to all three' surface values (Enriquez, 1988: 127) He goes on to say that another value, *kapwa*, is the very foundation of Philippine and human values, declaring that: 'Without *kapwa*, one ceases to be a Filipino and one is no longer human' (ibid). English translations of *kapwa* often render it in terms of 'others', but as Enriquez points out, whilst in English 'others' tends to be semantically opposed to self, in a Philippine ontology, *kapwa* actually refers to the 'unity of the "self" and "other"' (ibid: 139). In doing this, and related interpretations, Philippine culture via its supposed values is appropriated and represented in ways that fit within Western knowledge systems, frameworks of understanding and ideological and material interests.

The work of Andres, whilst on the one hand seeking to function as an indigenous interpretation of management, actually participates in processes of cultural appropriation and relocation. Enriquez offers the same trajectory of misinterpretation for other surface values that have been reiterated in the literature over the years (including the misrepresentation of 'confrontive' values, and the misinterpretation of *bahala na*). Enriquez represents a good illustration of a localized re-interpretation, a 'writing back' that relocates and recontextualizes such representations, reinvesting them with alternative, more positive meanings. Western, or Western-inspired, interpretations have had policy implications, for example in education, and have been used by some to account for failures in economic and social development within the Philippines. Indeed, as Enriquez points out, some Philippine social scientists have even gone so far as suggesting the eradication of traditional Filipino values as a necessary step towards development. Enriquez not surprisingly demurs, wanting to offer a different and, in his view, proper interpretation of Filipino values, one that is compatible with 'progressive change and development' (ibid: 146).

We began this section pointing out that the Western dominance is challenged in part by the production of localized texts away from the centre by and for people within those locales of the periphery and non-periphery. The Andres text appeared as an example, but it became apparent that things are not so simple and that the flows, intersections and hybridities are complex and dynamic. Andres's application of Filipino values is hybridized, if Enriquez is right, through absorbing Western-led or influenced interpretations of Philippine values. It is also hybridized through his attempt to relate the values to aspects of American management. Andres has produced at least ten texts that pursue this line in one way or another, including some quite recently (Andres, 1995, 1998), and others have continued to deploy the values Enriquez decries as surface and decontextualized to describe Philippine management (Franco, 1986; Gupta & Kleiner, 2001; Selmer & de Leon, 2003; Warner, 2000).

Nonetheless, the point remains that localized work on MOS/ICCM can be located in many places around the world. The issue with respect to the discourse of the centre in ICCM is one of visibility and impact. The work most often becomes visible when some portion of it does get taken up or published in the Western publishing machine or adjacently. So, for example, collections such as that of Putti (1991), do surface work produced on specific locations and often drawing on work produced locally, in this case from around Asia. This localized work is sometimes informed by indigenous perspectives, but is also often hybridized and syncretic with respect to Western texts, theories and frameworks.

Hybridization

From the outset, the notion of hybridity has been a central concern within PCT. Originally the term referred to the explicit crossing of the boundary of 'race' and 'ethnicity' through processes of miscegenation – it is already a deeply loaded term since it derives from the cross-fertilization of species in botany and implies the notion of different species of humans. It led to fine calibrations of 'race' – white, creole, mestiso, mulatto, quarteron, zambo, chino, negro (Stevenson, 1825) – and was deeply implicated in the racial discourses of the colonial period. Indeed, Young (1995) cautions against the term's carriage of this racist baggage. PCT has adopted the term, but in ways that challenge and undermine this original use. Within PCT, hybridity more typically (but not exclusively) refers to 'the creation of new transcultural forms within the contact zone produced by colonisation' (Ashcroft, Griffiths & Tiffin, 2000: 118). An important aspect of hybridity, and significant with respect to all periphery-centre relations, is the recognition that there is a relationship, an adjacency. Hybridity occurs precisely at, and because of, the contact zones between centre and periphery, between the colonizer and the colonized. There are hybridizing potentialities at every interstices of postcoloniality and it can occur at a linguistic, cultural, political or individualized level and, we might add, at an institutional or organizational level.

It is argued that it is important to 'discriminate between the diverse modalities of hybridity, for example forced assimilation, internalised self-rejection, political co-optation, social conformism, cultural mimicry, and creative transcendence' (Shohat, 1993: 110). It might be suggested, however, that this stretches the construct too broadly. Certainly the use of the term in postcolonial discourse theory has been criticized for focusing on notions of cultural exchange and implying mutuality in cultural relations, thereby deflecting from issues of power, dominance and inequality (Ahmad, 1992; Parry, 1987). However, there is nothing intrinsic to the term that necessarily implies that power relations are somehow eschewed in favour of mutuality. One can still conceive of an interpenetration and interdependence within relations of unequal power, as Bhabha (1994) would affirm. Alternatively, some have also argued that a term like 'hybridity' draws attention to and ultimately reaffirms colonial and neo-colonial structures of difference and inequality. What might be argued instead is that hybridity offers the potential to contest such structures by inserting a moment that challenges and subverts any claim for pristine independence and superiority made by a colonial or neo-colonial power. As Young (1995: 23) has it, reflecting on Bhabha's formulation, hybridity can operate: 'depriving the imposed imperialist culture, not only of the authority that it has for so long imposed politically... but even of its own claims to authenticity'.

Within contemporary PCT, hybridity, as Young suggests, is perhaps most closely associated with Bhabha (for example Bhabha, 1994), but there are clear and significant precursors in the work of Fanon and Memmi, among others. All point initially to the tendency for the colonial experience to generate a response of mimicry wherein the colonized, in the face of obvious power and dominance, seek to mimic the colonizer. This may take many forms and include aping modes of dress and behaviour. Naipaul (1967) wrote about the 'mimic men' somewhat disparagingly, but also in recognition of the psychological tensions and distortions the colonized experience engenders. This takes us back to the racialized roots of the term and the concern of colonizers to construct a knowledge system around race and racial difference that made encounters with difference more manageable and that justified strategies of dominance and superiority. In the dynamics of colonial relations it was advantageous to the colonizer to have the colonized recognize the superiority of their values, behaviours, systems and institutions, to have them as objects of desire and to embrace and mimic them. Such a dynamic created mechanisms for co-optation and control. Hybridity then is a power effect that stimulates a desire in the colonized to approach that power and superiority so as to be part of or participate in it. It is advantageous to the colonizer, since it both draws the colonized in and facilitates control, and serves as a justificatory civilizing process. However, the colonizer also wants to preserve difference and distance; it does not suit their purposes to validate any presumption that the colonized and the colonizer are the same. The politics of alterity demand that distance and difference be sustained and affirmed. Hence it is mimicry and not absorption, a copy of the original, but still different from it, preserving cultural (racial) integrity and a distance within which control and dominance can function.

Concomitantly, the dynamic from the perspective of the colonized was similarly to have the colonizer's world perceived as an object of desire, something to be aspired to and emulated, but which could never be fully attained. The colonized was drawn away from his/her own culture but never able to fully enter that of the colonizer. The colonized can approach, mimic, but never reproduce the original, never become the colonizer, never attain their status or form. It is this failure and the self-realization of it that sustains the power distance and instantiates hierarchical relations of dominance and enables them to persist. It is precisely this dynamic that Fanon (1952/1986) analysed in *Black Skins/White Masks*, pointing to the tortuous double-bind that the colonized wrestles with: the stimulated desire to become white, to don the white mask and shed the black skin, and the recognition of the impossibility of that, of shedding the black skin. It is the traumatizing psychoanalytic consequences of this that most concern Fanon and it is a dynamic that Memmi (1968) and others have dissected.

Analyses of the debilitating and stultifying effects of the mimic experience were an important and influential contribution in PCT and the ramifications are still with us and have a possible analytical place within ICCM that has yet to be taken up. Bhabha, however, offers a different and somewhat more positive interpretation of the dynamics of hybridization. Whilst acknowledging the apparently impossible location the colonized find themselves in, and the radical ambivalence that Fanon reveals, Bhabha maintains that hybridity actually represents an *aporia* in the colonial project, a lesion in its power effects. He argues that in hybridization there is a failure of the colonial to reproduce itself and that what is actually constructed – both materially and discursively – is the hybrid, a mutated and imperfect replication. The mimic man, whilst on the one hand apparently serving colonial interests and standing, as it were, as an authorized version of 'otherness', on the other hand is an imperfect copy, a deformation or, as Bhabha (1994: 88) points out, ultimately 'inappropriate cultural subjects'. The invited mimicry backfires, and the colonizer is confronted by a deformed mirror that does not reflect a likeness, but a difference and a doubling, a hybrid in which the self can be discerned but now penetrated and occupied by a difference. This subtly subverts colonial discourse and practice and its attempts to penetrate and occupy the Other. Here is a space to play with. Here is a space of interrogation, new positions of intelligibility, and fresh spaces of articulation. This is Bhabha's 'Third Space' of enunciation in which cultural encounters occur and identities form (Bhabha, 1994). Indeed, it is the space for all cultural system and identity formation, since all cultures are formed in confluence and interaction with others. Hybridity offers the grounds for a questioning of boundary and of margin-centre relations. There are grounds, then, for a less gloomy reading of hybridization.

We take the view that there is, as yet, relatively untapped scope for applying the notion of hybridity within MOS and a most obvious and potentially fruitful terrain in which to do so is in international management and organization. Indeed, as noted in Chapter 1, Frenkel and Shenhav (2006) have already taken up this challenge. They embrace a non-binary epistemology and work towards dismantling the binaries inherent in the Western ICCM canon in three ways. Firstly, they provide an analysis that reveals the emergence of early ideas about management and organization directly from the colonial encounter and colonial practice. Secondly, they examine the processes of exclusion, wherein aspects of the colonial experience embedded in thinking and texts about MOS have been ignored and expunged from the management canon. Thirdly, they seek to illuminate where 'remnants of Orientalism' can be discerned, despite the masking, in the work of some texts that are in the canon. We differ from Frenkel and Shenhav in that we feel that Orientalisms have persisted in the MOS/ICCM canon right the way through to the present, and that they constitute more than fragments. They do, however, pursue the emergence of ICCM through the work of Harbison and Myers as we have done here and earlier (for instance, Westwood, 2001) suggesting that it can be read as exhibiting the interplay between purification (the masking of hybridities through the insertion of binaries and distances) and hybridity (Frenkel & Shenhav, 2006: 866). We now move on to illustrate processes of hybridization in the field of management theory and practice with respect to the relationship between 'Japan and the West'.

Japan and the West: Hybridizations and flows in management

There is clear evidence of hybridization processes at work in the flows of management theory and practice between the US and Japan. As noted in Chapter 6, the success of the Japanese economy starting in the 1980s gave rise to some intense interactions between Japan and the

West. Flows across this zone of contact have a much longer history, however. It is common to refer to the visit of the US naval fleet under Commodore Perry in 1853 as bringing to an end a period of supposed isolation of Japan and to see the Meiji Restoration during the latter half of the 19th century as the starting point for Japan's emergence as a major international economic force. It needs to be noted that the US pushed Japan into signing the Harris Treaty of 1858, which forced Japan to abandon its isolationist policy toward foreigners. These events certainly signalled the emergence of modern, imperial Japan, but Japan had already witnessed interactions with explorers, traders and missionaries from Spain, Portugal, England and Holland before then. And by the 19th century, Japanese were visiting Europe to study Western technology (Pacey, 1991).

The 'openness' following the Meiji Restoration had significant precursors. Indeed it is argued that:

> In Japan, the adoption and development of technologies transferred from the West may seem to have begun abruptly soon after the Meiji Restoration of 1868. However, the reality is that Japan was able to use those technologies effectively because a technically innovative culture had been evolving for a long time. This had been stimulated by a selective adoption of Western techniques since the sixteenth century, and by a much longer tradition of borrowing and developing technology from Korea and China (Pacey, 1991: 204).

The latter point is noteworthy since we are conscious that we are pursuing a West – The Rest structure to our work here and we need to remain mindful of the complex and multidirectional nature of flows, not just in East Asia, but in any zone of the world. Japan has, throughout its history, engaged with China and Korea; for example, as early as the Han dynasty in China (206 BCE to 220 ACE) Japan was importing iron and bronze-making technologies, rice farming methods and other ideas from the Korean Peninsula and China.

Japan, then, has an extremely extensive history of the flow of ideas and technologies across its borders and had become adept at adopting, modifying and incorporating them into its own systems. This continued in its engagements with the West from the 16th century onwards. Prior to the Meiji Restoration, Japan had a developed merchant class and refined commercial and organizational competences. The Mitsui corporation has roots that go back as far as 1683 (Pacey, 1991). This led Pacey (1991: 154) to argue that: 'Undoubtedly, the greatest of all

Japanese industrial skills inherited from before the Meiji period were those relating to organization and commerce, and these skills were clearly demonstrated by the way in which the introduction of new technologies was managed'. He also argued that there were important continuities between the pre- and post-Meiji periods in terms of technology 'both with respect to the long-standing Japanese interest in Western techniques, and in the persisting importance of traditional technology and local innovation' (ibid: 153) thereby acknowledging the confluence of indigenous and 'imported' knowledge and organizational systems. This already signals then, flows and interdependencies between Japan and China/Korea as well as Europe well before the Meiji restoration, which included ideas and processes associated with not only technology, but also commerce, organization and management. Thus when the West starts to refer to 'Japanese management' style in the 20th century, particularly post-1980s and relates it to unique Japanese cultural sources, it has already effaced, or to use Frenkel and Shenhav's (2006) term (via Latour), 'purified' it of, these hybridizing processes.

The above notwithstanding, the Meiji Restoration certainly did signal a significant reorientation within Japanese society at a political, economic and cultural level, and increased openness to the outside, and the West particularly was part of that, as was the more or less express drive for modernization. From 1868 onwards, Japan experienced significant economic development, with some of it attributable to various types of engagements with the West, including sending thousands overseas for Western education. The government was proactive in creating a context in which entrepreneurship and industrialization could flourish. However, it is the post-World War Two period that witnessed a period of phenomenal economic growth and development. The economy grew through a mix of factors, some unique to Japan, some the result of international engagements and flows. Importantly, there was a flow of ideas, both practical and academic, and we will focus firstly on one management practice around such intersections.

The circulations of quality control

As the modern economy grew, so did the institutions associated with business and management. For instance, the Japan Management Association was inaugurated in 1942 and it acknowledged the Scientific Management movement initiated in the US. In Japan, this was translated into the pursuit of efficiency and early projects were concerned with seeking efficiencies in heavy industrial production processes with

Mitsubishi and Toyota. It began to examine quality control issues in 1949. However, it was the engineer Kaoru Ishikawa who focused on and extended the examination of quality control and quality improvement methodologies in the post-War period. What is of significance is not the general awareness of Scientific Management, but the translation and uptake of the work of American W. Edwards Deming on statistical methods for quality control and Joseph Juran's work on quality management principles and practices. Juran visited Japan in 1954 at the invitation of the *Japanese Union of Scientists and Engineers* (JUSE), lecturing and visiting corporations. There was extensive promulgation of Juran's work and its local interpretation across the country, first to engineers and then managers and supervisors. Ishikawa, following Juran's focus on the *management* of quality (see Juran, 1995, 1999) and not just its technical and statistical monitoring, recognized the significance of front line workers and their 'leading hand' *(gemba-cho)*. It seemed sensible to him to extend the training to leading hands and have them work with their teams to focus on continuous, on-the-job quality improvements. The training was conducted with teams of around ten workers sitting around a table and thus 'Quality Control Circles' were born, formally launched by Ishikawa (then a professor at the University of Tokyo) and *JUSE* in 1962 (Ishikawa, 1980).

Juran familiarized himself with the development and use of Quality Control Circles and became a keen advocate of them back in the USA (Juran, 1964). In this sense Juran was appropriating and importing a Japanese management technique that was itself already a hybrid of US and Japanese ideas and practices. Juran founded the Juran Institute in 1979 and continued to advocate and promote quality management in the US right through to the 1990s (for example Juran, 1992). Quality Control Circles have been adopted all round Asia and beyond. They had a spell of popularity in the USA, adopted by Lockheed for example, but it was not sustained.

There are, then, some important flows and hybridities mediated in part by Juran, but Edwards Deming also had a profound impact on Japanese organization and management. Trained in engineering and mathematics, Deming found himself working on the post-war census in Japan. Once again, it was the JUSE that, having encountered the work of Walter Shewhart of Bell Laboratories (who had taught and inspired Deming) on statistical control techniques, invited Deming to talk to them and teach courses in 1950. Deming was to return to Japan on numerous occasions to consult, teach and advise. His approach was much broader than mere statistical quality control and encompassed a whole management outlook and set of methods; it was this that he passed on to senior Japanese executives. It is argued that his input, and the application of his principles, was extremely influential in aiding Japanese industry to alter radically its stance and achieve the gains in productivity and quality that enabled it to come to compete so successfully in the international market – including the domestic US markets (Aguayo, 1991). Deming has been significantly honoured in Japan, but his influence in the US remained rather limited until the US awoke to the economic global success of Japan and its increasing intrusions into its own markets. His star rose after the airing of an NBC documentary *If Japan can...Why can't we* in 1980 in which his ideas featured. The Ford Motor Company employed him to help them lift their quality, but they were surprised that he talked more about management style and approach than he did about quality control techniques. This broader management philosophy was articulated in his popular book *Quality, Productivity, and Competitive Position*, which was originally published by MIT in 1982, but was rebranded as *Out of the Crisis* in 1986 (Deming, 1986). Deming was actually dismissive of Quality Control Circles, but his work became influential. It has been argued that Deming had reintroduced quality management into the USA (Gabor, 1992) and his work resonates with various total quality improvement programmes that have since become popular in the US and elsewhere. With Deming there are again some interesting flows, interactions and hybridities back and forth between the US and Japan.

P-M as a hybridized leadership theory

In another example, we focus on an area of organizational behaviour and specifically on leadership theory. There have been few theories or models developed in Japan that relate to organizational behaviour in the sense that the term is used in the Western academy, and barely any influential leadership theories. An exception is the so-called P-M model of leadership developed by Misumi (Misumi, 1985; Misumi & Peterson, 1985). To be brief, the model argued that effective leadership, in the Japanese context, depends upon simultaneous attention being paid by the leader to both Performance (P) matters and Maintenance (M) matters, and that an interdependent relationship exists between the two such that one enables the other. If one is absent or weak, then the whole impact of leader behaviour is impaired: for leadership to be effective, both functions need to be present to a moderately high degree. The Performance function is focused on task-related issues, achievement and the specification and delivery of outcomes, whereas

Maintenance behaviours are focused on the nature and quality of leader-member relations, and is concerned with such issues as being inclusive, supportive and maintaining harmony and social cohesion. Misumi argued, though, that the requirements and operation of these leadership functions were variant across contexts, for example in public versus private sector organizations. Consequently, he formulated slightly different dimensions and survey questions for application and determination of P and M functions in diverse settings corresponding broadly to different industrial sectors, as well as variation by hierarchical level.

It is suggested that Misumi's work on leadership was 'highly influenced by the work of Western social scientists' (Dorfman, 2004: 300). There is an apparent similarity in Misumi's formulation with the leadership behaviour dimensional models referred to as the Michigan studies (for instance Fleishman et al., 1955) and the Ohio studies (for instance Stogdill & Coons, 1957), but there are differences. Misumi actually acknowledges that he was heavily influenced by Kurt Lewin and his ideas about leadership and work relations. It is argued, rather puzzlingly, that Misumi 'maintained the contextual and configurational themes of Lewin's field theory' (Smith & Peterson, 2002: 228) and that this is 'consistent with Japanese holistic thinking' (ibid). By contrast, the Michigan leadership theorists, also influenced by Lewin, pursued US cultural inclinations to analyse phenomena 'into a series of separate elements, whose independent effects on one another can then be assessed' and then dissected the themes and transformed them into dimensions (ibid). Leaving aside the inherent essentialisms here, what is puzzling is how Lewin somehow transcends his cultural background and develops a theory that is consistent with Japanese holism, whilst both the Michigan scholars and Misumi are represented as somehow culturally trapped and only able to construct theoretical models that match their cultural locations. It needs to be noted that Smith and Peterson's discussion of Misumi is in a section on 'non-US theories of leadership', which they open by asking what precisely a 'non-US' theory is. They problematize, and to some extent provincialize, the issue by noting that Lewin was German and that his theories reflected interests in his 'home country' (Smith & Peterson, 2002: 226). They are comfortable to assert that this Germanic background does not invalidate the application of the ideas to the US.

The Misumi model has been tested within Japan, but also beyond (Misumi & Peterson, 1987; Peterson, 1988). One interesting instance is the application of Misumi's P-M measures to the Chinese context, where it found some support, but the analysis suggested the need to add a further dimension, labelled 'C', which connotes concerns for character and morals in the Chinese leadership context (Xu, 1987). This structure was subsequently confirmed by others (Ling & Fang, 2003; Wang & Satow, 1994). Furthermore, an additional aspect of cross-national and cross-cultural flow is indicated not only by Smith and Peterson's work with Misumi (Misumi & Peterson, 1985; Peterson, 1988; Smith, Wang & Leung, 1997), but also by the influence of Misumi's work on the development of the 'event management' approach to studying leadership (Peterson et al., 1990; Smith & Peterson, 1988; Smith, Peterson & Misumi, 1994) that has some visibility in the US and elsewhere.

We have offered here just two examples of hybridizing moments in MOS/ICCM, and we could go on to many more (for example Gopinath, 1998; Parikh & Garg, 1990). But, as noted by Frenkel and Shenhav, in a statement that provides a useful summary of this section:

> The apparent adoption in Japan of 'Western' canonic management knowledge in the 19th century (Westney 1987), its translation in the Japanese context, and its absorption of local content before being exported afresh to Western countries in the 1980s, provide us with an important example of management knowledge as a product of a long hybrid history (2006: 869–870).

Appropriation, reappropriation and return

We have intimated already in our discussion of Enriquez's corrective to the misinterpretations of Philippine values by Western social scientists, but also by local social scientists and others, the notion of 'writing back'. We see Enriquez as 'writing back' to the centre and its social sciences, pointing out their errors and misunderstandings and 'setting them straight'. But, and in another way, we might also see Andres as 'writing back', since he too is appropriating Western management theory, resituating it in a local context and aligning it with local values to suggest a locally relevant and meaningful mode of management. The complication is that Enriquez sees the types of interpretations of Filipino values that Andres uses as themselves misreadings and Orientalisms resulting from Western social science appropriations. A number of complex issues ensue here.

The notion of 'writing back' has become central in PCT, particularly in relation to postcolonial[4] literature (Ashcroft, Griffiths & Tiffin, 1989). Ashcroft et al. (1989) point out how colonial writing was appropriative and how literature was used in establishing hegemonic relations and controlling the colonized. It is a notion also captured and exemplified by Salman Rushdie when he talks explicitly about 'the Empire writing back to the Centre' (cited in Brennan, 1989). Writing back is concerned with the formerly subjugated using the power of language to rewrite or reinscribe themselves and their cultures back into not only literature, but also into history and memory, and into social science too. It concerns writers from the formerly colonized and periphery writing about and reconstructing accounts of their experiences and histories of the colonial and postcolonial conditions they endured. This writing back serves as a counterpoint or a reversal to the situation in colonial times when the colonized were written about and inscribed into the accounts and discourses of colonizers. As we have seen, they were so written about that the discursive space was almost entirely filled and there was little space left in which the colonized could speak except through the discourses and indeed the language of the colonizer. Thus, even in the postcolonial moment, Western hegemony still means that the English language is dominant and for many writers of the non-centre to be heard is to write in English (or other dominant language of the centre, such as French).

However, writing back also connotes acts of appropriation, including appropriation of the colonizer's language and turning it, adapting it and using it to write back their accounts, histories, experiences and interpretations – and on their terms. As one of the leading writers of postcolonial literature, Chinua Achebe (1996: 384) says: 'I feel that the English language will be able to carry the weight of my African experience. But it will have to be a new English, still in full communion with its ancestral home but altered to suit new African surroundings'. And that is what he does in his writing; he disturbs the original edifice of the English of colonial England by introducing into it additions from his own language, and hybrid forms and structures.

In 'writing back', we are concerned with acts of appropriation and reappropriation, of reversals and hybridizations through which the colonized or peripherized resist and challenge the colonizer or centre. One might consider writers and scholars from the non-centre who adopt the techniques and discourses of the centre for MOS/ICCM as appropriating or reappropriating. But we are on difficult ground here. Simply taking up the tools of the West and deploying them locally is not resistive or subversive and can simply reproduce the structures of asymmetry and domination. Is, then, Tomas Andres writing back, or is he, unwittingly perhaps, reinscribing the dominant discourses and knowledge systems of the West? There is a certain ambiguity here. But it is an uncertainty that contains the possibility that the hybridity might prove otherwise. In this potentiality, we could assert that the strategies of appropriation, return and hybridization are very viable ones for at least mounting an assault and constructing a turn in the discourse and power/knowledge systems of the centre and the orthodoxy. We next turn to an insight from an ethnographic study that displays, perhaps, a more positive view. It is often the case that the complexities of everyday life and encultured behaviour contain greater capacity for active resistance, nuance and change than textual strategies and theoretical representations from within academia. The example illustrates strategies of resistance through reappropriation, from which ICCM scholars might be able to take something useful.

I am a buffalo

Evans-Pritchard (1989) conducted ethnographic work with Native Americans about their perceptions and relations to others, notably tourists, and deals with the complex interactions that occur in touristic cross-cultural encounters. She notes how the local is not a mere passive recipient or dupe to the tourist in such encounters. The study shows that the tourist gaze cuts both ways – that its Others are typically aware of how visiting groups see them and the stereotypes they hold. Interestingly, and contrary to some of the views taken by other researchers, Evans-Pritchard suggests that touristic stereotypes can also serve an indigenous group positively. In short, her work demonstrates the agency, the subversion and the resistance of Native Americans, as well as the way they are actively aware of and use stereotypes for their own benefit. It also shows locals in the non-centre functioning as agents of social and economic change.

Indeed, there is a long history of Native American folklore and mythology that, to use Evans-Pritchard's terminology, 'burlesques' the Other (1989: 89), and provides parodies and criticisms of the 'whiteman' and his impact on local communities. She notes how:

> Indian responses to the whitemen have varied with the times, historically following a pattern of astonishment, messianic worship, armed revolt, and finally bitterness....They have caricatured the fire and brimstone of the missionaries, the financial gouging of the traders, the hypocrisy of the great white chiefs, and the credulity of the anthropologists (ibid: 90).

Her three-year fieldwork study investigated Pueblo and Navajo silversmiths in New Mexico and their perceptions and interactions with tourists visiting their shops and buying their work. The power of this paper is the detailed description of accounts of face-to-face interactions between the Native Americans and the tourists when selling crafts and arts. She suggests that there is a common set of representations of tourists that Native Americans have built up over time that illustrate an acute awareness of the preconceived ideas tourists have of them. This awareness informs how they deal with tourists in situationally-specific interactions such as selling arts and crafts. Evans-Pritchard gives examples of many different types of interactions that show 'perception, expression and manipulation of stereotypes' (ibid: 95) through strategies of trickstering, self-objectification, silence and various kinds of managed emotional reaction. These are embedded within developed marketing strategies and practices. She describes how one of the most frequent questions tourists ask local Native American artists is about the cultural significance of art, a question that assumes that they produce art for purely aesthetic, cultural or spiritual reasons, a trapping of the Other in a non-commercial sphere. Oftentimes, there is no cultural significance for the artist, but to fulfil tourists' need for a narrative and thus to turn a profit, Native American silversmiths will sometimes make one up, telling the tourists what they want to hear. The editing and invention of tradition is not just a practice of the dominant group; it is also part of minority engagement with the economic and cultural practices of and complex relations with industry.

Evans-Pritchard argues that stereotypes of Native Americans propagated by tourists can 'function to defend and protect as well as to discriminate' (ibid: 89); in short, they are not just negative forms of psychological attribution; they can also be mobilized to protect the privacy of the Native Americans. In cases such as the following, one can see why this is necessary. Evans-Pritchard describes how Native American Laureen responded to one female tourist woman's comment: '"Dear, are you a real Indian? ... I hope you don't mind my asking. But you look so American" with the retort: "I am a buffalo"'. This example suggests the power of strategies of reappropriation and return; how Western touristic practices and stereotypes of the Other can be reappropriated and reconstituted to advantage the Other and position them to benefit more from the exchanges that tourism presents. We wonder how this insight has been and can be applied for the benefit of future ICCM scholars not based in its centre.

Avoidance, isolationism and silence

In the discussion so far it might appear that we are insisting on the adoption of positions and strategies to enable those from the periphery and semi-periphery to participate more fully in the discourse(s), knowledge circuits and institutions of ICCM. There is, of course, a risk in this. Given prevailing power asymmetries and Western hegemonic dominance, such a move might actually compel those from the non-centre to accommodate, if not be assimilated by, the centre and to have any indigenous voice, perspective or knowledge either subsumed, transliterated and bastardized in the process. Lest there be any misunderstanding, that is not our insistence, and we do not wish to participate in any such move if those are the consequences. Any decision to participate in the discourse(s), knowledge circuits and institutions of ICCM needs to be at the discretion of institutions and individuals, made on an informed basis and with the potential choice not to participate. It needs to be acknowledged that for certain people, institutions or locations there are various options available that sustain distance and that such options may become enacted unwittingly, by default or strategically. We hold that these are viable, legitimate and sometimes wholly justified options.

Our analysis in Chapter 3 reveals that the institutions and discourses of ICCM have routinely and persistently excluded large parts of the world, particularly in Africa, the Middle East and Latin America. For many, participation is not a choice, as there are exclusionary practices at work that prevent or curtail participation in any case. For many individual academics confronting such a situation there is not a choice, but for some there is. Scholars of MOS/ICCM located in the periphery may confront a dilemma. Do I ignore the machinations and seductions of the centre, including its institutional paraphernalia (academies, journals and so on), and pursue purely domestic and local studies from an entirely indigenous perspective? Do I focus on local research, but make use of the theories and research from the centre seeking to adapt and reposition them? Or do I strive to achieve inclusion in the centre and participate fully in its discourses, knowledge circuits and institutions? Further, if the last, do I seek to do so through the adoption of Western theory and methods, or do I seek to do so by carrying my local or indigenous perspectives with me? Our analysis suggests that the latter is a difficult road to travel – to say the least. The reality is that many locations, institutions and individuals are disengaged to varying degrees from participation in the activities of the academic centre. However, it is not clear whether people and institutions from the periphery are deliberately choosing avoidance, disengagement or silence, and we are not aware of much direct evidence or research to help determine this. An exception would be those involved in the *Multiversity*, such as

Alvares (2001, 2008), who have expressly turned their back on Western education systems, but there may well be others.

There is a sense of imposed exclusion and silencing here. In the manner implied in the subaltern studies, it might be viewed that Western discourse with respect to management and organization is so pervasive and totalizing that it carves out a space and leaves no room for genuinely other or alternative accounts. To speak at all is to speak in ways that are always refracted though a Western epistemic and ontological lens so as to be accommodated and legitimated in the discourse, or else be condemned to speak outside the discourse and in that sense be silent. This dilemma can be stultifying and has forced some into silence. Indeed, the Kenyan writer Ngugi wa Thiong'o adopted the radical position of ceasing entirely to write in English and to only write in his own language of Gĩkũyũ. He does so in full recognition of the fact that language organizes thinking and the way we construct meanings, including sense of self (Ngugi wa Thiong'o, 1981). This may appear to assume that the language of the colonized has remained pristine and uncontaminated by the categories and organizing principles of the colonizer.

Confronting the same dilemma, but in this case with respect to the dominance of Western scientific discourse, Tibi (1995) struggles with the issue of escaping the circuits of that discourse, which he sees as anchored in the culturally-bound interests of Cartesian dualism and Weberian rationality, objectivity and instrumentalism. He seeks to articulate a science that avoids these 'Weberian' values and is not impelled by motives of intervention to alter the world so that it better serves human material interests. Both Guha and Spivak (Guha, 1983; Guha & Spivak, 1988) adopt a different response. They perceive the difficulty of stepping outside the circuits of dominant Western power/knowledge and so conclude that the most viable strategy is to enter those circuits, open them up and work for reinterpretations and reconfigurations from within. This is more akin to Achebe's (1975) response to his writing dilemma – to use English, but to Africanize and in other ways open it up. These are all possible responses, but one of us has known at least one would-be scholar who ceased her PhD studies because she could not find a resolution to the dilemma!

Conclusion

This chapter completes Part III in which we have explored the representational strategies inscribed in the discourses of ICCM and some responses to them. Our analysis has revealed the persistent and entrenched reliance on strategies that reproduce ethnocentric, essentialist, universalist and exoticized reproductions that echo Orientalist tropes. Chapters 7 and 8 have shown quite clearly that the texts of ICCM work Orientalist strategies that produce West-the Rest, centre-periphery binaries, claim the field for the West, efface hybridizations and so sustain structures of dominance. In this chapter we have discussed how cultural and other flows are a ceaseless productivity and that all knowledge systems, cultures, discourses and texts are, to some degree, the product of hybridizing processes. More particularly, we have addressed some of the modes of response open to individuals and institutions confronted by the centre's dominant and appropriating discourses and inclusion/exclusion practices. Such responses include resistive strategies that range from appropriation, reappropriation and return, writing back, deliberate hybridizing, as well as avoidance and retreats to silence. Each is a possible and legitimate response, one that individuals and institutions need to be free within limits to make based on their own assessments. We do not want to pretend that any such decision is easy or without important consequences.

Part IV
Reframing ICCM

10
Decolonizing Methodology in ICCM

Introduction

The critical analyses presented in the previous two parts of the book suggest that ICCM can be viewed as Western and Eurocentric discourses that exhibit historical as well as contemporary resonance with what might broadly be labelled 'the colonial project'. Part II located ICCM within the historical development of a political-commercial-military complex whose evolution links Europe's erstwhile empires with present-day geopolitics. Part III identified and discussed the continuing presence of Orientalism and appropriating representational practices, as well as alternatives and resistances to these colonizing forms, in a selection of texts that formed part of an emerging ICCM canon. In sum, these two sections reveal a latent structure of domination in ICCM as a system of knowledge. In this final part of the book, we move on to ask where we can go from here.

We call for PCT, in its various guises, to be mobilized in order to rupture the ICCM hegemony and transform the field theoretically, methodologically, institutionally and politically. The most pertinent question for guiding our endeavour in this section is: how might we decolonize theory, methodology and institutional practice in ICCM? The answer to this question is multifaceted and covers issues of onto-logy, epistemology, method, politics, ethics and the institutions of the academy. Our intention is not to 'insert' a postcoloniality sensitivity into ICCM as an addition, an addendum or 'issue', capable of being kept at the margins as a 'perspective'; rather, it is to deploy the theoretical and political resources of PCT so as to bring about a significant reconfiguration of the field. This is an ambitious goal to be sure and certainly one that cannot be contained adequately within the three chapters that comprise the final part of this book. Accordingly, we see this book as a contribution to the beginnings of a conversation regarding the decolonization of knowledge and research practice in ICCM. Such a conversation takes place against a horizon of hope that the field might eventually move from a postcolonial to a 'past-colonial' mode (Butz & Besio, 2004: 355).

For scholars wishing to join this conversation, the road ahead is long and difficult and with professional and personal challenges. This is so because the decolonization of research is 'a long-term process involving the bureaucratic, cultural, linguistic and psychological divesting of colonial power' (Smith, 1999: 98). As Overing (2006) suggests, though talking about the decolonization of her own discipline of anthropology, we must avoid a 'silver bullet' mentality – the quest for the monologic single shot – through which academic work can be transformed. The kind of transformatory process we have in mind is a messy business, with no clear rules to follow. PCT assists us, however, in at least two regards. First, and in a generic sense, its demands can be used to rupture and open up new conversational spaces and a reconfigured epistemological terrain for ICCM. Second, and in a more specific sense, it can be used to delineate and inflect particular forms of research – historical, theoretical, empirical and so on.

We have chosen to place a primary focus in this chapter on methodological questions and recommendations. The reason for this is quite simple: compared to other modes of academic work, there exist few attempts to conduct empirical research and fieldwork from a postcolonial perspective. We believe that, in part, this paucity of postcolonial empirical research is the result of a lack of discussion on the methodological choices and issues that might be involved. How might we create research designs and in which research practices could we engage that are potentially less appropriating of the cultural and organizational life of others? How might we render our methodologies less presumptive of a 'superior gaze', and rebalance and recentre our methodological relationships with the researched along more dialogical lines? These are the questions that drive this chapter.

Decolonizing theory

Whilst our primary focus is on methodology, we do not want, nor believe it possible, to omit commentary on theoretical issues in ICCM. The various theoretical recommendations offered in Table 10.1 could each fill the pages of a single monograph on their own. As such, we offer selective commentary on some of the issues. To begin, we draw upon Tsui's (2007)

Table 10.1   Recommendations for the Reconfiguration of ICCM

Theoretical Recommendations

- Scrutinize and critique claims of the universal application of ICCM theory
- Provincialize and thus decentre US-centric and Eurocentric theories of ICCM
- Foster context-specific and indigenous theory, especially where it brings in previously excluded questions, voices, issues and groups of people
- Enhance levels of epistemic reflexivity
- Challenge and move beyond the field's reliance on functionalist, positivist, quantitative as well as naive interpretive approaches
- Work towards a state of epistemic pluralism in ICCM by taking account of post-positivist theoretical discourse available through greater interdisciplinary engagement
- Conduct more theoretical work from critical, feminist, deconstructive and indigenous perspectives whilst recognizing the philosophical and political tensions between and within them
- Inculcate more dialogical approaches into our research philosophies that recognize a diversity of social identities and power relations

Methodological Recommendations

- A reiteration of the need for reflexivity
- Dialogically-informed research designs that explicitly articulate collaborative and participatory sensitivities in an attempt to escape a US-centric and Eurocentric 'world-picturing'
- Dialogically-informed research designs that explicitly articulate emancipatory ideals in order to contribute to social justice and social change and attempt to escape a Eurocentric 'world-picturing'
- To conduct a greater number and more diverse forms of ethnographic fieldwork in ICCM (including collaborative, Participatory Action Research (PAR), global and autoethnographies)
- To think more carefully about issues of writing, positionality and accountability
- To engage in collaborations with and face the methodological, epistemic and political challenges of indigenous research

recommendation that IM researchers produce more context-specific and exploration theory through the following principles:

- *Seek valid understanding through deep contextualization.* IM scholars should develop deep forms of knowledge that will provide a culturally-situated understanding of local modes and categories of knowing, with research findings carefully embedded in their specific and multiple contexts. Tsui suggests (*pace* Peterson, 2001) using 'native informants', or native/local scholars, to enhance levels of contextualization within a study and to pay attention to the multiple contexts of a particular national location.

- *Develop theoretical innovations through contextualized theory building.* Contextual specificities can also become the basis for generating new theory. Tsui is guided here by Whetten's (2002) distinction between 'contextualized theory' and 'context-effects theory', the former involving the development of theories in context or contextualizing extant theories (with the potential to challenge North American views), the latter denoting theories of context, or the deployment of context to generate novel theory.

- *Regenerate intellectual excitement through novel questions in new contexts.* Tsui echoes criticisms from other areas of the management academy that the field of IM has shied away from big and important questions. This has created a situation of intellectual stagnation and an over-interest in 'technical precision and manageable research projects' (Pfeffer, 2005: 99, in Tsui, 2007: 1359). We need to ask 'big-picture' questions.

A postcolonial perspective can develop and extend these recommendations further.

Questioning our questions

To enter a conversation about decolonizing our field, we need to start at the very beginning of any research endeavour, be it philosophical or conceptual inquiry, or empirical work, by carefully considering what questions we ask. This is crucial, since the questions we set ourselves are generated by the particular values and benefits that can be accrued from the production of research, and these serve to prioritize the interests of some over the interests of others. We should ask ourselves:

- Who decides what the legitimate research questions are, either at the level of the individual research project, or institutionally in terms of the discipline's key themes?
- At the level of the field, which topics, whose questions and, therefore, whose interests are prioritized in research questions? Which topics and whose questions are left out of the picture?
- At the level of the group or individual researcher, why are we pursuing the research we are? What benefits are to be gained from it? And why set the particular questions we do?

- What does a 'novel' question look like? Missing questions, revisionary questions, dialogically-formed and emergent questions, questions defined by the Other for the benefit of the Other?

To ask a novel question is to address an issue, location or group of people or subjectivity previously or typically excluded from consideration in our main journals and funding agencies, or overlooked by received wisdom and conventional imagination. Novel questions could be generated through collective debate, or, more appropriately in a postcolonial context, through dialogue with a greater diversity of stakeholders that relies less on the perspectives of 'northern experts' (Escobar, 1995).

Missing subjectivities

The Global South[1] (Braveboy-Wagner, 2009) as a geographical, cultural, political, epistemic and economic reality needs to be central to the ICCM agenda. How are asymmetrical economic, political and cultural relations between the FW and the Global South, between the minority (rich) and the majority (poor) world reproduced? What is ICCM's responsibility for this? We need to be wary of invoking the Global South simply as a 'research site' for the generation of data and/or using this data to develop theory elsewhere. More broadly, we need to extend our visions beyond the fractured modernities of the West, and pay attention to alternative modernities, alternative histories, alternative capitalisms and/or exchange systems, and alternative cultural developments to those either at the metropolitan centres, or its key satellites. Furthermore, we might study international and cross-cultural issues beyond the confines of the managerial classes who form the intended recipients of ICCM knowledge. Making social class, and its various national and international machinations, a core analytic category for ICCM is an important starting point, but only when combined with other markers of difference, most notably gender and race. Placing these issues within transnational and migrational contexts can assist in the development of global and local perspectives on a number of conceptual and empirical questions. In terms of historical research, we ought to be looking not just at the histories of leading organizations, industries and managerial elites, but also at 'histories from below'. We could gain much by consulting interdisciplinary resources, for example by looking at labour historians and historical sociologists.

Postcolonial contexts

We recommend that researchers ask: what is the colonial, postcolonial, neo-colonial or imperial context of the people and places we are studying? With regard, first, to the colonial context, what we have in mind here is a historical sensitivity to the nature and impact of formal colonial regimes on the current nature of management and organizational practice and experience within a particular nation. It would be imprudent to generalize about the colonial experience: first, across nations – in this regard we need to follow Hoogvelt's (2001) lead in exploring the specificities of different postcolonial formations; and second, within nations, since social divisions between elite and non-elite populations have served, and continue to mediate, the experience and respective fortunes from colonization and the problematic legacies with which certain groups continue to live. What are the particular and continuing forms of economic and cultural dependency and/or subjugation within nations that mediate social relations and whose provenance is linked to formal European colonization? How do new and old forms of empire and imperialism work together? Where do they complement each other, and where are there disjunctures? How might the analysis in Chapter 9 of the varied modes of response to Western hegemonic culture inform our answers to these questions?

Problematize the native informant

One of the most common recommendations for more culturally-sensitive research is the inclusion of 'native informants'. From epistemological and historical perspectives, there are a number of complexities that attend this injunction and ICCM needs to grapple with them to a much greater extent. In epistemological terms, the idea of the native informant as a local cultural expert, entitled and able to speak on behalf of a culture and represent faithfully and neutrally its core categories of knowledge is problematic. As prefaced in our discussion of representationalism in Chapter 7, the epistemological problems are several: the construction of a boundary between the native and the non-native, which traps the former into the realm of a particular cultural tradition; the essentialization of the cultural identity of the Other and, by extension, the Self; the assumption of a correspondence model of representation and communication. A more useful epistemological proposition, in our view, is to talk about transcultural knowledge and to replace 'native informant' with transcultural knower (a move partly inspired by Spivak's writing in her *Critique of Postcolonial Reason*). According to Katz (2001: 504): 'This is not a project of getting "others" to speak as all knowing subjects of otherness ... but rather to undermine this very construction and recognize that none of us are all knowing subjectivities'. The Western researcher thus loses his/her grip as the 'originating subject' whence knowledge springs, and also becomes an object. It is premised on the idea that knowledge is generated inter-subjectively and refuses to privilege one form of knowledge as more complete or essentially more appropriate than another.

Relatedly, we are also of the view that the term 'indigenous' is used in too weak a way in current management discourse as an adjective pertaining to ideas, objects or phenomena native to a particular place. The term 'indigenous' is a loaded one in colonial and postcolonial con-texts and relates to the struggles of subjugated groups, of intergroup rivalry, poverty, violence and calls for self-determination, as well as celebrations of cultural identity and alternative modes of knowing and being. We need to be cognizant of these complexities, and to specify carefully whom we mean when we talk about a native or indigenous informant.

Moreover, we urge strongly that the concept of the subaltern and the condition of subalternity be introduced into the deep contextualizing practices and theoretical development of future ICCM, where specific locations and contexts render appropriate use of this term. Importantly, as Spivak notes, whilst we might wish to work with the category, this is not to say that this is a condition of which we are politically supportive. As a socioeconomic location and state of disenfranchisement, we ought to be organizing against the subaltern status of researched groups.

Unthinking privilege and ethnoscience

We see two potential risks in the pursuit of context-specific theorizing. The first is that we risk connecting context-specificity too closely with societies and cultures outside the West/North Atlantic orthodoxy, and thereby making context a burden that only 'they' have to attend to. For instance, within the work of Tsui and others on Chinese manage-ment theory, the laudable focus on contextualization could have the unintended consequence of losing sight of the metropolitan centres that generated context-related problems in the first place. Put another way: why do advocates of the North American paradigm not take the burden for contextualizing and thus articulating the local specificities of their own work, before it is ever exported to novel contexts for dis-cussion? Why does contextualizing work have to start 'elsewhere'?

The second challenge is to avoid inadvertently reinscribing the meta-theoretical status quo of ICCM research. Tsui argues that: 'In essence, taking the context seriously, either within a single nation or across mul-tiple nations, is simply practising good science' (2007: 1358). What is intended by the phrase 'simply practising good science'? And just whose science is 'good science'? Tsui's work implicitly uses the yardsticks of Western normal science to make judgements about the sound practice of context-sensitive theory development. For us this is a contradiction – in calling for an indigenization of research through deep contextualization, this advocated mode of theory development serves to translate and subject indigenous knowledge to neo-positivist precepts for theory development. The danger then is that the structural functionalist and positivist orthodoxy of ICCM will continue to exist until we properly address it at the root.

Postcolonial work might approach the question of unthinking privilege by framing it as a pedagogical problem: how does a dominant social group learn to recognize its privilege and change it? How does the US and Eurocentric axis share the burden of contextualization and turn it into a source of reflexive strength? Debate is urgently needed on these questions. To situate theory in this way means taking account of how: 'theorization ... incorporates people differently in different parts of the (post)colonial world' (Raghuram & Madge, 2006: 280). To do innovative, context-specific theory is not only to ensure that theory development from the Third World is taken seriously, but also that Western science is seen as one local knowledge system, or one specific ethnoscience amongst several other competing ones.

We need to witness a radical disjuncture from the unexamined reliance on Western positivist theory development. Greater levels of epistemic and ethical reflexivity, as well as epistemic pluralism, are also vital for the future development of innovative theory. Epistemic reflexivity involves a reconnection, and reflection on the connections of theory and method. We call for ICCM to stop treating methods as merely technical solutions to data-gathering problems derived from an abstractly determined theoretical position in a manner that reinforces neo-positivist assumptions. The field needs to become more conversant with interdisciplinary discourse in the social sciences about the nature and logic of scientific inquiry under the rubrics of the paradigm wars or the crisis of representation. Discourse about post-positivism is helpful in this respect. Whilst post-positivist discourses of feminism and critical theory have been an important condition of possibility for the positive reception and growth of indigenous perspectives in the Western academy, they also reflect the limitations of their cultural and institutional provenance (Smith, 1999) and thus need to be engaged with carefully.

Finally, we call for a recognition of the fundamentally relational and dialogical conditions that underpin the construction and naming of any kind of knowledge or experience. Buber's principle of 'I-Thou', also called his dialogical principle or principle of alterity, suggests that there is no such thing as an independent, autonomous human agent; that is, no pre-existing Self or Other. From such a dialogical approach for understanding human relations, certain implications flow of foundational importance for decolonizing theory about culture in ICCM. Specifically, culture would cease to be viewed as a pre-existing reality that can be neutrally described. Instead, it becomes an unfinished outcome of human relations which, in the particular institutional context of research, involves the continual and selective process of seeing, hearing and writing. Culture is thus a process, something we do rather than something we are. This theoretical position has a number of further implications in terms of methodology, to which we turn next.

Decolonizing methodology

PCT demands epistemic reflexivity, not just at the broad disciplinary level, but also in the individual and team research practices of ICCM scholars. Reflexivity demands an account of the localized particularities of the research – historical, ideological, cultural, economic, geopolitical. It calls on us to be mindful of the positionality – that is to say, the particular social structures and socially structured knowledge that we embody and experience – of both researcher and researched. It impels us to become much more explicit about the ontological and epistemological assumptions, and political and ethical goals, underpinning our research methodology.

Debates about the nature, status and production of ethnographies offer ICCM considerable potential for pluralizing its philosophical and methodological bases, and understanding fully the demands of reflexivity. As noted earlier, there is a small but established ethnographic tradition in ICCM scholarship (Brannen, 1996; Chio, 2005; Sharpe, 2004). We would like to see ICCM researchers build and extend this tradition by engaging in more and a greater diversity of ethnographic research studies. We are recommending ethnography because it is a form of writing culture (Clifford & Marcus, 1986) that 'utilizes an epistemology that prioritizes the particularity and context-dependent nature of knowledge' (Besio & Butz, 2004: 433).

It is important to note that whilst ethnographers have traditionally relied on methods of participant-observation, local language learning and long periods in the field to record the realities of daily life, it would be wrong to assume that ethnography is and always has been an interpretive or politically progressive methodology. Early ethnographies, especially those associated with the British social anthropologists discussed in Chapter 4, held realist assumptions; some still do. And as Chapter 4 also makes all too clear, anthropology has had a hand in facilitating colonizing relations. Ethnography can be as appropriative, essentializing and exclusionary as any methodology framed within neo-positivism. However, it is anthropology, and ethnographic writing within that discipline, that has led the way in experimenting with and embedding dialogical modes of research.

Collaborative ethnography

In calling for more 'relational research', we are recognizing the inter-subjectivity of knowledge creation and believe that the degree of reciprocity between the researcher and the researched should be taken as an explicit criterion for judging whether research is good or not (*pace* Lincoln, 1995). Collaborative research is typically based on a partnership model, where an attempt is made to negotiate the shared control of all parts of the research process amongst researchers and the group or community studied. Collaborative engagement of research participants spans the whole research process, from input into the choice of topic and co-definition of research questions to: data collection; scanning and discussion of interpretations through respondent validation and group feedback; co-authorship and input into the production of research texts; discussion of recommendations and how these should best be implemented, where and by whom; publication strategies and forms of writing; sharing in the rewards from the research. Such co-operative research principles have a long history in action research (Reason, 1994; Torbert, 1976).

In MOS, Peterson's (2001) review of modes and practices of international collaboration in OB research summarizes the multiple contextual factors that impact upon the working success of international research teams. The purpose of a research project is a key variable, since it 'triggers various effects of institutional context' (Peterson, 2001: 62), such as: the role expectations employers have for collaborators, and collaborators for colleagues at their university; collaborative norms in their country; and aspects of funding and resourcing. Peterson cites the *Meaning of Work Project* (1987) as a creative and carefully considered example of a global research project in which a single brief is applied uniformly across all the partners to minimize the bias of any single country. His review suggests that 'horsetrading', manipulation and expropriation are recurrent problems in this set-up, and he goes on to discuss different ways for exerting control in multimember projects without too much centralization (including the use of social contracts, fostering trust and using hierarchy). Interestingly, Peterson notes how 'the most egalitarian projects have been either very slow to get into print or have had less influence' (ibid: 77).

Moving more specifically to collaborative anthropology, and then collaborative ethnography, we are aided by the work of Lassiter, who quotes (2005: 84) at length from the American Anthropological Association's (2002) El Dorado Task Force. It defined collaboration as a model for research that:

> (...) involves the side-by-side work of all parties in a mutually bene-
> ficial research program. All parties are equal partners in the enter-
> prise, participating in the development of the research design and in
> other major aspects of the programme as well, working together
> toward a common goal. (...). Only in the collaborative model is
> there a full give and take, where at every step of the research know-
> ledge and expertise is shared. In collaborative research, the local
> community will define its needs, and will seek experts both within
> and without to develop research programs and action plans. In the
> process of undertaking research on such community-defined needs,
> outside research may very well encounter knowledge that is of inter-
> est to anthropological theory. However, attention to such interest,
> or publication about them, must itself be developed within the
> collaborative framework, and may have to be set aside if they are
> not of equal concern to all the collaborators.

Lassiter (2005) argues that whilst much collaborative anthropological work succeeds in most of these injunctions, it is less successful in the co-production of textual outputs from ethnographic study. Hence, he discusses collaborative ethnography in terms of extending 'fieldwork collaboration more systematically into the writing of the actual ethnography' (Lassiter, 2005: 84). Drawing upon innovative work from his own area of Native American anthropology, Lassiter describes a number of strategies that anthropologists have used in collabor-ative ethnographies, stating that most ethnographers employ a com-bination of these strategies depending on the contingencies of their fieldwork.

- Locals act as principal consultants as either readers, editors or both during the writing. Few researchers, Lassiter notes, document how divergent interpretations are negotiated, and calls for this to form part of the 'writing-up'.

- Use of focus groups: Meet with small groups of people to review individual pieces of writing, as in the case of research that used Yuchi focus groups to create community-based texts.
- Editorial boards: Formal editorial boards will be appointed by a community, a common activity in Native American studies. He cites one collaboration of a university press with the Salish Kootenai tribal government in the production of an oral history of the tribe.
- Collaborative ethnographer/consultant teams: For studies with large numbers of people – put together community advisers and student ethnographers.
- Discussion in community forums.
- Texts fully co-authored with a local.

Whilst these examples go some way to enacting the collaborative mode, Lassiter notes that written output in collaborative ethnographies is not always co-authored. In critiquing the so-called 'second-generation' anthropological texts (those most influenced by the postmodern turn), he points out that many texts written with multivocality and multiple perspectives in mind, perhaps using a number of different representational genres, have still not necessarily involved the researched directly in the writing process. We recommend that fully collaborative research should include methods and practices for co-writing, and that these are described in texts (Gottlieb, 1995). Lassiter (2005) cites Severt Young Bear and RD Theisz's (1994) *Standing in the Light: A Lakota Way of Seeing* as an exemplary co-written text. According to Lassiter, Theisz 'engages the consultant as narrator and the ethnographer as compiler and translator: Theisz recorded Young Bear's narratives and organized the material on paper, maintaining Young Bear's style and delivery as best he could, and the two edited the text together as it developed' (ibid: 96).

One particular challenge faced by researchers producing ethnographic, or indeed any form of academic text that utilizes a cross-cultural and/or a multilingual methodological strategy, is the impact of language and translation on the creation and writing up of research results. This theme is tackled by Lincoln and Gonzalez y Gonzalez (2008), who present a comparative analysis of six studies (taken from US-based doctoral research) that enacted different cross-cultural and cross-language research methodologies in attempts to promote liberatory and democratic research. The different strategies used all had to tackle the difficult question of translation. Translation was not only a 'technical' challenge in these research studies; it was also of a cultural and political nature, largely due to the fact that, as Temple (2006) points out, translation in most research contexts works from a minority language into a majority language (usually English).

The question is one of how we explicitly incorporate the translator and translation into our texts whilst retaining the linguistic integrity of the original data. Lincoln and Gonzalez y Gonzalez (2008) identify three key strategies:

- Produce a bilingual dissertation: Data are presented in both the original language of the respondent as well as translated into the target language of the reader. Methodology sections would include a technical account of how the translation worked, especially the translation of important and difficult concepts.
- Present accounts of reflexivity in mixed languages: Previous researchers have written up reflexive accounts of their positionality, research design and data collection using terms from a foreign language. This is partly a strategy for embedding the researcher in a home culture, and of helping understand how their own cross-cultural and cross-linguistic worlds might have impacted their research.
- Get a native speaker to assist with cross-cultural interview methodology.

Lincoln and Gonzalez y Gonzalez favour the use of the first strategy – bilingual texts. (We address the issue of publishing multilingually in Chapter 11). It allows future researchers to discuss, for instance, the identity effects of the researcher on the translation (for example their class or gender), and the use of their first and second languages. Retaining first language expressions in the text allows certain nuances and colloquialisms to be maintained, since often these can be victims of translation. As for reflexive accounts in mixed languages, this strategy could be a practical way for researchers to reveal a kind of cultural 'double consciousness'. Lincoln and Gonzalez y Gonzalez quote from one study by a Nicaraguan immigrant and bilingual teacher in the US talking about the embodied nature of her research practice. The author thinks of her body, her womanhood, her femaleness in one language (Spanish) but other parts of her social and professional life in another (English). Though this strategy is demanding for the reader, since it requires a certain level of linguistic and cultural proficiency, it foregrounds certain dilemmas for researchers whose culture and language of professional work is not their first.

Public/Activist ethnography and PAR

Collaborative ethnography and anthropology are, according to Lassiter (2005), about much more than recentring the relationship between researcher and researched, and working towards full co-production, especially in terms of written output. He writes:

> Collaborative ethnographic practice is now converging with an engaged, public anthropology, and an important component of this emergent public anthropology is written for publics beyond the boundaries of anthropological discourse. This may be among our biggest challenges if we want to speak more powerfully to public issues and concerns. A collaborative ethnographic practice encourages us to address the publics with which we work ... (Lassiter, 2005: 96–97).

According to Lassiter (2005) then, collaborative ethnography shares important concerns with public and activist anthropology and there is some convergence between the two. In part, Lassiter argues, this is because recent feminist and postmodern approaches to the ethnographic endeavour have drawn anthropologists' attention to the important historical, social and political contexts in which their work takes place. Critics (notably Hymes, 1974) argued that anthropology needed to reconnect and bridge gaps between theory and practice, between the elite positions of anthropologists in universities, and the applied and public aspects of their discipline. Much discussion has taken place within anthropology on what such a public anthropology should look like under a number of different contemporary rubrics, including applied anthropology, activist anthropology or ethnography from below.

In such contexts, collaborative ethnography is often mixed with participatory action research (PAR) as anthropologists have recognized their multiple responsibilities to communities beyond the academy. Kemmis and McTaggart (2005), whilst pointing to the diversity of assumptions and practices that constitutes participatory research, underline that its goal is to both unmask exploitation and subjugation, and transform it. It is also to question how we might go about ensuring that we create a 'more materially grounded and relevant research agenda' (Raghuram & Madge, 2006: 277) by committing to take up the issues raised by those who are researched and to contribute to change. Thus, PAR can be viewed as part of an emancipatory tradition.

When applied in non-Western contexts, especially in development or decolonizing contexts or amongst subjugated groups in Western contexts, it is often inspired by Freirian principles that use conscientization processes as part of a more ethical knowledge generation process. Kemmis and McTaggart argue that its emancipatory intent needs to be connected to concrete outcomes. This could be something basic like getting fresh water for a community – or improving language skills – but the key is that the local community should define what will bring them more benefit, and they should derive advantage from the research.

What has this to do with ICCM? The idea that a core research objective of ICCM might be to contribute to local community development might not be seen as 'our business'. Surely this belongs to development studies, geography or anthropology perhaps? We believe that ICCM needs to bring such issues into its broader research agenda. Our point here is twofold. First, that we need to recognize that ICCM has a hand in a system that produces unequal power relations and material and discursive outcomes between different groups in the world. From a critical perspective, we need to broaden our research agenda to recognize how this might be so, and to tackle it. Perhaps given the prevailing structural interests that current work in ICCM represents, there are few instances to do this type of emancipatory research. As Brewis and Wray-Bliss (2008) suggest, it is to make research ethics the 'central warrant' of our research. Second, PCT demands political action – it is a political enterprise. As such, an ICCM recontextualized through PCT requires forms of political action.

This is certainly not to suggest that PAR or research with an explicit emancipatory goal is without is challenges and limitations. Brewis and Wray-Bliss (2008) warn us of the dangers of participatory research, including the temptation to romanticize disenfranchised communities, and essentialize or view them as passive victims or homogeneous entities. They also draw our attention to the question of how far dialogue can really change the wider systemic problems that blight a community. Importantly, they warn of the potential dangers of what Benton (1981) labelled the 'paradox of emancipation'. The problem here lies in Western researchers assuming the 'God's eye' perspective in which only they can see the oppression of others, and assume that it is their job to help others see it and change it. Benton sees the paradox lying in the other-ascription of interests rather than the self-ascription, as in the case where researchers identify the false consciousness of the researched.

Similarly, Mohan (1999) describes how PAR can actually reinscribe and strengthen rather than challenge relationships of power between experts and others in the particular context of developing countries. In terms of specific research practices, Mohan describes examples from India of outside facilitators treating PAR data collection exercises as informal events (for example by wearing casual clothes, using open air settings) out of kilter with local perceptions of a formal event requiring appropriate attire and etiquette. Language use has also proved problematic, with locals conversant in Western media and modes of communication dominating public PAR meetings at the expense of others (usually women). Consequent decisions, Mohan argues, have tended to favour local elites. As such, the idea of 'the local' as a harmonious community that needs intervention becomes difficult and promotes an overly consensual view. Researchers need to be aware of the limitations of their interventions and accept the idea that our research communities have a different kind of power to them: 'The key is to acknowledge that inequalities of power exist and to work productively within them rather than attempting to minimize a differential which cannot readily be removed' (Mohan, 1999: 50).

Autoethnography

Autoethnography has emerged as a novel methodological approach in a number of social scientific disciplines in the last two decades. Most typically, it involves the author viewing and enacting research as autobiographical writing – in short, taking the imperative for reflexivity to its full conclusion (Ellis & Bochner, 1996). However, there is another, less well-known conception of autoethnography articulated by Mary Louise Pratt in her seminal postcolonial text *Imperial Eyes* (1992). Pratt conceptualized autoethnography as activities where: 'members of colonized groups strive to represent themselves to their colonizers in ways that engage with colonizers' terms while also remaining faithful to their own self-understandings' (1992: 7, quoted in: Butz & Besio, 2004: 350). In these terms, autoethnography can be viewed as a cultural expression of both collaboration with, but also resistance to, appropriation of the 'idioms of the conqueror' (ibid). In a fascinating discussion of Pratt's work, geographers Butz and Besio (2004) suggest the appropriateness of autoethnography as a research practice for postcolonial scholars. Their discussion over two articles[2] in *The Professional Geographer* is highly instructive for ICCM scholars.

On the one hand, Butz and Besio endorse and exemplify the practice of autoethnography in the context of their respective research in two different villages in northern Pakistan. Butz gives one example of his involvement in autoethnographic practice with members from the

Shimsal community whom he witnessed and assisted with the production of a text that would describe their Nature Trust. This text was subsequently placed on the Web. Following Pratt, Butz and Besio emphasized that the production of such autoethnographic forms is more than just a cultural issue, or resistant psychology. It is also framed as a 'set of material global/local struggles' (ibid: 354) aimed at clawing back greater levels of local control over broader historical processes of nation-building and globalization. On the other hand, the significance of Butz and Besio's work is more than just an endorsement and illustration of how researchers can facilitate indigenous self-expression. They extend Pratt's treatise by calling for researchers to engender an 'autoethnographic sensibility' in their work *via* an 'attentiveness to the autoethnographic characteristics of things that are going on in our research settings' (ibid: 354). Butz and Besio express different levels of optimism about the fruitfulness of such an endeavour. Butz, the keener of the pair, outlines three key injunctions of an autoethnographic sensibility:

- To recognize ontologically and analytically the subjectivity of our respondents but not to end up treating them as 'native informant' [see our earlier discussion].
- To detect and understand the implications of our involvement in our respondents' world and for the information we get from them. Butz talks about the moments and modes in which the researcher becomes an audience for the self-representations of a cultural group.
- To understand how researchers are involved in the production, dissemination and reproduction of autoethnographic expressions, and to organize our research in ways that support our research participants' projects of self-representation.

To address the first point, Butz also recommends the injunctions of a transcultural discourse. As for the last two, Butz describes how he was used by the Shimsal elite to help the community express their auto-ethnographic document using developmentalist and conservation idiom through which they felt they would be heard. Butz was able to use his access to national documentation archives and Western evidence to buttress the community's historical claim to land. The local community felt he could disseminate their documents to a wider set of audiences – *via* the joint presentation of work at workshops and conferences in Pakistan. He thus became, in his view, both a useful audience for and supporter of local needs and interests.

Besio, however, is more cautious than Butz though still supportive of the cultivation of autoethnographic sensitivities. Crucially, she notes how: 'The political efficacy of an autoethnographic sensibility remains, to my mind, very much context dependent and one that researchers would have to reckon with on a case-by-case basis' (Besio & Butz, 2004: 436). The contextual contingencies reported by Besio relate to her particular experiences as a feminist researcher studying the lives of women and girls in the village of Askole. First, she argues that the nature and possibility of autoethnographic expressions depend on the social group studied. Her male colleague Butz worked with the elite groups in Shimsal – elders, porters and educated activists, in the main men: 'a group of highly skilled, transcultural communicators in a community which is quite well positioned to manipulate some transcultural interactions to its advantages'. Compared to the more explicit and formalized nature of autoethnography in Butz's community, Besio's group of females did not have the same access to these autoethnographic possibilities, for historical and social reasons. This is not to say they did not engage in autoethnography and forms of political action, but that the forms it took were more informal, secretive and away from the public fora dominated by men and local elites.

As for her own autoethnographic sensibilities, Besio argues that, compared to Butz, her position as a researcher was too tenuous a site from which to do autoethnographic work. She draws attention to the effects of the gendered positioning of researchers by local communities on the conduct of research and suggests that her colleague was less restricted by his male gender. Besio further describes how her positioning by the community was dependent upon the gendered history of previous researchers in the villages, or a succession of 'sahibs'. She says:

> I am clearly one of the sahibs, aligned with them by my 'race', class, and 'outsiderness', if not by gender and sex. I position myself as a Western woman and feminist, and simultaneously – through local constructions of 'researcher' – as masculine and colonial (ibid: 433).

She describes this paradoxical positioning within a masculine knowledge system as a 'double displacement: I am a gendered male and marked as colonialist' (ibid: 434). Consequently she argues that her male research partner – who constructs himself and is constructed as masculine by the men he works with – enjoys a more comfortable position for research. Such a contradiction raises fascinating and complex questions about our positionality in relation to the communities we study, as well as issues of how we account for them and write their contradictory and complex nature into our work.

Writing, reflexivity and critical praxis

The previous discussion summarized an exemplary and nuanced illustration of reflexivity in academic practice, albeit not one based on the more usual conception of reflexivity in the social sciences. In this subsection we explore further the possibilities and pitfalls of a reflexive turn, drawing upon aspects of feminist methodology. We begin with feminist geographer Rose (1997) who critiques what she refers to as a model of 'transparent reflexivity'. Rose argues not only that achieving reflexivity is difficult in practical terms, but also that it is a conceptually contradictory thing to do.

Rose explains that the problems with the model of transparent reflexivity (that is, where we are able to clearly demarcate our positionalities, interests and values and how they impact our research) lie in two conceptual arenas – a rhetoric of space and a rhetoric of vision. In terms of visibility, the model presumes an inwards look to the identity of the researcher and an outwards look to the Other and the outer world. It presumes a conscious, knowable agent who is able to bring a certain analytical order to the world around her *via* the organizing device of scale (micro and macro) and a distributional model of power. The contradiction, according to Rose, lies in the fact that you can only map the relationship between the researcher and the researched in two ways. First, as a relationship of difference based on an objectified distance; second as a relationship of sameness where researcher and researched occupy the same position. She argues that the first is unacceptable, and the second impossible, so there is no space left for understanding across difference.

The point, however, is not to drop reflexivity, but to think about the consequences of its contradictions and to try to use this in a more productive manner. It is about understanding across difference, and thinking about how difference is constituted. To do this, Rose draws upon the work of translation expert Fiona Smith (1996), arguing that we need to take a relational approach to reflexivity that addresses psychic processes such as fetishism and paranoia in relation to researching Others. We should account for the connections that make our research possible and attempt to address the variety of uncertainties that attend our research.

> The feminist task becomes less one of mapping difference – assuming a visible landscape of power with relations between positions of

distance between distinctly separate agents – and more one of asking how difference is constituted, of tracing its destabilizing emergence during the research process itself (Rose, 1997: 313).

Further complexity in the practice of reflexivity is expressed in the work of certain transnational feminist writers located in the non-West. Raju (2002), an Indian scholar, describes her experience at a conference in the UK where Western researchers were highly concerned with reflexivity and positionality. She wrote that she considered it an 'academic luxury that we from the "Third World" cannot afford' (Raju, 2002: 173). Raju's text is one of three in a debate between feminist researchers in the journal *Gender, Place and Culture* on the role and accountabilities of the Western researcher in 'Third World' or developing contexts. Also part of this debate, Nagar (2002) argues that existing models for being reflexive, and accounting for one's positionality are based on a model of the individual researcher that underplays how researcher identities 'intersect with institutional, geopolitical, and material aspects of their positioning' (Nagar, 2002: 182). As a result, she argues that key political questions that attend the research process are overlooked, notably, she argues, the theoretical frameworks and particular kinds of language used by researchers in producing their texts. In thinking to a greater extent about the languages we use and the writing we do, we should ask:

- Whom are we writing for? How? And why?
- What does it mean to co-produce knowledge across a variety of different kinds of border?
- What are the implications of the answers to the questions above for the structure of the academy?

To address the first two questions in Nagar's list, further discussion of commonality and difference from a feminist perspective is useful. In this regard, Raju cites Friedman's (1998) concept of 'locational feminism'– one in which feminist research is located and aware of its location, but is global in scope, and working between these two analytical levels. In her implicit criticism of Western poststructuralism, Raju suggests that 'even as deconstructed specificities remain in focus, we need not lose perspective of structures such as colonial history, neoclassical economic and political frameworks, and patriarchy' (ibid: 175–176). She takes a materialist feminist view that despite individual or locational differences, the wider structures of patriarchy and capitalism contain women in a disadvantaged position. We need to find forms of commonality such that Western researchers can take the responsibility, when needed and desired by local communities, to find ways that express agency and make possible particular kinds of struggles. Nagar urges us to consider not just what is theoretically trendy in the West but 'what is considered politically imperative by the communities we work with or are committed to over *there*' (ibid: 184, italics in the original). She urges us to ask: 'What kinds of struggles did my analysis make possible for them?' (Larner, 1995: 187, in Nagar, 2002: 183).

Finally, in embedding such concerns more explicitly into a critical ICCM, we need to consider options for critical praxis. That is to say, we need to think practically about our political action as academics. Wakefield (2007) outlines and discusses different kinds of praxis that should enable our work to become practically and politically relevant for the communities with whom we research. She defines praxis as a blend of theory and reflection with practice and action, that should involve a conscious attempt to transform chosen aspects of the world. She calls for a broader approach to academic praxis that goes beyond traditional forms such as teaching and academic writing. She distinguishes between praxis from inside the academy (including teaching/radical pedagogy, writing for publication, changing the system from within) and outside (incorporating one's values into everyday activity, involvement with groups and organizations, explicit political action). She then goes on to outline forms of praxis that bridge this divide, including teaching and writing in non-academic venues (for example public lectures, popular education, writing for newspapers, magazines, art installations, direct policy engagement, PAR).

Global ethnography

Global ethnography describes a set of methodological approaches that, whilst placing an emphasis on local and naturally-occurring behaviour, widens the analytic scope in terms of geographical and cultural imagination. It is a methodological device that enables the creation of a 'translocal countertopography' (Katz, 2001) – a concept in which disparate places are linked analytically in ways that try to enhance struggles through a common interest.

Global ethnography emerged from two inter-related facets of recent anthropological and sociological debate. First, the crisis of anthropology noted in Chapter 4 encouraged anthropologists to take greater cognizance of 'external factors' – i.e. those historical, political and economic issues – in the study of local societies and cultures. Second, and relatedly, it spanned from a need to rethink some highly entrenched assumptions about ethnographic fieldwork. Both anthropologists, such as Marcus (1998), and sociologists, such as Burawoy (1998, 2000), had noted the limitations of traditional studies of cultures as bounded, integrated and consensual systems with clear and hermetically-sealed boundaries found in realist ethnographies. Marcus refers to this as the 'fiction of the whole' – a nod to the rhetorical ontological status of culture – and calls for a shift away from 'an ethnography that is so centrally place- and local-world determined toward an ethnography that emphasizes a link-up with the more pluralistically sensitive systems perspectives' (Marcus, 1998: 34).

For Burawoy, similarly, the question for 'global' ethnographers was how to reimagine the ethnographic site as 'permeated by broader power flows in the form of local racial and gender orders, free-flowing public discourses, economic structures and so on' (2000: p. xii). What is needed is an 'understanding of cultures increasingly in circulation, making all locales and sites of sustained fieldwork partial perspectives' (Marcus, 1998: 5). To this end, Burawoy makes two suggestions: multi-sited ethnography; and a multi-sited research imaginary. Theoretically, he suggests that both strategies should combine postmodern anthropological concerns with polyphony and the representation of multiple voices and perspectives in an ethnographic text, together with political economy and systems theoretical concerns with flows and processes that connect different locales. He is clear, however, that he does not believe in theoretical monoliths or grand narratives that posit one universal historical trajectory whence local life can be read as one segment. Instead, he advocates a pluralistic systems perspective. Together, this all means:

> The aim is to represent a whole local world and simultaneously a world system, by attempts either to represent an intensively studied locale penetrated by larger systems, or to represent larger systems in human terms by revealing as intersubjective processes the multiple centers of activity that constitute the systems, conventionally labelled the market, capitalism, or the state. (...) The idea is that any cultural identity or activity is constructed by multiple agents in varying contexts, or places, and that ethnography must be strategically conceived to represent this sort of multiplicity, and to specify both intended and unintended consequences in the network of complex connections within a system of places (ibid: 39, 52).

The multisited research imaginary acknowledges the practical and pragmatic reality of much international research: that, for reasons of time, money and access, it is not always possible to travel to conduct ethnography in multiple and dispersed geographical sites. In such a case, Marcus suggests a 'site-specific, intensively investigated and inhabited scene of fieldwork but framed and partially investigated by a multi-sited imaginary that provides the special context of significance and argument for ethnography' (ibid: 14). He says that we need to look beyond research subjects' extant discourses and towards 'cultures of connection, association, and circulation' (ibid: 16). Archival research *inter alia* can enable us to attend to the world system context. Within a single site 'the crucial issue concerns the detectable system-awareness in the everyday consciousness and actions of subjects' lives' (ibid: 96).

As for multisited strategies, these represent a significant change to what traditionally constitutes ethnographic knowledge, since they examine cultural circulation across and within multiple sites. Such ethnography facilitates both a comparative dimension as well as the potential to trace objects across sites. In order to produce this kind of ethnography, Marcus' first injunction is that the research practice needs to be or become multilingual. Second, he suggests an array of 'mapping strategies' to do the tracing work outlined above, including:

> Follow the people; follow the thing (money, intellectual property, art); follow the metaphor; follow the plot, story or allegory; follow the life or biography; follow the conflict.

The Global Ethnography Project conducted by Michael Burawoy and his students at Berkeley in 1996 gives a number of excellent illustrations of their view on what constitutes a global ethnography. The Project is inspired by the same kind of concerns as Marcus', taking an interest in global forces, connections and imaginaries. To make ethnography more globally relevant, their solution is a shift from studying 'sites' to studying 'fields', that is, the relations between sites. The resultant book describes a number of individual studies of different social groups spread across different parts of the world (for instance nurses in Kerala, India, software engineers in Ireland, welfare clients in Hungary) that deployed transnational, multisited ethnography.

> We sought to understand the incessant movement of our subjects, the mosaic of their proliferating imaginations, by ourselves continually switching places, moving among sites within the field ... our fieldwork had to assemble a picture of the whole by recognizing

diverse perspectives from the parts, from singular but connected sites (Burawoy, 2000: 4–5).

All the authors situated their analyses in the particular histories of the places in which they came to dwell, and drew upon a number of secondary sources to build up a historical picture. They used these ethnohistories 'to spiral outward and explore changes in globalization' (ibid: 5) – moments of dwelling before moments of travel, aimed at exploring external forces, connections and wider imaginations. Whilst the group's theoretical frames varied, to some degree, between discursive and material approaches, the Marxist credentials and previous methodological writings of Burawoy dominate this collection. Burawoy is explicitly influenced by the 1960s Manchester School of anthropology and its extended case study method, which is premised on the following (Burawoy, 1998: 4):

1. Extending the observer into the world of the participant.
2. Extending observations over time and space – in different places and for extended periods of time.
3. Extending out from micro processes to macroforces, 'from the time-space rhythms of the site to the geographical and historical context of the field' (ibid: 27). A key analytical issue here is avoiding the objectification of extralocal forces (more below).
4. Extending theory.

Burawoy explains that not all studies will cover all these aspects; they will tend to focus on one or two of them. Of particular note is his very explicit message that the extended case method does not 'erase' the effects of the researcher's power. What it can do, however, is to make us aware of the variety of power effects that attend the extended case method, including silencing, domination, objectification and normalization.

The potential for objectification, for example, was of particular concern in the Global Ethnography project. The authors followed three strategies to counter the potential for objectification of global forces:

> The first is to consider global forces as constituted at a distance. The focus of the ethnography then is on the way global domination is resisted, avoided and negotiated. The second strategy is to see global forces as themselves the product of contingent social processes. Here forces become the topic of investigation; they are examined as the

product of flows of people, things, and ideas, that is, the global connections between sites. The third strategy, the most radical, sees global forces and global connections as constituted imaginatively, inspiring social movements to seize control over their immediate but also their more distant worlds (Burawoy, 2000: 29).

Indigenous research methodologies

The final sub-section in this chapter, and in many ways the most important one, is dedicated to a call for the fostering of indigenous research on and in IM. Our use of the term 'indigenous' comes with an awareness of significant historical, cultural and political baggage associated with the term. This baggage is usually overlooked in current discussions in MOS/ICCM. The significance of indigenous approaches to research lies in their valuation and development of the knowledge and experience of indigenous populations often in resistance to the normative conventions and power structures of Eurocentric social science (Denzin, Lincoln & Smith, 2008). As a research agenda defined by and for indigenous communities, indigenous research also indexes a decolonization project whose goal of self-determination is both a political and a social justice issue.

We take a very small slice of this large literature, mainly from Maori research, to outline the historical background, key concerns and implications of indigenous research methodology. Smith's (1999) *Decolonizing Methodologies: Research and Indigenous Peoples* is a classic text on indigenous methodology, located in her own Maori identity and in Maori research. She clarifies why even the question of conducting research amongst indigenous communities is such a challenge. The first half of her text describes powerfully how indigenous communities, with particular regard to Maori, have a deep suspicion and mistrust of research based on their historical experience of exploitation at the hands of researchers. She argues that research is a site of struggle for indigenous peoples and that one cannot discuss any aspect of research, epistemology or methodology, without doing so within the context of imperialism or colonialism. She says (Smith, 1999: 1):

> (...) it galls us that Western researchers and intellectuals can assume to know all that it is possible to know of us, on the basis of their brief encounters with some of us. It appalls us that the West can desire, extract and claim ownership of our ways of knowing, our imagery, the things we create and produce, and then simultaneously reject the people who created and developed those ideas and seek to

deny them further opportunities to be creators of their own culture and own nations.

Research has been deeply embedded in colonial practices, and it would be infelicitous to assume that it has ceased to be a problem for indigenous communities since the formal end of colonial regimes. Smith describes, in a section called 'Trading the Other', several contemporary and disturbing examples of the cultural appropriation and economic exploitation of Maori life, with some graphic instances including the farming of the umbilical cord blood of aborted babies, the scientific reconstruction of previously extinct indigenous people and the patenting of cultural institutions. As well as these historical and contemporary practices, the problem is also one of the impact of Western positivism, which brings 'a different conceptualization of things such as time, space and subjectivity, different and competing theories of knowledge, highly specialized forms of language, and structures of power' (ibid: 42) to local communities through research. To redress this situation, Smith calls for the decolonization of research and describes attempts by indigenous researchers to develop research by and for indigenous peoples. But who are they?

> Indigenous peoples can be defined as the assembly of those who have witnessed, been excluded from, and have survived modernity and imperialism. They are peoples who have experienced the imperialism and colonialism of the modern historical period beginning with the Enlightenment (Smith, 2005: 86).

She uses the term 'indigenous' to cover a vast diversity of peoples (Sami, Aboriginals, Hawaiians, Native Americans, Basque) rather than other terms such as First Peoples, Native Peoples, First Nations, People of the Land and so on. Smith firmly locates her own work within the context of the modern indigenous peoples' project and the political struggles of these varied indigenous communities and impels other researchers interested in indigenous perspectives to do likewise. She describes how, from the 1960s onwards, communities began to work towards the 'development of global indigenous strategic alliances' (ibid: 108), agitating for a diversity of issues, notably land rights, but also linguistic and cultural preservations, as well as human rights. Rather than communities working on separate decolonizing projects, this quasi-social movement allowed them to work under a collective banner whilst retaining individual identities. This energization of a more collective indigenous movement led to networks and alliances between different indigenous groups and supportive publishing networks from Europe and North America.

A wide-ranging indigenous agenda has emerged from such collectivization, with the aim of constituting a self-determining indigenous world and a concomitant research agenda for effecting it. The goals of this indigenous research agenda are described by Smith (1999) as survival, recovery, development and self-determination, and include elements such as decolonization, healing, mobilization and transformation. Smith gives examples of 25 indigenous projects situated within this agenda with names such as claiming, testimonies, storytelling, remembering, intervening, gendering, democratizing, protecting. These project titles are evocative and point to the important and strategic role of 'naming' research in an indigenous research context. Smith argues that indigenous peoples have distinctive ways of conceiving of research, underpinned by historical and epistemological specificities, and manifest in particular methodological approaches and research protocols. This is significant because it serves to render visible the specificity of indigenous approaches rather than 'disguising them within Westernized labels such as "collaborative research"' (Smith, 1999: 125). It is part of a 'researching back'.

What are the ontological and epistemological assumptions of an indigenous approach? How would we proceed methodologically, and what kinds of data collection techniques and research ethics might be appropriate? There is no one answer; it will depend on the particular indigenous researcher and community being studied. To give one example, we stay with Smith and other Maori researchers to examine briefly kaupapa Maori research, which has been used as a lens for the indigenous study of management and organization in New Zealand. Kaupapa Maori methodology is a well-established research approach underpinned by Maori epistemology, cosmology and methodological protocols grounded in Maori cultural codes. Kaupapa Maori literally means 'the Maori way or agenda' (Henry & Pene, 2001: 235) where research is based on a radically different worldview to so-called Pakeha (non-Maori or Eurocentric) research, which views 'knowledge as cumulative, whose component parts can be drawn together to discover universal laws' (ibid). Henry and Pene (2001: 37) summarize as follows:

> *kaupapa* Maori is both a set of philosophical beliefs and a set of social practices (*tikanga*). These are founded on the collective (*whanaungatanga*) interdependence between and among humankind

(*kotahitanga*), a sacred relationship to the 'gods' and the cosmos (*wairuatanga*), and acknowledgment that humans are guardians of the environment (*kaitiakitanga*), combining in the interconnection between mind, body and spirit. Taken together, these ethics inform Maori ontology and assumptions about human nature; that is, 'what is real' for Maori.

In addition to these ontological and epistemological assumptions, kaupapa Maori research practice is reflective of and embedded in particular cultural protocols and modes of ethical conduct. One example is the mentorship of community elders embedded within the concept of 'Whanau', which provides a 'supervisory and organizational structure for handling research' (Smith, 1999: 195). Research comes with a set of obligations to the community and is a collectivist task – conducting research with respect, working with others and sharing knowledge, community consultation, using community modes of communication, feedback and a long-term commitment to the community. In embedding these practices in research design, research is able to address the following Maori concerns: initiation (how the research process begins and whose interests and concerns define results); benefits (who gains directly from it); representation (whose research constitutes an adequate portrayal of reality); legitimacy (the authority we claim for our texts); accountability (who has control over research procedures) (Bishop, 2005). In persuading Maori peoples that research can work for them rather than exploit them, kaupapa methodology positions research within the struggles for autonomy and self-determination.

Indigenous research comes with its own distinctive challenges, which can be articulated around the concept of insider-outsider relations. For 'outsiders', or non-indigenous researchers wishing to conduct research in indigenous communities, four strategies for culturally sensitive research include (G. Smith, in: L. Smith, 1999): tiaki (based on mentoring by community elders); whangai (based on the research becoming incorporated into daily Maori life and developing long-term relationships); power-sharing; and an empowering outcomes model based on community-relevant priorities. Whilst Smith believes that indigenous communities should accept the potential help of interested non-indigenous researchers where they see benefit, there is also the argument that non-indigenous researchers should cease to be allowed into the community.

It would be wrong to assume, however, that indigenous research carried out by 'insiders' or indigenous researchers is necessarily free of problematic issues and a simple panacea for issues of cultural appropriation or exploitation. Smith (1999) describes at length how indigenous researchers face their own pressures and changing insider/outsider relations. For one, gender and age can affect the success of research especially when (young female) researchers are working with male elders: protocols of respect and reciprocity mean that access and consent can take a long time. Smith argues that there are multiple ways of being an outsider and an insider in an indigenous context, and the problem is that those inside the community have to live with the consequences of their research.

Bishop (2005) also reminds us to be wary of essentializing about indigenous researchers and simply assuming that all will necessarily conduct more sensitive and responsive research. Some may be viewed as more biased, too close to community concerns and therefore without a dispassionate distance. Moreover, Smith (1999) suggests that Western-trained indigenous researchers can also employ techniques that marginalize local participants' contributions and appropriate local understandings. In short, some do not automatically behave in culturally appropriate ways in their own community, and so a critical reflexivity is still needed here.

But critical reflexivity is needed not only at the personal or group levels of research; we also need to apply it at the institutional level. As Smith (2005: 88) argues:

> Decolonizing research (...) is not simply about challenging or making refinements to qualitative research. It is a much broader but still purposeful agenda for transforming the institution of research, the deep underlying structures and taken-for-granted ways of organizing, conducting, and disseminating research and knowledge.

We turn to these issues next.

11
Towards an Alternative Institutional Frame

Introduction

We have argued that a radical transformation of ICCM is not merely a matter of methodological refinement, but also one of trenchant reconfiguration of the ontological, epistemological, ethical and political commitments of research practice in the field. Such a reframing is a necessary precursor to any reconsideration of methodology and methods. Given our assessment of the institutional present of ICCM in Chapter 3, it is apparent that any reconsideration of theoretical and methods commitments in ICCM needs to be supported at the institutional level. The field's current institutional framework maintains and perpetuates the damaging modes of representation discussed in Chapters 6 and 7, and contributes simultaneously to the reproduction of the hegemony of Western knowledge systems. In this chapter, we address the possibilities of an alternative, more inclusive institutional frame that is compatible with the reconfigured commitments and alternate methods we have articulated. The central goal of this reconfiguration is to allow for the proper and effective inclusion of non-Western voices.

In Chapter 3, we discussed the work of Loubser (1988), who identified a comprehensive set of factors he felt constrain indigenous social science, many of them related to the structures of dependence and the vertical relationships he saw as characterizing the relationship between the academies and scholars of the centre and periphery. One consequence of these structures of inequality and dependency is that scholars from the periphery, or even semi-periphery, are in danger of becoming 'captive minds' (Alatas, 1974). The current institutional arrangements perpetuate a form of academic dependency (Alatas, 2000, 2003), if not educational imperialism, that colonizes the mind (Ngugi,

1981). We also noted in Chapter 3, citing Alatas (2003), that the current institutional frame for ICCM is constituted by a division of labour within which scholars from the periphery are frequently confined to empirical but not theoretical labour, the investigation of domestic contexts not international, and the single case not comparative work.

We are seeking to reconstitute the field so that this division of labour is dismantled and scholars from anywhere can be as engaged and play as full a part as they wish. This requires changes to the many elements that are part of the institutional present of ICCM discussed in Chapter 3. These include: the broad societal context and local support environment; national research councils; a place within international educational systems; universities and their management regimes; professional and academic associations; textbook publishing and pedagogy; and the apparatus of academic journals. In our reconfiguration we shall consider each of these again, seeking to offer suggestions for alternative arrangements, structures and processes. Before we do so we need to make some prefatory comments.

Firstly, we want to acknowledge that we remain deeply aware of our own privileged backgrounds and location (we return to this at the start of the concluding chapter), and of the danger of repeating and reproducing the very binary relations, structures and asymmetries that we seek to problematize and dismantle. The last thing we want to do is participate in the centre-periphery structures of dominance that are taken to give permission to those of the centre to represent, intervene and change things for those of the periphery. We want to avoid being read as 'speaking for' or 'talking to'. It needs to be acknowledged, therefore, that those in the periphery – be they individual scholars, academic institutions or other bodies – are at liberty, quite legitimately, to choose not to become engaged in the international education and research system, to choose not to engage with the academic machinations surrounding MOS/ICCM, and to choose to sustain a position of independence or isolation. There may well be plausible and persuasive arguments for doing so and we certainly support the right of people to make that determination if they so wish. We would note the establishment of the *Multiversity*, the disgust with academic imperialism that led to its foundation, and its turning away from the Western educational establishment (see Alvares, 2001, 2008), as a fascinating example of such academic independence. This is an understandable response. Having said this, our work here is premised on a commitment to ICCM and to its betterment at an international level. It is also premised on the assumption that the field is already internationalized, albeit partially and with biases and distortions, and that it would benefit from proper internationalization, but only if that involves a reconfiguration that lowers barriers, broadens inclusiveness, lessens dependencies and dismantles asymmetries. It is to that end that we have undertaken this work, and to that end that we offer the suggestions below as possible steps along the way.

Secondly, lest we appear naïve, we need to acknowledge that some of our suggestions in what follows must, at this stage, be considered to some degree as idealizations with extensive obstacles standing in the way of their realization. We would note that despite his own suggestions for improvement, Loubser (1988) remained somewhat pessimistic and stated that the wider factors limiting indigenous social science that need changing are largely beyond the scope of the academic community and that genuine, foundational, change rests on the establishment of a new international socioeconomic order. We understand and are sympathetic to that perspective, but seek to be more optimistic whilst remaining realistic about the challenges and the horizons of possibility.

Societal context and local support environment

Our assessment of ICCM shows that it remains ethnocentric and parochial; that most of the work is done by scholars and institutions from the centre, about organizations from the centre or located in countries in which the centre has a strategic or commercial interest; and is published by the centre's publishing machine. Large parts of the world are peripheral players in all of this or are excluded altogether. Furthermore, there is a Western intellectual hegemony, if not a form of academic imperialism, that continues to dominate the field and to marginalize alternative perspectives, knowledge systems and methods. There is a pressing need for indigenous research that begins to build up conceptualizations, models and theories that are rooted in, reflect and resonate with local concerns and problems and that act as a rebalancing or counterpoint to Western dominance. To develop localized, alternative or indigenous approaches to research, local scholars need to be free to choose or indeed develop conceptualizations, theories and methods that are relevant and appropriate to local epistemological predilections, problems and issues prevailing in that society at that time. Denzin (2005: 945–946) summarizes five imperatives for indigenous researchers:

- Be proactive and name the world for themselves;
- Craft their own version of science, including how science and scientific understandings will be used in their world;

- Develop a participatory model of democracy;
- Use theory proactively, as an agent of change, but act in ways that are accountable to the indigenous community and not just the academy;
- Resist new forms of colonization.

For this to happen, indigenous researchers need an institutional frame at the national societal level that is supportive and enabling – materially, ideologically and intellectually. Loubser argued that the prospects for a viable and vibrant local, indigenous social science depend very much upon a supportive local context, and he is talking mainly here in national societal terms. He envisages a situation of potential mutuality in which local national governments and other institutions support local scholars and academic institutions to pursue localized research and theory development. In return, the local community benefits from research and theory that is relevant and that addresses the issues and problems faced by society. It is hard to argue against such a structure of mutuality, but Loubser pointed out barriers that currently militate against its realization.

We suggested that local national support needs to come in both material and ideological forms. The former is possibly the easier of the two. Local governments, social institutions, businesses and philan-thropists might refocus their budgets and provide greater levels of material support for the pursuit of indigenous research and theory development. This ought to be feasible. The pay-offs ought to be calcu-lable, albeit within a timeframe demanding patience as local theory development and local methods are built up. More at issue is the ideo-logical support, and we suggest that material support is unlikely to flow unless the ideological support is there. By that we mean that local institutions need to buy into the idea that there are local alternatives to Western knowledge systems, theories and methods, and that these can deliver knowledge, understanding and solutions for locally rele-vant issues and problems. One of the problems, as Loubser noted, is that local elites, including scholars, are often enamoured by – one might even say seduced by – the knowledge systems, theories and methods of the centre, and prefer to adopt, utilize and support them rather than anything 'home-grown'. Unless there is a shift in the per-spective of such elites, the importation will continue, thereby bolstering relations of dependence and retarding local understandings.

However, the positive symbiosis ought to be achievable with some political will, ideological adjustment, patience and investment. It is clearly not simply a matter of financing or other resources. As Alatas

(2003) points out, Japan, which is economically developed and has a social science infrastructure that does intersect with the West, has not really been able to exert much influence internationally in the social sciences. This demonstrates that it is not economic power alone that produces influence in these domains and what is needed is the political will to follow through with appropriate policies and practices. As Alatas suggests: 'There has to be a conscious effort on the part of social scientists and the administrators of research and teaching institutions to formulate and implement policies designed to help social science communities break out of the current division of labour' (2003: 605). In sum, there needs to be an act of political will on the part of domestic governments to support local MOS research, to legitimate alternative and indigenous approaches to theory and research, and to back that up with material support in terms of funding and institution building.

In even more concrete terms, the role of national research councils and/or equivalent bodies is also important. In many respects the comments made above also apply in the case of these bodies. As instruments of government (typically), they are often also in the thrall of Western equivalents and the knowledge systems they support. Consequently, we sometimes see national research councils more inclined to support research that has international links, or that deploys known Western theories and methods, than local research and academic work. Such bodies need to be encouraged and empowered to have the confidence to support more indigenous research and theory development. Indeed, Loubser (1988) argues that the support of an indigenous research community ought to be the '*raison d'être*' of national research councils. They can support indigenous work and contribute to the whole tone of research practice locally, supporting local academics in pursuit of locally relevant research agendas. They can also play a part in institution building, in fostering appropriate international collaborations, and in the generation of systems of publication and communication that are geared towards supporting indigenous effort.

Smith (1999), for example, argues that there are two principal pathways for the development of indigenous research that research councils could foster: funding community action projects that derive from indigenous problem-identification; and funding spaces within institutions for indigenous research centres and studies. Smith's (1999) discussion of the institutional barriers and frustrations involved in setting up the Research Unit for Maori Education at the University of Auckland is particularly instructive. We might add the following to this list of new priorities for national research councils: grant funding for longer-term projects (from five to ten years) that would enable the kinds of participative, longitudinal and transformative ethnographic methodologies outlined in Chapter 10 to be realized fully rather than 'jammed' into a shorter time period; PhD funding targeted specifically at indigenous researchers and addressing indigenous research topics; providing money for research training for PhD students in the particular challenges of indigenous research and, importantly, for meaningful and long-term language learning.

These are important changes and we fully recognize that they are often outside the scope of the academic community itself, although that community could take the lead, undertake locally relevant research and demonstrate its local value. In general though, changes at this level require political acts of readjustment and a form of ideological shift as a precursor to the provision of more substantive material support.

International location and networks

The history of MOS/ICCM purportedly rests in the West – in Europe and in the US – and is self-defined that way. The colonial period saw Western dominance not just militarily, politically, and economically but also culturally and educationally. Western education systems were exported around the world, or else copied, often with the support and collusion of local elites. In the postcolonial era this imbalance has continued, with continued Western domination in many respects. In particular, in terms of management education, the US model has been widely exported and/or adopted (Engwall & Zamagni, 1998; Gourvish & Tiratsoo, 1998; Leavitt, 1957). The influence of US management systems internationally has been extensive and strategic (Gemelli, 1996; Kipping & Bjarnar, 1998; Westwood & Jack, 2008), but variable (Gourvish & Tiratsoo, 1998; Kipping, Üsdiken & Puig, 2004). It has certainly served to foster and cement US educational dominance and contribute to its cultural hegemony.

However, there are assertions of greater levels of independence and an increasing diversity of management education systems slowly emerging from what was a strong US, or at least North Atlantic, dominance. Europe as a whole, and specific countries within Europe in particular, have begun to demarcate some different territory and to pursue differentiated trajectories *vis-à-vis* the US (Amdam, 1996). Scandinavian business schools and education, for example, are sustaining and strengthening some degree of independence, both institutionally and through perspective. Whilst we recognize that this is a region belonging to the privileged centre, we can use some of the things done in Scandinavia to suggest ways of asserting a degree of independence from the US-dominated scene whilst not pursuing an isolationist stance. One example is the establishment of the Scandinavian Consortium for Organizational Research (SCANCOR) in 1988. As the organization says on its website (SCANCOR, 2009) the aim was to:

> create a foundation for internationalizing research and education in organization and leadership. Through cooperation among Scandinavian business schools and universities, SCANCOR hopes to promote an international perspective in research and education, as well as to strengthen ties among Scandinavian researchers and encourage joint research projects.

It currently has members across Scandinavia and ties with Stanford University in the US. There is also the *Scandinavian Journal of Management*, which was established in 1985, has a solid reputation and publishes papers of local, regional and international interest. The journal is the official publication of the Nordic Academy of Management; hence the region has its own professional association too. There is also an academic publisher focused on MOS issues, The Copenhagen Business School Press, which publishes in conjunction with Liber AB of Sweden for some titles. In other words, Scandinavia has a full set of regional institutions that serve the countries of the region and that provide support for a network, a means of publication, and institutional location of MOS scholars. This has provided ground for some degree of localized theorization and research and some degree of independence. At the same time an international focus has also been sustained. We need to note that although there are pan-Scandinavian bodies, there are differences and unique institutions and approaches in the individual countries within the region.

This example suggests the value of (a) local and/or regional networks, perhaps supported by a professional association; (b) the establishment of national/regional research centres or research networks; (c) the criticality of having a local publishing house and particularly a credible local journal as a means of dissemination for local work. Of great significance, as we have suggested, is that there is support from local government and other bodies that value, support and provide legitimacy for local MOS/ICCM work. We argue that these elements are part of what is required in regions of the periphery to help strengthen the local MOS/ICCM scene and to move towards the facilitation of a quasi-independent and indigenously focused practice.

Our choice of Scandinavia is somewhat arbitrary and there are plenty of other places around the world where localized solutions to the issues of location and networking have been addressed. For example, Asia-Pacific Researchers in Organization Studies (APROS) was established in 1982 in Australia as a networking vehicle for organization studies scholars within the Asia-Pacific region. It has a conference within the region every second year and mounted its thirteenth at the end of 2009. It is loosely modelled on, but is also a counterpoint to, the European Group for Organizational Studies (EGOS), which was established in Europe in the early 1970s to provide a similar network there. This is an important network for the Asia-Pacific region and for some of those of the semi-periphery. Still more localized is the OIL network established by Prichard, Holmes and others in New Zealand that we have noted before. It was established at least in part to consider precisely the issue of location and the problematics of research and theorization from beyond the centre.

Loubser (1988) also emphasized the significance of the development of local and regional networks for those within the periphery or semi-periphery. He stressed the importance of facilitating interaction and co-operation among non-Western researchers and institutions and of diverting from, or at least supplementing, centre-periphery linkages. Again, national associations can play a part by forging regional links with counterparts. Local universities likewise can forge networked relationships. On this issue of local and regional networks and as part of a more general set of strategies to reduce academic dependency, Alatas (2003: 610) has this to say:

> these efforts can be significantly aided by greater interaction among the social scientists of the Third World. This cannot be left to chance. While there are ample opportunities for scholars from the Third World to meet each other, they tend to gravitate to the West for conferences and research opportunities. It is necessary, therefore, to form regional associations. For example, there is a need for an Asian sociological association. Such a regional association could consciously strive to organize events that bring together scholars from all over the world with similar concerns.

We support this statement and note that such collaboration and networking within Third World or developing regions is at present not common. As Altbach and Hoshino (1995) explain in comments about the publishing industry, partly as a reflection of colonial history, the lines of contact tend to be from individual Third World countries to the centre, rather than links between countries within the Third World.

Universities and their management regimes

We argued in Chapter 3 that universities and related institutions are a critical element in the institutional frame for a number of reasons, principally through their: involvement in the production and dissemination of knowledge; role in the establishment of research agendas; promotion of research methods and pedagogy; policing of the discursive boundaries; and role in the management of employment and careers. In terms of knowledge production and dissemination, we have clearly demonstrated how this remains very ethnocentric and Western-dominated. We will return to some of these other aspects of university systems later, but for now we want to address them in terms of their role in the management of employment and careers.

We reflected in Chapter 3 how a range of employment and HR practices impact on academics wherever they are located and send signals that determine how they approach their task. We argued that, increasingly, there has been an internationalization of these practices and that Western models are exerting an increasing influence internationally. The presence of these practices is serving to further impel people in the non-centre to engage with Western theory and research practice to the neglect of alternative and indigenous ones. Principal among these employment and research practices are recruitment, training and development and performance management systems.

In order for academic dependence to be broken or weakened, and for localized, alternative and/or indigenous perspectives to develop, local academic institutions need to be able to recruit and develop staff capable of contributing to that effort. The first step is, naturally, to recruit local people as much as possible and not to rely on expatriate academics from the centre. However, as we discussed in Chapter 3, simply recruiting local people is no guarantee of a localized orientation. Firstly, there has been a tendency for universities from the non-centre to either recruit local people who have received their critical tertiary education in the West or to send their people overseas for such training. Secondly, unless the local environment is supportive of efforts to adopt a localized or alternative perspective, particularly in terms of its performance management systems, there is no incentive for even local staff to embark on such a path.

A problem we identified in Chapter 3 is the 'brain drain'. This was meant in two senses, firstly and concretely the migration of scholars from the periphery to the centre(s). The reasons are varied and may have to do simply with better remuneration and career opportunity, but they may also relate to a perceived desirousness or need to participate in the main circuits of MOS/ICCM, and these might be supposed to reside in the centre. For some this is a permanent migration, for others it is temporary and for the purposes of graduate study. The second notion associated with brain drain is that once educated in the Western academy, scholars often become so imbued with the philosophy, knowledge systems, theories and methods they are exposed to that they are unable or unwilling to think about or work with alternatives. They become in that sense 'captive minds'. To reconfigure the field it would seem desirable to slow or halt this brain drain – in both senses. They are related and working on one has an impact on the other.

To limit the actual migration of talent, at one level the local context must be made more desirable in employment and career terms. This is largely the responsibility of local governments and institutions, and may mean more investment and the production of better material terms and conditions. An academic career in the periphery is often not seen as particularly desirable. Commenting on the high staff turnover in Malaysian management education tertiary institutions, it has been suggested that this is often the result of disillusionment resulting from: 'lack of support from the top management, poor administrative support with lazy administrators, absence of autonomy in academic and non-academic matters, poor monetary rewards, unappealing or uninteresting work load, and inability to cope with student demands' (Muniapan, 2008: 84).

However, again material support is not the only issue: what is also critical is that local work, and local work conducted from an indigenous perspective, is legitimized, validated and supported. Academics might always be motivated to move towards the centre in search of career and money, but many feel compelled to do so because they perceive that little value is placed on work that has a purely local or indigenous perspective. Obviously there are complex linkages here. For example part of the impulsion to seek engagement with the centre is because the system of the centre maintains that the best journals are there. So in terms of engagement, impact and career, it is felt that one must publish there. Writing outside the centre makes it difficult to publish in those journals; it is easier if one is in the centre – as our analysis has shown.

Furthermore, increasingly local higher education systems in MOS/ICCM are adopting the standards of the centre and applying their metrics in recruitment and performance management systems. At the heart of such systems are metrics related to journal publication and comprised of ranking and citation regimes. These systems are based on Western-criteria and Western journals. We will comment more on this shortly. The point here is that stemming the brain drain depends not just on material support for local conditions, but also an institutional shift to give more value to local/indigenous work and to eschew the performance regimes promulgated by the West. Such an institutional shift might involve some or all of the recommended strategies for building indigenous research capacity offered by Smith (2005: 92) including:

- The training of indigenous people as researchers;
- The employment of indigenous people as researchers;
- Participation by indigenous people in a wide range of research projects employing different kinds of approaches and methodologies;
- The generating of research questions by communities;
- Developing indigenous research methodologies;
- Developing research protocols for working with communities;
- The support by various individuals and communities of research-based decision making;
- The establishment of indigenous research organizations;
- Presentation of research by indigenous researchers to other indigenous researchers;
- Engagements and dialogue between indigenous and non-indigenous researchers and communities.

One of the issues we discussed in Chapter 3 in terms of both recruitment and training and development was the resources to develop local talent. The dilemma, as we put it then, was that the extant dominance of Western MOS/ICCM meant that most of the available pedagogy is Western-produced or produced locally in mimicry of Western materials. Local institutions tend to adopt known Western texts. A senior human resource consultant in Malaysia bemoaned the reliance on Western theories, concepts and materials, and insinuated that a change of attitude locally is needed to alter that. He commented that:

> ...most Malaysian students and managers are still mentally colonised and feel that anything from the West must be good. Management educational programmes in IHL[1] tend to place too much emphasis on Western management theories and concepts, which were written in a different cultural context (Muniapan, 2008: 84).

The knock-on effect is that people are schooled in those materials, become imbued with them, potentially intellectually captive, and so the capacity to pursue alternative indigenous perspectives is further retarded. This circle needs to be broken. There needs to be support, encouragement and legitimization of locally produced materials. That ultimately depends upon the support and valorization of local/indigenous research and theory development that can feed into the production of local materials. Commenting on management education in Malaysia for instance, Muniapan (2008: 85) points to the reliance on Western theories, concepts and materials and calls for an increase in Malaysian-based 'research and textbook publications' as well as local theory development. He argues that the government 'through the Ministry of Higher Education, needs to provide incentives to local management authors and researchers to conduct research and publish in Malaysian management contexts and Malaysian-based management case studies'. The production of local materials provides a place for and encouragement of localized research and theory development as well as providing the necessary means to train and develop local people in more meaningful ways and equipping them to go and further focus on local and indigenous research and theory development.

It is quite apparent that the performance management systems and reward and incentive systems of academic institutions impact on and shape the behaviour of individual academics and will, in turn, shape the whole ethos and orientation of the institution and the field in that locale. As we have already stated, a tendency has developed whereby universities and higher education systems in the periphery and semi-periphery are starting to adopt standards and criteria for evaluating outcomes and performance that have become commonplace in the West. The fact that these criteria and outcomes primarily relate to publishing in the journals of the centre seems almost masochistic. In addition, the databases upon which citations are based and upon which journal rankings are established, and subsequently scholars and institutions are judged by, are loaded towards researchers/institutions from the centre, and more particularly from the US and Europe, not least because of the almost exclusive reliance on journals published in English. We would endorse the call from Adler and Harzing (2009) for a moratorium on rankings and a re-examination of the whole issue of ranking journals and judging output.

Some countries however have already decided to opt out of the Western publications-performance game. As Alatas (2003: 606) points out 'the Japanese social science establishment, while very much influenced by Western models, does not gauge success according to publications in Western periodicals and Western languages. There is, in a sense, an opting out of that game'. He argues that the same is true of Germany where the social science establishment rewards people for publishing in local journals and monographs and in German. National governments and academic establishments can, then, choose not to participate in the regimes of the centre and there are good grounds for doing so in many cases.

Local institutions need to have proactive policies to encourage and reward people for pursuing localized, alternative and alternatively-orientated work rather than work in the Western mainstream. Only if such systems are in place are individuals likely to feel able to pursue that path and to resist the seductions of the Western game. This element is vital if other things such as developing local journals and learned institutions are to have a chance of being really successful.

Professional and academic associations

We have demonstrated that despite their claims to be international, many of the large, indeed dominating, professional academies of the centre are actually rather parochial in terms of their membership, certainly in terms of their governance, and sometimes in terms of their orientation. With respect to membership they are often disconnected from large tracts of the globe. Further, as Loubser (1988) argues, through the way they currently function, they tend to reinforce and perpetuate the vertical relationships of international academia. International academies need to examine their assumptions, particularly to question the universalist assumptions often inherent in the practices they advocate and support in research and publishing, and examine what it really means to be international in the sense of being positively and actively inclusive. This requires a fundamental shift in intellectual orientation and position. More pragmatically and positively, they can examine their mission statements, philosophy and policies with respect to the non-Western world and actively work to promote genuine inclusiveness. In terms of the current structural imbalances, they can take more proactive steps to reach out and locate members from non-Western and Third World contexts – particularly in Latin America, Africa and the Middle East – through explicit outreach programmes. Similarly with respect to the imbalances within their governance structures, they also need to outreach and appoint more officials from non-Western and Third World contexts. Mechanisms such as affirmative action or proportional representation might have a place. Many such institutions and academies also publish or support lead journals; they can influence editorial policy and practice as well as address the issue of editorships and editorial board composition. The Western academies can further work to ensure a greater diversity through other strategies and activities such as: locating conferences and workshops in non-centre locations on a number of fronts; providing language translation and editing services; acting as a portal for research partnerships; offering reduced prices on services for scholars from countries with a low GDP per head, or travel and conference scholarships.

In terms of local academies situated in locations out of the centre, there is a need to be strong and confident enough to resist the bland-ishments of the academies and other institutions of the centre, and focus primarily on building and supporting local scholars and their localized agendas and activities. Indeed, Loubser (1988: 185) urged that national learned societies be 'discouraged from following the fads and fashions of the dominant social science centres and from uncritically applying models, theories, methods, techniques, and so-called "univer-sal" standards of excellence in their work, reward and incentive systems'. This feeds back into the issues of adopting Western standards and criteria and applying them to performance management regimes locally.

Textbook and pedagogy

We have already touched on the issue of textbooks and other aspects of pedagogy in our brief exploration of employment practices in general and the training and development of staff in particular. The problem, as noted, is the dominance of Western texts and pedagogy and the tendency of scholars and institutions to elect to adopt Western texts. Altbach and Hoshino (1995) point to the ongoing power of 'metropolitan' publishers, especially in the Third World. Underlying the scarcity of locally-produced texts with local content is the deficiency in localized research and theory development that can provide the necessary material for the texts. This is the priority area. As we have already signalled, this requires material sup-port but also intellectual and ideological support. Local institutions must concretely support this by policy orientation, priority establishment, pro-vision of funding, and the construction of appropriate HRM and perfor-mance-reward systems that provide incentives and encouragement to pursue localized, indigenous or alternative research and theory. Such research and theory development must, in turn, become the basis for pedagogic content for the training and development of new local staff.

Commenting on scientific publishing in China, for example, Phua (2001: 60)[2] suggests that although local publishing has expanded and improved since 'openness', it still needs to develop further. He suggests a number of strategies to facilitate that including: government subsidies for local publications; the government providing incentives for scientists to publish in local journals rather than international ones; and improving the quality of local publications. He does note the work of the national publishing house *Science Press*. Incidentally, cognizant of the preclusive costs of journals and texts in the Third World, he also advocates returning copyright to scientists and having cheaper or freer dissemination around the world. Altbach and Hoshino (1995) also point to the continued control of copyright by the centre. Electronic distribution systems are starting to help with this, but in developing contexts they are a mixed blessing (ibid). Phua also points to the need for translation services.

National academic associations might play a role not only in encouraging this trajectory, but perhaps could establish their own publishing operations, not just for journals, but also for locally produced academic material – texts and monographs. Equally, local universities or conglomerations or co-operatives of local universities might take on such a role. Phua (2001) calls for the establishment of regional publishing associations in Third World regions. Altbach and Hoshino (1995) point to the colonially-established commercial lines running from the colonizing countries of the centre to colonized countries in the TW and maintains that it is still easier, for example, for a book buyer in Nigeria to secure book supplies from England than it is from, say, Kenya, or Angola. Even local publishing houses might do more to encourage, publish and disseminate locally produced materials. Altbach and Hoshino (1995) argue that it is imperative that all but the very smallest of Third World countries develop an indigenous publishing industry. They describe enormous difficulties in Africa and elsewhere, but do note some successful indigenous publishing operations in, for example, Kenya and South Africa. Claude Alvares' 'Other India' publishing house is an example of an independent operation that supports and encourages indigenous (and critical) work.

International (i.e. Western) publishing houses can make a contribution. They can in general be more open and sensitive in their editorial and publishing policies. They can *inter alia:* establish operations in more diverse places (Sage's New Delhi operations demonstrate the viability of this); engage in outreach activities to locate writers and work outside the centre; relax copyright restrictions and allow reprints; offer price discounts; offer translation and other text development services for authors; publish more often in a wide range of languages; appoint for diversity in their own management and editorial teams.

We pointed out in Chapter 3 that a barrier to the localized training and development of academics, schooled in localized material as a basis for relevant pedagogy, is the presumed deficiency of local, indigenous theory. The consequence is the importation or mimicking of Western texts and other pedagogy and the continued reliance on Western derived theory. One response to this in some parts of the world is for local scholars to investigate indigenous intellectual heritage and to examine that heritage for theory, conceptualization and insight that, sometimes with reinterpretation, has contemporary currency. Thus, Alatas (2003) urges that textbooks be developed (in his case for the social sciences in general) that not only include core Western theory such as Marx, Weber and Durkheim, but also the ideas of non-Western thinkers, and he cites the Indian Scholar Sarkar and the Philippine scholar Rizal as examples. Sarkar was a thinker and writer who was active in the early part of the 20th century and made an early challenge to Western social science imposition and hegemony. Alatas (2003) quotes Sarkar who castigates the captive minds of Asian thinkers who have become 'victim to the fallacious sociological methods and messages of the modern West, to which the postulate of an alleged distinction between the Orient and the Occident is the first principle of science' (Sarkar, 1937/1985: 19). Rizal, Alatas says (ibid: footnote 12), was concerned about the colonial erosion of Philippine history and memory and reproduced an annotated and reinterpreted version of Antonio de Morga's *Sucesos de las Islas Filipinas*, which was a Spanish history of the Philippine Islands.[3] Rizal was a reformer and advocate of peaceful resistance.

In another example, Gopinath (1998) points to the situation in India where scholars are re-examining some key indigenous texts for insights relating to contemporary management and organization. He cites the work of Sen (2004) and Subramaniam (1990), both of whom have offered reinterpretations of the *Arthasasthra* of Kautilya and Vishnagupta, which Gopinath describes as being a treatise on politics, strategy and statecraft akin to Machiavelli's *The Prince*.[4] We might also note that Sun Tzu's *The Art of War* has also been similarly scrutinized by both Western and Chinese scholars (such as McNeilly, 1996; Michaelson, 2001). Others have turned to Hindu and Buddhist texts (Chakraborty, 1991; Simha, 1992). The risk is to romanticize and revise these older works, but as Chakraborty argues, the aim is not a regressive return to the past, but rather an attempt to ground contemporary management practice in Indian thought and values rather than imported Western thought and values. In his view it is important to ground management practice in relevant and meaningful values and then supplement that with skills and methods, not the other way round (Gopinath, 1998: 266).

As Altbach and Hoshino (1995) argue, textbook publishing is critical in Third World contexts for a whole host of reasons, some pragmatic and material (such as trying to reduce costs), some political and ideological, which have to do with systems of dependence and the decolonization of the mind. They also recognize a whole range of difficulties in developing an indigenous publication industry. They point, for instance, to the persistent strength and influence of colonial languages, the typical diversity of indigenous languages, the failure of inter-regional co-operation, and the scarcity of resources and talent. There is unlikely to be a single solution and all parties, such as international publishing houses, local governments, academic bodies and associations and others, can make a contribution. For ICCM it is a highly significant element of the institutional frame. We have argued about the circular trap: textbooks are imported because there are no good local alternatives with local content; there is no good local content because scholars are not incentivized to produce local, indigenous research and theory; those absences mean that would be scholars are schooled in Western texts and Western theory and methods, further eroding the capacity and will to produce indigenous research and theory. A concerted effort is required to break this destructive cycle.

Journals and journal publishing apparatus

If textbook publishing is important to ICCM outside the centre, then journal publishing might be even more so given its centrality not only to knowledge dissemination, but to the very practice of ICCM research and to careers within ICCM. We have offered something of a critique of the Western publishing machine and its role in exclusionary practices and the maintenance of Western hegemony. It is obvious that an independent, localized and indigenized MOS/ICCM is dependent on breaking the bounds of the Western publishing machine and developing the means to disseminate and communicate its findings through local and independent media. Given prevailing standards of performance (although these might be challenged and reconfigured), it is journal publishing that is most at issue. However, other modes of communication and dissemination are also of importance, including monographs, textbooks, audio-visual materials, websites as well as symposia, conferences, and the like.

The first issue here is whether or not scholars from the non-centre ought to pursue publication in the journals of the centre. They are likely to want to continue to do so when the incentives from their institutions and/or governments continue to reward that. This again is where the solutions and alternatives become compacted. Increasingly, academic institutions in the periphery are entering performance regimes that depend upon the metrics of journal publication. They are, therefore, increasing incentives to publish in those journals and, at the same time, further neglect and not support or reward publication in local journals. Individual scholars, naturally attuned to the signals that affect their careers, reputations and impact become less motivated to publish locally and hence less likely to set their research agendas to local themes and problems. Local theory development is retarded. Local journals are further diminished (a) because of fewer contributions and (b) because the content is impoverished, since there is a failure to address local issues and develop local theory and method. Once again, this matrix is in urgent need of reconfiguration, but also once again it is a fiendishly impacted and entrenched set of problems and issues that like a Gordian knot will not be readily unravelled.

With respect to journals, local academic societies and institutions can play a role by supporting or even publishing relevant journals. Of course, the mere existence of a local journal is not the whole story; there are already quite a number of localized MOS/ICCM journals in existence. Examples from just within Africa include: the *African Journal of Business Management* (published by Academic Journals out of Nigeria); *Management Dynamics* (published on-line by the Southern African Institute for Management Scientists); *African Administrative Studies* (published in Morocco by the *African Training and Research Centre in Administration for Development*, CAFRAD); *African Journal of Finance and Management* (published in Dar es Salaam, Tanzania by The Institute of Finance Management); *Lagos Business School Management Review* (published through the Lagos Business School). This does not include those journals that may be published in languages other than English, which remain somewhat invisible to our Western search methods. There are, naturally, other locally and regionally orientated journals that are published in the West. Again, an example with respect to Africa is *The Journal of African Business*, which is published and produced in Toronto by Haworth Press. The issue is one of visibility, impact and location in the field of MOS/ICCM discourse. These issues again have a bearing on local writers' pragmatic calculations and choices of where to publish. So mere existence is not enough; local publication outlets must be given value and encouragement and academic institutions need to incentivize academic staff to publish in them, as we have already discussed. A further point identified by Loubser is noteworthy; that it is not just the presence or development of local journals, publishers and annual meetings, but also the 'question of an independent set of information systems through which information about the products of its social science activities can be disseminated efficiently' (Loubser, 1988: 182). This means access to or development of things such as databases, bibliographies, citation indices and directories. These are all well developed adjuncts to the Western publishing machine, but they are not always readily available or accessible by those in the non-West.

Of significance in this regard is the establishment of the International Network for the Availability of Scientific Publications (INASP), which was established by the International Council for Science (ICSU) in 1992. It was established, as their website (INASP, 2008) states, 'as a direct response to a study on how to meet the information needs of scientists in the developing world'. INASP now operates out of the UK as a registered charity. The vision of the organization is concerned with helping to ensure the free and valid provision and availability of information as vital to 'democracy, good governance and poverty reduction' (ibid). Whilst this pertains to all types of information, the organization has focused on research-based information and ensuring that researchers have proper access to, and can freely and effectively disseminate, research information. Their mission, hence, is stated as being to 'enable a sustainable network of stakeholders that owns and drives access, use, dissemination and communication of research information' (ibid). The INASP provides a range of services – advisory, training and research – that are designed to work with stakeholders such as publishers, libraries and research institutions to ensure effective communication and dissemination of research-related information, particularly for those individuals and institutions in developing or Third World contexts. One of its keystone programmes is the Programme for the Enhancement of Research Information (PERI), through which INASP works to forge a functioning network of publishers, libraries and research institutes. Publishers involved include key Western publishing houses such as Taylor/Francis, Palgrave/Macmillan and Sage, aggregate providers such as JSTOR, EBSCO and Thomson-Reuters Web of Science, as well as more specialized publishers and providers such as the American Physical Society, The Geological Society and various university presses.

There are other key issues and changes that would be valuable with respect to journals and journal publishing. As our analysis in Chapter 3 shows, most Western-journals are ethnocentric and biased towards their own authors and those of a limited number of countries. They are also biased in their management and governance structures. Hence, as with academic institutions, there are strategies that could be pursued to improve this situation:

1. The policies and practices of the journals need to be reconsidered and made more explicitly inclusive. This includes being not only open to authors and issues from a wider range of national and cultural locations, but also to more significant shifts in editorial and intellectual policy. This entails: a) examining policies and practices for assumptions of universality; b) ensuring equal requirements regarding context; c) being more open to alternative epistemological and ontological positions; d) being more open to indigenous perspectives; e) being more inclusive with respect to methods and research designs.

2. There could be outreach activities to locate and invite contributions from a wider range of locations and about a wider range of issues. Such activities might include, for example, greater presence of editorial and publishing teams and officials at conferences and other events in the periphery.

3. Greater attempts need to be undertaken to broaden governance structures. As we have recorded, editors and editorial teams tend to be drawn from a very narrow set of locations. Again, explicit strategies can be undertaken to broaden that. One step in that direction is to appoint area or regional editors from a range of locations. Other strategies might again include some notion of proportional representation or affirmative action type policies. What needs to be avoided is tokenism or the empty gesture of the type that Özbilgin (2004) reported and that we noted in Chapter 3.

4. Language issues are extremely problematic. Journals could work to address their typical monolingualism. One path is to provide translation services so that people can write and submit to English language journals in their own language, but have their work professionally translated. A second strategy is to actually publish in more than one language. Examples already exist: *Transtext(e)s Transcultures* publishes in English, French and Chinese. It describes itself as a *Journal of Global Cultural Studies*, and the lead statement from its website home page is worth quoting in full:

> *Transtext(e)s Transcultures [and here should appear Chinese characters representing Transtext(e)s]* is a tri-lingual research journal created in 2006. It is intended to be a forum transcending disciplinary as well as spatial boundaries for writers and academics throughout the

global community. Its ambition is to provide a space for the imagining of new frameworks of accounting for and representing the world, a space in which different approaches and trans-disciplinary methods, may jostle to express the complexity and the diversity of human (hi)stories and societies.

We might also note *Traces* (2009), which is described as publishing a series of books, but is very close to a periodic journal. It is a multilingual series related to translation and cultural theory, published in English, Chinese, Japanese and Korean.[5] It is a series/journal that explicitly emphasizes and works in relation to ties among Northeast Asian cultures.

Captive minds and constructive imitation

We concluded Chapter 3 with a discussion of 'captured minds' (Alatas, 1974) and our comments and suggestions here and in the preceding chapter are largely intended to avoid captured minds and to offer alternative approaches and institutional contexts in which scholars from the non-centre can pursue theory and research in MOS/ICCM as they see fit and in light of the heritage, traditions, interests, values and conditions within their locations. However, Alatas quite rightly reminds us that societies have always been influenced by others and that there has always been a confluence and a flow of ideas, methods and peoples. To our minds, it is both unrealistic and potentially hazardous and self-defeating to shun ideas from outside and to cut oneself off in some attempted splendid isolation. It is equally hazardous to presume that one can push back international influence and return to some presumed originary location; some pristine, uncontaminated premodern indigenous state. Alatas notes this in his search for the solution to the problem of 'captive minds' and as Subramani and Kempner (2002: 242) interpret him, it is 'obviously prudent to imitate' provided that it is 'constructive imitation' (Alatas, 1974) and not imposed or unthinking and unreflexive imitation. Constructive imitation is possible when:

- It is based on a conscious and rational choice;
- It supports existing and sound values;
- It considers the problems, if any, surrounding the adoption of the innovation;
- Its non-adoption would be inhibiting to society;

- It increases the understanding of phenomena surrounding the innovation;
- It does not disrupt other aspects of social life considered valuable;
- It does not create great strains detrimental to the purpose of the undertaking;
- It enters the collective value system in the sense that it is recognized as valuable by large groups of people;
- It is not the effect of manipulation by external groups motivated by their own interests to the detriment of the adopter (Alatas, 1974: 692).

In sum, this chapter has attempted to revisit key elements of the institutional frame that supports scholarship in ICCM with a view to reconfiguring them such that they can become more inclusive. A key problematic in this regard is the question of how indigenous research that legitimizes and valorizes non-Western forms of knowledge can be fostered. We have tried to outline a comprehensive set of concrete actions that the variety of different actors that constitute the institutional frame of ICCM nationally and internationally can engage in to transform its multiple parochialisms. We now turn to our final chapter, in which we offer a reflexive evaluation of our argument, and its conditions of possibility.

12
Conclusion

In this short concluding chapter to the book, our aim is to provide a reflexive evaluation of the conditions of possibility, significance and limitations of our argument. In consonance with our calls for ICCM researchers to demonstrate reflexivity, we too attempt to speak of our own social identities, structural and epistemic positions, values and interests. We do so in order to acknowledge the forms of privilege and power that enabled the production of this book, and the contradictions attendant to it, and to situate it in its specific locations. Against this reflexive context, we provide a conclusion and evaluation of our argument, outlining its significance for the field of ICCM in general, and postcolonial modes of critique in MOS in particular. But we also try to articulate the silences and point to the limitations and constraints of the text we have produced here. In this particular regard, we emphasize the potential disjuncture between our predominantly cultural critique and the wider conditions of possibility for such a critique to be heard. The limitations of our own privilege, and the silences, distortions, and biases to which they inevitably give rise, produce a range of choices and directions for future researchers wishing to pursue a critique of international and cross-cultural management studies.

Identities and carriers of privilege

In his intriguing reflections on gender and diversity research, Jacques (1997) self-identifies as a 'pale, stale, male' – a straight, white, man. He discusses the implications and ethical responsibilities of these intersecting subject positions, and the forms of privilege of which they speak, for/as a researcher(s) in these areas. He notes: 'we of dominant identities are obligated to identify and resist the operation of this structural dominance in theory and practice' (1997: 82). So, what about us? Are we similarly "pale, stale, males"? And what difference does this make to the production and evaluation of this text?'

We do not think it possible theoretically, nor necessarily desirable to hold a mirror up to ourselves expecting to 'isolate' or 'capture' easily and transparently the values, interests, desires, fantasies, structural conditions, and epistemic positions that have enabled and constrained the production of our text. We share Rose's (1997) reservations described in Chapter 10 about transparent models of reflexivity that supposedly enable the researcher to glimpse him-/herself in some kind of fullness or wholeness. Instead we make an attempt to articulate something of a 'displacement' of ourselves, first locating our personal forms of identification within wider structural positions, and then noting some of the attendant ambiguities and uncertainties on which the text and our own subjectivities as 'originating authors' rest. Whilst this textual process will involve naming and labelling our identities, interests, and those forms of knowledge that seem certain enough for us to proclaim, we also try to listen to the silences that haunt our text. Ultimately though, it is the situated perceptions of our readers holding this book right now that will locate our work into their own positions of intelligibility and identify gaps, omissions and limitations beyond our own reflexive capacities and possibilities for articulation.

In spite of the philosophical difficulties associated with the notion of a reflexive subject, and more pressingly the practical challenges of how one accounts for the self in academic writing, our PCT framework demands, as an ethical obligation, that we attempt to take responsibility for the enabling and constraining power conditions and effects of our work. To return to Jacques (1997), it is to demonstrate that despite our epistemological and political locations, we share structural positions that, in the main, are the bases for reproducing and enacting relations of dominance and subjugation. Jacques (ibid: 103) puts it thus:

> We who experience social life from dominant positions male, straight, white, dominant culture, middle class, middle age – must come to better understand that the problem is structural as well as personal. (...) when others point to the existence of asymmetrical power and voice, relative privilege and marginality, or even outright oppression, I must accept that, as a producer of research, as an organization

member, as a citizen, *to fail to resist these systemic forces is as much an act of dominance as is face-to-face discrimination.* (italics in the original)

For the most part, our own personal identities line up with the structural issues pointed to by Jacques (with the exception of the axis of sexuality in one of our cases). We also need to add that we are creatures from the centre. We were, and continue to benefit from being, born British with all that means for subject locations of privilege and within circuits of power. We therefore need to take responsibility for these structural locations that accordingly enable and limit the production of our text and its contents, as well as the contradictions and distortions that may attend that. Whilst we attempt to articulate these contradictions below, ultimately it is impossible for us to realize them all. We would therefore like to acknowledge these other forms *a priori*.

This book has been a number of years in the making and was produced collaboratively by two white men, born and educated in the United Kingdom. We completed our undergraduate degrees in the British higher education system (GJ in languages and international business; RW in philosophy and psychology) before undertaking higher research degrees in business schools on different topics (GJ on intercultural management communication; RW on organizational change and theory). We have both worked in schools or faculties of management/business for the majority of our professional lives. GJ worked for nine years in three different management schools in the UK, before emigrating in 2009 to Australia. RW has worked in universities for close to 30 years, taking a more circuitous route to Australia *via* Fiji, Macau, Hong Kong. He left the UK in 1983. RW now works at UTS following more than ten years at other universities in Australia. Thus our professional and personal identities are rooted in the Northern centre and are deeply embedded in its education system. We have also though, to varying degrees, spent time in the periphery or semi-periphery as well as in colonial and formerly colonial contexts. These are formative exposures but do not efface white privilege which is carried through these other spaces. They are also highly important in helping shape the interests, motives and perceptions that are enabling and constraining conditions of possibility for this text.

We are native English speakers and have researched and published, to different degrees, on international and comparative management. In institutional terms, we are currently relatively privileged to work in universities that fund research well and provide structures for good careers, advancement and material rewards for 'internationally recognized' (sic) research output. We therefore have money to travel to the metropolitan and elite conference circuits of the USA and Europe, attend both mainstream and critical conferences (from AOM to EGOS and CMS). Both have benefited materially and symbolically from the opportunities offered by these structural positions. These too are conditions enabling of the production and dissemination of our text.

By contrast, and in epistemic and political terms, the values and interests that guide our research might well be considered marginal relative to the mainstream of MOS and ICCM described at length in this book. Both of us have quite wide and varied academic and intellectual interests. In the domain of ICCM, while RW has published many articles and book chapters on a number of substantive areas, neither of us can be said to be well-known in mainstream, positivistic ICCM circles. We have not regularly attended the IM division of the AOM (though GJ is a more recent participant), nor been regular contributors to the AIB for instance (although RW attended a few earlier in his career).

Moreover in epistemological terms, earlier chapters in this book outlined our social constructionist position and located it within a critical and radical management tradition. We write with critical intent since we believe not only that our field has been overly preoccupied with a narrow range of topics, interests and studies that contribute to the reproduction of a narrow status quo, but also that ICCM is currently too disconnected from the material realities and shocking inequities of the material world and contemporary global relations. We feel a sense of outrage that the field, through its orthodox practices, actually contributes to a cultural circuit of knowledge and capital that propagates and reproduces this state of affairs, as we noted in Chapter 6. Outrage too that it seems to do little about acknowledging this situation, and less still about making moves to rectify it. The field has shown few signs thus far of either widening its critical lens or reflecting on its ethical and political commitments and modifying them. We intend these comments at ICCM to be considered collectively and institutionally, not at individuals within it, many of whom might well share different ethical and political commitments.

Taking these points altogether, we might say that we have been situated in positions of privilege within the Western academy, but have remained somewhat on the fringe of the orthodox and mainstream as embodied in the US academy. This would not be atypical for academics from, for example, Australasia. So we emanate from the centre and have drifted to what, in some ways, might be taken as the semi-periphery, with RW moving through the periphery en route. We have continued to occupy positions of privilege relative to the periphery, and although we have chosen not to participate fully in the orthodoxy of the American academy, we do engage with it periodically through our publishing, networking and conference attendance.

From this semi-peripheral institutional, epistemically marginal but socially and culturally dominant location, a number of prejudices and limitations ensue for the arguments we have pursued in this book. In large part, these relate to the fact that our writing is epistemically located in Eurocentric frames of reference, and materially facilitated by the disciplinary regimes of our locations in English-speaking and well-funded universities. These frames of reference and disciplinary regimes are the very same ones that form the objects of our critique and consequently, a number of tensions and ambiguities can be discerned. For one, we are using primarily Western philosophical and theoretical resources to mount a critique of Western research and theory practice and particularly on the grounds of its parochialism, ethnocentrism and universalism. We have also critiqued the orthodoxy for ignoring or not adequately engaging with the non-centre. But we have not been able to transcend our own locations and bring to bear very many critical theoretical resources from outside the centre. Within MOS/ICCM we are critical of mainstream traditions and inspired by critical works by writers in MOS (and other parts of the humanities and social sciences) largely, but not entirely, based in European, American and Australian/ New Zealand institutions. Our text relies upon knowledge produced in the English language; we have not been in a position to examine texts in other languages, particularly those located in the periphery. We are publishing in a well-known Western publishing house whose distribution channels are primarily geared to Western markets. In all likelihood the readership, if we may so presume, are likely to be fellow academics from the centre (although we hope not just there!)

Furthermore, we are British white men, social identities that took the lead in organizing Empire and that continue to dominate sites of power, including the international university system, and certainly the particular academic field we critique. In material terms, we have gained money from our institutions to travel to write together, and to attend international conferences to help shape our arguments. We have also presented drafts of certain chapters to other colleagues in British and American management schools. We would expect to gain some reward from the writing of this text, not necessarily financial, but through its contribution to our demonstration of an 'international research profile'. We recognize and acknowledge mixed motivations within ourselves in relation to this project.

Given the substantive concerns of our book with the after-effects of colonialism, and extant forms of neo-colonialism and imperialism, these loosely assembled, but related set of points about our locations and identities offer some unsettling contrasts and we own up to feeling a bit uneasy as we set them down in text. In short, our conditions of possibility are those of the centre, feeding from the possibilities of interaction with elite institutional formations, open to us through our privilege. They are possibilities that have become available through the historical sedimentation of modernity and the multiple forms of British colonial encounter. They are conditions formed by and embedded in the histories and structures of dominance and hegemony about which we seek to speak, criticize and dismantle. They are conditions that allow us to speak out from the centre and be heard.

Our task as writers has been enabled and constrained by these various biographical, structural, institutional and epistemic conditions of possibility. They represent our own indigenous ways of knowing and doing, our 'ethnoscience', conditioned by the specificities of our particular cultural, political, ideological and historical locations and by the structural privileges accorded to us through our social and professional identities. They are also simultaneously our forms of 'un-knowing', of lacunae, of ignorance, and ethical impossibility. We cannot 'know' what it is to be 'on the other side' of a colonial binary, to be forced to work within and between reified oppositions of the self and other that do not speak to our own sense of who we really are. We are not usually forced to work with the cultural structures of Others in order to be heard, in order to make a contribution, although RW has experienced that working in parts of Asia. With these points in mind, we next attempt to articulate the significance of our argument.

Conclusion and implications

We set out in this book to ask critical questions, informed in the main by postcolonial theory, about the values, interests and dominant forms of cultural knowledge contained within the broad field we labelled as ICCM – International and Cross-Cultural Management Studies. Who is represented? Who does the representing? What do we claim to know, and how? For what purposes and with what effects? In short, we set out to provincialize our field through strategies of historical contextualization and textual critique, and to begin a conversation about how we might collectively set about decolonizing theory, methodology and the institutional context of ICCM.

At the end of this journey, we come to the following conclusion: ICCM are Western and Eurocentric discourses that exhibit historical as well as contemporary resonances with colonial, neo-colonial and imperial projects. These are pursued by an evolving set of actors embedded in and constituted by a fluid commercial-military-political complex. In this respect, ICCM is a thoroughly modern project, but one that sits ill-at-ease with the realities of the contemporary global cultural economy and its various effects. Today, our field exhibits an incredibly narrow set of interests and voices, with knowledge-creation skewed towards the interests of elite audiences, and unwittingly reproductive of representational strategies and practices that can be considered orientalizing in nature. The evidence for this position has been laid out over three sections in the book.

The historical evidence in section two, for example, illustrated how science, anthropology and commercial practice, as well as the key discourses and material practices that underpin ICCM, have a particular set of colonial histories. The historiography of MOS in general, and ICCM in particular, has tended to overlook or efface how key assumptions and practices of the 'science' of ICCM can be located in the colonial encounter. Despite the end of formal colonialism and the demise of formal European Empires, section two illustrated the continuing impact of imperial economic and cultural structures on ICCM, in this instance associated with a US commercial-military complex. Discourses of modernization, industrialization and development, artefacts of contemporary US domestic and foreign policy, became sedimented into the early classics of ICCM, rendering them ideological artefacts of US cultural imperialism.

In section three, our mode of analysis moved from the historical to the textual, an attempt to surface the values, interests and dominant modes and strategies for representing the Other in a selection of central and influential ICCM texts. Here, we identified a latent structure of domination in ICCM manifest in the particular ways that knowledge of Others is appropriated, domesticated and controlled through representational forms that are universalizing, essentializing and resonant with Orientalism. Importantly, we also highlighted forms of hybridized cultural knowledge, reappropriation and resistance in the realms of MOS/ICCM, demonstrating that these dominant cultural forms are not totalizing in impact even though they may be in intent. Instead they point to the manner in which hegemonies and the texts and discourses that constitute them necessarily contain aporia and points of opposition that offer the grounds for challenge, deconstruction and decomposition.

In light of the perpetuation of US hegemony and the failure to transform radically the economic and cultural dependencies of colonial times, PCT insights tell us that neo-colonialism and imperialism have not gone away, but mutated into new postcolonial configurations in the economic and cultural spheres. The existence and nature of these new postcolonial configurations is barely acknowledged within ICCM yet alone the implications systematically explored. The impact these changes might have on our present history and the manner in which we translate them into knowledge, and text, offer critical challenges and opportunities for our field. We believe that ICCM, if we are to take a postcolonial approach seriously, should view the current times as a point of disjuncture, and an opportunity for radical reconfiguration.

The implications of our conclusions for ICCM could be significant. Given the centrality accorded to the culture concept and modes of analysis in this book, it is perhaps appropriate that the most profound implications pertain to culture in ICCM. We need to reconceive radically our understanding of the culture concept, and how we conduct cultural analysis. To begin, we need to stop trading in essentialist and reductionist views of culture, either through the rubric of national or societal cultures, or inflected by positivist or naïve interpretivist modes of analysis. Relatedly, we need to stop imagining that when two individuals (be they managers, workers, tourists, customers, migrants etc) of different cultural and linguistic groupings come together, they should be understood *a priori* as interlocutors of two pre-existing, fixed and homogenously organized cultures. And furthermore, that what exists in their interactions over time is some kind of hybrid or third culture, a syncretic mix of the two. This kind of 'Venn diagram' approach to culture is equally unhelpful. Our conclusion impels a different way forward.

We need to understand culture as a relational and a processual construct. Let us give up on fixed and essential notions of culture and instead work with more fluid notions that highlight the making and unmaking of new subjectivities, meanings, structures and localities. We need to do more border thinking, seeking to grasp, conceptualize and work with the complexities inherent in the making and unmaking of boundaries and cultures in particular power constellations. We need to see culture as a historical outcome and a power effect; one that inherits the baggage of convention, but is also structured and shaped by the wider configuration of economic and cultural structures and processes. And most importantly, we need to realize that culture, both as an everyday practice 'out in the world' and as a discourse used by academics to conduct their work, is intricately bound with the legacy of modernity, colonialism and imperialism from which it cannot be abstracted or disconnected. These concepts are not optional add-ons for the cultural analysis of organizations – they are basic starting points.

Relatedly, we have argued that the self-other divisions used to produce comparisons of all manner of managerial and organizational behaviours and practices on an international basis are deeply problematic. We believe that the logical conclusion of such a view is that the field should give up producing 'comparative' knowledge in the manner that we currently do. A reformist strategy would, for example, look to Burawoy's extended case method as an alternative methodology for constructing comparative understandings of concepts and issues in different locales. A more radical strategy still would be to desist from doing any form of comparative work until the field engages in a more serious, epistemically diverse and politically aware discussion of the complex representational issues it entails. We suspect, though, that the current investments of institutions and scholars in the field render this an unlikely prospect.

A further implication of our argument is that the current institutional arrangements of ICCM support and reproduce the problems in the discourse and the practice of ICCM that we have sought to address. Furthermore, they are inadequate for the task of responding to the vicissitudes of the contemporary global cultural economy. Whilst increasing demographic diversity in the ranks of the AOM, for example, can be viewed as progress to some degree, the underlying lack of epistemic diversity, the lack of indigenous (in the sense articulated in this book) perspectives as well as the mechanisms associated with intellectual and institutional gatekeeping need urgent attention. Our book is an invitation to a collective conversation involving individuals and institutions to find strategies through which we might transform our discipline. We might take the positive strides that anthropology has made in recent years in these areas as something of an exemplar (see for instance Harrison, 2008), but ICCM has its own particularities and problems. A key part of such institutional transformation is the need for political organizing amongst us.

One instance of this would be to instigate political organization with the audience of our institutions – to lobby for change, and change it from the inside through academic debate, and by assuming positions of responsibility. But more importantly, given the PCT context of this book, to pursue change through more concerted and sustained efforts to engage meaningfully with the 'outside world' and working to help address the pressing problems and concerns therein. The present lack of a well-developed emancipatory interest in the field is a major challenge if it is to set itself on a fresh trajectory for transformation and aims to deal with relevant and big world problems. PCT is a political project that demands a response to the inequities associated with colonialism, neo-colonialism and imperialism that continue to structure the world. One question to begin to organize around politically is this: What role might ICCM play as a change agent in national and institutional contexts (*pace* Cooke, 2004)?

Our silences, new futures?

All readers bring their particular biographies, interests, areas of expertise and, of course, critical eye to a text. As we read others' texts, we usually see and perceive issues that we feel are missing, underdone or that do not speak to our experiences and concerns with the world. For a book such as this, the experience of reading will certainly be no different. It is incumbent upon us to try to articulate the limitations and more especially the 'silences' of our work. Other than what we might call technical deficiencies that are attendant to the production of all texts, these silences are a consequence of the manner in which our social identities, structural positions, and personal interests select ways of seeing the world that make certain topics and concerns of more interest to us, than others.

To begin, this book takes a very particular route through postcolonial studies. We have focused our predominant conceptual interests on areas of discourse, representation and ethics. Our principal goal has been to provincialize and recontextualize our field and particularly as it represents itself and its presumed subject matters textually. It is, in that sense a 'negative' form of critique, as we noted earlier. We have attempted to understand how our field has been organized in ways that perform acts of inclusion and exclusion feeding from and reproducing colonial and imperial cultural and economic structures. Our book has perhaps said less about more 'positive' forms of postcolonial critique, including insights into the ways that cultural structures, performances, art, drama, music, and knowledges can enrich our lives. Further, whilst we have attended in a number of places to institutional and economic issues this has not been our sustained focus. There is perhaps an inevitable critique pointing to those absences and taking our text to task for not being sufficiently cognizant of political economy perspectives. Some, perhaps taking the strong steers offered by Dirlik, JanMohamed or others, might come to the view that our focus on representation and the cultural is dated, even aestheticizing and depoliticizing.

For some, the 'cultural turn' in postcolonial studies, might be taken as already done and well-rehearsed. We do not believe this to be the case for postcolonial modes of critique in MOS, and certainly not in ICCM. It is true that what there is of postcolonial work in organizational analysis speaks largely from a discourse basis, and is interested in cultural formations and representation. But this hardly means that we have exhausted this line of interrogation. There are other theoretical and critical resources, authors, texts, cultural issues and complexities that the work so far has barely scratched the surface of. In that sense our work is selective, and admittedly so, but part, we would hope, of an emergent and growing critical interrogation and process of change and reconfiguration. Our focus on culture is partial, and is one of personal interest admittedly, but nonetheless we have tried where appropriate to connect it to institutional politics, and broader trends in international political economy. We are fully aware that this needs to be taken further and we fervently hope that it will be. Perhaps more than this, the idea that this, or any other issue, topic or problem is somehow ever 'done' and dispatched, seems to place unnecessary restrictions on the intellectual imagination.

For others, the 'cultural strain' of postcolonial critique is a fatal distraction, one that obscures our vision from the 'real' matters of poverty, disadvantage, disenfranchisement and structural and material inequality, and lacks a politics for meaningful social change. We do not share the view that cultural analysis has little of political merit in relation to structural issues; we believe that cultural asymmetries facilitate and legitimate inequitable material relations as well as being outcomes of them. There is a deep and implicate relationship between the domains. Research approaches that combine discursive, material and institutional relations might offer a more complete picture of postcolonial relations in the fields and concepts of interest to ICCM.

However, we do need to ask ourselves some hard questions about the practical politics of this text. Firstly, is anyone actually willing or able to hear this critique? Or, to put it another way, are the current structural conditions of our discipline and the wider communities in which it is nestled, open to this discourse? Given the loading of interests towards capitalist relations of production and neo-liberal institutional forms within and outwith the management academy, how can a text like ours make any difference? On the one hand, the primary audience for this book is an academic one, and so our book might make a difference in the classroom and in the research orientations of some academics and academic institutions. Whether this is able to have momentum and begin to impact on other stakeholders and, in particular, policy-makers is a moot point and we can only be aspirational about that. In light of the current global financial crisis, it is perhaps the case that conditions for listening to critiques of our global cultural economy, even if indirectly and obliquely made as in our text, are propitious. On the other hand, we view our politics as a collective endeavour, one that is cumulative and accretional. Its potential to effect any kind of change relies on collective, discursive and material interventions into the world over time. We hope that this text takes part in that.

To address the omissions in the text, we are perhaps silent, or not vocal enough, on the following two issues. First, race and racism. Nkomo (1992), and Harney and Nyathi (2007), all correctly point to the exclusion of discussions of race and racism from the management academy. The paradox here is that managerial discourse and practices, organizational forms and corporate activities played a central role in colonial and postcolonial times in structuring relations between different races in workplace contexts that privileged and asserted the superiority of white subjectivities over non-white subjectivities. We have stopped short of levelling a charge of racism at researchers in ICCM, since, in interpersonal terms, we find it implausible that many would consciously set out to exercise a racist worldview. Having said this, we have to point to explicit instances (mainly historical) of the manner in which problematic racial differences have been organized for the benefit of private interests. Moreover, we might argue that the problem of racism is a structural one, beyond interpersonal interaction and the particular intentions and actions of the individual. We therefore need to ask, just as Harding and others have done in relation to science, what are the structures in our field that organize and support problematic racial differentials? In short, is there a structural basis for racism in our field, be it in the language we use, the metaphors that structure the process of scientific research, or the professional workings of our community? We suspect that there is, and that we need to address this head on. Debate about the politics of whiteness in the academy might contribute to answering these questions to some degree.

Relatedly, we recommend that future research in ICCM and its critique adopt a more explicit 'gender-lens' on the panoply of issues addressed in this book. We have mentioned the marginal and exploitative position of women in the current international division of labour, and alluded to the androcentric and masculine structures of knowledge at the foundation of 'scientific' forms of knowledge construction. Researchers might wish either to take a 'sex'-based approach to the critique of ICCM – so taking their cue from the study of men or women in ICCM, or instead examine how gender relations are organized, and lead to particular forms of femininity and masculinity, in the construction of knowledge about ICCM. We think there is particular future merit in the application of transnational feminist insights and, in particular, transnational feminist politics for the historicization and politicization of the field. We have merely alluded to this possibility in the book, but certainly believe that its tenets and politics would be sympathetic to our project. Transnational feminisms combine cultural sensitivities with those of materialist politics within a global frame, thus combining a number of threads that can usefully produce a fuller analytical picture of the fate of various gendered, racialized and class-specific subjectivities in the contemporary global economy.

On a final note, we would reiterate that the kind of transformation process of ICCM we have in mind is anticipated to be a messy business with no clear rules to follow and a lack of clarity of what the future might or ought to look like. Furthermore, the inertia embedded within the current orthodoxy, with the monumental institutional apparatus supporting it, will ensure that the current order of things exhibits robustness and intransigence. Loubser (1988) might have been right in his pessimism that the prospects for the emergence of a genuinely independent indigenous social science might ultimately rest on reconfigurations of the core socioeconomic structures that presently dominate. We do not subscribe to responses of inactivity or passivity in the face of these challenges. We encourage future researchers to join us, and others that have gone before, in critiquing the epistemic and institutional basis of ICCM in order to move the field forward. It is vital that the kinds of critique and future options we have begun to open up are not just articulated by 'well-meaning' Westerners like us, nor the 'pale, stale, males' whose voices are all too audible in both mainstream and critical management research. It is time that our research and our institutions resonate with other voices, other knowledges and other visions of a different, more just, democratic and secure world in which academic research in ICCM plays a positive role.

Notes

Chapter 1

1   By 'the management academy', we mean both the American and Western European institutions responsible for the production of what is considered orthodox and therefore dominant management knowledge at the time of writing. These institutions include the Academy of Management and its core journals, EGOS, BAM and EURAM for instance.

2   The term 'subaltern' was originally coined by Gramsci (1971) to refer to those elements of society that were subject to the hegemony of the ruling class. Gramsci sees the mechanisms of domination operating subtly through the construction of hegemonic relations in which the subaltern is 'solicited' or seduced into 'civil society'. It is not merely more overt forms of unequal structural relations that reproduce the conditions of domination, but also the processes of cultural reproduction and related cultural practices. For Said (1978), it is cultural hegemony that lends the cultural practices that constitute Orientalism its animus and force. The term 'subaltern' was adapted by a group of primarily Indian scholars to denote the general attribution of subordination of sectors of society, including colonial and neo-colonial subordination. Subaltern historians in particular drew attention to the difficulty of subaltern groups speaking and accounting for themselves since the space for such accounts and explanations was dominated by Western historical and other discourses. Only those Western accounts were accepted as legitimate and valid (see for example Chaturvedi, 2000; Guha, 1982).

3   Leader of the Ghanaian independence movement and the first leader of the postcolonial state.

4   It is not especially appropriate to use postcolonialism as an umbrella term in this way. The significant tensions between, for instance, scholars who would identify an interest in anticolonialism and decolonization, as opposed to postcolonialism, render this kind of bracketing problematic. But we do so for analytic convenience at this early stage in the text.

5   This convention is a problem since it leads readers to overlook the important writings and political struggles of earlier anticolonial activists such as Frantz Fanon, Aimé Césaire or Mahatma Gandhi *inter alia*. As noted in the section introducing postcolonialism, however, there is a current trend towards remembering and revaluing the insights and protests of these earlier writers as a better 'originary moment' for postcolonial studies.

6   In his well-known piece on management and slavery plantations, Cooke is careful to articulate that he views this essay as a study in white supremacism and racism, rather than postcolonialism as such.

7   Thanks to Jo Maltby, University of York for providing some good pointers and references on the colonial context of accounting (and taxation) history.

8   In the management academy, the emergence of organizational discourse as a field of study is principally based on the insight that representational

practice, through different systems of signification (from writing and art to photography), has reality-constitutive properties. In contrast to correspondence theories of representation, discourse theories explore how reality comes into being through discursive practice. Having said that, organizational discourse is a field with a marked lack of interest in postcolonial themes, despite Said's well-known use of a Foucauldian/genealogical perspective.

9 This interpolation of modes of self-knowing was very much the point of the subaltern studies project (see Guha, 1982).

10 Moore-Gilbert (1997) summarizes the following principal criticisms of Said's argument in *Orientalism*. It has a tendency: to homogenize colonial discourse and thus to ignore the divergences between British, French and Portuguese Empires for instance; to ignore resistance to colonial discourse, and thus to underplay the complex, contradictory and often ambivalent nature of the colonial encounter; to sideline the gender dynamics of Empire, as well as the material/economic contexts of production for these sets of images and representations. He is also criticized for ignoring the previous writers (especially Arabic writers) who made many of the same points about the nature of Orientalism in their publications before 1978. Moore-Gilbert (1997) suggests that Said's later works do show greater acknowledgement of these writers.

Chapter 2

1 It is coincidental that Boyacigiller et al. (1996) use the term ICCM. They use it to stand for International and Cross-Cultural Management. We add 'Studies' to this for the purposes of the book but do not include it in the abbreviation for reasons of pure convenience.

2 It is important to note that the fifth dimension was originally developed by Michael Bond from the Chinese University of Hong Kong. For a critique of this fifth dimension see Fang, 2003.

3 By way of illustration, this issue is engaged in the 'debate' between Ashkanasy (2003) and Chan (2003) in Westwood and Clegg's (2003) *Point and Counterpoint in Organizational Studies*, albeit with respect to organizational cultures.

4 Australia might be better conceived of as part of the semi-periphery.

5 Readers are invited to go to the OIL website for a very interesting resource here: http://tur-www1.massey.ac.nz/~cprichar/oil.htm

6 Professor Tsui has been a Fellow of the Academy since 1997 and was Editor of the *Academy of Management Journal* from 1997–9. She is also the founding President of the *International Association for Chinese Management Research* which she helped form in 2001, and Editor of the journal *Management and Organization Review*, the official journal of the Association.

7 We hasten to add that not all those cited above as calling for a turn to anthropology in MOS are guilty in this regard.

8 It needs to be acknowledged that the appearance of such a piece of work in the AMJ is something of a departure. The record shows that the journal only infrequently publishes qualitative empirical studies, let alone studies with a seemingly progressive anthropological orientation.

9 Jack et al. (2008) noted the work on the MNE has been considerably more open to the insights of other disciplines, principally economic sociology, in reflecting upon questions of ontology and epistemology.

Chapter 3

1 And, of course, not only in non-Western contexts.
2 The exception was the Chinese University of Hong, which always had a majority of local staff.
3 Figures as of mid-2008. This figure includes executive, student and emeritus members – ordinary academic members number 11,009.
4 On its official website it claims members from 71 countries on its home page, but on its 'community' page it only claims them from 65 countries (AIB, 2008).
5 As of mid-2008.
6 The other associations under the aegis of EIASM are primarily academic associations formed around disciplinary areas within management and business studies. They are: the European Accounting Association (EAA), European Association for Research in Industrial Economics (EARIE), European Finance Association (EFA), European Marketing Academy (EMAC), European Operations Management Association (EUROMA), European Doctoral Programmes Association in Management and Business Administration (EDAMBA), as well as the European Academy of Management (EURAM) and the European International Business Academy (EIBA).
7 Other estimates put it much higher and the price of textbooks has become a contentious issue in the US and elsewhere.
8 Although this is made up not just of new books but also a healthy second-hand market as well as course packs and other in-house materials sold to students on campus.
9 We acknowledge that there are some limitations in using survey work to aid our outline of the state-of-knowledge of ICCM. Wong-MingJi and Mir (1997) note that journals and evaluation criteria selected to produce surveys are arbitrary. The evaluation criteria in particular are already specific to Western knowledge systems, and are skewed as a result in the favour of Western authors. Surveys rely on nation-states as a unit of designation for authorship. However, we should not assume that institutional affiliation (taken as a proxy of the nationality of authors) indicates the national origin of any author. By contrast just because a piece of research comes from a non-American author does not always exclude it from adopting a Westernized perspective. Many Indian scholars, to give one example, belong to Indian business schools modelled on US business schools and often complete PhDs in the US. India's colonial history also means that its schooling system makes central use of the English language and a certain Eurocentric curriculum.
10 *Management International Review* is edited and published out of Germany but its language of publication is English.
11 Danell reports that 86.6 per cent of *Administrative Science Quarterly* authors for 1981–92 were American. Comparatively, nearly 30 per cent of the authors of the European-based *Organization Studies* were American too.
12 Of the remaining work, 27 per cent was classified as 'polycentric and 14 per cent as comparative in orientation and design'.
13 Base rate referring to the ratio of submissions from North American and non-North Americans.
14 There is a methodological weakness here since the geographical location of authors was decided on the basis of the location of the university they

reported as affiliated to. This does not take account of academics on sabbatical, secondments or in temporary expatriate conditions.

15   There was, naturally, wide variation across journals with respect to these numbers and percentages.

16   In fact he cites just one co-authored paper from South America (Brazil) out of the 1948 papers.

17   This is a potentially significant point and one not taken into account by Kirkman and Law.

18   Determined by the stated institutional affiliation of at least one of the chief authors being outside of North America.

19   It might be noted that 30 per cent of the international papers had no non-North American author, i.e. were entirely written by North American authors.

20   In terms of both submissions to the journal, as well as final article publications.

21   Based on Caligiuri's (1999) classification of IHRM journals.

22   Özbilgin notes the limitations in the method, recognizing that current address does not necessarily signal national or cultural identity. His assumption that current country of residence colours intellectual orientation is not really warranted. In the geopolitics of international academia it is likely that some of the editorial members reporting residence outside of the North Atlantic are actually expatriates or immigrants from there.

23   This is informed speculation on our part and not asserted as such by Özbilgin, although he does note that 'Europe' is Western Europe dominated.

24   It might be noted that Hong Kong and Singapore have housed significant numbers of academic expatriates from Europe and North America – although this has declined over the last decade.

25   Based in Turkish universities we need to add, i.e. not expatriate Turks in the Western academy.

26   Determined thus: Editor = 50 per cent, editorial team = 50 per cent, affiliation as reported on the journal's website. Where multiple affiliations are reported, they are shared in equal proportions. Note that affiliation and nationality may often vary, for instance most scholars from 'France' in this list are based at INSEAD and do not always have strong ties to the country.

27   Alatas (2003) provides a partial analysis.

28   The notion of the captive mind resonates to some extent with the notion of 'mimic men' discussed by Fanon and Memmi.

Chapter 4

1   In the original text, Basalla places the adjective 'non-scientific' in quotation marks in order to mark his intention not to deploy the term in a pejorative fashion. Instead he uses 'non-scientific' to signify 'the absence of modern Western science and not to a lack of ancient, indigenous scientific thought of the sort to be found in China or India' (1967: 611).

2   Francis Bacon was on board the HMS Challenger and offered 17th century planters of colonies advice in their scientific endeavours.

3   Prakash locates the impetus for this scientific project in the 19th century in the developing history of the East India Company. India moved from

company governance to crown rule in the mid-nineteenth century, and this called for new forms of control. Prakash notes what he calls an intensification of colonial despotism at the time, and science was to contribute to this.

4 We have taken the title of this section from Bowen's (2006) book of the same title.

Chapter 5

1 An elite class of officials based on Confucian education and policed by a rigorous examination system.

2 Fenn was an influential figure in academia, business and government. He was an assistant editor of the *Harvard Business Review* and editor of the *Business School Bulletin;* a Faculty member of Harvard Business School from 1955–1961; staff assistant to President Kennedy (1961–1963); Tariff Commissioner (1963–1967); president, Center for Business-Government Relations (1969–1971); Director, John F. Kennedy Library (1972–1986); faculty member (again), Harvard Graduate School of Business Administration (1976–1980). Taken from an entry on Fenn at the John F. Kennedy Library National Archives and Records Administration, http://www.jfklibrary.org/fa_fenn.html#admin, accessed Sept, 15th 2008.

3 John McCloy was Assistant Secretary of War (1941–45), the US Military Governor of the US-zone in Germany and the US High Commissioner for Germany (1949–1952). It is also worth noting that he was also one of the contributors to the Fenn text and was explicit in warning about the Soviet threat.

4 We will have cause to comment more on their work later.

Chapter 6

1 We attempt, however briefly and selectively, to bring together globalization with postcolonial theory in this chapter. This is not an easy task, partly because the two discourses have rarely been brought together (Rizvi, 2007) (though notable exceptions include Hoogvelt, 2001), and for some there is a substantive discrepancy between them. Some globalization theorists dismiss modernistic categories like first and third world as irrelevant in the postmodern global world. Some postcolonial analysts would view this as a depoliticizing and conservative move. Dismissing these terms intellectually does not erase material conditions of poverty including third worlds in the first, and first worlds in the third (Banerjee et al., 2009). We share this latter view.

2 The Nazi state and the current status of Palestine and Guantanamo Bay are examples of 'states of exception' (Banerjee, 2008).

3 On this point, we depart from Appadurai, for reasons found in Endnote (1). We do not believe that getting rid of the vocabulary of dependency and world systems theory dispenses with the material inequalities to which they speak. As noted earlier, we prefer the notion of multiple centres and peripheries.

4 It must be noted that there are positive articulations of multiculturalism to be found amongst postcolonial critics. Most notably, Gilroy (2005) makes a

positive case for multiculturalism using the Freudian concept of melancholia. He argues that we have overlooked certain everyday forms of multiculturalism currently being practised in urban contexts, for instance London. The kind of organic and somewhat disordered form of multiculturalism provides hope for a future rescue of the concept.

Chapter 7

1   We need to note that as a US-centred project, it is not uncommon for Kerr and colleagues to represent parts of Europe as contrastive to the US, so the representational strategy extends beyond the non-West strictly speaking. In consequence we will mainly use the expression 'non-US' in this section of the chapter.
2   Clearly electing not to use the 'Three Worlds' nomenclature, which in any case was not popularized until about the mid-1960s.
3   Although results for only 25 of the countries are reported here.
4   The study generated 3500 responses and was conducted across 14 countries.
5   With the addition of Sarah Moran.
6   The focus is on Iran and Saudi Arabia.
7   With a focus on Puerto Rico.
8   Largely, as they acknowledge, because of the US' strategic interests in those countries at that time.

Chapter 8

1   We provided an analysis of Harris and Moran in the preceding chapter.
2   There appears to be some similarity with Richard Lewis' LMR model, which we tackle later in the chapter, although there is no reference to Samovar in that book.
3   A whole list of other essentialisms in relation to Arabic culture can be found on page 116 of Ronen.
4   He does also cite a non-Western scholar, Maruyama (1974), who criticizes the ethnocentrism of the hierarchy of needs and its validity for 'Oriental' cultures – but note even Maruyama uses the designation 'Oriental'.
5   Nath and Sadhu were both at the Joseph M. Kratz Graduate School of Business, University of Pittsburgh; Banai, Levicki and Sethi were all from Baruch College, City University of New York; Allen and Miller were at the University of Michigan; Boyce at Michigan Technical University; Kiggundu at the School of Business, Carleton University, Ottawa; Namiki was from California State University (Sacramento); and Tung from the University of Wisconsin. Fernando Quezada was something of an exception and was working as project director of the Biotechnology Center of Excellence in the Executive Office of Economic Affairs of the Commonwealth of Massachusetts. He was, however, also an adjunct professor of cross-cultural technology transfer at the Lesley College Graduate School in Cambridge, Massachusetts.
6   The exceptions are Quezada (Mexico and Brazil) and Namiki (not stated).
7   We are using 'Asia' and 'Latin America' here because that is what the discourse signifies, not because we accept that there is such a thing as Asian culture or Latin American culture.

8 Of course our selection of the 'late 1970s' is itself an interesting choice and perhaps reflects embeddedness in Western preoccupations. Change in China was monumental around 1949, through the mid-1960s and so on.
9 Note the use of Hofstede's cultural dimensions again here.
10 There is also significant self-citing.
11 This according to the publisher.
12 WASPS – seen to be culturally dominant within the US.
13 Very brief coverage is given to Kazakhstan, Uzbekistan, Kyrgyzstan, Turkmenistan, Tajikistan and Azebaijan.
14 At the end of each section on a country or region, Lewis provides a separate, graphically boxed out, section on motivation, which is intended as advice for (presumably US) managers on what motivates people in the featured country.

Chapter 9

1 We say 'despite' because a Foucauldian view of power would see it as contiguous with forms of resistance. Forms of resistance to Orientalism are lacking in Said's text.
2 The English translation of the first three is provided by Soriano (1991), the latter by Andres (1985).
3 Andres cites and makes use of, for example, the work of Peter Drucker, Frederick Herzberg, Keith Davis, Warren Bennis and Douglas McGregor.
4 Postcolonial is used in the temporal sense here to refer to periods after formal independence.

Chapter 10

1 A recent and more encompassing term for the 'Third World' and 'developing countries'.
2 Both articles are co-authored. In the first article, the author order is Butz and Besio, to reflect the fact that autoethnography is written about, in a positive light, by Butz. In the second, they reverse it to Besio and Butz, to reflect the change of principal authorial voice.

Chapter 11

1 IHL is a Malaysian government body with responsibility for higher education.
2 Dr. K.K. Phua is himself Chairman of the World Scientific Publishing Co. based in Singapore.
3 He was executed by the Spanish for sedition, rebellion and conspiracy in 1896. Although he argued for freedom through education and peaceful reform, some see his ideas as instrumental for the Philippine Revolution.
4 The text is probably from the 2nd century BCE, but relying on older material, and is often cited as being constructed in the 3rd century BCE.
5 For an account of the journal and its rationale go to www.news.cornell.edu/chronicle/01/11.15.01/Traces.html for an interview with its founder Naoki Sakai.

References

AAP (American Association of Publishers Inc) (2006) *The Higher Education Textbook Market*. Washington, DC: AAP.

Abegglen, J.C. (1958) *The Japanese Factory*. Glencoe, ILL: The Free Press.

Achebe, C. (1975/1996) 'The African Writer and the English Language', in: M.K. Asante & Abu Shardow Abarry (eds) *African Intellectual Heritage: A Book of Sources*, pp. 379–384. Philadelphia: Temple University Press.

Adams, W. & Garraty, J.A. (1960) *Is the World Our Campus?* East Lansing, MI: Michigan State University Press.

Adler, N. (1983) 'Cross-Cultural Management Research: The Ostrich and the Trend', *Academy of Management Review*. 8: 226–232.

Adler, N. (1986) *International Dimensions of Organisational Behavior*. Boston, MA: Wadsworth.

Adler, N. & Graham, J.L. (1989) 'Cross-Cultural Interaction: The International Comparison Fallacy?' *Journal of International Business Studies*. 20(3): 515–537.

Adler, N.J. & Harzing, A.W. (2009) 'When Knowledge Wins: Transcending the Sense and Nonsense of Academic Rankings', *Academy of Management Learning and Education*. 8(1): 72–95.

Aguayo, R. (1991) *Dr. Deming: The American Who Taught the Japanese about Quality*. New York: Simon and Schuster.

Ahmad, A. (1992) *In Theory: Classes, Nations, Literatures*. London: Verso.

AIB (2008) Academy of International Business, official website, http://aib.msu.edu/aboutaib.asp, accessed May 2008.

Ailon, G. (2008) 'Mirror, Mirror on the Wall: *Culture's Consequences* in a Value Test of Its Own Design', *Academy of Management Review*. 33(4): 885–904.

Ajiferuke, B. & Boddewyn, J. (1970) 'Culture and Other Explanatory Variables in Comparative Management Studies', *Academy of Management Journal*. 13: 153–165.

Alatas, S.H. (1974) 'The Captive Mind and Creative Development', *International Social Science Journal*. 36(4): 691–700.

Alatas, S.H. (1977) *The Myth of the Lazy Native*. London: Frank Cass.

Alatas, S.F. (1996) 'Western Theory and Asian Realities: A Critical Appraisal of the Indigenisation Theme', Paper presented at the Asia Pacific Regional Conference of Sociology, Quezon City, Philippines, May 28–31.

Alatas, S.F. (2000) 'Academic Dependency in the Social Sciences: Reflections on India and Malaysia', *American Studies International*. 38(2): 80–96.

Alatas, S.F. (2003) 'Academic Dependency and the Global Division of Labour in the Social Sciences', *Current Sociology*. 51: 599–633.

Alatas, S.H. (2000) 'Intellectual Imperialism: Definition, Traits and Problems', *Southeast Asian Journal of Social Science*. 28(1): 23–45.

Altbach, P.G. (1987) *Higher Education in Third World: Themes and Variations*. New York: Advent Books.

Altbach, P.G. & Hoshino, E.S. (eds) (1995) *International Book Publishing: An Encyclopedia*. London and New York: Routledge.

Alvares, C. (1988) 'Science, Colonialism and Violence: A Luddite View', in: A. Nandy (ed.) *Science, Hegemony and Violence*, pp. 68–112. Bombay: Oxford University Press.

Alvares, C. (2001) *Recapturing Worlds – The Original Multiversity Proposal.* Goa: Other India Press. Reproduced on the Multiversity: USA Chapter Website: http://vlal.bol.ucla.edu/multiversity/Right_menu_items/Claude_proposal.htm, accessed December 2008.

Alvares, C. (2002) *The Multiversity Enterprise.* Presentation at the Inaugural Conference of Multiversity, February 2002, Penang, Malaysia, reproduced on the Multiversity: USA Chapter Website: http://vlal.bol.ucla.edu/multiversity/Right_menu_items/2002conf/conf2002.htm, accessed December 2008.

Alvares, C. (2008) *Multiversity Mission Statement* The Multiversity Website, http://www.swaraj.org/multiversity/vision.htm, accessed August 2008.

Alvarez, J.L. (ed.) (1997) *The Diffusion and Consumption of Business Knowledge.* London: Macmillan.

Amable, B. (2003) *The Diversity of Modern Capitalism.* Oxford: Oxford University Press.

Amdam, R.V. (1996) *Management Education and Competitiveness: Europe, Japan and the United States.* London and New York: Routledge

Andersen, P.H. & Skaates, M.A. (2004) 'Ensuring Validity in Qualitative International Business Research', in: R. Marschan-Piekkari & C. Welch (eds) *Handbook of Qualitative Research Methods for International Business*, pp. 464–485. Cheltenham, UK and Northampton, MA, USA: Edward Elgar.

Andres, T.D. (1981) *Understanding Filipino Values: A Management Approach.* Quezon City, Philippines: New Day.

Andres, T.D. (1985) *Management by Filipino Values.* Quezon City, Philippines: New Day.

Andres, T.D. (1989) *Management Filipino Style.* Makati, Philippines: St Paul.

Andres, T.D. (1995) *The Effective Manager.* Quezon City, Philippines: New Day Publishers.

Andres, T.D. (1998) *People Empowerment by Filipino Values.* Quezon City, Philippines: Rex Bookstore.

AOM Online (2008) The Academy of Management, official website, http://www.aomonline.org/, accessed June 2008.

Appadurai, A. (1990) 'Disjuncture and Difference in the Global Cultural Economy', *Theory, Culture and Society.* 7: 295–310.

Argyris, C. (1957) *Personality and Organisation: The Conflict between the System and the Individual.* New York: Harper and Brothers.

Asad, T. (ed.) (1973) *Anthropology and the Colonial Encounter.* London: Ithaca Press.

Ashcroft, B., Griffiths, G. & Tiffin, H. (1989) *The Empire Strikes Back: Theory and Practice in Post-Colonial Literatures.* London: Routledge.

Ashcroft, B., Griffiths, G. & Tiffin, H. (eds) (1995) *The Postcolonial Studies Reader.* London: Routledge.

Ashcroft, B., Griffiths, G. & Tiffin, H. (2000) *Post-Colonial Studies: The Key Concepts.* London: Routledge.

Ashton, T.S. (1948) *The Industrial Revolution 1760–1830.* Oxford: Oxford University Press.

Ashkanasy, N.M. (2003) 'The Case for Culture', in: R.I. Westwood & S. Clegg (eds) *Debating Organisation: Point and Counterpoint in Organisation Studies*, pp. 300–311. Oxford: Blackwell.

Badawy, M.K. (1980) 'Styles of Mideastern Managers', *California Management Review.* 22: 51–58.

Bajaj, J.K. (1988) 'Francis Bacon, the First Philosopher of Modern Science: A Non-Western View', in: A. Nandy (ed.) *Science, Hegemony and Violence: A Requiem for Modernity*, pp. 24–67. Bombay: Oxford University Press.

Ballon, R.J. (ed.) (1967) *Doing Business in Japan*. Rutland: Sophia University, Tokyo in cooperation with Charles E. Tuttle Company.

BAM (2008) The British Academy of Management, official website, http://www.bam.ac.uk/, accessed June 2008.

Banai, M. & Levicki, C.J. (1988) 'Europe', in: R. Nath (ed.) *Comparative Management: A Regional View*, pp. 97–137. Cambridge, MA: Ballinger.

Banerjee, S.B. (2000) 'Whose Land is it Anyway? National Interest, Indigenous Stakeholders, and Colonial Discourses: The Case of the Jabiluka Uranium Mine', *Organization & Environment*. 13(3): 3–38.

Banerjee, S.B. (2003) 'Who Sustains Whose Development? Sustainable Development and the Reinvention of Nature', *Organization Studies*. 24(1): 143–180.

Banerjee, S.B. (2008) 'Necrocapitalism', *Organization Studies*. 29(12): 1541–1563.

Banerjee, S.B., Carter, C. & Clegg, S. (2009) 'Managing Globalization', in: M. Alvesson, H. Willmott & T. Bridgman (eds) *Handbook of Critical Management Studies*, pp. 186–212. Oxford: Oxford University Press.

Banerjee, S.B. & Linstead, S. (2001) 'Globalization, Multiculturalism and Other Fictions: Colonialism for the New Millennium?', *Organization*. 8(4): 683–722.

Banerjee, S.B. & Linstead, S. (2004) 'Masking Subversion: Neocolonial Embeddedness in Anthropological Accounts of Indigenous Management', *Human Relations*. 57(2): 221–248.

Banerjee, S.B. & Prasad, A. (eds) (2008) 'Critical Reflections on Management and Organization Studies: A Postcolonial Perspective', *Special Issue of Critical Perspectives on International Business*. 4(2/3).

Banerjee, S.B., Chio, V. & Mir, R. (eds) (2009) *Organizations, Markets and Imperial Formations: Towards An Anthropology of Globalization*. Cheltenham: Edward Elgar.

Barrett, G.V. & Bass, B.M. (1976) 'Cross-Cultural Issues in Industrial and Organizational Psychology', in: M.D. Dunette (ed.) *Handbook of Industrial and Organizational Psychology*, pp. 1639–1686. New York: Rand McNally.

Baruch, Y. (2001) 'Global or North American?: A Geographical Based Comparative Analysis of Publications in Top Management Journals', *International Journal of Cross Cultural Management*. 1(1): 109–126.

Bass, B.M. (1981) 'Leadership in Different Cultures', in: B.M. Bass (ed.) *Stogdill's Handbook of Leadership*, pp. 522–549. New York: Free Press.

Basalla, G. (1967) 'The Spread of Western Science', *Science*. 156 (May): 611–622.

Bate, S.P. (1997) 'Whatever Happened to Organizational Anthropology? A Review of the Field of Organizational Ethnography and Anthropological Studies', *Human Relations*. 50(9): 1147–1171.

Beamish, P.W., Killing, J.P., Lecraw, D.L. & Crookel, H. (1991) *International Management: Text and Cases*. Homewood, IL.: Richard D. Irwin.

Benton, T. (1981) '"Objective Interests" and the Sociology of Power', *Sociology*. 15(2): 161–184.

Berry, J.W. (1980) 'Introduction to Methodology', in: H. Triandis & J.W. Berry (eds) *Handbook of Cross-Cultural Psychology*. Volume Two, pp. 1–28. Boston: Allyn and Bacon.

Berry, J.W. (1999) 'Emics and Etics: A Symbiotic Conception', *Culture and Psychology*. 5: 165–171.

Besio, K. & Butz, D. (2004) 'Autoethnography: A Limited Endorsement', *The Professional Geographer.* 56(3): 432–438.

Betts, R.F. (2004) *Decolonization.* 2nd edition. London and New York: Routledge.

Bhabha, H. (1994) *The Location of Culture.* London: Routledge.

Bishop, R. (2005) 'Freeing Ourselves from Neo-Colonial Domination in Research: A Kaupapa Maori Approach to Creating Knowledge', in: N.K. Denzin & Y. Lincoln (eds) *The Sage Handbook of Qualitative Research,* pp. 109–138. Thousand Oaks, CA: Sage.

Blaut, J.M. (1993) *The Colonizer's Model of the World.* New York: Guildford Press.

Blommaert, J. & Verscheuren, J. (1998) *Debating Diversity: Analysing the Discourse of Tolerance.* London: Routledge.

Blough, R., Smith, D.T., Waugh, S.C. & Mills, L. (1957) 'Government Policy and Business Abroad', in: D.H. Fenn Jr. (ed.) (1957) *Management Guide to Overseas Operations,* pp. 199–217. New York: McGraw-Hill Book Co.

Bond, M.H. & Hofstede, G. (1989) 'The Cash Value of Confucian Values', *Human Systems Management.* 8: 195–200.

Bowen, H.V. (2006) *The Business of Empire: The East India Company and Imperial Britain, 1756–1833.* Cambridge: Cambridge University Press.

Boyacigiller, N.A. & Adler, N.J. (1991) 'The Parochial Dinosaur: Organizational Science in a Global Context', *Academy of Management Review.* 16(2): 262–290.

Boyacigiller, N.A., Kleinberg, M.J., Phillips, M.E. & Sackmann, S.A. (1996) 'Conceptualizing Culture', in: B.J. Punnett & O. Shenkar (eds) (1996) *Handbook for International Management Research,* pp. 157–208. Cambridge, MA: Blackwell.

Brake, T., Walker, D.M. & Walker, T. (1994) *Doing Business Internationally: The Guide to Cross-Cultural Success.* New York: McGraw-Hill.

Brannen, M.Y. (1996) 'Ethnographic International Management Research', in: B.J. Punnett & O. Shenkar (eds) (1996) *Handbook for International Management Research,* pp. 115–143. Cambridge, MA: Blackwell.

Brantlinger, P. (1985) 'Victorians and Africans: The Genealogy of the Myth of the Dark Continent', *Critical Inquiry.* 12: 166–203.

Braveboy-Wagner, J.A. (2009) *Institutions of the Global South.* London: Routledge.

Brennan, T. (1989) *Salman Rushdie and the Third World.* London: MacMillan.

Brett, J.M., Tinsley, C.H., Janssens, M., Barsness, Z.I. & Lytle, A.L. (1997) 'New Approaches to the Study of Culture in Industrial/Organizational Psychology', in: P.C. Earley & M. Erez (eds) *New Perspectives on International Industrial Organizational Psychology,* pp. 75–129. San Francisco: New Lexington Press.

Brewis, J. & Wray-Bliss, E. (2008) 'Re-searching Ethics: Towards a More Reflexive Critical Management Studies', *Organization Studies.* 29(12): 1521–1540.

Brummelhuis, H.T. (1984) 'Abundance and Avoidance: An Interpretation of Thai Individualism', in: H. ten Brummelhuis & J.H. Kemp (eds) *Strategies and Structures in Thai Society,* pp. 39–54. Amsterdam: Anthropologisch-Sociologisch Centrum, Universiteit van Amsterdam.

Buckley, P.J. (2002) 'Is the International Business Research Agenda Running Out of Steam?' *Journal of International Business Studies.* 33(2): 365–373.

Burawoy, M. (1998) 'The Extended Case Method', *Sociological Theory.* 16(1): 4–33.

Burawoy, M. (2000) 'Introduction: Reaching for the Global', in: M. Burawoy et al., *Global Ethnography. Forces, Connections and Imaginations in a Postmodern World,* pp. 1–40. Berkeley: University of California Press.

Burawoy, M., Blum, J.A., George, S., Gille, Z., Gowan, T., Haney, L., Klawiter, M., Lopez, S.L., O'Riain, S. & Thayer, M. (2000) *Global Ethnography. Forces,*

Connections and Imaginations in a Postmodern World. Berkeley: University of California Press.

Bush, B. & Maltby, J. (2004) 'Taxation in West Africa: Transforming the Colonial Subject into the "Governable Person"', *Critical Perspectives on Accounting*. 15: 5–34.

Butz, D. & Besio, K. (2004) 'The Value of Autoethnography for Field Research in Transcultural Settings', *The Professional Geographer*. 56(3): 350–360.

Calás, M.B. & Smircich, L. (2003) 'To Be Done with Progress and Other Heretical Thoughts for Organization and Management Studies', in: E.A. Locke (ed.) *Postmodernism and Management: Pros, Cons and the Alternative*. Research in the Sociology of Organizations, Volume 21, pp. 29–56. Oxford: Elsevier Science.

Caldwell, M. (2004) 'Domesticating the French Fry: McDonald's and Consumerism in Moscow', *Journal of Consumer Culture*. 4: 5–26.

Caligiuri, P.M. (1999) 'The Ranking of Scholarly Journals in International Human Resource Management', *The International Journal of Human Resource Management*. 10(3): 515–519.

Cameron, A. & Palan, R. (2004) *The Imagined Economies of Globalization*. London: Sage.

Carnoy, M. (1974) *Education as Cultural Imperialism*. New York: David McKay.

Carter, L. (2006) 'Postcolonial Interventions within Science Education: Using Postcolonial Ideas to Reconsider Cultural Diversity Scholarship', *Educational Philosophy and Theory*. 38(5): 677–691.

Cavanaugh, J.M. (1997) '(In)corporating the Other? Managing the Politics of Workplace Differences', in: P. Prasad, A.J. Mills, M. Elmes & A. Prasad (eds) *Managing the Organizational Melting Pot: Dilemmas of Workplace Diversity*, pp. 31–53. Thousand Oaks, CA: Sage.

Cavusgil, S.T. & Das, A. (1997) 'Methodological Issues in Empirical Cross-Cultural Research: A Survey of the Management Literature and a Framework', *Management International Review*. 37(1): 71–96.

Césaire, A. (1955/1972) *Discourse on Colonialism*. (Translated by Joan Pinkham). New York: Monthly Review Press.

Chakrabarty, D. (2000) *Provincializing Europe*. Princeton: Princeton University Press.

Chakraborty, S.K. (1991) *Management by Values: Towards Cultural Congruence*. New Delhi: Oxford University Press.

Chan, A. (2003) 'Instantiative versus Entiative Culture: The Case for Culture as Process', in: R.I. Westwood & S. Clegg (eds) *Debating Organisation: Point and Counterpoint in Organisation Studies*, pp. 311–320. Oxford: Blackwell.

Chan, K.C., Fung, H.G. & Lai, P. (2005) 'Membership on Editorial Boards and Rankings of Schools with International Business Orientation', *Journal of International Business Studies*. 36(4): 452–469.

Chandrasekara, I. (2009) *Ethnofinance: A Study of the Daily Accounting and Finance Practices of a Sinhalese Women's Community*. Unpublished PhD Thesis. University of Leicester.

Chatterjee, P. (1986) *Nationalist Thought and the Colonial World: A Derivative Discourse*. London: Zed Books.

Chatterjee, P. (1993) *The Nation and Its Fragments: Colonial and Postcolonial Histories*. Princeton, NJ: Princeton University Press.

Chaturvedi, V, (ed.) (2000) *Mapping Subaltern Studies and the Postcolonial*. London and New York: Verso.

Chen, M. (1995) *Asian Management Systems: Chinese, Japanese and Korean Styles of Business*. London: International Thomson Business Press.

Chester, E.T. (1995) *Covert Network: Progressives, the International Rescue Committee, and the CIA*. New York: M.E. Sharpe.

Chia, R. (1996) *Organizational Analysis as Deconstructive Practice*. New York and Berlin: De Gruyter.

Chio, V. (2005) *Malaysia and the Development Process: Globalization, Knowledge Transfers and Postcolonial Dilemmas*. New York: Routledge.

Chio, V. (2008) 'Transfers, Training and Inscription: The Production of Modern Market Citizens in Malaysia', *Critical Perspectives on International Business*. 4(2/3): 166–183.

CIBER (2008) Center for International Business Education and Research, University of Wisconsin, http://www.bus.wisc.edu/ciber/aboutciber/about-ciber.asp, accessed November 2008.

CIBERWeb (2008) Centers International Business Education and Research, http://ciberweb.msu.edu/about.asp, accessed November 2008.

Clark, T., Grant, D. & Heijltjes, M. (1999–2000) 'Researching Comparative and International Human Resources Management: Key Challenges and Contributions', *International Studies of Management and Organization*. 29(4): 6–23.

Clarke, J. & Newman, J. (1997) *The Managerial State*. London: Sage.

Clegg, S.R., Linstead, S. & Sewell, G. (2000) 'Only Penguins: A Polemic on Organization Theory from the Edge of the World', *Organization Studies*. 21: 103–127.

Clegg, S.R., Redding, S.G. & Cartner, M. (eds) (1990) *Capitalism in Contrasting Cultures*. Berlin: de Gruyter.

Clifford, J. & Marcus, G.E. (eds) (1986) *Writing Culture: The Poetics and Politics of Ethnography*. Berkeley, CA: University of California Press.

Coates, D. (2005) (ed.) *Varieties of Capitalism, Varieties of Approaches*. New York: Palgrave Macmillan.

Cochrane, J. (1979) *Industrialism and Industrial Man in Retrospect*. Ann Arbor: University of Michigan Press.

Coleman, P. (1989) *The Liberal Conspiracy: The Congress for Cultural Freedom and the Struggle for the Mind of Postwar Europe*. New York: The Free Press.

Connell, R.W. (1991) 'A Thumbnail Dipped in Tar Or: Can We Write Sociology from the Edge of the World?' *Social Analysis*. 30: 68–76.

Consadine, M. & Painter, M. (1997) *Managerialism: The Great Debate*. Melbourne: Melbourne University Press.

Cooke, B. (1998) 'Participation, "Process" and Management: Lessons for Development in the History of Organization Development', *Journal of International Development*. 10(1): 35–54.

Cooke, B. (2003a) 'The Denial of Slavery in Management Studies', *Journal of Management Studies*. 40(8): 1895–1918.

Cooke, B. (2003b) 'A New Continuity with Colonial Administration: Participation in Development Management', *Third World Quarterly*. 24(1): 47–61.

Cooke, B. (2003c) 'Managing Organizational Culture and Imperialism', in: A. Prasad (ed.) *Postcolonial Theory and Organizational Analysis: A Critical Engagement*, pp. 75–94. New York: Palgrave Macmillan.

Cooke, B. (2004) 'The Managing of the (Third) World', *Organization*. 11(4): 589–615.

Crang, M. (1998) *Cultural Geography*. London: Routledge.

Crosby, A.W. (1993) *Ecological Imperialism: The Biological Expansion of Europe, 900–1900*. Cambridge: Cambridge University Press.

Czarniawska, B. (2008) *A Theory of Organizing*. Cheltenham, UK & Northampton, MA : Edward Elgar.

Czarniawska-Joerges, B. (1992) *Exploring Complex Organizations. A Cultural Perspective*. London: Sage.

Danell, R. (1998) 'Does the North American Dominance in Business Studies Prevail?', Paper presented at the 14th EGOS Colloquium, Maastricht, The Netherlands, July.

Dash, J.M. (1989) 'Introduction', in: E. Glissant, *Caribbean Discourse: Selected Essays*, pp. xi–xiv. Translated and with an introduction by J.M. Dash. Charlottesville: University Press of Virginia.

Davis, S.M. (1971) *Comparative Management: Organizational and Cultural Perspective*. Englewood Cliffs, NJ: Prentice-Hall.

Deal, T.E. & Kennedy, A.A. (1982) *Corporate Cultures: The Rites and Rituals of Corporate Life*. Harmondsworth: Penguin Books.

De Bettignies, H.C. & Evans, P.L. (1977) 'The Cultural Dimension of Top Executives Careers: A Comparative Analysis', in: T.D. Weinshall (ed.) *Culture and Management*, pp. 277–292. Harmondsworth: Penguin Books.

Deem, R. (1998) '"New Managerialism" and Higher Education: The Management of Performances and Cultures in Universities in the United Kingdom', *International Studies in Sociology of Education*. 8: 48–63.

DeMaria, B. (2008) 'Neo-Colonialism through Measurement: A Critique of the Corruption Perception Index', *Critical Perspectives on International Business*. 4(2/3): 184–202.

De Mente, B.L. (2004) *Chinese Etiquette and Ethics in Business*. 2nd edition. McGraw-Hill Professional.

Deming, W.E. (1986) *Out of the Crisis*. Cambridge, MA: MIT Press.

Denzin, N.K. (2005) 'Emancipatory Discourses and the Ethics and Politics of Interpretation', in: N.K. Denzin & Y. Lincoln (eds) *The Sage Handbook of Qualitative Research*, pp. 933–958. Thousand Oaks, CA: Sage.

Denzin, N.K. & Lincoln, Y.S. (eds) (2005) *The Sage Handbook of Qualitative Research*. 3rd edition. Thousand Oaks, CA: Sage.

Denzin, N.K., Lincoln, Y.S. & Smith, L.T. (eds) (2008) *Handbook of Critical and Indigenous Methodologies*. Thousand Oaks, CA: Sage.

Deresky, H. (1993) *International Management: Managing Across Borders and Cultures*. London: HarperCollins.

Derrida, J. (1982) *Margins of Philosophy*. Chicago, IL: University of Chicago Press.

DeWalt, B.R. (1994) 'Using Indigenous Knowledge to Improve Agriculture and Natural Resource Management', *Human Organization*. 53(2): 123–131.

Diamond, S. (1992) *Compromised Campus: The Collaboration of Universities with the Intelligence Community, 1945–1955*. New York: Oxford University Press.

Dirks, N.B. (ed.) (1992) *Colonialism and Culture*. Ann Arbor: University of Michigan Press.

Dirlik, A. (1997) *The Postcolonial Aura: Third World Criticism in the Age of Global Capitalism*. Boulder, CO: Westview Press.

Dore, R.P. (1973) *British Factory – Japanese Factory: The Origins of Diversity in Industrial Relations*. Berkeley, CA: University of California Press.

Dorfman, P.W. (2004) 'International and Cross-Cultural Leadership Research', in: B.J. Punnett & O. Shenkar (eds) *Handbook for International Management Research*. 2nd edition, pp. 265–355. Ann Arbor: University of Michigan Press.

Dorfman, P.W. & Howell, J.P. (1988) 'Dimensions of National Culture and Effective Leadership Patterns: Hofstede Revisited', *Advances in International Comparative Management*. 3: 127–150.

Dossa, S. (2007) 'Slicing Up "Development": Colonialism, Political Theory, Ethics', *Third World Quarterly*. 28(5): 887–899.

Drucker, P. (1942) *The Future of Industrial Man*. New York: John Day.

Drucker, P. (1946) *Concept of the Corporation*. New York: John Day.

Drucker, P. (1954) *The Practice of Management*. New York: Harper and Row.

DuBois, F.L. & Reeb, D. (2000) 'Ranking the International Business Journals', *Journal of International Business Studies*, 31(4): 689–704.

Dugan, K.G. (1987) 'The Zoological Exploration of the Australian Region and Its Impact on Biological Theory', in: N. Reingold & M. Rothenberg (eds) *Scientific Colonialism: A Cross-Cultural Comparison*, pp. 97–100. Washington, D.C.: Smithsonian Institution Press.

DuGay, P. & Pryke, M. (eds) (2002) *Cultural Economy: Cultural Analysis and Commercial Life*. London: Sage.

Dunlop, J. (1958) *Industrial Relations Systems*. New York: Holt, Rinehart and Winston.

Dunlop, J., Kerr, K., Harbison, F. & Myers, C. (1975) *Industrialism and Industrial Man Reconsidered*. Princeton: Interuniversity Study of Labor Problems in Economic Development.

Earley, P.C. (2006) 'Leading Cultural Research in the Future: A Matter of Paradigms and Taste', *Journal of International Business Studies*. 37: 922–931.

Echtner, C.M. & Prasad, P. (2003) 'The Context of Third World Tourism Marketing', *Annals of Tourism Research*. 30(3): 660–682.

Eden, D. & Rynes, S. (2003) 'Publishing Across Borders: Furthering the Internationalization of *AMJ*', *Academy of Management Journal*. 46: 679–683.

Eggers, E.R. (1977) 'How to do Business with a Frenchman', in: T.D. Weinshall (ed.) *Culture and Management*, pp. 136–139. Harmondsworth, Middlesex: Penguin Books.

EIASM (2008) The European Institute for Advanced Studies in Management. Official website, http://www.eiasm.org, accessed June 2008.

EIBA (2008) The European International Business Academy, official website, http://www.eiba-online.org, accessed August 2008.

Ellis, C. & Bochner, A.P. (1996) *Composing Ethnography: Alternative Forms of Qualitative Writing*. Walnut Creek, CA: Alta Mira Press.

England, G.W. (1978) 'Managers and Their Value Systems: A Five Country Comparative Study', *Columbia Journal of World Business*. 13(2): 35–44.

England, G. (1986) 'National Work Meanings and Patterns – Constraints on Management Action', *European Management Journal*. 4(3): 176–184.

England, G.W., Dhingra, O.P. & Agarwal, N.C. (1974) *The Manager and the Man*. Kent, OH: Kent State University Press.

England, G.W. & Lee, R. (1971) 'Organizational Goals and Expected Behavior among American, Japanese and Korean Managers – A Comparative Study', *Academy of Management Journal*. Dec: 425–438.

England, G.W. & Lee, R. (1974) 'The Relationship between Managerial Values and Managerial Success in the United States, Japan, India, and Australia', *Journal of Applied Psychology*. 59(4): 411–419.

Engwall, L. (1996) 'The Vikings versus the World: An Examination of Nordic Business Research', *Scandinavian Journal of Management*. 12(4): 425–436.

Engwall, L. & Zamagni, V. (eds) (1998) *Management Education in Historical Perspective*. Manchester: Manchester University Press.

Enriquez, V.G. (1977) 'Pakikisama o Pakikibaka: Understanding the Psychology of the Filipino'. Paper presented at the Conference on Philippine Culture; Bay Area Bilingual Education League, Berkeley, California, 29–30 April 1977.

Enriquez, V.G. (1988) 'The Structure of Philippine Social Values: Towards Integrating Indigenous Values and Appropriate Technology', in: D. Sinha & H.S.R. Kao (eds) *Social Values and Development: Asian Perspectives*, pp. 124–150. New Delhi: Sage.

Escobar, A. (1995) *Encountering Development: The Making and Unmaking of the Third World*. Princeton, NJ: Princeton University Press.

Evans-Pritchard, D. (1989) 'How "They" See "Us": Native American Images of Tourists', *Annals of Tourism Research*. 16: 89–105.

Fabian, J. (1983) *Time and the Other: How Anthropology Makes its Object*. New York: Columbia University Press.

Fabian, J. (2001) *Anthropology with an Attitude: Critical Essays*. Stanford, CA: Stanford University Press.

Fang, T. (2003) 'A Critique of Hofstede's Fifth National Culture Dimension', *International Journal of Cross Cultural Management*. 3(3): 347–368.

Fanon, F. (1952/1986) *Black Skin, White Masks*. London: Pluto.

Fanon, F. (1961/1967) *The Wretched of the Earth*. London: Penguin.

Farmer, R.N. (ed.) (1968) *International Management*. Belmont, CA: Dickenson Pub. Co.

Farmer, R.N. & Richman, B.M. (1965) *Comparative Management and Economic Progress*. Homewood, IL.: Irwin.

Fatehi, K. (1996) *International Management: A Cross Cultural Approach*. Upper Saddle River, NJ: Prentice Hall.

Featherstone, M. (1993) 'Global and Local Cultures', in: J. Bird, B. Curtis, T. Putnam, G. Robertson & L. Turner (eds) *Mapping the Futures: Local Cultures, Global Change*, pp. 169–187. London: Routledge.

Fenn, D.H. Jnr. (ed.) (1957) *Management Guide to Overseas Operations: Business Looks Abroad – At Its Opportunities and Responsibilities*. New York: McGraw Hill.

Fernando, J.L. (2003) 'NGOs and Production of Indigenous Knowledge Under the Condition of Postmodernity', *Annals of the American Academy of Political and Social Science*. 590: 54–72.

Feuchtzwang, S. (1973) 'The Discipline and Its Sponsors', in: T. Asad (ed.) (1973) *Anthropology and the Colonial Encounter*, pp. 71–102. London: Ithaca Press.

Fish, S. (1997) 'Boutique Multiculturalism, or Why Liberals are Incapable of Thinking about Hate Speech', *Critical Inquiry*. 23: 378–395.

Fleishman. E., Harris, E.F. & Burtt, R.D. (1955) *Leadership and Supervision in Industry*. Columbus, OH: Ohio State University Press.

Fleischman, R.K. & Tyson, T.N. (2004) 'Accounting in Service to Racism: Monetizing Slave Property in the *Ante Bellum* South', *Critical Perspectives on Accounting*, 15(3): 376–399.

Ford Foundation, The (2008) Website of the Ford Foundation, http://www.ford-found.org/, accessed on 10/07/2008.

Forster, P. (1973) 'A Review of the New Left Critique of Social Anthropology', in: T. Asad (ed.) *Anthropology and the Colonial Encounter*, pp. 23–40. London: Ithaca Press.

Fougere, M. & Moulettes, A. (2006) *Development and Modernity in Hofstede's Culture's Consequences: A Postcolonial Reading*. Lund, Sweden: Lund Institute of Economic Research.

Foucault, M. (1976/1981) *The History of Sexuality: Volume One*. Translated by Robert Hurley. London: Penguin.

Frank, A.G. (1975) *On Capitalist Underdevelopment*. Bombay and New York: Oxford University Press.

Frank, A.G. (1978) *Development Accumulation and Underdevelopment*. London: Macmillan.

Franco, E.A. (1986) *Pinoy Management*. Metro Manila: National Bookstore.

Frenkel, M. (2008) 'The Multinational Corporation as a Third Space: Rethinking International Management Discourse on Knowledge Transfer Through Homi Bhabha', *Academy of Management Review*. 33(4): 924–942.

Frenkel, M. & Shenhav, Y. (2003) 'From Americanization to Colonization: The Diffusion of Productivity Models Revisited', *Organization Studies*. 24: 1537–1561.

Frenkel, M. & Shenhav, Y. (2006) 'From Binarism Back to Hybridity: A Postcolonial Reading of Management and Organization Studies', *Organization Studies*. 27: 855–876.

Friedman, J. (1994) *Cultural Identity and Global Process*. London: Sage.

Friedman, S.S. (1998) *Mappings: Feminism and the Cultural Geographies of Encounter*. Princeton, NJ: Princeton University Press.

Freire, P. (1970) *Pedagogy of the Oppressed*. New York: Seabury Press.

Gabor, A. (1992). *The Man Who Discovered Quality: How W. Edwards Deming Brought the Quality Revolution to America*. New York and London: Penguin.

Gandhi, L. (1998) *Postcolonial Theory: A Critical Introduction*. St Leonards, NSW: Allen and Unwin.

Geertz, C. (1983). *Local Knowledge: Further Essays in Interpretive Anthropology*. New York: Basic Books.

Gemelli, G. (1996) 'American Influence on European Management Education – The Role of the Ford Foundation', in: R.P. Amdam (ed.) *Management, Education and Competitiveness: Europe, Japan and the United States*, pp. 38–68. London: Routledge.

Giacalone, R.A. (2009) 'Academic Rankings in Research Institutions: A Case of Skewed Mind-Sets and Professional Amnesia', *Academy of Management Learning and Education*. 8(1): 122–126.

Gilmartin, D. (1994) 'Scientific Empire and Imperial Science: Colonialism and Irrigation in the Indus Basin', *The Journal of Asian Studies*. 53(4): 1127–1149.

Gilroy, P. (2005) *Postcolonial Melancholia*. New York: Columbia University Press.

Glissant, E. (1981/1989) *Caribbean Discourse: Selected Essays*. Translated and with an introduction by J. Michael Dash. Charlottesville: University Press of Virginia.

Goodman, P.S. & Moore, B.E. (1972) 'Critical Issues of Cross Cultural Management Research', *Human Organization*. 31(1): 39–45.

Gopinath, C. (1998) 'Alternative Approaches to Indigenous Management in India', *Management International Review*. 38(3): 257–275.

Gottlieb, A. (1995) 'Beyond the Lonely Anthropologist: Collaboration in Research and Writing', *American Anthropologist*. 97(1): 21–26.

Gourvish, T.R. & Tiratsoo, N. (eds) (1998) *Missionaries and Managers: American Influences on European Management Education, 1945–1960*. Manchester: Manchester University Press.

Graham, W.K. & Roberts, K.H. (1972) *Comparative Studies in Organizational Behavior*. New York: Holt, Rinehart and Winston.

Gramsci, A. (1971) *Selections from the Prison Notebooks of Antonio Gramsci*. Edited and translated by Q. Hoare and G. Nowell-Smith. London and New York: Lawrence & Wishart International Publishers.

Graves, D. (ed.) (1973) *Management Research: A Cross Cultural Perspective*. San Francisco: Jossey Bass.

Guha, R. (ed.) (1982, 1983, 1984, 1985, 1987) *Subaltern Studies I–V: Writings on South Asian History and Society*. Delhi: Oxford University Press.

Guha, R. & Spivak, G.C. (1988) *Selected Subaltern Studies*. New York: Oxford University Press.

Gupta, A. & Kleiner, B.H. (2001) 'Effective Personnel Management Practices in the Philippines', *Management Research New*. 24(3/4): 149–153.

Haire, M., Ghiselli, A. & Porter, L. (1966) *Managerial Thinking: An International Study*. New York and London: John Wiley.

Hall, E.T. (1976) *Beyond Culture*. New York: Anchor/Doubleday.

Hall, P.A. & Soskice, D. (eds) (2001) *Varieties of Capitalism: The Institutional Foundations of Comparative Advantage*. Oxford: Oxford University Press.

Hamilton, G.G. (2006) *Commerce and Capitalism in Chinese Societies*. London and New York: Routledge.

Harbison, F.H. & Dubin, R. (1947) *Patterns of Union-Management Relations: United Automobile Workers (CIO)*. General Motors, Studebaker. Chicago: Science Research Associates.

Harbison, F. & Ibrahim, A.I. (1958) *Human Resources for Egyptian Enterprise*. New York: McGraw-Hill.

Harbison, F.H., Burns, R.K. & Dubin, R. (1948) *Toward a Theory of Labor-Management: Insights in Labor Relations*. New York: Macmillan.

Harbison, F. & Myers, C.A. (1959) *Management in the Industrial World: An International Analysis*. New York: McGraw-Hill.

Harding, S. (1986) *The Science Question in Feminism*. Ithaca, NY: Cornell University Press.

Harding, S. (1991) *Whose Science? Whose Knowledge?: Thinking from Women's Lives*. Milton Keynes: Open University Press.

Harding, S. (1996) 'European Expansion and the Organisation of Modern Science: Isolated or Linked Historical Processes', *Organization*. 3(4): 497–509.

Hardy, C. (2001) 'Researching Organizational Discourse', *International Studies of Management & Organization*. 31(3): 25–47.

Harney, S. & Nyathi, N. (2007) 'Race, Revolution and Organisation', in: C. Jones and R. ten Bos (eds) *Philosophy and Organisation*, pp. 132–139. London: Routledge.

Harris, M. (1964) *The Nature of Cultural Things*. New York: Random House.

Harris, M. (1976) 'History and Significance of the Emic/Etic Distinction', *Annual Review of Anthropology*. 5: 329–350.

Harris, M. (1979) *Cultural Materialism: The Struggle for a Science of Culture*. New York: Vintage.

Harris, P.R. & Moran, R.T. (1979) *Managing Cultural Differences*. 1st edition. Houston, TX: Gulf Pub. Co.

Harrison, F.V. (2008) *Outsider Within: Reworking Anthropology in the Global Age*. Urbana and Chicago: University of Illinois Press.

Hartmann, H. (1959) *Authority and Organization in German Management*. Princeton, NJ: Princeton University Press.

Hayhoe, R. & Pan, J. (eds) (1996) *East-West Dialogue in Knowledge and Higher Education*. New York: M.E. Sharpe.

Headland, T.N., Pike, K.L. & Harris, M. (eds) (1990) *Emics and Etics: The Insider/ Outsider Debate*. Newbury Park, CA: Sage.

Hedmo, T., Sahlin-Andersson, K. & Wedlin, L. (2005) 'Fields of Imitation: The Global Expansion of Management Education', in: B. Czarniawska & G. Sevon (eds) *Global Ideas, How Ideas, Objects and Practices Travel in the Global Economy*, pp. 190–212. Malmo: Liber & Copenhagen Business School Press.

Heidegger, M. (1977) 'The Age of the World Picture', in: M. Heidegger (trans. W. Lovitt), *The Question Concerning Technology*. New York: Harper and Row.

Helfrich, H. (1999) 'Beyond the Dilemma of Cross-Cultural Psychology: Resolving the Tension between Etic and Emic Approaches', *Culture and Psychology*. 5(2): 131–153.

Henry, E. & Pene, H. (2001) '*Kaupapa Maori*: Locating Indigenous Ontology, Epistemology and Methodology in the Academy', *Organization*. 8(2): 234–242.

Hickson, D.J., Hinings, C.R., McMillan, C.J. & Schwitter, J.P. (1974) 'The Culture-Free Context of Organization Structure: A Tri-National Comparison', *Sociology*. 8(1): 59–80.

Hirst, P. & Thompson, G. (1998) *Globalization in Question*. Cambridge: Polity.

Hickson, D.J., Hinings, C.R., McMillan, C.J. & Schwitter, J.P. (1977) 'The Culture Free Context of Organization Structure: A Trinational Comparison', in: T.D. Weinshall (ed.) *Culture and Management*, pp. 354–382. Harmondsworth: Penguin.

Hickson, D.J. & Pugh, D.S. (1995) *Management Worldwide: The Impact of Societal Culture on Organizations around the Globe*. London: Penguin Books.

Hobson, J.A. (1902) *Imperialism*. Ann Arbor: University of Michigan Press.

Hobson, J.M. (2004) *The Eastern Origins of Western Civilization*. Cambridge: Cambridge University Press.

Hobsbawm, E.J. (1968) *Industry and Empire: An Economic History of Britain since 1750*. London: Weidenfield & Nicolson.

Hodgetts, R. & Luthans F. (2002) *International Management: Culture, Strategy, and Behaviour*. 5th edition. International edition. Boston, MA and London: McGraw-Hill Irwin.

Hoecklin, L. (1995) *Managing Cultural Differences*. Workingham: Addison-Wesley.

Hofstede, G. (1980) *Culture's Consequences: International Differences in Work-Related Values*. Beverly Hills, CA: Sage.

Hofstede, G. (1984) 'The Cultural Relativity of the Quality of Life Concept', *Academy of Management Review*. 9(3): 389–398.

Hofstede, G. (2006) 'What did GLOBE Really Measure? Researchers' Minds versus Respondents' Minds', *Journal of International Business Studies*. 37: 882–896.

Hofstede, G. & Bond, M.H. (1988) 'The Confucian Connection: From Cultural Roots to Economic Growth', *Organisational Dynamics*. 16(4): 4–21.

Hollnsteiner, M. (1965) 'Philippine Organizational Behaviour: Personalism and Group Solidarity', *Bulletin of the Philippine Library Association*. 1(2): June.

Hoobler, J.M. (2005) 'Lip Service to Multiculturalism: Docile Bodies of the Modern Organization', *Journal of Management Inquiry*. 14(1): 49–56.

Hoogvelt, A. (2001) *Globalization and the Postcolonial World*. 2nd edition. Basingstoke: Palgrave.

Huggan, G. (2001) *The Postcolonial Exotic: Marketing the Margins*. London: Routledge.

Hymes, D. (1974) *Reinventing Anthropology*. New York: Vintage Books.

Ibarra-Colado, E. (2006) 'Organization Studies and Epistemic Coloniality in Latin America: Thinking Otherness from the Margins', *Organization*. 13(4): 463–488.

INASP (2008) International Network for the Availability of Scientific Publications, Official Website http://www.inasp.info/file/68/about-inasp.html, accessed January 2009.

Inkpen, A.C. (2001) 'A Note on Ranking the International Business Journals', *Journal of International Business Studies*. 32(1): 193–196.

Inzerilli, G. (1981) 'Preface: Some Conceptual Issues in the Study of the Relationships Between Organizations and Societies', *International Studies of Management and Organization*. 10(4): 3–14.

Ishikawa, K. (1970/1980) *QC Circle Koryo: General Principles of the QC Circle*. Tokyo: QC Circle Headquarters, Union of Japanese Scientists and Engineers.

Jack, G. (2008) 'Postcolonialism and Marketing', in: M. Tadajewski and D. Brownlie (eds) *Critical Marketing: Contemporary Issues in Marketing*, pp. 367–387. Chichester: John Wiley and Sons.

Jack, G.A., Calás, M.B., Nkomo, S.M. & Peltonen, T. (2008) 'International Management and Critique: An Uneasy Relationship', *Academy of Management Review*. 33(4): 870–884.

Jack, G. & Lorbiecki, A. (2003) 'Asserting Possibilities of Resistance in the Cross-Cultural Teaching Machine: Re-viewing Videos of Others', in: A. Prasad (ed.) *Postcolonial Theory and Organizational Analysis: A Critical Engagement*, pp. 213–232. New York: Palgrave.

Jack, G.A. & Westwood, R. (2006) 'Postcolonialism and the Politics of Qualitative Research in International Business', *Management International Review*. 46(4): 481–501.

Jacques, R. (1997) 'The Unbearable Whiteness of Being: Reflections of a Pale, Stale, Male', in: P. Prasad, A.J. Mills, M. Elmes & A. Prasad (eds) *Managing the Organizational Melting Pot: Dilemmas of Workplace Diversity*, pp. 80–106. Thousand Oaks, CA: Sage.

James, W. (1973) 'The Anthropologist as Reluctant Imperialist', in: T. Asad (ed.) *Anthropology and the Colonial Encounter*, pp. 71–102. London: Ithaca Press.

Jamieson, I. (1980) *Capitalism and Culture: A Comparative Analysis of British and American Manufacturing Organisations*. Farnborough: Gower.

JanMohamed, A.R. (1983) *Manichean Aesthetics: The Politics of Literature in Colonial Africa*. Amherst: University of Massachusetts Press.

Jasanoff, S. (ed.) (1995) *Handbook of Science and Technology Studies*. Thousand Oaks, CA: Sage.

Javidan, M., House, R.J., Dorfman, P.W., Hanges, P.J. & De Luque, M.S. (2006) 'Conceptualizing and Measuring Cultures and Their Consequences: A Comparative Review of GLOBE's and Hofstede's Approaches', *Journal of International Business Studies*. 37: 897–914.

Jaya, P.S. (2001) 'Do We Really "Know" and "Profess"? Decolonizing Management Knowledge', *Organization*. 8(2): 227–233.

Jeffcutt, P. (1994) 'From Interpretation to Representation in Organizational Analysis: Postmodernism, Ethnography and Organizational Symbolism', *Organization Studies*. 15(2): 241–274.

Jocano, F.L. (1981) 'Management and Culture – A Normative Approach'. Paper presented at the 18th National Conference of the Personnel Association of the Philippines, Baguio City, the Philippines.

Jones, G. (2000) *Merchants to Multinational: British Trading Companies in the Nineteenth and Twentieth Centuries*. Oxford: Oxford University Press.

Juran, J. (1992) *Juran on Quality by Design: The New Steps for Planning Quality into Goods and Services*. New York: Free Press.

Juran, J. (1964/1995) *Managerial Breakthrough: The Classic Book on Improving Management Performance*. New York: McGraw-Hill.

Juran, J. (1951/1999) *Quality Control Handbook*. 5th edition. New York: McGraw-Hill.

Kanungo, R.N. (1983) 'Work Alienation: A Pancultural Perspective', *International Studies of Management and Organization*. 13: 119–138.

Kaplan, A. (1964) *The Conduct of Inquiry*. New York: Crowell.

Katz, C. (2001) 'On the Grounds of Globalization: A Topography for Feminist Political Engagement', *Signs*, 26: 1213–1234.

Kaufman, B.E. (2005) 'Clark Kerr and the Founding of the Berkeley IIR: A Celebratory Remembrance', *Industrial Relations*. 44(3): 405–415.

Kelley, L. & Worthley, R. (1981) 'The Role of Culture in Comparative Management: A Cross-Cultural Perspective', *Academy of Management Journal*. 24(1): 164–173.

Kelly, J.D. (1999) 'Time and the Global: Against the Homogeneous, Empty Communities in Contemporary Social Theory', in: B. Meyer & P. Geschiere (eds) (1999) *Globalization and Identity: Dialectics of Flow and Closure*, pp. 239–272. Oxford: Blackwell.

Kelly, G.P. & Altbach, P.G. (eds) (1984) *Education and the Colonial Experience*. New Brunswick: Transaction.

Kemmis, S. & McTaggart, R. (2005) 'Participatory Action Research: Communicative Action and the Public Sphere', in: N.K. Denzin & Y. Lincoln (eds) *The Sage Handbook of Qualitative Research*, pp. 559–603. Thousand Oaks, CA: Sage.

Kerr, C., Dunlop, J.T., Harbison, F.H. & Myers, C.A. (1960) *Industrialism and Industrial Man: The Problems of Labor and Management in Economic Growth*. Cambridge, MA: Harvard University Press.

Kerr, C., Dunlop, J.T., Harbison, F.H. & Myers, C.A. (1973) *Industrialism and Industrial Man: The Problems of Labor and Management in Economic Growth*. 2nd edition. Harmondsworth: Penguin.

Kiggundu, M.N. (1988) 'Africa', in: R. Nath (ed.) *Comparative Management: A Regional View*, pp. 169–243. Cambridge, MA: Ballinger.

Kim, K.I., Park, H.J. & Suzuki, N. (1990) 'Reward Allocation in the United States, Japan, and Korea: A Comparison of Individualistic and Collectivist Cultures', *Academy of Management Journal*. 33: 188–198.

Kipping, M. & Bjarnar, O. (1998) *The Americanisation of European Business: The Marshall Plan and the Transfer of US Management Models*. London/New York: Routledge.

Kipping, M., Üsdiken, B. & Puig, N. (2004) 'Imitation, Tension, and Hybridization: Multiple "Americanizations" of Management Education in Mediterranean Europe', *Journal of Management Inquiry*. 13(2): 98–108.

Kirkman, B. & Law, K. (2005) 'International Management Research in AMJ: Our Past, Present, and Future', *Academy of Management Journal*. 48(3): 377–386.

Kirkman, B.L., Lowe, K.B. & Gibson, C.B. (2006) 'A Quarter Century of *Culture's Consequences*: A Review of Empirical Research Incorporating Hofstede's Cultural Values Framework', *Journal of International Business Studies*. 37: 285–320.

Kluckhohn, C.K. (1951) 'Values and Value Orientations in the Theory of Action', in: T. Parsons & E.A. Shils (eds) *Toward a General Theory of Action*. Cambridge, MA: Harvard University Press.

Kluckhohn, C. & Kroeber, A.L. (1952) *Culture: A Critical Review of Concepts and Definitions*. Cambridge, Mass: The Museum.

Kluckhohn, F.R. & Strodtbeck, F.L. (1961) *Variations in Value Orientations*. Evanston, Ill.: Row Peterson.

Kolde, E.J. (1968) 'Business Enterprise in a Global Context', in: R.N. Farmer (ed.) *International Management*, pp. 8–32. Belmont, CA: Dickenson Pub. Co.

Kraut, A.I. (1975) 'Some Recent Advances in Cross-National Management Research', *Academy of Management Journal*. 18: 538–549.

Kwek, D. (2003) 'Decolonizing and Re-presenting Culture's Consequences: A Postcolonial Critique of Cross-Cultural Studies in Management', in: A. Prasad (ed.) *Postcolonial Theory and Organizational Analysis: A Critical Engagement*, pp. 160–194. New York: Palgrave.

Lackner, H. (1973) 'Colonial Administration and Social Anthropology: Eastern Nigeria 1920–1940', in: T. Asad (1973) *Anthropology and the Colonial Encounter*, pp. 123–152. London: Ithaca Press.

Lane, H.W. & DiStefano, J.J. (1988) *International Management Behavior*. Scarborough, ONT: Nelson Canada.

Landau, O. (2006) 'Cold War Political Culture and the Return of Systems Rationality', *Human Relations*. 59(5): 637–663.

Larner, W. (1995) 'Theorising Difference in Aotearoa/New Zealand', *Gender, Place and Culture*, 2: 177–190.

Lassiter, L.E. (2005) 'Collaborative Ethnography and Public Anthropology', *Current Anthropology*. 46(1): 83–106.

Laurent, A. (1983) 'The Cultural Diversity of Western Conceptions of Management', *International Studies of Management and Organization*. 13(1/2): 75–96.

Leavitt, H.J. (1957) 'The Export of American Management Education', *Journal of Business*. 30(3): 153–162.

Leclerc, G. (1972) *Anthropologie et Colonialisme*. Paris: Fayard.

Lee, S.H. (2000) 'The Rise of East Asia and East Asian Social Science's Quest for Self-Identity', *Journal of World-Systems Research*. 6(3): 768–783.

Lenin, V.I. (1916) 'Imperialism, the Highest Stage of Capitalism', *Collected Works of V.I. Lenin*. Moscow: Foreign Language House.

Leung, K., Bhagat, R.S., Buchan, N.R., Erez, M. & Gibson, C.R. (2005) 'Culture and International Business: Recent Advances and Their Implications for Future Research', *Journal of International Business Studies*. 36: 357–378.

Levy, D. (2008) 'Political Contestation in Global Production Networks', *Academy of Management Review*. 33(4): 943–963.

Lewis, R.D. (2006) *When Cultures Collide: Managing Successfully Across Cultures*. London: Nicholas Brealey Publishing.

Likert, R. (1953) *Motivation: The Core of Management*. New York: American Management Association. Personnel Series, 55: 3–21.

Lim, L. & Firkola, P. (2000) 'Methodological Issues in Cross-Cultural Management Research: Problems, Solutions, and Proposals', *Asia Pacific Journal of Management*. 17(1): 133–154.

Lincoln, Y. (1995) 'Emerging Criteria for Quality in Qualitative and Interpretive Research', *Qualitative Inquiry*. 1(3): 275–289.

Ling, W. & Fang, L. (2003) 'The Chinese Leadership Theory', *Advances in Global Leadership*. 3: 183–204.

Lincoln, Y.S. & Gonzalez y Gonzalez, E.M. (2008) 'The Search for Decolonizing Methodologies in Qualitative Research', *Qualitative Inquiry*. 14(5): 784–805.

Lindberg, D.C. (1992) *The Beginning of Western Science: The European Scientific Tradition in Philosophical, Religious, and Institutional Context, 600 B.C. to A.D. 1450*. Chicago and London: University of Chicago Press.

Linstead, S.A. (ed.) (2003) *Text/Work: Representing Organization and Organizing Representation*. London: Routledge.

Litvin, D. (1997) 'The Discourse of Diversity: From Biology to Management', *Organization*, 4(2): 187–210.

Loomba, A. (1998) *Colonialism/Postcolonialism*. London: Routledge.

Loubser, J.J. (1988) 'The Need for the Indigenization of the Social Sciences', *International Sociology*. 3(2): 179–187.

Lowe, H.D. (1968) 'Doing Business in the Developing Countries', in: R.N. Farmer (ed.) *International Management*, pp. 52–63. Belmont, CA: Dickenson Pub. Co.

Lowe, S. (2001) 'In the Kingdom of the Blind, the One-Eyed Man is King', *International Journal of Cross Cultural Management*. 1(3): 313–332.

Ludden, D. (1992) 'India's Development Regime', in: N.B. Dirks (ed.) *Colonialism and Culture*. Ann Arbor: University of Michigan Press.

Lustig, J. (2004) 'The Mixed Legacy of Clark Kerr: A Personal View', *Academe* (on-line), 90(4), http://www.aaup.org/publications/Academe/2004/04ja/04jatoc.htm, accessed 20/7/2005.

Luthans, F. & Hodgetts, R.M. (1990) *International Management: Culture, Strategy and Behavior*. New York: McGraw-Hill.

Malinowski, B. (1930/1961) *The Dynamics of Culture Change: An Inquiry into Race Relations in Africa*. New Haven, CT: Yale University Press.

Marcus, G.E. & Fischer, M. (1986). *Anthropology as Cultural Critique*. Chicago: University of Chicago Press.

Marcus, G.E. (1998) *Ethnography through Thick and Thin*. Princeton: Princeton University Press.

Marschan-Piekkari, R. & Welch, C. (eds) (2004) *Handbook of Qualitative Research Methods for International Business*. Cheltenham, UK and Northampton, MA, USA: Edward Elgar.

Martin, J.S. & Chaney, L.H. (2008) *Global Business Etiquette: A Guide to International Communication and Customs*. Westport, CT: Praeger.

Maruyama, M. (1974) 'Paradigmatology and Its Application to Cross Disciplinary, Cross Professional and Cross Cultural Communication', *Dialectica*. 28.

Maurice, M. (1976) 'Introduction – Theoretical and Ideological Aspects of the Universalistic Approach to the Study of Organizations', *International Studies of Management & Organization*. 6(3): 3.

Maurice, M. (1979) 'For a Study of "The Societal Effect": Universality and Specificity in Organisation Research', in: C.J. Lammers & D.J. Hickson (eds) *Organizations Alike and Unlike*, pp. 42–60. London: Routledge and Kegan Paul.

Maurice, M., Sorge, A. & Warner, M. (1980) 'Societal Differences in Organizing Manufacturing Units: A Comparison of France, West Germany and Great Britain', *Organization Studies*. 1(1): 59–86.

McClelland, D.C. (1961) *The Achieving Society*. Princeton: Van Nostrand Reinhold.

McClelland, D.C. & Winter, D.G. (1969) *Motivating Economic Achievement*. New York: Free Press.

McClintock, A. (1995) *Imperial Leather: Race, Gender and Sexuality in the Colonial Conquest*. New York and London: Routledge.

McGregor, D. (1957) 'The Human Side of Enterprise: An Adventure in Thought and Action'. Proceedings of the Fifth Anniversary Convocation of the MIT School of Industrial Management. Cambridge, MA. June.

McNeilly, M (1996) *Sun Tzu and the Art of Business: Six Strategic Principles for Managers*. New York: Oxford University Press.

McSweeney, B. (2002) 'Hofstede's Model of National Cultural Differences and Their Consequences: A Triumph of Faith – A Failure of Analysis', *Human Relations*. 55(1): 89–118.

Mead, R. (1994) *International Management: Cross-Cultural Dimensions*. 1st edition. Oxford: Blackwell.

Mead, R. (1998) *International Management: Cross-Cultural Dimensions*. 2nd edition. Oxford: Blackwell.

Meaning of Work International Research Team (1987) *The Meaning of Work*. London: Academic Press.

Memmi, A. (1968) *Dominated Man: Notes Towards a Portrait*. London: Orion Press.

Meriläinen, S., Tienari, J., Thomas, R. & Davies, A. (2008) 'Hegemonic Academic Practices: Experiences of Publishing from the Periphery', *Organization*. 15(4): 584–597.

Meyer, B. & Geschiere, P. (eds) (1999) *Globalization and Identity: Dialectics of Flow and Closure*. Oxford: Blackwell.

Meyer, H.D. (2002) 'The New Managerialism in Education Management: Corporatization or Organizational Learning?' *Journal of Educational Administration*. 40(6): 534–552.

Meyer, K.E. (2006) 'Asian Management Research Needs More Self-Confidence', *Asia Pacific Journal of Management*. 23(2): 119–137.

Michaelson, G. (2001) *Sun Tzu: The Art of War for Managers; 50 Strategic Rules*. Avon, MA: Adams Media.

Miller, G.A. (1987) 'Meta-Analysis and the Culture-Free Hypothesis', *Organization Studies*. 8(4): 309–326.

Miller, S.W. & Simonetti, J.L. (1974) 'Culture and Management: Some Conceptual Considerations', *Management International Review*. 11(60): 87–100.

Mir, R., Banerjee, S.B. & Mir, A. (2008) 'Hegemony and Its Discontents: A Critical Analysis of Organizational Knowledge Transfer', *Critical Perspectives on International Business*. 4(2/3): 203–222.

Mir, R. & Mir, A. (2009) 'From the Colony to the Corporation: Studying Knowledge Transfer Across International Boundaries', *Group & Organization Management*. 34(1): 90–113.

Mir, R.A., Mir, A. & Upadhyaya, P. (2003) 'Toward a Postcolonial Reading of Organisational Control', in: A. Prasad (ed.) *Postcolonial Theory and Organizational Analysis: A Critical Engagement*, pp. 47–74. New York: Palgrave Macmillan.

Mishra, V. & Hodge, B. (1991) 'What is Post(-)Colonialism?', *Textual Practice*. 5: 399–414.

Misumi, J. (1985) *The Behavioral Science of Leadership*. Ann Arbor: University of Michigan Press.

Misumi, J. & Peterson, M.K. (1985) 'The Performance-Maintenance Theory of Leadership: Review of a Japanese Research Program', *Administrative Science Quarterly*. 30: 198–220.

Misumi, J. & Peterson, M.F. (1987) 'Supervision and Leadership', in: B. Bass, P. Weisenberg & P.J.D. Drenth (eds) *Advances in Organizational Psychology: An International Review*. pp. 273–298. Beverly Hills, CA: Sage.

Mohan, G. (1999) 'Not So Distant, Not So Strange: The Personal and the Political in Participatory Research', *Ethics, Place and Environment*. 2(1): 41–54.

Moore-Gilbert, B. (1997) *Postcolonial Theory: Contexts, Practices, Politics*. London and New York: Verso.

Moran, R.T. & Harris, P.R. (1982) *Managing Cultural Synergy*. Houston, TX: Gulf Publishing.

Moran, R.T., Harris, P.R. & Moran, S.V. (2007). *Managing Cultural Differences: Global Leadership Strategies for the Twenty-First Century*. 7th edition. Butterworth-Heinemann.

Morgan, G. (1986) *Images of Organization*. Beverly Hills, CA: Sage.

Morgan, G., Whitley, R.D. & Moen, E. (eds) (2006) *Changing Capitalisms? Internationalisation, Institutional Change and Systems of Economic Organisation*. Oxford: Oxford University Press.

Morley, D. and Robins, K. (1992) 'Techno-Orientalism: Futures, Foreigners and Phobias', *New Formations*. 16: 136–156.

Morris, M.W., Kwok, L., Ames, D. & Lickel, B. (1999) 'Views from Inside and Outside: Integrating Emic and Etic Insights about Culture and Justice Judgment', *Academy of Management Review*. 24(4): 781–796.

Morrison, T., Conaway, W.A. & Borden, G.A. (1994) *Kiss, Bow, or Shake Hands: How to Do Business in Sixty Countries*. Palm Springs, CA: Adams, Inc.

Mufti, A. (2005) 'Global Comparativism', *Critical Inquiry*. 31(2): 472–489.

Muniapan, B. (2008) 'Perspectives and Reflections on Management Education in Malaysia', *International Journal of Management in Education*. 2(1): 77–87.

Munro, J.F. (2003) *Maritime Enterprise and Empire: Sir William MacKinnon and His Business Network, 1823–93*. Woodbridge, UK: The Boydell Press.

Murata, S. & Chittick, W.C. (1994) *Vision of Islam*. New York: Paragon House.

NACS (National Association of College Stores) (2008) *Higher Education Retail Market Facts and Figures 2007*. Lorain St, Oberlin, Ohio: NACS, http://www.nacs.org/public/research/higher_ed_retail.asp

Nader, L. (1997) 'The Phantom Factor: Impact of the Cold War on Anthropology', in: N. Chomsky, I. Katznelson, R.C. Lewontin & D. Montgomery (eds) *The Cold War and the University: Toward an Intellectual History of the Postwar Years*, pp. 107–146. New York: The New Press.

Nagar, R. (2002) 'Footloose Researchers, "Traveling" Theories, and the Politics of Transnational Feminist Praxis', *Gender, Place and Culture*. 9(2): 179–186.

Naipaul, V.S. (1967) *The Mimic Men*. London: Penguin Books Limited.

Nandy, A. (ed.) (1988) *Science, Hegemony and Violence: A Requiem for Modernity*. Tokyo and Delhi: The United Nations University and Oxford University Press.

Nasr, S.H. & Leaman, O. (eds) (1996) *History of Islamic Philosophy*. London: Routledge.

Nath, R. (1975) 'Comparative Management and Organization Theory: Linking the Two', *Organization and Administrative Sciences*. 5(4): 115–124.

Nath, R. (ed.) (1988) *Comparative Management: A Regional View*. Cambridge, MA: Ballinger.

Needham, J. (1969) *The Grand Titration: Science and Society in East and West*. London: Allen & Unwin.

Negandhi, A.R. (1974) 'Cross-Cultural Management Studies: Too Many Conclusions, Not Enough Conceptualization', *Management International Review*. 14(6): 59–67.

Negandhi, A.R. (1983) 'Cross Cultural Management Research: Trends and Future Directions', *Journal of International Business Studies*. 14(2): 17–28.

Neu, D. (2000) '"Presents" for the "Indians": Land, Colonialism and Accounting in Canada', *Accounting, Organizations and Society*. 25: 163–184.

Ngugi, W.T. (1981) *Decolonising the Mind: The Politics of Language in African Literature*. Portsmith, NH: Heinemann.

Ngugi, W.T. (1983) *Barrel of a Pen: Resistance to Repression in Neo-Colonial Kenya*. Africa Research and Publications Project.

Nkomo, S.M. (1992) 'The Emperor has No Clothes: Rewriting "Race in Organization"', *Academy of Management Review*. 17(3): 487–513.

Nkomo, S. (2009) 'The Seductive Power of Academic Journal Rankings: Challenges of Searching for the Otherwise', *Academy of Management Learning and Education*. 8(1): 106–112.

Nyathi, N. (2008) *The Organisational Imagination in African Anti-Colonial Thought*. Unpublished PhD Thesis. University of Leicester.

Ohmae, K. (1995) *The End of the Nation State: The Rise of Regional Economies*. New York: Free Press.

Olds, K. & Thrift, N. (2005) 'Assembling the "Global Schoolhouse" in Pacific Asia: The Case of Singapore', in: P.W. Daniels, K.C. Ho and T.A. Hutton (eds) *Service Industries and Asia-Pacific Cities*, pp. 199–215. Abingdon: Routledge.

Olds, K. & Thrift, N. (2007) 'Global Assemblage: Singapore, Foreign Universities, and the Construction of a "Global Education Hub"', *World Development*. 35(6): 959–975.

Omanovic, V. (2006) *A Production of Diversity: Appearances, Ideas, Interests, Actions, Contradictions and Praxis*. Goteborg: BAS Publishing.

Ong, A. (2006) *Neo-Liberalism as Exception: Mutations in Citizenship and Sovereignty*. Durham, NC: Duke University Press.

Orpen, C. (1978) 'The Relationship between Job Satisfaction and Job Performance among Western and Tribal Black Employees', *Journal of Applied Psychology*. 63(2): 263–265.

Oseen, C. (1997) 'The Sexually Specific Subject and the Dilemma of Difference: Rethinking the Different in the Construction of the Nonhierarchical Workplace', in: P. Prasad, A.J. Mills, M. Elmes & A. Prasad (eds) *Managing the Organizational Melting Pot: Dilemmas of Workplace Diversity*, pp. 54–79. Thousand Oaks, CA: Sage.

Osland, J. & Osland, A. (2001) 'International Qualitative Research: An Effective Way to Generate and Verify Cross-Cultural Theories', in: B. Toyne, Z.L. Martinez & R.A. Menger (eds) *International Business Scholarship*, pp. 198–214. Westport, CT: Quorum.

Ouchi, W.G. (1981) *Theory Z: How American Business Can Meet the Japanese Challenge*. Reading, MA: Addison-Wesley.

Overing, J. (2006) 'The Backlash to Decolonizing Intellectuality', *Anthropology and Humanism*. 31(1): 11–40.

Owens, R. (1997) 'Diversity: A Bottomline Issue', *Workforce*. 76(3): 3–6.

Özbilgin, M. (2004) '"International" Human Resource Management: Academic Parochialism in Editorial Boards of the "Top" 22 Journals on International Human Resource Management', *Personnel Review*. 33(2): 205–221.

Özbilgin, M.F. (2009) 'From Journal Rankings to Making Sense of the World', *Academy of Management Learning and Education*. 8(1): 113–121.

Pacey, A. (1991) *Technology in World Civilization: A Thousand-Year History*. Cambridge, MA: MIT Press.

Parikh, U. & Garg, P.K. (1990) 'Indian Organisations: Value Dilemmas in Managerial Roles', in: A. Jaeger & R.N. Kanungo (eds) *Management in Developing Countries*, pp. 175–190. London: Routledge.

Parry, B. (1987) 'Problems in Current Theories of Colonial Discourse', *Oxford Literary Review*. 9(1/2): 27–58.

Parsons, T. (1951) *The Social System*. New York: Free Press.

Parsons, T. & Shils, E.A. (1951) *Towards a General Theory of Action*. Cambridge, MA: Harvard University Press.

Parsons, T. (1967) *Sociological Theory and Modern Society*. New York: Free Press.

Parsons, T. (1973) 'Culture and Social System Revisited', in: L. Schneider & C. Bonjean (eds) *The Idea of Culture in the Social Sciences*, pp. 33–46. Cambridge: Cambridge University Press.

Parsons, T. (1977) *The Evolution of Societies*. Englewood Cliffs, NJ: Prentice-Hall.

Pascale, R.T. & Athos, A.G. (1981) *The Art of Japanese Management*. New York: Simon and Schuster.

Pazam, A. & Reichel, A. (1977) 'Cultural Determinants of Managerial Behavior', *Management International Review*. 17: 65–72.

Peng, M.W. (2004) 'Identifying the Big Question in International Business Research', *Journal of International Business Studies*. 35(2): 99–108.

Peng, T.K., Peterson, M.F. & Shyi, Y.P. (1991) 'Quantitative Methods in Cross-National Management Research: Trends and Equivalence Issues', *Journal of Organisational Behaviour*. 12: 87–107.

Pennycook, A. (1996) 'English, Universities, and Struggles Over Culture and Knowledge', in: R. Hayhoe & J. Pan (eds) *East-West Dialogue in Knowledge and Higher Education*, pp. 64–80. New York: M.E. Sharpe.

Perlmutter, H.V. (1977) 'Emerging East to West Ventures: The Transideological Enterprise', in: T.D. Weinshall (ed.) *Culture and Management*, pp. 140–162. Harmondsworth, Middlesex: Penguin Books.

Peters, T. & Waterman, R. (1982) *In Search of Excellence: Lessons From America's Best-Run Companies*. New York: Harper and Row.

Peterson, M.F. (1988) 'PM Theory in Japan and China: What's in for the United States?' *Organizational Dynamics*, pp. 22–39. Spring.

Peterson, M.F. (2001) 'International Collaboration in Organizational Behavior Research', *Journal of Organizational Behavior*. 22: 59–81.

Peterson, M.F, Smith, P.B., Bond, M.H. & Misumi, J. (1990) 'Personal Reliance on Alternative Event-Management Processes in Four Countries', *Group and Organization Studies*. 15(1): 75–92.

Peterson, R.B. (2004) 'Empirical Research in International Management: A Critique and Future Agenda', in: R. Marschan-Piekkari & C. Welch (eds) *Handbook of Qualitative Research Methods for International Business*, pp. 25–55. Chelthenham: Edward Elgar.

Pfeffer, J. (2005) 'Why Do Management Theories Persist? A Comment on Ghoshal', *Academy of Management Learning and Education*. 4: 96–100.

Phene, A. & Guisinger, S. (1998) 'The Stature of the *Journal of International Business Studies*', *Journal of International Business Studies*. 29(3): 621–631.

Phua, K.K. (2001) *Scientific Publishing in the Asia-Pacific Region*. Proceedings of the Second ICSU/UNESCO International Conference on Electronic Publishing in Science, UNESCO House, Paris 20–23 February.

Pierce, B. & Garven, G. (1995) 'Publishing International Business Research: A Survey of Leading Journals', *Journal of International Business Studies*. 26(1): 69–89.

Pike, K.L. (1967) *Language in Relation to a Unified Theory of the Structure of Human Behavior*. 2nd edition. The Hague: Mouton.

Pletsch, C.E. (1981) 'The Three Worlds, or the Division of Social Scientific Labor, circa 1950–1975', *Comparative Studies in Society and History*. 23(4): 565–590.

Pollitt, C. (1993) *Managerialism and the Public Services: Cuts or Cultural Change in the 1990's*. 2nd edition. Oxford: Basil Blackwell.

Prakash, G. (1992) 'Postcolonialism and Indian Historiography', *Social Text*. 10(1/2): 8–19.

Prakash, G. (1999) *Another Reason: Science and the Imagination of Modern India*. Princeton, NJ: Princeton University Press.

Prasad, A. (1997a) 'The Colonizing Consciousness and Representation of the Other: A Postcolonial Critique of the Discourse of Oil', in: P. Prasad, A. Mills, M. Elmes & A. Prasad (eds) *Managing the Organizational Melting Pot: Dilemmas of Workplace Diversity*, pp. 285–311. Thousand Oaks: Sage.

Prasad, A. (ed.) (2003) *Postcolonial Theory and Organizational Analysis: A Critical Engagement*. New York: Palgrave Macmillan.

Prasad, P. & Mills, A.J. (1997) 'From Showcase to Shadow: Understanding the Dilemmas of Managing Workplace Diversity', in: P. Prasad, A.J. Mills, M. Elmes & A. Prasad (eds) *Managing the Organizational Melting Pot: Dilemmas of Workplace Diversity*, pp. 3–27. Thousand Oaks, CA: Sage.

Prasad, A. & Prasad, P. (2003) 'The Postcolonial Imagination', in: A. Prasad (ed.) *Postcolonial Theory and Organizational Analysis: A Critical Engagement*, pp. 283–295. New York: Palgrave Macmillan.

Pratt, M.L. (1992) *Imperial Eyes: Travel Writing and Transculturation*. London and New York: Routledge.

Prichard, C., Sayers, J. & Bathurst, R. (2007) 'Franchise, Margin and Locale: Constructing a Critical Management Studies Locale in Aotearoa New Zealand', *New Zealand Sociology*. 22(1): 22–44.

Prichard, C. & Willmott, H. (1997) 'Just How Managed is the McUniversity?' *Organization Studies*. 18(2): 287–231.

Priyadharshini, E. (2003) 'Reading the Rhetoric of Otherness in the Discourse of Business and Economics Towards a Postdisciplinary Practice', in: A. Prasad (ed.) *Postcolonial Theory and Organizational Analysis: A Critical Engagement*, pp. 171–192. New York: Palgrave Macmillan.

Puri, S.K. (2007) 'Integrating Scientific with Indigenous Knowledge: Constructing Knowledge Alliances for Land Management in India', *MIS Quarterly*. 31(2): 355–379.

Putti, J. (ed.) (1991) *Management: Asian Context*. Singapore: McGraw-Hill.

Quezada, F. & Boyce, J.E. (1988) 'Latin America', in: R. Nath (ed.) *Comparative Management: A Regional View*, pp. 245–270. Cambridge, MA: Ballinger.

Radhakrishnan, R. (1996) *Diasporic Mediations: Between Home and Location*. Minneapolis, MN: University of Minnesota Press.

Raghuram, P. & Madge, C. (2006) 'Towards a Method for Postcolonial Development Geography? Possibilities and Challenges', *Singapore Journal of Tropical Geography*. 27: 270–288.

Rahman, S., Gabbay, D.M. & Van Bendegem, J.P. (eds) (2008) *The Unity of Science in the Arabic Tradition: Science, Logic, Epistemology and Their Interactions*. Dordrecht: Kluwer Academic Publishers.

Raju, S. (2002) 'We are Different, but Can We Talk?' *Gender, Place and Culture*. 9(2): 173–177.

Raman, A. (1983) *Intellectual Colonisation: Science and Technology in West–East Relations*. New Delhi: Vikas Publishing House.

Reason, P. (ed.) (1994) *Participation in Human Inquiry*. London: Sage.

Redding, S.G. (1990) *The Spirit of Chinese Capitalism*. Berlin: Walter de Gruyter.

Redding, S.G. (1994) 'Comparative Management Theory: Jungle, Zoo or Fossil?', *Organization Studies*. 15(3): 323–359.

Redding, S.G. (2002) 'The Capitalist Business System of China and Its Rationale', *Asia Pacific Journal of Management*. 19(2/3): 221–249.

Redding, S.G. (2005) 'The Thick Description and Comparison of Societal Systems of Capitalism', *Journal of International Business Studies*. 36(2): 123–155.

Redding, S.G. & Martyn-Johns, T.A. (1979) 'Paradigm Differences and Their Relation to Management, with Reference to South-East Asia', in: G.W. England, A.R. Negandhi & B. Wilpert (eds) *Organizational Functioning in a Cross-Cultural Perspective*, pp. 103–125. Kent, OH: Kent State University Press.

Reingold, N. & Rothenberg, M. (eds) (1987) *Scientific Colonialism: A Cross-Cultural Comparison*. Washington DC: Smithsonian Institution Press.

Rhodes, C. (2001) *Writing Organisation: (Re)Presentation and Control in Narratives at Work*. Amsterdam: John Benjamins.

Richman, B. (1965) 'The Significance of Cultural Variables', *Academy of Management Journal*. 8(4): 292–308.

Rist, S. & Dahdouh-Guebas, F. (2006) 'Ethnosciences – A Step Towards the Integration of Scientific and Indigenous Forms of Knowledge in the Management of Natural Resources for the Future', *Environment, Development and Sustainability*. 8(4): 467–493.

Rizvi, F. (2007) 'Postcolonialism and Globalization in Education', *Cultural Studies-Critical Methodologies*. 7(3): 256–263.

Roberts, K.H. (1970) 'On Looking at an Elephant: An Evaluation of Cross-Cultural Research Related to Organizations', *Psychological Bulletin*. 74(5): 327–350.

Robins, K. (1997) 'What in the World's Going On?' in: P. Du Gay (ed.) *Production of Culture/Cultures of Production*, pp. 11–66. London: Sage and The Open University Press.

Robinson, R.D. (1978) *International Business Management – A Guide to Decision Making*. 2nd edition. Hinsdale, IL: Dryden.

Ronen, S. (1986) *Comparative and Multinational Management*. New York: Wiley.

Ronen, S. & Kraut, A.I. (1977) 'Similarities among Countries Based on Employee Work Values and Attitudes', *Columbia Journal of World Business*. 12(2): 89–96.

Rose, G. (1997) 'Situating Knowledges: Positionality, Reflexivities and Other Tactics', *Progress in Human Geography*. 21(3): 305–320.

Rosenfeld, S. (2002) 'The FBI's Secret UC Files', *The San Francisco Chronicle*, Sunday June 9th.

Ross, A. & Pickering, K. (2002) 'The Politics of Reintegrating Australian Aboriginal and American Indian Indigenous Knowledge into Resource Management: The Dynamics of Resource Appropriation and Cultural Revival', *Human Ecology*. 30(2): 187–214.

Rostow, W.W. (1960) *The Stages of Economic Growth: A Non-Communist Manifesto*. Cambridge: Cambridge University Press.

Rousseau, D.M. & Fried, Y. (2001) 'Location, Location, Location: Contextualizing Organizational Research', *Journal of Organizational Behavior*. 22: 1–13.

Sabath, A.M. (1998) *International Business Etiquette: Asia and the Pacific Rim: What You Need to Know to Conduct Business Abroad With Charm and Savvy*. Franklin Lakes, NJ: Career Press Inc.

Sabath, A.M. (1999) *International Business Etiquette: Europe: What You Need to Know to Conduct Business Abroad With Charm and Savvy*. Franklin Lakes, NJ: Career Press Inc.

Said, E. (1978) *Orientalism: Western Conceptions of the Orient*. London: Penguin.

Said, E. (1993) *Culture and Imperialism*. London: Vintage.

Samovar, L.A., Porter, R.E. & Jain, N.C. (1981) *Understanding Intercultural Communication*. Belmont, CA: Wadsworth.

Sardar, Z. (1999) *Orientalism*. Buckingham: Open University Press.

Sarkar, B.K. (1937/1985) *The Positive Background of Hindu Sociology*. Delhi: Motilal Banarsidass.

Saunders, F.S. (1999) *Who Paid the Piper? The CIA and the Cultural Cold War*. London: Granta Publications.

Saunders, K. (2003) *Feminist Post-Development Thought: Rethinking Modernity, Post-Colonialism and Representation*. London: Zed Books.

SCANCOR, The Scandinavian Consortium for Organisational Research (2009) Official Website: *www.scancor.org/*, accessed January 2009.

Schaffer, B.S. & Riordan, C.M. (2003) 'A Review of Cross-Cultural Methodologies for Organizational Research: A Best-Practices Approach', *Organizational Research Methods*. 6(2): 169–215.

Schedvin, C.B. (1987) 'Environment, Economy, and Australian Biology', in: N. Reingold & M. Rothenberg (eds) *Scientific Colonialism: A Cross-Cultural Comparison*, pp. 101–128. Washington, D.C.: Smithsonian Institution Press.

Schollhammer, H. (1969) 'The Comparative Management Theory Jungle', *Academy of Management Journal*. 12: 81–97.

Schollhammer, H. (1975) 'Current Research on International and Comparative Management Issues', *Management International Review*. 15: 29–45.

Scholte, J.A. (2000) *Globalization: A Critical Introduction*. Basingstoke: Palgrave.

Segal, L.A. (1997) 'Diversify for Dollars', *HR Magazine*. 42(4): 134–140.

Selmer, J. & de Leon, C. (2003) 'Culture and Management in the Philippines', in: M. Warner (ed.) *Culture and Management in Asia*, pp. 152–170. London and New York: Routledge.

Selvaratnam, V. (1988) 'Higher Education Co-Operation and Western Dominance of Knowledge Creation and Flows in Third World Countries', *Higher Education*. 17(1): 41–68.

Sen, R. (2004) 'Glimpses of Social Structure in Ancient India: Kautilya's Relevance for Sociology in South Asia', in: Partha N. Mukherji and Chandan Sengupta (eds) *Indigeneity and Universality in Social Science*, pp. 233–254, New Delhi: Sage.

Servan-Schreiber, J.J. (1968) *The American Challenge*. Translated by R. Steel. New York: Atheneum.

Severt Young Bear & Theisz, R.D. (1994) *Standing in the Light: A Lakota Way of Seeing*. Lincoln, NE: University of Nebraska Press.

Shenkar, O. (2004) 'One More Time: International Business in a Global Economy', *Journal of International Business Studies*. 35(1): 161–171.

Shiva, V. (1988) 'Reductionist Science as Epistemological Violence', in: A. Nandy (ed.) *Science, Hegemony and Violence: A Requiem for Modernity*, pp. 232–256. Bombay: Oxford University Press.

Shohat, E. (1993) 'Notes on the Post-Colonial', *Social Text*. 31/32: 99–113.

Simha, S.L.N. (1992) *Management with Dharma All the Way*. Madras: Institute for Financial Management and Research.

Simon, H.A. (1944) 'Decision-Making and Administrative Organization', *Public Administration Review*. 4: 16–31.

Simon, H.A. (1945) *Administrative Behavior*. New York, NY: Macmillan.

Simon, H.A. (1952) 'A Comparison of Organisation Theories', *The Review of Economic Studies*. 20(1): 40–48.

Sinha, J.B.P. (1976) 'The Authoritarian Leadership: A Style of Effective Management', *Indian Journal of Industrial Relations*. 2: 381–389.

Sinha, J.B.P. (1978) 'Power in Superior-Subordinate Relationships: The Indian Case', *Journal of Social and Economic Studies*. VI(II): 205–218.

Sinha, J.B.P. (1980) *The Nurturant Task Leader*. New Delhi: Concept.

Sirota, D. & Greenwood, J.M. (1977) 'Understand Your Overseas Workforce', in: T.D. Weinshall (ed.) *Culture and Management*, pp. 261–276. Harmondsworth, Middlesex: Penguin Books.

Smart, B. (1996) '(Mis)Understanding Japan', *Theory, Culture and Society*. 13(3): 179–192.

Smith, B.E. & Thomas, J.M. (1972) 'Cross-Cultural Attitudes among Managers: A Case Study', *Sloan Management Review*. 13: 34–51.

Smith, F. (1996) 'Problematising Language: Limitations and Possibilities in "Foreign Language" Research', *Area*. 28: 160–166.

Smith, L.T. (1999) *Decolonizing Methodologies: Research and Indigenous Peoples*. London and Dunedin: Zed Books and University of Otago Press.

Smith, L.T. (2005) 'On Tricky Ground: Researching the Native in the Age of Uncertainty', in: N.K. Denzin & Y. Lincoln (eds) *The Sage Handbook of Qualitative Research*, pp. 85–107. Thousand Oaks, CA: Sage.

Smith, P.B. (2006) 'When Elephants Fight, the Grass Gets Trampled: The GLOBE and Hofstede Projects', *Journal of International Business Studies*. 37: 915–921.

Smith, P.B. & Peterson, M.F. (1988) *Leadership, Organizations and Culture*. London: Sage.

Smith, P.B. & Peterson, M.F. (2002) 'Cross-Cultural Leadership', in: M.J. Gannon and K.L. Newman (eds) *The Blackwell Handbook of Cross-Cultural Management*, pp. 217–235. Oxford and Malden, MA: Blackwell Business.

Smith, P.B., Peterson, M.F. & Misumi, J. (1994) 'Event Management and Work Team Effectiveness in Japan, Britain and USA', *Journal of Occupational and Organizational Psychology*. 67(1): 33–44.

Smith, P.B., Wang, Z. & Leung, K. (1997) 'Leadership, Decision-Making and Cultural Context: Event Management within Chinese Joint Ventures', *The Leadership Quarterly.* 8(4): 413–431.

Søndergaard, M. (1994) 'Hofstede's Consequences: A Study of Reviews, Citations and Replications', *Organization Studies.* 15(3): 447–456.

Sorge, A. (1991) 'Strategic Fit and the Societal Effect: Interpreting Cross-National Comparisons of Technology, Organisation and Human Resources', *Organization Studies.* 12(2): 161–190.

Sorge, A. & Maurice, M. (1990) 'The Societal Effect in Strategies and Competitiveness of Machine Tool Manufacturers in France and West Germany', *The International Journal of Human Resource Management.* (1/2): 141–172.

Soriano, E.V. (1991) 'Management in Pakikisama Society – Philippines', in: J.M. Putti (ed.) *Management: Asian Context*, pp. 61–77. Singapore and New York: McGraw Hill.

Spivak, G.C. (1985) 'Can the Subaltern Speak? Speculations on Widow Sacrifice', *Wedge.* 7(8): 120–130.

Spivak, G.C. (1987) *In Other Worlds: Essays in Cultural Politics.* New York: Methuen.

Spivak, G.C. (1988) 'Can the Subaltern Speak?', in: Cary Nelson and Lawrence Grossberg (eds) *Marxism and the Interpretation of Culture*, pp. 217–313. Basingstoke: Macmillan.

Springhall, J. (2001) *Decolonization Since 1945: The Collapse of European Overseas Empires.* Basingstoke: Palgrave Macmillan.

Steers, R.M., Bischoff, S.J. & Higgins, L.H. (1992) 'Cross-Cultural Management Research: The Fish and the Fisherman', *Journal of Management Inquiry.* 1(4): 321–330.

Steinbock, D. (2005) *US Business Schools: Origins, Rankings, Prospects.* Helsinki: The Finish Academy.

Stevenson, W.B. (1825) *Narrative of Twenty Years Residence in South America*, cited in Loomba, 1998.

Stogdill, R.M. & Coons, A.E. (eds) (1957) *Leader Behavior: Its Description and Measurement.* Columbus, OH: Ohio State University Bureau of Business Research.

Stoler, A.L. (1992) 'Rethinking Colonial Categories: European Communities and the Boundaries of Rule', in: N.B. Dirks (ed.) *Colonialism and Culture*, pp. 319–352. Ann Arbor: University of Michigan Press.

Subramani, S. & Kempner, K. (2002) 'Malaysian Higher Education: Captive or Post-Western?' *Australian Journal of Education.* 46(3): 231–254.

Subramaniam, V.K. (1990) *Maxims of Chaitanya.* New Delhi: Abhinav.

Sullivan, D. (1998) 'Cognitive Tendencies in International Business Research: Implications of "A Narrow Vision"', *Journal of International Business Studies.* 29(4): 837–862.

Sullivan, P. (2008) 'Bureaucratic Process as Morris Dance: An Ethnographic Approach to the Culture of Bureaucracy in Australian Aboriginal Affairs Administration', *Critical Perspectives on International Business.* 4(2/3): 127–141.

Tedmanson, D. (2008) 'Isle of Exception: Sovereign Power and Palm Island', *Critical Perspectives on International Business.* 4(2/3): 142–165.

Temple, B. (2006) 'Representation Across Languages: Biographical Sociology Meets Translation and Interpretation Studies', *Qualitative Sociology Review*, II(1), http://www.qualitative sociologyreview.org, accessed 17.02.09.

Terpstra, V. (1978) *Cultural Environment for International Business.* Cincinnati, OH: Southwestern.

Theodorson, G.A. (1953) 'Acceptance of Industrialisation and Its Attendant Consequences for the Social Pattern of Non-Western Societies', *American Sociological Review.* 18(5): 476–485.

Thomas, N. (1994) *Colonialism's Culture: Anthropology, Travel and Government.* Cambridge: Polity Press.

Thomas, A.S., Shenkar, O. & Clarke, L. (1994) 'The Globalization of Our Mental Maps: Evaluating the Geographic Scope of Journal of International Business Coverage', *Journal of International Business.* 25: 675–686.

Tibi, B. (1995) 'Culture and Knowledge: The Politics and Islamisation of Knowledge as a Postmodern Project? The Fundamentalist Claim to De–Westernization', *Theory, Culture and Society.* 12: 1–24.

Torbert, W.R. (1976) *Creating a Community of Inquiry: Conflict, Collaboration, Transformation.* New York: Wiley.

Traces (2009) Official Website http://www.arts.cornell.edu/traces/, accessed 18 January 2009.

Transtext(e)s Transcultures (2009) *Journal of Global Cultural Studies*, Official Website, http://www.transtexts.net/, accessed January 15th 2009.

Trevor, M. (1983) *Japan's Reluctant Multinationals: Japanese Management at Home and Abroad.* London: Pinter.

Triandis, H. (1972) *The Analysis of Subjective Culture.* New York: Wiley.

Triandis, H. (1982/3) 'Dimensions of Cultural Variations as Parameters of Organisational Theories', *International Studies of Management and Organisation.* 132(4): 139–169.

Trompenaars, F. (1993) *Riding the Waves of Culture: Understanding Cultural Diversity in Business.* London: Nicholas Brealey.

Trow, M. (1994) *Managerialism and the Academic Profession: Quality and Control.* London: SRHE and the Open University Press.

Tsui, A.S. (2004) 'Contributing to Global Management Knowledge: A Case for High Quality Indigenous Research', *Asia Pacific Journal of Management.* 21: 491–513.

Tsui, A.S. (2007) 'From Homogenization to Pluralism: International Management Research in the Academy and Beyond', *Academy of Management Journal.* 50(6): 1353–1364.

Tsui, A.S., Nifadkar, S.S. & Ou, A.Y. (2007) 'Cross-National, Cross-Cultural Organizational Behavior Research: Advances, Gaps, and Recommendations', *Journal of Management.* 33(3): 426–478.

Tsui, A.S., Schoonhoven, C.B., Meyer, M.W., Lau, C.M. & Milkovich, G.T. (2004) 'Organization and Management in the Midst of Societal Transformation: The People's Republic of China', *Organization Science.* 15: 133–144.

Tucker, V. (1999) 'The Myth of Development', in: R. Munck & D. O'Hearn (eds) *Critical Development Theory*, pp. 1–26. London: Zed Books.

Tung, R.L. (1984) *Key to Japan's Economic Strength: Human Power.* Lexington, MA: Lexington Books.

Tung, R.L. (1988) 'China', in: R. Nath (ed.) *Comparative Management: A Regional View*, pp. 139–168. Cambridge, MA: Ballinger.

Tyson, T.N., Fleischman, R.K. & Oldroyd, D. (2004) 'Theoretical Perspectives on Accounting for Labor on Slave Plantations of the USA and British West Indies', *Accounting, Auditing and Accountability Journal.* 17(5): 758–778.

Van den Ven, A. (1989) 'Nothing is Quite So Good as a Good Theory', *Academy of Management Review.* 14: 486–489.

Vogel, E. (1979) *Japan as Number One: Lessons for America*. Cambridge, MA: Harvard University Press.

Wakefield, S.E.L. (2007) 'Reflective Action in the Academy: Exploring Praxis in Critical Geography Using a "Food Movement" Case Study', *Antipode*. 39(2): 331–354.

Walbridge, J. (2000) 'Logic in the Islamic Intellectual Tradition: The Recent Centuries', *Islamic Studies*. 39(1): 55–75.

Wallace, W. (1971) *The Logic of Science in Sociology*. Chicago: Aldine.

Wallerstein, I. (1974) *The Modern World-System*. New York: Academic Press.

Wallerstein, I. (1990) 'Culture as the Ideological Battleground in the Modern World-System', *Theory, Culture and Society*. 7: 31–55.

Wang, Z.M. & Satow, T. (1994) 'Leadership Styles and Organizational Effectiveness in Chinese-Japanese Joint Ventures', *Journal of Managerial Psychology*. 9: 31–36.

Warner, M. (2000) *Regional Encyclopedia of Business and Management: Management in Asia-Pacific*. New York: Business Press – Thomas Learning.

Warner, M. & Ying, Z. (1998) 'Re-Assessing Chinese Management: The Influence of Indigenous versus Exogenous Models', *Human Systems Management*. 17(4): 245–256.

Webber, R.A. (1969) 'Convergence or Divergence?', *Columbia Journal of World Business*. 4(3): 75–83.

Webber, R.A. (1977) 'Convergence or Divergence?', in: T.D. Weinshall (ed.) *Culture and Management*, pp. 39–55. Harmondsworth, Middlesex: Penguin Books.

Weber, M. (1905/2002) *The Protestant Ethic and the Spirit of Capitalism and Other Essays*. Translated by Peter R. Baehr & Gordon C. Wells. London: Penguin.

Weber, M. (1915/1951) *The Religion of China: Confucianism and Taoism*. Translated and edited by Hans H. Gerth. Glencoe: Free Press.

Weber, M. (1958) *The Religion of India: The Sociology of Hinduism and Buddhism*. Translated and edited by Hans H. Gerth and Don Martindale. Glencoe: Free Press.

Webster, A. (1994) 'University-Corporate Ties and the Construction of Research Agendas', *Sociology*. 28(1): 123–143.

Weinshall, T.D. (ed.) (1977) *Culture and Management*. Harmondsworth, Middlesex: Penguin Books.

Weinshall, T.D. (1977a) 'Multinational Corporations – A Total System Approach to Their Role and Measurement: Some Reflections on Their Supranational, Intercultural and Multistructural Aspects', in: T.D. Weinshall (ed.) *Culture and Management*, pp. 383–432. Middlesex: Penguin Books.

Weinshall, T. (ed.) (1993) *Societal Culture and Management*. Berlin: De Gruyter.

Werbner, R. & Ranger, T. (eds) (1996) *Postcolonial Identities in Africa*. London: Zed Books.

Westney, E.D. (1987) *Imitation and Innovation: The Transfer of Western Organizational Patterns to Meiji Japan*. Cambridge, MA: Harvard University Press.

Westwood, R.I. (2001) 'Appropriating the Other in the Discourses of Comparative Management', in: R.I. Westwood & S. Linstead (eds) *The Language of Organisation*, pp. 241–282. London: Sage.

Westwood, R. (2004) 'Towards a Postcolonial Research Paradigm in International Business and Comparative Management', in: R. Marschan-Piekkari & C. Welch (eds) *Handbook of Qualitative Research Methods for International Business*, pp. 56–83. Cheltenham, UK: Edward Elgar.

Westwood, R.I. & Clegg, S. (2003) (eds) *Debating Organisation: Point and Counterpoint in Organisation Studies*. Oxford: Blackwell.

Westwood, R.I. & Everett, J. (1987) 'Culture's Consequences: A Methodology for Comparative Management Studies in South East Asia?', *Asia-Pacific Journal of Management*. 4(3): 187–202.

Westwood, R.I. & Jack, G. (2007) 'Manifesto for a Post-Colonial International Business and Management Studies: A Provocation', *Critical Perspectives on International Business*. 3(3): 246–265.

Westwood, R.I. & Linstead, S. (eds) (2001) *The Language of Organisation*. London: Sage.

Westwood, R.I. & Jack, G. (2008) 'The US Commercial-Military-Political Complex and the Emergence of International Business and Management Studies', *Critical Perspectives on International Business*. 4(4): 367–388.

Whetten, D.A. (2002) 'Modelling-as-Theorizing: A Systematic Methodology for Theory Development', in: D. Partington (ed.) *Essential Skills for Management Research*, pp. 45–71. London: Sage Publications.

White, S. (2002) 'Rigour and Relevance in Asian Management Research: Where are We and Where can We Go?' *Asia Pacific Journal of Management*. 19: 287–352.

Whitely, W. & England, G.W. (1977) 'Managerial Values as a Reflection of Culture and the Process of Industrialization', *Academy of Management Journal*. 20(3): 439–453.

Whitely, W. & England, G.W. (1980) 'Variability in Common Dimensions of Managerial Values Due to Value Orientation and Country Differences', *Personnel Psychology*. 33: 77–89.

Whiteman, G. & Cooper, W.H. (2000) 'Ecological Embeddedness', *Academy of Management Journal*. 42(6): 1265–1282.

Whitley, R.D. (1991) 'The Societal Construction of Business Systems in East Asia', *Organization Studies*. 12(1): 1–28.

Whitley, R. (1992) *Business Systems in East Asia: Firms, Markets and Societies*. London/Thousand Oaks, CA: Sage.

Whitley, R. (1999) *Divergent Capitalisms: The Social Structuring and Change of Business Systems*. Oxford: Oxford University Press.

Whitley, R. (2002) *Competing Capitalisms: Institutions and Economies*. Cheltenham: Elgar.

Whitley, R.D. (2006) 'Understanding Differences: Searching for the Social Processes that Construct and Reproduce Variety in Science and Economic Organization', *Organization Studies*. 27(8): 1153–1177.

Wilk, R. (1995) 'Learning to be Local in Belize: Global Systems of Common Difference', in: D. Miller (ed.) *World Apart: Modernity through the Prism of the Local*, pp. 110–133. London: Routledge.

Wolf, M.J. (1985) *The Japanese Conspiracy: The Plot to Dominate Industry Worldwide – And How to Deal with It*. Sevenoaks: New English Library.

Wong, S.L. (1985) 'The Chinese Family Firm: A Model', *The British Journal of Sociology*. 36(1): 58–72.

Wong-MingJi, D. & Mir, A.H. (1997) 'How International is International Management? Provincialism, Parochialism, and the Problematic of Global Diversity', in: P. Prasad, A.J. Mills, M. Elmes & A. Prasad (eds) *Managing the Organisational Melting Pot: Dilemmas of Workplace Diversity*, pp. 340–364. London: Sage.

Wright, L.R. (1996) 'Qualitative International Management Research', in: B.J. Punnett & O. Shenkar (eds) (1996) *Handbook for International Management Research*, pp. 63–81. Cambridge, MA: Blackwell.

Wright, P. (1981) 'Organizational Behavior in Islamic Firms', *Management International Review*. 21: 86–94.

Wright, S. (ed.) (1994) *Anthropology of Organizations*. London and New York: Routledge.

Xu Lian, C. (1987) 'A Cross-Cultural Study on the Leadership Behaviour of Chinese and Japanese Executives', Asia-Pacific Journal of Management. 4(3): 203–209.

Xu, Q. (2008) 'A Question Concerning Subject in *The Spirit of Chinese Capitalism*', *Critical Perspectives on International Business*. 4(2/3): 242–276.

Yeh, R.S & Lawrence, J. J. (1995) 'Individualism and Confucian Dynamism: A Note on Hofstede's Cultural Root to Economic Growth', *Journal of International Business Studies*. 26(3): 655–669.

Young, R.J.C. (1995) *Colonial Desire: Hybridity in Theory, Culture and Race*. London: Routledge.

Young, R.J.C. (2001) *Postcolonialism: A Historical Introduction*. Oxford: Blackwell.

Young, R.J.C. (2003) *Postcolonialism: A Very Short Introduction*. Oxford: Oxford University Press.

Zaide, G.F. &. Zaide, S.M. (2004) *Philippine History and Government*. 6th edition. Quezon City, Philippines: All-Nations Publishing Company.

Zimmerman, J.L. (2001) *Can American Business Schools Survive?* Rochester, NY: Unpublished manuscript. Simon Graduate School of Business Administration.

Index

Note: Page number in italics refers to tables

Moran, R.T., *168*, 180, 189–91, 195
Morley, D., 156, 157
Mufti, A., 20–1
multicultural, 155, 220
 see also culture; multiculturalism
multiculturalism, 155, 157–63,
  319–20n4
 boutique, 160, 162–3
 criticisms on, 160–3
 see also culture
multinational corporations (MNCs),
  188–9
multinational enterprise (MNE), 30,
  31, 32, 110
multi-sited ethnography, 272
 see also ethnography
multi-sited research imaginary,
  272–3
Muniapan, B., 291
Murata, S., 213
Myers, C.A., 114, 118, 120, 128, 129,
  130, 131, 132, 133, 135, *168*, 173,
  174, 180, 183, 186, 199

Nader, L., 122
Nagar, R., 270, 271
Naipaul, V.S., 234
Nath, R., 32, 33, *168*, 193, 202–5
national cultural identity, 154
nation-state, 144, 154–7
native informants, 256–7
necrocapitalism, 150
 see also capitalism
neo-colonial discourse analysis,
  18–24
 politicization, 19
 provincialization, 19
 recontextualization, 19
 see also neocolonialism
neo-colonialism, 12
 see also neo-colonial discourse
  analysis
nepotism, 214
Netherlands, the
 journal publishing, institutional
  bias in, 77
network(s)
 international location and, 285–7
Neu, D., 109

New Zealand, 51, 57, 218
 dominance of Western knowledge
  in management theory and
  practice, 17
 indigenous studies of management
  and organization in, 57, 277
 journal publishing, institutional
  bias in, 77
 Performance Based Research
  Programme in, 61
 professional academics and
  associations, 66
Ngugi, W.T., 80
Nifadkar, S.S., 6
Nkomo, S.M., 44, 46, 313, 316n9
non-governmental organizations
  (NGOs), 49, 126, 144
North America (NA), 29, 35, 38, 49,
  50, 56, 202, 254, 257
 editors/editorial process in, 78, 79
 Eurocentrism in, 20, 21
 journal publishing, institutional
  bias in, 72
 professional academics and
  associations, 65, 66
 see also United States
North Atlantic intellectual hegemony,
  50
 see also hegemony
Nyathi, N., 17, 313

Occidental, *200*
Office of Strategic Services (OSS), 123
Oldroyd, D., 108, 109
Olds, K., 158–9
ontology, 11, 22, 39, 41, 42, 51, 52,
  53, 81, 121, 170, 232, 272, 277,
  278
open systems theory, 202
organizational behaviour (OB), 5, 30,
  31, 44, 71, 187, 229–30, 260
 see also attitude/behaviour;
  P-M model
organizational discourse
 emergence of, 22, 315–16n8
 Foucauldian/genealogical
  perspective on, 316n8
Organizational Theory (OT), 18, 30,
  50–1, 187